Delictual Liability

For Annie Thomson

Delictual Liability

Fifth Edition

Joe Thomson

Formerly Regius Professor of Law, University of Glasgow
and Commissioner, Scottish Law Commission

Bloomsbury Professional

Bloomsbury Professional Ltd, Maxwelton House, 41–43 Boltro Road, Haywards Heath, West Sussex, RH16 1BJ

© Bloomsbury Professional Ltd 2014

Bloomsbury Professional is an imprint of Bloomsbury Publishing Plc

A CIP Catalogue record for this book is available from the British Library.

ISBN: 978 1 78043 467 4

Typeset by Phoenix Photosetting, Chatham, Kent
Printed and bound in Great Britain by CPI Group (UK) Ltd, Croydon, CR0 4YY

Preface

It is 20 years since the first edition of this book. While there have been many statutory and judicial developments during this period, nevertheless the contours of the subject remain basically the same.

For this edition I owe an immense debt to Katarzyna Chalaczkiewicz-Ladna who was my research assistant. Without her, the production of this edition would have been so much more difficult, if not impossible.

For the last 15 years, my wife, Annie, has been a great source of support in all my academic endeavours. More importantly, she has given me so much happiness during our marriage. As a token of the esteem in which I hold her, I would like to dedicate this edition to her.

The law is stated as at 1 May 2014.

Joe Thomson
Campbeltown
1 May 2014

Contents

Table of Statutes

Table of Statutory Instruments

Table of Cases

M

Q

Introduction

The essence of the modern Scots law of delict is the obligation of a person, A, to compensate another person, B, for the losses B has sustained as a result of harm caused to B by the wrongful actions of A. This obligation to pay compensation is called reparation. The obligation to make reparation when loss has been suffered as a result of a person's wrongful actions is obediential; it arises *ex lege* regardless of the will of the wrongdoer. In this respect, delictual obligations differ from contractual obligations which arise as a result of the agreement of the parties to a contract. However, a delictual obligation is similar to the obligation to reverse an unjustified enrichment, since the latter obligation also arises *ex lege*. But unlike unjustified enrichment the delictual obligation to make reparation arises only when the loss has arisen as a result of the wrongful act of the person who caused the harm. It is only when a person has been at fault that the obligation to make reparation arises. In Scots law we use the term '*culpa*' to describe fault. *Culpa* covers both intentional and unintentional conduct which causes harm to another but before there is liability the law must regard the conduct as wrongous. This is encapsulated in the brocard *damnum injuria datum*, ie harm caused by wrongous conduct.

Some examples will make the point clearer. If A intentionally assaults B, causing him harm, A is under a delictual obligation to compensate B for the losses he has sustained from his injuries: A is guilty of *culpa* because he deliberately intended to harm B by assaulting him, which the law regards as a wrongous act. If A drives his car carelessly on a public highway and as a result injures B, a pedestrian, then A is under a delictual obligation to compensate B for the losses he has sustained from his injuries: A is guilty of *culpa* because of his careless driving which the law regards as a wrongous act. Thus we can say that modern Scots law begins from the premise that there is an obediential obligation on a person to make reparation to another who has sustained losses as a consequence of suffering harm as a result of the *culpa* or fault of the wrongdoer, ie the wrongdoer's intentional or unintentional, but careless, conduct, which caused the harm. Its function is corrective justice – to put the victim, so far as an award of damages can, into the position he would have been if the wrong had never taken place.

It is not the case that a person who suffers loss from harm caused by another's intentional or unintentional, but careless, conduct will always be entitled to reparation. The act which causes the harm must be regarded by the law as wrongful (*injuria*). For policy reasons, certain acts are not regarded as wrongful in this sense. So for example, as we shall see,[1] A is free to undercut the prices of his competitor, B, even if B suffers economically; nor does it matter if A deliberately undercuts B's prices with the intention of putting B out of business. The reason for this is that in our society competition is to be encouraged even if persons suffer economically as a result. This is an example of *damnum absque injuria*, ie harm without wrongful conduct.

Before there is an obligation to make reparation, the victim must suffer harm. But, in addition, this harm must arise from an intrusion by the wrongdoer upon a right of the victim which is recognised by the law as reparable. One of the fascinating aspects of the law of delict is to see when the courts are prepared to recognise rights as reparable and when they are not.

For example, the law has long recognised as reparable a person's right to physical integrity so that if there is an intrusion of that right as a result of culpable conduct, the wrongdoer must make compensation for pain and suffering, ie non-patrimonial loss and any patrimonial, ie economic, loss arising from the injuries sustained, such as loss of earning capacity. But the Scots law of delict has, hitherto, not recognised as a reparable right a person's privacy per se[2] although it has, for example, protected a person's confidential information.[3]

An area which has caused controversy is whether the law should recognise as a reparable right economic loss sustained by a person where the economic loss does not derive from injury to that person's body or damage to his property.[4] So, for example, if A carelessly damages an electric cable owned by B with the result that there is a loss of power to C's factory, should C be able to obtain compensation for his loss of production (pure economic loss) if the power cut did not cause any physical damage to the machinery in his factory? B, of course, can seek reparation from A in respect of the physical damage to B's cable.

1 Para 2.1 below.
2 *Wainwright v Home Office* [2003] All ER (D) 279, discussed at para 1.2 beyond.
3 Breach of confidence is discussed at para 1.19 beyond.
4 This matter is discussed at length in Chapter 4.

Scottish lawyers maintain that Scots law is based on principle rather than remedies. It is probably true to argue that the modern Scots law of delict is based on the general principle of an obediential, *ex lege* obligation to make reparation for loss sustained as a result of conduct which constitutes *culpa*. This was not always the case and is, indeed, a comparatively recent development. In medieval times, before there was a centralised system for the prosecution of criminal offences, there was a close relationship between what would now be considered delictual actions and the enforcement of the criminal law. What we discover is that there were specific remedies to deal with particular situations which were common in those turbulent times. *Stair* lists the following:[1]

'besides those of a special name and nature, which are chiefly these, assythment, extortion, circumvention, spuilzie, intrusion, ejection, molestation, breach of arrestment, deforcement, contravention, forgery, which comes in more properly in the process of improbation'.

Three of these deserve further consideration to illustrate the close relationship which existed at that time between delictual liability and the enforcement of the criminal law.

Assythment was concerned with the regulation of acts which caused death and was an attempt to avoid blood feuds. The remedy of assythment was an action for a sum of money:

'to be payit be the commirtaris of slaughter, to the kin, bairnis and friends of any person that is slane ... gevin to thame in contentatioun of the hurt, damnage and skeith sustenit be thane throw the wanting of the person who is slane, and for the skaith incurrit be thame thairthrow, and for the pacifying of their rancor'.[2]

Several features of the action should be noted. There had to be a crime which caused death or physical injury to the victim. The action could be brought by any person, however remote, who was a relative of the deceased or injured person. The damages depended on the wrongdoer's means, ie they were not simply compensatory, and, finally, no assythment was due if the wrongdoer was executed. Assythment arose either if the wrongdoer was convicted and because of his position received a lesser penalty than was due or if there was no conviction and the family of the deceased issued a document known as a letter of slains acknowledging receipt of assythment and petitioning the Crown not to proceed with a prosecution. The latter situation was more important because it short-circuited the need for a criminal trial. With the establishment of a centralised system of public prosecution it became contrary to public policy that the victim or his family should be able to circumvent the normal prosecution process by issuing letters of slains. In practice, actions for assythment died out though they were still theoretically possible if the wrongdoer had been prosecuted but had not suffered the due pains of the law. At the same time, the common law developed an action under which the spouse and ascendants and descendants of a person who had been killed as a result of the defender's *culpa* could obtain reparation in respect of the death, ie they could bring an action in delict.

1 *Institutions* IX, 5, 6.
2 Balfour *Practicks* p 516.

An attempt to revive an action of assythment was made in *McKendrick v Sinclair*.[1] A workman was killed by an electric shock allegedly due to the negligence of his employer. He had financially supported his sister and two brothers. They could not bring an action in delict because at common law brothers and sisters of the deceased had no title to sue.[2] However, the Lord Advocate was not prepared to prosecute the defender or to concur if the relatives had sought a private prosecution. The old practice of letters of slains was inappropriate as the employer denied liability for culpable homicide. Accordingly, assythment would only have been available on the old authorities if there had been a conviction. As this was not the case, the action failed since it did not fall within the recognised parameters of the remedy.[3] Lord Simon of Glaisdale was prepared to dismiss the action on a more radical ground: that in spite of being a common law remedy assythment had fallen into desuetude, ie had become obsolescent:

'This Brunnhilde [assythment] would awake in our uncongenial modern Niebelheim. This Rip van Winkle would find *Eisten's* case firmly embodied in the law, that private prosecutions are extinct, that capital punishment for homicide has been abolished, and that damages are related to loss to the pursuer and not to the means of the defender. Even if this Sleeping Beauty were so attractive as to tempt your Lordships to favour her with your kisses she could not live happily ever after.'[4]

Assythment was finally laid to rest when it was abolished by section 8 of the Damages (Scotland) Act 1976 which extended title to sue in respect of the death of a relative to include the deceased's brothers and sisters[5] thus closing the lacuna revealed in the *McKendrick* case.

1 1972 SC (HL) 25, 1972 SLT 110.
2 *Eisten v North British Railway Co* (1870) 8 M 980.
3 *McKendrick v Sinclair* 1972 SLT 110 at 113 per Lord Reid and at 120 per Lord Kilbrandon, 1972 SC (HL) 25.

4 1972 SLT 110 at 117.
5 For discussion of the right to sue in respect of the death of a relative, see Chapter 13. The 1976 Act has been repealed and replaced by the Damages (Scotland) Act 2011.

The second old remedy we should consider is contravention of lawburrows. This was a method of primitive law enforcement in the absence of an effective police force and system of public prosecution of criminal offences. If a person had reasonable grounds to believe that he or his family or their property was in danger from another person, he could apply to a court to have that person find caution (ie to lodge a sum of money in court) not to harm him or his family or their property. This was known as lawburrows. In other words, the defender was ordered not to molest the pursuer or the family or their property on pain of losing caution, ie the money lodged in court. If the defender contravened the non-molestation order, he could be sued in an action of contravention of lawburrows for forfeiture of the caution.[1] With the advent of effective law enforcement agencies, the use of lawburrows declined, though there is no doubt that the action is still technically competent.[2]

Finally there was the action of spuilzie. This action arose when the defender interfered with the possession of another's moveable property, for example, stole cattle or sheep. The pursuer was the owner or the lawful possessor of the property.[3] The action was to have the property returned, or its value. But the quasi-criminal nature of the action is illustrated by the fact that the pursuer was entitled to violent profits, ie all the profits which the pursuer might have made from the property while in possession of the defender. In many situations, spuilzie has been overtaken by the general principle of liability for *culpa*.[4]

1 Lawburrows Acts 1429 and 1581.
2 On lawburrows generally, see 13 *Stair Memorial Encyclopaedia* paras 901–926; *Morrow v Neil* 1975 SLT (Sh Ct) 65; *Liddle v Morton* 1996 SLT 1143.
3 *FC Finance Ltd v Brown & Son* 1969 SLT (Sh Ct) 41.
4 See, for example, *Harris v Abbey National plc* 1997 SCLR 359 (liability based on gratuitous deposit of property rather than spuilzie).

We have seen, then, how these specific remedies had important quasi-criminal aspects. While it is clear that lawburrows and spuilzie remain, theoretically at least, part of Scots law, in practice they have largely been overtaken by the development of effective law enforcement agencies and the general principle of liability to make reparation for loss caused as a result of the defender's *culpa*. *Stair* laid the basis for the general principle of delictual liability when he recognised that to cause damage by delinquence gave rise to an obediential obligation to make reparation for the damage caused: *damnum injuria datum*. This was a general innominate remedy based on the defender's *culpa* which included deliberate as well as careless conduct. *Stair* treated the nominate Scottish remedies as simply aspects of the general obligation to make reparation for loss caused by *culpa*.[1] This general obligation was accepted by the later institutional writers.[2] In attempting this synthesis, reliance was, of course, placed on Roman law and in particular liability under the Lex Aquilia which included liability for unintentional, but careless, conduct.

Although the modern Scots law of delict can be traced back to the institutional writers, their treatment is not extensive. Instead, the principles of the law of delict are largely the creation of the courts. The judges have had to develop the law to take account of the increase of potential injury to persons and damage to property created by industrialisation, mass production and distribution of goods, easier access to information, and the motor car. At the same time, they have also appreciated that there must be limits on a person's liability, particularly for unintentional conduct, if that person is to continue to engage in conduct which is socially and economically desirable, even if it is potentially harmful. The traditional Scots law solution has been to restrict liability by insisting that it is only triggered by the defender's fault and by refusing to recognise certain kinds of harm as reparable rights. This book is largely concerned with the rules of common law and statute which have developed to achieve this balance. However, in some areas it has been considered socially and economically desirable that persons should recover compensation for losses resulting from physical injury or damage to property without the need to establish fault on the part of the defender. While the concept of *culpa* has proved flexible enough to create liability where the degree of moral blame on the part of the defender is small,[3] nevertheless, some degree of fault is required.[4] Accordingly, legislation has been necessary to introduce into Scots law what is known as strict liability, ie where a person can be liable in delict for breach of duties imposed by a statute without the need for the person who suffers loss from the injury or damage to establish fault. In a modern context, it is therefore important to discuss the principles of strict liability in relation to the breach of statutory duties imposed by some, at least, of the most important statutes.

1 *Stair* I, 9, 2.
2 See, for example, Erskine *Institute* III, 1.
3 Particularly as the criterion for fault in the context of unintentional conduct is the failure to reach the standards of the reasonable person, as opposed to the standards which the particular defender could morally be expected to reach: see Chapter 5 below.
4 But, for example, where a person has used his property in a potentially very dangerous way, the degree of fault is small: *Kerr v Earl of Orkney* (1857) 20 D 298, 30 SJ 158: see para 10.1 below.

The Human Rights Act 1998 makes the European Convention on Human Rights directly effective in Scots – and English – domestic law. As a consequence, the Convention is having a profound effect on how the law is being developed by the courts in such areas as protection of confidential information,[1] the delictual liability of state agencies[2] and the law of defamation.[3] Moreover, where a public authority has infringed a Convention right, the victim may be entitled to damages under the 1998 Act,[4] whether or not the violation of the Convention right amounts to a delict. It should be noted that damages are only available against a public authority, not a private individual. Detailed discussion of damages for breach of Convention rights is outwith the scope of this book.

It is the author's primary intention to concentrate on the common law principles which underlie delictual liability for *culpa*, ie intentional and unintentional wrongdoing. These are becoming more difficult to explain in a coherent way. While it has always been accepted that the imposition of a duty of care in novel situations involves the courts making decisions on grounds of legal policy,[5] once that decision was made the rules of the law of delictual liability could be applied more or less mechanically to determine whether or not the defender was liable and the extent of that liability. However, it is now clear that the superior courts are prepared to abandon the logical application of these rules or make exceptions to these rules when their application would produce a result which is not conducive to the judges' conception of what is a 'fair' or 'just' result or what is in accordance with 'practical' or 'distributive' justice. Moreover, there is now a marked reluctance to lay down comprehensive general principles. This makes the modern law of delict extremely complicated because it has become so fact sensitive. Such instances of judicial creativity are highlighted in the text.[6]

The book begins with a study of delictual liability for intentionally harmful conduct; the second part contains an analysis of the general principles of liability for unintentional, but careless, conduct; the third part considers delictual liability in the context of some important social and economic relationships. Included in this part is a chapter on defamation and verbal injury where different principles apply. The book ends with a chapter on damages.

1 For discussion, see beyond paras 1.19–1.23.
2 For discussion, see beyond paras 11.5–11.9.
3 For discussion see Chapter 15.
4 Human Rights Act 1998, s 8(3).
5 See generally beyond Chapter 4.
6 See Joe Thomson 'Principle as Policy' (2003) 56 CLP 123.

Part I

INTENTIONAL DELICTS

CHAPTER 1

Intentional wrongs in respect of persons and property

A. INTRODUCTION

1.1   As we have seen,[1] *culpa* includes (a) deliberate conduct intended to harm the victim or the victim's property and (b) unintentional, but careless, conduct which has harmed the victim or the victim's property. In the case of unintentional conduct, the range of victims is prima facie indeterminate, ie it could potentially include any person who has been harmed by the conduct. Because of this, the law has had to invent devices for limiting the number of persons who are entitled to sue in delict if they suffer harm as a result of another's careless conduct. The most important of these devices is the concept of a duty of care:[2] it is only a person to whom the defender owes a duty of care who can sue in delict for harm arising from the defender's careless conduct.[3]

Where an act is done deliberately to harm a particular person, there is not the same degree of difficulty since the potential pursuer is normally determinate:[4] the pursuer is the person whom the defender *intended* to harm by his conduct and there is no need to invoke the concept of a duty of care. Intentional delicts in relation to persons and property are discussed in this chapter.

1 Introduction above.
2 There are other devices such as remoteness of injury and causation: see para 5.17 and Chapter 6 below.
3 The duty of care is discussed at Chapter 3 below.
4 There can be cases where this might not be so: A may intend to harm B by blowing up B's house but injure C instead; while it is thought that A will be liable to C, such cases are rare in practice.

B. INTENTIONAL WRONGS RELATING TO PERSONS

(1) Assault

1.2   'Everyone who lives under the protection of the law has an absolute right to the safety of his person; and wherever this right is invaded there is in Civil law a provision for redress of injury, as well as in penal law a punishment for the crime.'[1] A physical assault is a common law crime provided there is the necessary evil intent on the part of the perpetrator *(dolus)*. Assault also constitutes a civil wrong. But even though an assault is not criminal because of the absence of *evil* intent, it is still an actionable delict provided the defender intended to invade the physical integrity of the pursuer. So where A playfully attacked B in order to make B engage in sport, it nevertheless constituted an actionable wrong even although it was done 'for a lark'.[2] If the assault does not result in serious physical harm, the damages awarded will not be substantial in spite of the insult caused to the victim.[3]

In *Wainwright v Home Office*[4] the House of Lords refused to extend the concept of assault to include the infliction of humiliation and distress without more. The plaintiffs claimed that they had suffered mental harm as a consequence of being asked to undress for the purpose of a strip search when visiting a relative in prison. Their Lordships maintained that there was no liability at common law for invasion of privacy. Where the only mental harm was distress as opposed to a recognised psychiatric disorder, there was no liability unless it could be shown that the defendant had known his conduct was unjustifiable and intended to cause mental harm. The strip searches were attempts to inhibit drug smuggling and there was no evidence that the defendants intended to cause distress. This was an English case but it is thought that a similar approach would be taken by the Scottish courts.

An assault may amount to a breach of Article 3 of the European Convention of Human Rights: 'No one shall be subjected to torture or to inhuman or degrading treatment or punishment.' Where this is so, it is competent to seek damages at common law for assault and compensation for a breach of Article 3 in the same action.[5]

1 Bell *Principles* para 2028.
2 *Reid v Mitchell* (1885) 12 R 1129.
3 See, for example, *Downie v Chief Constable of Strathclyde Police* 1997 SCLR 603 (the pursuer was awarded £1,500 in respect of an assault by two policemen; the victim had recovered without the need of medical treatment).
4 [2003] UKHL 53, [2004] 2 AC 406, [2003] 3 WLR 1137, [2003] 4 All ER 969, HL.
5 *Ruddy v Chief Constable of Strathclyde* [2012] UKSC 57 (alleged assault by police on the pursuer when he was arrested and detained in custody).

1.3   Where the 'victim' consents to the act, it does not amount to an assault for the purposes of delict[1] since the essence of the wrong is *non-consensual* invasion of bodily integrity. Where this principle is important is in respect of medical procedures. If a doctor or dentist carries out a medical procedure on an adult[2] without the patient's consent, then the doctor or dentist is liable to make reparation.[3] Although this will usually not be a crime because of the absence of evil intent on the part of the doctor or dentist, it is still a delict. The patient can obtain reparation not only for any resulting patrimonial loss but also for *contumelia*, ie the insult suffered as a result of the non-consensual invasion of bodily integrity. The fact that the procedure was carried out for the patient's benefit is irrelevant.[4]

The question then arises as to when the patient's consent is valid in order that the doctor or dentist concerned can avoid potential delictual liability. It is clear that a patient must be given sufficient information upon which to give consent. All medical and dental procedures involve a risk to the patient even if *properly* carried out, for example, side effects of a drug or an operation or other medical procedure. In the United States,[5] there has evolved a doctrine known as 'informed consent'. Under this doctrine, if the patient is not informed of all the risks inherent in the proposed medical procedure which a reasonable *patient* should know, then the patient's apparent consent is vitiated and the doctor or dentist can be sued for assault.

An attempt to introduce this doctrine into English law was rejected by a majority of the House of Lords in *Sidaway v Board of Governors of the Bethlem Royal Hospital.*[6] Instead, it was held that a doctor need only disclose to a patient the risks inherent in a medical procedure which are regarded by *a responsible body of medical opinion* as proper to disclose. Two important points follow. First, provided the doctor or dentist has disclosed those risks which a responsible body of medical or dental opinion would disclose, the patient's consent is valid and the patient cannot sue in assault where she sustains harm, the risk of which it was *not* necessary to disclose. The harm must, of course, be inherent in the medical procedure when properly carried out; if the harm arose as a result of careless treatment, the patient can sue the doctor or dentist for breach of a duty of care since the patient has *not* consented to the risk of harm as a result of professional incompetence.[7] Second, if the doctor or dentist has not disclosed those risks which a responsible body of medical or dental opinion would disclose, then if the patient sustains *any* harm which is inherent in the medical procedure when properly carried out, the patient can sue the doctor or dentist; but it would appear from *Sidaway* that the patient sues for a breach by the doctor or dentist of the duty of care which they owe to their patients to disclose those risks inherent in the medical procedure which a responsible body of medical or dental opinion would disclose, ie for an unintentional wrong and not assault. In other words, the general principles of liability for *culpa* rather than assault apply to this particular issue. While *Sidaway* is an English case, it has been followed in Scotland.[8]

1 In criminal law, if there is evil intent on the part of the accused, the consent of the 'victim' is irrelevant: a person cannot consent to a crime: *Smart v HM Advocate* 1975 JC 30, 1975 SLT 65.
2 A person under the age of 16 will have legal capacity to consent if the doctor or dentist is of the view that the young person is capable of understanding the nature and probable consequences of the medical treatment or procedure: Age of Legal Capacity (Scotland) Act 1991, s 2(4).
3 In an emergency, if the patient is, for example, unconscious, a doctor may proceed without the patient's consent if it is *necessary* for the patient's wellbeing to do so.
4 'Even when his or her own life depends on receiving medical treatment, an adult of sound mind is entitled to refuse it': *St George's Healthcare NHS Trust v S; R v Collins, ex parte S* [1998] 3 WLR 936, [1998] 3 All ER 673, CA at 685 per Judge LJ.
5 *Canterbury v Spence* (1972) 464 F 2d 772.
6 [1985] AC 871, [1985] 1 All ER 643, HL (Lord Scarman dissenting).
7 On professional delictual liability, see Chapter 7 below.
8 *Moyes v Lothian Health Board* 1990 SLT 444. There it was observed by the Lord Ordinary (Caplan) at 447 that provided there was a failure to warn of risks, which amounted to a breach of a duty of care (ie that a responsible body of medical opinion would have disclosed some risks), it did not matter that the harm sustained by the pursuer was one the risk of which it was not necessary to disclose. See also *Glancy v Southern General Hospital NHS Trust* [2013] CSOH 35.

1.4   In practice, most patients simply sign a general consent form in respect of risks inherent in treatment. Nor is it clear when a reasonably prudent doctor should inform a patient of a particular risk inherent in a medical procedure. In *Sidaway* the risk of harm was slight, less than 1 per cent, but if it materialised the injury could have been severe. Yet the House of Lords took the view that since a majority of responsible medical practitioners would not have informed the patient of such a risk, no delictual liability was incurred.[1]

It had generally been thought that the normal rules of causation would apply in these cases and that the patient would have to establish that if he had been informed of the risks he would not have undergone the surgery. However, in *Chester v Afshar*,[2] the House of Lords held by a majority that it was not necessary for the usual 'but for' test to be satisfied: the claimant did not have to establish on the balance of probabilities that she would not have consented to the surgery had she known about the risks of harm. By not informing her, the claimant had lost the opportunity to explore the risks involved and the chance to have a second opinion before deciding whether or not to have the medical procedure, which might, of course, be carried out without the harm materialising. This was the reason for imposing a duty to inform in the first place. To restrict damages to those patients who could establish that they would not have had the operation, would deny a remedy to other patients whose doctors had also been in breach of their duty to warn and who had sustained the very injury the risk of which the doctors should have warned against. Therefore, unless a more liberal attitude to causation was taken in these cases, the duty to warn of risks inherent in medical procedures would be 'a hollow one, stripped of all its practical force and devoid of all content'.[3] But while every failure to warn is a wrongful intrusion of a patient's autonomy, it is difficult to see why a patient who would have had an operation even if she knew of the risks involved, should have damages assessed on the basis of the physical harm sustained. As we shall see,[4] in cases of wrongful conception the parents can obtain a conventional, non-compensatory, award of damages (approximately £15K–£20K) to recognise the invasion of their rights to plan their family. It is thought that such a conventional award would also have been appropriate for patients whose rights to be informed have been infringed but who nevertheless would have undergone the medical procedures even if they had been told of the risks involved.

1 It has been held that a significant risk of the order of 10 per cent should be disclosed while a risk of 0.2 per cent need not be disclosed: *Pearce v United Bristol NHS Trust* [1999] PIQR P53.
2 [2005] 1 AC 134. On causation generally, see beyond Chapter 6.
3 Ibid per Lord Hope at 162–163. He also accepted that the issue of causation cannot be separated from issues of policy *viz* whether in the unusual circumstances of the case, justice required the normal approach to causation to be abandoned: ibid.
4 Beyond para 16.6.

1.5 As we have seen, consent of the victim prevents delictual liability for assault from arising. This explains why there is no liability for assault in sports involving physical contact: boxing, rugby, soccer etc.[1] But the players give consent only to the physical contact inherent in the sport, so that there will be liability if injury is sustained as a result of conduct outwith the rules of the sport; if, for example, a rugby player punches, as opposed to tackles, an opponent. While an assault usually takes the form of physical contact this is not strictly necessary; thus to spit at a person or shake a fist in a threatening manner is an assault.[2]

There is a complete defence to an action of assault if it was the result of an unavoidable accident or carried out in self-defence provided the defender's belief that he was under threat of imminent attack was reasonably held.[3] If the assault took place as a result of the pursuer's provocation, the damages can be reduced. 'No verbal provocation whatever can justify a blow ... But ... verbal provocation is a good ground for mitigating damages ... '.[4] The rationale is that since reparation for intentional wrong is based on *culpa*, the pursuer must come to the court with clean hands; if the pursuer's hands are not clean, the pursuer's damages can be reduced.[5]

1 Cf non-physical sports, for example, golf: *Lewis v Buckpool Golf Club* 1993 SLT (Sh Ct) 43.

2 But not all conduct which causes humiliation and distress will be treated as an assault, for example requesting a person to undress for the purpose of a strip search: *Wainwright v Home Office* [2003] UKHL 53, [2004] 2 AC 406, [2003] 3 WLR 1137, [2003] 4 All ER 969, HL.

3 *Ashley v Chief Constable of Sussex Police* [2008] 1 AC 962; it is a defence to a criminal assault that the accused had acted in an honest but mistaken belief that he was under threat of imminent attack. While *Ashley* is an English case, it is thought that it would be followed in Scotland.

4 *Anderson v Marshall* (1835) 13 S 1130 at 1131 per the Lord President (Hope). See also *Ashmore v Rock Steady Security Ltd* 2006 SLT 207.

5 *Ross v Bryce* 1972 SLT (Sh Ct) 76. In *Ashmore v Rock Steady Security* 2006 SLT 207, the Lord Ordinary (Emslie) thought that because of his provocation, the pursuer's damages should be reduced by 20 per cent: the pursuer had been punched by a security guard at a club.

1.6 Assaults on children by parents may be justified as an exercise of a parental right physically to chastise a child. The force used by a parent when physically chastising a child must be reasonable but it is irrelevant that a parent loses his or her temper at the time.[1] Parents can delegate the right physically to chastise their children to persons who have de facto care of the child.[2] In determining whether the assault is justifiable, the court must have regard to: (a) the nature of what was done, the reason for it and the circumstances in which it took place; (b) its duration and frequency; (c) any effects – physical or mental – which it has been shown to have had on the child; (d) the child's age; and (e) the child's personal characteristics (including sex and state of health) at the time of the parent's conduct.[3] If the assault on the child included or consisted of a blow to the head, shaking or the use of an implement, the court must hold that the assault was unjustifiable.[4] When the assault cannot be justified, the child will be able to sue the parent in delict. In *A v United Kingdom*,[5] the European Court of Human Rights held that the parent's 'reasonable chastisement' defence was a breach of the child's right under Article 3 to be protected from 'inhuman or degrading treatment or punishment':

in this case a caning. Such an assault would not be justifiable in Scots law because it involves the use of an implement.

Where an assault constitutes a crime, the victim may receive compensation under the Criminal Injuries Compensation Scheme.

1 *B v Harris* 1989 SCLR 644, 1990 SLT 208 (mother strapped her seven-year-old child who had called the mother 'a fucking bastard'). Cf *Cowie v Tudhope* 1987 GWD 12-395 (father hit 15-year-old son with the leg of a table).
2 *Stewart v Thain* 1981 JC 13, 1981 SLT (Notes) 2.
3 Criminal Justice (Scotland) Act 2003, s 51(1).
4 CJ(S)A 2003, s 51(3).
5 [1998] 2 FLR 959.

(2) Unauthorised post mortem and removal and retention of organs from a dead body

1.7 It is a wrong to a deceased person's family if a post mortem is carried out without the family's consent.[1] It is also a wrong if organs are removed from the corpse and retained without the deceased's family's consent. In *Stevens v Yorkhill NHS Trust*[2] a mother who had agreed reluctantly to a post mortem on her baby suffered acute distress when she learned that the baby's brain had been removed during the operation and retained by the hospital. She had not been told that this would be done. The court held that the mother had been the victim of an actionable wrong. Temporary Judge Macaulay said:[3]

'In my opinion Scots law recognises as a legal wrong for which damages by way of solatium[4] can be claimed the unauthorised removal and retention of organs.'

The judge took the view that this was an independent wrong that had its juridical basis in the Roman *actio injuriarum* which provided reparation when the defender's conduct was insulting and caused affront to the victim. We may also say that the doctor's conduct in not seeking the mother's consent was an invasion of her right as the dead child's mother to be informed of what would happen to the baby: the failure to ask her permission was an invasion of the mother's personality rights. It is thought that the defender must intend not to ask the mother's permission and to that extent at least it is an intentional wrong.[5]

1 *Pollock v Workman* (1900) 2F 354; *Conway v Dalziel* (1901) 3F 918; *Hughes v Robertson* 1913 SC 394.
2 2006 SLT 889.
3 Ibid at 902.
4 Ie compensation for hurt feelings, pain and suffering.
5 A similar action will probably lie where parents were told that there were no ashes when their dead babies were cremated.

(3) Seduction and entrapment

1.8   Closely related to assault is the delict of seduction. In a case of assault the essence of the wrong is the invasion of a person's bodily integrity without consent. Thus, for example, rape is actionable as an assault because sexual intercourse was obtained without the woman's consent. Conversely, if a woman consents to sexual intercourse, no assault is committed as she has consented. In the case of seduction, the woman gives consent to sexual intercourse but her consent is vitiated because it was obtained by the man as a result of deception or abuse of position. In *Murray v Fraser*,[1] a young girl who was naive in sexual matters allowed a trusted member of the family to have sexual intercourse with her on his assurance that nothing would happen to her; in fact she became pregnant. The defender was held liable in seduction because he had abused a position of trust and had taken advantage of the girl's innocence. A common example of deception was where a girl allowed a man to have sexual intercourse with her because he promised to marry her but had no intention to do so.[2]

Entrapment arises when a person has been fraudulently induced to enter into a marriage which is void. The most common example is when the defender purports to marry the pursuer, knowing that he is already married to another and has therefore fraudulently misrepresented that he was in a position validly to marry the pursuer.[3]

1 1916 SC 623.
2 It is thought that an action in seduction would continue to arise in these circumstances in spite of s 1(1) of the Law Reform (Husband and Wife) (Scotland) Act 1984 which declares *inter alia* that a promise to marry does not create any rights or obligations; this is because the wrong of seduction does not arise solely from the breach of promise.
3 See, for example, *Burke v Burke* 1983 SLT 331, OH. There is no authority on whether entrapment will be extended to include fraudulent inducement to register a civil partnership.

(4) Enticement

1.9   It is a wrong for A to entice B to leave B's family without justification. The most obvious reason why A would wish to entice B away from B's family is for sexual purposes but it could, for example, arise if A wished B to join A's religious sect. The pursuers are B's family.[1] There is no longer delictual liability if A induces B to leave his or her spouse.[2] A *husband* no longer has the right to sue his wife's paramour in damages;[3] these damages were awarded as solatium to the husband in respect of the unlawful sexual intercourse, ie his wife's adultery with the defender. It is arguable that a husband can still sue a man for solatium if he raped the husband's wife; the wife, of course, would sue the rapist in assault.

1 It has been held that parents cannot sue for the loss of society of a child where the child has been removed from the parents as a result of intervention by the police in the interests of the child: *McKeen v Chief Constable, Lothian and Borders Police* 1994 SLT 93, OH. If the removal is not justified, the *child* may have the right to sue for infringement of liberty. In England, it was held in *Hamilton Jones v David and Snape* [2004] 1 All ER 657, that the loss of the company of a child is not actionable at common law. On wrongful removal of children by local authorities exercising statutory powers, see beyond para 11.6.
2 Law Reform (Husband and Wife) (Scotland) Act 1984, s 2(2).
3 Divorce (Scotland) Act 1976, s 10.

(5) Injuries to liberty

1.10 'Next to life is liberty; and the delinquence against it are restraint and constraint. And though liberty itself be inestimable, yet the damages sustained through these delinquencies are reparable.'[1] A slight infringement of liberty is prima facie actionable: so, for example, where a lady was alleged to have been detained against her will for a quarter of an hour by the manager of a hydropathic establishment, her action in delict was held to be relevant.[2] As a general principle, no one can be detained against his or her will; if this occurs, there is liability in delict. The loss suffered is both the loss of liberty and the affront caused to the pursuer. However, detention can be justified at common law if, for example, a store detective arrests a person suspected of shoplifting and detains that person for a reasonable time until the police arrive.[3]

In practice, cases of wrongful detention by ordinary members of the public are rare; instead, they arise when the person has been held under what purports to be lawful legal process. Even so, an action in delict may still arise, but the onus rests on the pursuer to show that the exercise by the authorities of their powers was neither reasonable nor necessary and accordingly unjustified.[4]

Where a person is wrongfully imprisoned by a court, superior court judges are immune from liability. Inferior judges, such as justices of the peace or magistrates, can be liable if the sentence is imposed maliciously and without probable cause.[5] If, for example, a magistrate lacks jurisdiction, he will be acting *ultra vires* but there is no liability for a bona fide error in relation to the statutory interpretation of his jurisdiction. Before he can succeed, the pursuer must also prove that the magistrate was acting maliciously.[6] Where there has been a miscarriage of justice by the superior courts, the Secretary of State may make an *ex gratia* award of compensation to the victim.

1 *Stair* I, 9, 4.
2 *Mackenzie v Cluny Hill Hydropathic Co* 1908 SC 200, 15 SLT 518. In the course of his judgment, Lord Low said: 'It is averred that the manager detained this lady for fifteen minutes ... and refused to let her go until she made an apology. If that be true it was an outrage ... ': 1908 SC 200 at 206.
3 Where, as in the example, the arrest is made without a warrant, the defender must establish that the suspicions were justified: *Pringle v Bremner and Stirling* (1867) 5 M (HL) 55; *Dahl v Chief Constable, Central Scotland Police* 1983 SLT 420, OH. If an arrest is made under authority of a warrant, it is presumed that the detention was lawful and the onus rests on the pursuer to show that the detention was not justified.
4 See, for example, *Henderson v Chief Constable, Fife Police* 1988 SLT 361, OH. (Staff staged a 'work-in'. They were arrested. When they were put in police cells, a man was handcuffed and a woman told to remove her brassiere. The use of handcuffs was conceded to be unjustified. While it was normal practice to ask women to remove underwear to prevent suicide attempts, this was not justified in this case as the woman had co-operated, made no attempt to escape and was not a danger to herself or others.)
5 Criminal Procedure (Scotland) Act 1995, s 170(1).
6 *McPhee v Macfarlane's Exor* 1933 SC 163, 1933 SLT 148. Similarly, malice must be proved if a pursuer seeks reparation on the grounds of malicious prosecution: *McKie v Strathclyde Joint Police Board* 2004 SLT 982.

1.11   The right to liberty is enshrined in Article 5(1) of the European Convention of Human Rights: 'Everyone has the right to liberty and security of person.' This is a fundamental right. No one is to be deprived of their liberty unless it falls within one of six exceptions expressly listed in Article 5: these deal with lawful arrest and detention for various purposes and are to be narrowly interpreted. Otherwise the right is absolute and unqualified. The revulsion of detention without charge or trial trumps all other interests even the interests of national security.[1] But while the right to liberty cannot be restricted, liberty of movement can be restricted in the interests of public safety or to maintain public order. The paradigm case of deprivation of liberty is literal imprisonment where the prisoner 'has no freedom of choice about anything. He cannot leave the place to which he has been assigned. He may eat only when and what his gaoler permits. The only human beings he may see or speak to are his gaolers and those whom they allow to visit. He is entirely subject to the will of others.'[2]

But outwith the paradigm, it is a question of degree on whether a restriction on freedom of movement has become a deprivation of liberty within Article 5. In *Austin (FC) v Commissioner of Police of the* ser.

Metropolis[3] a demonstrator was held in a police cordon for seven hours. The cordon was necessary in order to prevent violence. The measures were done in good faith,[4] were proportionate and enforced for no longer than reasonably necessary: therefore they were not arbitrary. In these circumstances, the restriction on freedom of movement as a result of the cordon did not amount to an arbitrary deprivation of liberty and therefore did not amount to a breach of Article 5.[5] Because there was no breach of Article 5, the appellant had been lawfully detained at common law to prevent a breach of the peace and therefore no wrong had been committed.

Article 5(4) provides: 'Everyone who is deprived of his liberty by arrest or detention shall be entitled to take proceedings by which the lawfulness of his detention shall be decided speedily by a court and his release ordered if the detention is not lawful.' Where a person is sentenced to life imprisonment, the judge must impose a minimum sentence or 'tariff' to be served for the purposes of retribution or deterrence. Once the tariff has expired, the prisoner may apply to the Parole Board which can order his release if satisfied that the prisoner is no longer a danger to the public, ie that he has been rehabilitated. Where the prisoner's right to apply to the Parole Board has been delayed, his detention after the tariff has expired is not unlawful and he has no claim for damages at common law for wrongful imprisonment.[6] Nor will there normally be a breach of Article 5(4) or Article 5(1), although the prisoner may receive compensation if he can prove that the Parole Board would have released him earlier.[7] Where there was a failure to provide programmes or courses to help the prisoner's rehabilitation, the House of Lords held there was no breach of Article 5(4) or Article 5(1).[8] However, the European Court of Human Rights has taken the view that failure to provide rehabilitative courses can amount to a breach of Article 5(4), which would render the detention arbitrary and result in a breach of Article 5(1).[9] There is clearly a tension between the approaches. In spite of the decision in the House of Lords being binding upon him, in *Arthur Duncan Petitioner*[10] the Lord Ordinary (Glennie) held that a failure to provide rehabilitative programmes could amount to a breach of Article 5(4) and consequently Article 5(1).[11]

1 *Secretary of State for the Home Department v JJ and others* [2008] 1 AC 385.
2 Ibid per Lord Hoffmann at para 37.
3 [2009] UKHL 5.
4 Cf if they had been used to punish the demonstrators or treat them a lesson; ibid per Lord Neuberger at para 63.
5 Ibid per Lord Hope at paras 33, 34 and 37. This approach was indorsed by the European Court of Human Rights; *Austin v United Kingdom* (2012) 55 EHRR 14.

6 *R (on the application of Faulkner) (FC) (Appellant) v Secretary of State for Justice*
  [2013] UKSC 23.
7 Ibid. Where a prisoner has received a determinate sentence but has been
  detained for breaking the conditions of the licence under which he was freed
  after serving part of his sentence, a delay in his right to take his case to the
  Parole Board does not constitute unlawful detention or a breach of Article 5:
  Brown v Parole Board of Scotland [2013] CSOH 200.
8 *R (James) v Secretary of State for Justice* [2010] 1 AC 553.
9 *James v the United Kingdom* (2013) 56 EHRR 12.
10 [2014] CSOH 24.
11 Living arrangements made for mentally incapacitated persons may amount
   to a deprivation of liberty and a breach of Article 5: *Chester West and Chester
   Council v P* [2014] UKSC 19.

(6) Harassment

1.12 Every individual has a right to be free from harassment.[1]
Where a person pursues a course of conduct which amounts to
harassment, the victim can bring a civil claim against him:[2] this
is known as an action of harassment.[3] Before the pursuer will
succeed it must be established that the defender intended his
behaviour to amount to harassment, or his behaviour occurred in
such circumstances that a reasonable person would conclude that
it amounted to harassment.[4] The course of conduct can include
speech and must have occurred on at least two occasions.[5]

Harassment is *not* defined in the legislation but 'includes
causing the person alarm or distress'.[6] In the context of alleged
harassment at work, when 'the quality of the conduct said to
constitute harassment is being examined, courts will have in
mind that irritations, annoyances, even a measure of upset arise
at times in everybody's day-to-day dealings with other people.
Courts are well able to recognise the boundary between conduct
which is unattractive, even unreasonable, and conduct which is
oppressive and unacceptable.'[7] An employer is vicariously liable
for harassment carried out by an employee on a fellow employee
or a third party.[8] If the action is successful, the court can award
damages:[9] these can include compensation for anxiety and financial
loss caused by the harassment.[10] The court can also grant interdict
or a non-harassment order.[11] Breach of a non-harassment order is
a criminal offence.[12] It is a defence to an action of harassment that
the course of conduct was authorised by law or was pursued for
the purpose of preventing or detecting crime or was reasonable in
the particular circumstances of the case.[13]

There is a similar regime where the harassment amounts to
domestic abuse.[14]

1 Protection from Harassment Act 1997, s 8(1). It is arguable that conduct which deliberately caused fear and alarm, even in the absence of physical harm, was delictual at common law: *Ward v Scotrail Railways Ltd* 1999 SC 255. Such conduct could certainly be controlled by an interdict (molestation) and, in theory, should have been sufficient cause for a claim in damages. However in *G v S* 2007 SCLR 137, Lord Turnbull observed at 142 para 18 that '… a claim for damages arising out of anxiety would not normally sound in damages. It is only the statutory provision in section 8(6) of the [1997] Act which permits this.' It has been held in England that the infliction of humiliation and distress by conduct calculated to humiliate and distress, without more, does not give rise to liability at common law: *Wainwright v Home Office* [2003] All ER (D) 279.

2 Individual instances of harassment will make up a course of conduct, but it is the course of conduct which has to have the quality of amounting to harassment rather than the individual instances of conduct. See *Iqbal v Dean Manson, Solicitors* [2011] EWCA Civ 123; *Marinello v City of Edinburgh Council* [2011] CSIH 33.

3 Protection from Harassment Act 1997, s 8(2).

4 PHA 1997, s 8(1)(a), (b).

5 PHA 1997, s 8(3). Thus, a single assault will not amount to harassment unless it is the cumulation of a course of conduct which amounts to harassment: *Vaickuviene v Sainsbury* [2013] CSIH 67.

6 PHA 1997, s 8(3).

7 *Majrowski v Guy's and St Thomas's NHS Trust* [2007] 1 AC 224 per Lord Nicholls at para 30.

8 Ibid. PHA 1997, s 10(1) adds a new s 18B to the Prescription and Limitation (Scotland) Act 1973 where it is clear that Parliament anticipated that an action could be brought against the employer of a person alleged to have harassed the complainer. Lord Hope's reasoning in *Majrowski* is a remarkable example of literal construction of a statute overriding policy considerations: ibid at para 43. See also *Vaickuviene v Sainsbury* [2013] CSIH 67 discussed beyond para 12.14.

9 PHA 1997, s 8(5)(a). But an action of damages for non-harassment is not an action for personal injuries: *G v S* 2007 SCLR 137.

10 PHA 1997, s 8(6).

11 PHA 1997, s 8(5)(b). Although an interim interdict is competent, an interim non-harassment order is not: *Heenan v Dillon* 1999 Fam LR 62. On non-harassment orders, see, for example, *McCann v McGurran* 2002 SLT 592; *McGuire v Kidston* 2002 SLT (Sh Ct) 66.

12 PHA 1997, s 9.

13 PHA 1997, s 8(4). To succeed, the defender has to show that he had acted rationally: *Hayes v Willoughby* [2013] UKSC 17.

14 PHA 1997, s 8 A.

C. INTENTIONAL WRONGS RELATING TO PROPERTY

(1) Heritable property

(a) Trespass

1.13 It is often wrongly assumed that Scots law does not recognise the wrong of trespass. Indeed, it has been judicially opined that the word 'trespasser' means nothing more in Scots law than 'a person who intrudes on the lands of another without that other's permission'.[1] However, as we shall see, a person who deliberately enters another's land may be interdicted from doing so again and is liable to pay damages if he has caused any harm to the property. Trespass is a *temporary* intrusion into property owned by another without the permission of the owner: for example, playing football in the owner's field or taking a short cut through his garden. Because heritable property is owned *a coelo usque ad centrum* (from the heavens to the centre of the earth) trespass protects an owner's air space as well as his land and the ground below his property. Thus for example, the owner of a house successfully obtained an interdict preventing the respondent's crane from sweeping over his property when the respondent was building on adjacent land.[2] Because of this, statute provides that aircraft may fly over a person's land without liability for trespass.[3]

The primary remedy for trespass is interdict. No compensation is available unless there has been actual damage to the property as a result of the intrusion. There is therefore no liability for damages in Scots law merely for entering another's property. But the proprietor is entitled to use self-help to remove a trespasser provided it is reasonable in the circumstances; for example, the owner could ask a trespasser playing football in his field to leave but not threaten him with violence if the trespasser refuses to do so.[4] Interdict is an equitable remedy and is not granted automatically merely on proof of an unauthorised entry onto land. Before an interdict will be granted, further intrusions must be likely and the intention of the trespasser is important. Any potential damage to the land as a result of the trespass will also be a relevant consideration. In *Winans v Macrae*,[5] for example, a shooting tenant of a lease of 200,000 acres was, perhaps understandably, refused an interdict to prevent a cottar's pet lamb from entering the property.

In summary, apart from specific statutory offences, in Scots law trespass is not per se criminal, does not give rise to an action in damages unless actual damage has been done to the property and will only result in an interdict if likely to recur again and any potential damage is not *de minimis*. However, the landowner is allowed a reasonable degree of self-help to remove the trespasser.

In this section, trespass has been defined as a *temporary* intrusion onto land. If a person enters onto another's property with the intention of occupying it for an indefinite period, for example a squatter, he does commit a criminal offence under the Trespass (Scotland) Act 1865. If the owner is not in possession at the time, the squatter is liable for the wrong of intrusion; if the owner is in possession and has been wrongfully removed by the squatter, the squatter is liable for the wrong of ejection. The rightful owner can seek summary ejection, violent profits[6] and compensation for actual losses incurred.

Trespass is concerned the temporary intrusion by a person onto the land of another. Sometimes property may intrude on a person's land without his consent, for example if a person builds beyond his boundaries and on his neighbour's land. This is an actionable wrong and is known as encroachment. The remedies are interdict, an order for removal or damages: self-help while sometimes unwise is nevertheless lawful.[7]

1 *Dumbreck v Robert Addie & Sons (Colleries) Ltd* 1928 SC 547 at 554 per the Lord President (Clyde), 1928 SLT 341.On trespass see Gordon Cameron, SULI *Delict* paras 14.114 ff.
2 *Brown v Lee Constructions Ltd* 1977 SLT (Notes) 61, OH.
3 Civil Aviation Act 1982, s 76.
4 If the self-help is excessive and results in physical harm to the trespasser, the owner can be liable for assault or negligence: *Revill v Newberry* [1996] QB 567, [1996] 1 All ER 291 (owner shot the trespasser!).
5 (1885) 12 R 1051.
6 Violent profits are the greatest profits the owner could have made if he was in actual possession of the land. It is thought that this should have been the remedy awarded in *Saeed v Waheed* 1996 SLT (Sh Ct) 39, 1995 SCLR 504, rather than damages for negligence.
7 For a discussion of encroachment, see Gretton and Steven *Property, Trusts and Succession* (Tottel, 2009) paras 17.10ff.

(b) *In aemulationem vicini*

1.14 When A owns land (X) which adjoins B's land (Y), A will be liable to B if he uses his land (X) in a way that is detrimental to B's enjoyment of his land (Y). Before A is liable for using his land *in aemulationem vicini*, A must use his land with the predominant motive of harming B and not to further A's legitimate interests. If A's predominant motive is not to harm B, then A cannot be liable for this wrong but A's conduct may amount to nuisance.[1]

An example of use of land *in aemulationem vicini* would be where A intercepted water flowing below his land with the predominant purpose of preventing the water percolating onto his neighbour, B's, land.[2] However, when these facts were litigated in the English case of *Bradford v Pickles,*[3] the House of Lords held that *in aemulationem vicini* was not part of English law. The case is important because Lord Watson, the Scottish Lord of Appeal in Ordinary, stated *obiter* that *in aemulationem vicini* was also not part of Scots law.[4] This *obiter dictum* was contrary to institutional authority. In *Campbell v Muir*[5] where the defender spitefully exercised his right to fish from a boat in a river in such a way that it prevented anglers on the opposite bank from being able to cast their rods, the Lord President (Dunedin) held that the pursuer would have been entitled to interdict because 'the defender was on the particular occasion acting *in aemulationem vicini* against his neighbour's right, and that that was a just ground for complaint'.[6] In *More v Boyle*[7] it was accepted by the sheriff that the doctrine of *in aemulationem vicini* is still part of Scots law.

Liability arises only if it can be shown that the defender acted with the predominant motive of harming the pursuer. It is, of course, difficult to establish malice, so an objective assessment must be made of the defender's conduct in order to infer malice. But unlike nuisance, which is usually concerned with a continuing wrong,[8] liability for use of land *in aemulationem vicini* can arise from a single act of the defender provided the predominant motive of harm to the pursuer can be established.

1 On nuisance, see paras 10.6–10.8 below.
2 See Kames *Principles of Equity* (4th edn, 1800) p 42.
3 [1895] AC 587, HL.
4 [1895] AC 587 at 597–598.
5 1908 SC 387, 15 SLT 737.
6 1908 SC 387 at 393.
7 1967 SLT (Sh Ct) 38.
8 See para 10.6 below.

(2) Moveable property

(a) Trespass

1.15 In *Leitch v Leydon*[1] the complainers sold soda water to their customers. Since the bottles were more expensive than the contents, it was a term of the contract with their customers that the complainers retained the ownership of the siphons which should be returned to them when the contents were finished. Instead, some customers went to the respondent to have the bottles filled with his soda water. The House of Lords held that the complainers were not entitled to an interdict preventing the respondent from filling their bottles with soda water. While the complainers might have an action for breach of contract against their customers, the respondent had not incurred any delictual liability in filling the bottles with soda water at the request of the complainers' customers who had lawful possession of the siphons. In the course of his speech, Viscount Dunedin said that the concept of trespass to moveables[2] 'in a Scottish lawyer's mouth is a perfectly unmeaning phrase'.[3]

Nevertheless, where there have been 'sit-ins' on board a ship[4] or offshore oil installations,[5] it has been held that the delict of trespass was committed even although neither the ship nor off-shore oil installations constitute heritable property. The Lord Ordinary (Dunpark) maintained that 'Scots law offers remedies for the unlawful *occupation* of property, be it heritable or moveable'.[6] It would appear, therefore, that where the trespass consists of the unlawful occupation of moveable property, for example, a car or caravan, a ship or an oil installation, there is delictual liability even though the property concerned is technically moveable rather than heritable. Where the moveable property cannot be occupied, like the soda siphons in *Leitch v Leydon*,[7] merely to handle the property does not per se constitute the delict of trespass.

1 1931 SC (HL) 1.
2 Delictual liability would arise if the respondent had intended to 'pass off' the soda water as that of the complainer. On passing off, see paras 1.17–1.18 below.
3 1931 SC (HL) 1 at 12.
4 *Phestos Shipping Co Ltd v Kurmiawan* 1983 SC 165, 1983 SLT 388.
5 *Shell UK Ltd v McGillivray* 1991 SLT 667.
6 *Phestos Shipping Co Ltd v Kurmiawan* 1983 SLT 388 at 391.
7 1931 SC (HL) 1. For this reason there was no liability in trespass when the defender handled the pursuer's gas cylinders in *Calor Gas Ltd v Express Fuels (Sc) Ltd* 2008 SLT 123.

(b) Wrongful interference with moveable property

1.16 Unless moveable property is actually occupied, in Scots law the delict of trespass is not available to the owner. This does not mean that the owner of moveable property is without legal redress if a person wrongfully interferes with the property. But the owner's remedy may lie in areas of the law other than the law of delict. Consider the following examples:

(1) A owns a horse. B steals the horse. Under the law of property, A is entitled to sue B for the return of the horse, ie A can vindicate (claim ownership of) the horse. If B had sold the horse to C, a bona fide purchaser for value, A can still vindicate against C because a *vitium reale* attaches to the horse.
(2) A owns a horse. B steals the horse and sells it to C. C slaughters the horse and boils it down to make glue. Under the law of

property, the glue belongs to C. A can no longer vindicate since the horse, ie A's property, no longer exists. What remedies are available to A? First, if the delict still exists, A could sue B for spuilzie.[1] Second, he may have a delictual action against C on the general principles of *culpa*. If C knew the horse belonged to A, then A can sue C for intentionally destroying the horse. But even if C did not know that the horse belonged to A, A may be able to sue C if, in the circumstances, C was at fault in going ahead in boiling down the horse without inquiring whether or not B was the animal's true owner. Thus, in *Faulds v Townsend*,[2] a thief stole a horse which he sold in the middle of the night to the defender who turned the unfortunate animal into chemicals. Because of the circumstances of the sale and the fact that the horse was in good condition, the court held that the defender was under a duty to inquire as to the ownership of the horse; he had not done so and was therefore at fault and the owner could sue for damages under the general principles of *culpa*.[3] Finally, even if fault could not be established, on principles of unjustified enrichment, A may seek recompense from C in respect of his use of the horse and, indeed, could obtain any profits which C made from the sale of the glue.

(3)   The modern equivalent of the horse is, of course, the motor car. As a general rule, the same principles would apply if A's car was stolen. Difficulties can arise where A is technically the owner of a car, for example a finance company, the car being purchased by B, a hirer, on a contract of hire purchase; what is A's remedy if B sells the car in breach of the hire contract to C, a third party? These difficulties are illustrated by *FC Finance v Langtry Investment Co Ltd*[4] FC Finance owned a motor car which was hired to Allan under a contract of hire purchase. In breach of the contract, Allan sold the car to McKay who traded as Medwin Motors. McKay sold the car on hire purchase to Kennedy. The hire purchase was financed by Langtry Investment Co and Kennedy paid the instalments. Part III of the Hire Purchase Act 1964 provides an exception to the *nemo dat quod non habet* principle and Kennedy as an innocent private purchaser acquired a good title to the car.[5] Therefore FC Finance could not vindicate against Kennedy. McKay was a man of straw. FC Finance had registered the car with HP Information Ltd; any finance company could telephone HP Information Ltd and discover, before buying the car, whether it was subject to an existing hire purchase agreement. These complex facts are summarised in the diagram below.

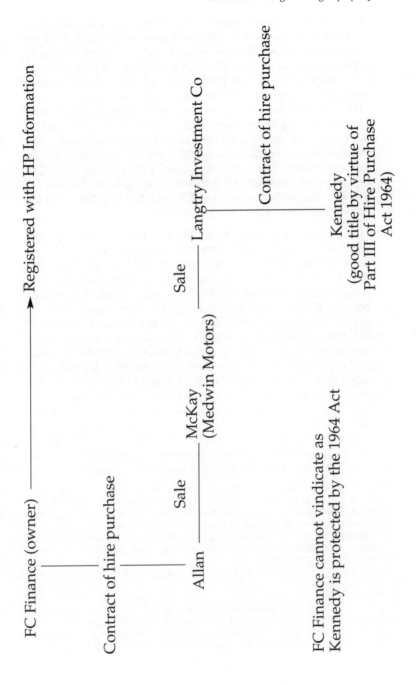

FC Finance's primary remedy was to sue Allan for breach of contract. However, Allan had emigrated to Canada. In these circumstances, FC Finance sought redress against Langtry Investment. It was held that there was no duty on Langtry Investment to check with HP Information Ltd before financing Kennedy's hire purchase of the motor car. But because Medwin Motors had offered them cars subject to subsisting hire purchase agreements on previous occasions, Langtry Investment should have been on their guard and were therefore at fault – like the defender in *Faulds v Townsend*[6] – for not making inquiries. Therefore they were liable on general principles of *culpa*. The parties agreed that if the defenders were liable, the measure of damages would be the balance of the outstanding hire purchase payments owed by Allan to FC Finance.

This decision is controversial. The pursuer's loss was purely economic – there was no physical damage to the car. As we shall see below, in cases of unintentional wrongs the courts have been reluctant to allow recovery for pure economic loss. It is therefore doubtful whether there was sufficient proximity between the parties to impose a duty of care on the defender to prevent the pursuer suffering pure economic loss as a result of the defender's careless conduct. This might have been a case where spuilzie should have been resurrected, since the defender had wrongfully interfered with the possession of the pursuer's moveable property. Another solution might have been for the pursuer to have sued in unjustified enrichment for the amount that the defender was *lucratus* as a result of the mistaken dealings with the car. Whatever the answer, the case is an important example of how the law of delict cannot be treated in isolation from other areas of law when considering the difficult issues that can arise in modern commercial dealings.

1 See Introduction above. For an attempt to revive the delict see *FC Finance Ltd v Brown & Son* 1969 SLT (Sh Ct) 41. In *Calor Gas Ltd v Express Fuels Ltd* 2008 SLT 123 the pursuer's customers were entitled to possession of the pursuer's gas cylinders. They voluntarily transferred them to the defender who returned them to the pursuer. Because possession was given voluntarily to the defender and the defender had returned the cylinders, the defender could not be liable in spuilzie.
2 (1861) 23 D 437, 33 SJ 224.
3 Ie because of his careless conduct in not satisfying himself as to the true ownership of the horse.
4 1973 SLT (Sh Ct) 11.
5 Before Part III of the 1964 Act applies, there must be a valid contract of hire between the finance company and the person who sells the car to the bona fide private purchaser: if the contract of hire is void the 1964 Act does not apply and the bona fide private purchaser does not acquire title to the property: *Shogun*

Finance Ltd v Hudson (FC) [2004] 1 AC 919. For further discussion see MacQueen and Thomson *Contract Law in Scotland* (3rd edn, 2012) paras 4.41ff.
6 (1861) 23 D 437, discussed above.

(c) Goodwill – passing off

1.17 The goodwill and reputation of a business can be a very valuable asset. Important elements of goodwill are the marketing devices used to enable customers to recognise the product and distinguish it from the products of competitors. These devices include trade names, personal and geographical names associated with a product, for example Rennie Mackintosh jewellery[1] or Glenfiddich whisky,[2] and the 'get up' of the product, for example a distinctive container.[3] If a competitor markets a product using a similar name or get up, this may cause confusion among actual or potential customers resulting in damage to the goodwill of the original trader through loss of custom or loss of reputation if the rival product is inferior. In order to protect a trader's goodwill, the delict of 'passing off' has been developed.

Goodwill consists of the features of a business which attract customers to trade with that business. Before there is an action for passing off it must be established that there is a close association between the trader and the particular device which identifies the product or services for existing or potential customers, ie that the device is part of the goodwill of the trader. It may be very difficult, particularly in relation to ordinary words, as opposed to invented words, to show that the word is a marketing device peculiar to the goodwill of a particular trader. Some words, such as 'hoover', may become part of ordinary usage and lose their distinctive quality of being associated with a particular manufacturer. On the other hand, other words, such as 'Scotch', while describing a geographical situation, may, as in relation to whisky, acquire a secondary meaning peculiar to a particular product. Similar difficulties can arise if a trader claims that the shape of a product is sufficiently distinctive to constitute a protectable device; but a lemon-shaped container of lemon juice has been held to have a secondary meaning associated with a particular product.[4] Once it is established that the device is part of his goodwill, the law will protect the goodwill of the trader from being undermined by a competitor passing off his own product by using a similar name or get up.

1 *Carrick Jewellery Ltd v Ortak* 1989 GWD 35-1624, OH.
2 *William Grant & Sons Ltd v William Cadenhead Ltd* 1985 SC 121, 1985 SLT 291.

3 *John Haig & Co Ltd v Forth Blending Co Ltd* 1954 SC 35, 1954 SLT 2, OH (dimple bottle); *Reckitt and Colman Products Ltd v Borden Inc* [1990] 1 All ER 873, HL (Jif plastic lemon).
4 *Reckitt and Colman Products Ltd v Borden Inc* [1990] 1 All ER 873, HL.

1.18 The criteria of the wrong were articulated by Lord Diplock in the leading case of *Erven Warnink BV v J Townend & Sons (Hull) Ltd*.[1] Passing off consists of:

'(1) a misrepresentation (2) made by a trader in the course of trade, (3) to prospective customers of his or ultimate consumers of goods or services supplied by him, (4) which is calculated to injure the business or goodwill of another (in the sense that this is a reasonably foreseeable consequence) and (5) which caused actual damage to a business or goodwill of the trader by whom the action is brought or (in a *quia timet* action) will probably do so'.[2]

The essence of the wrong is that by using the same or similar device which forms part of the goodwill of the pursuer, the defender misrepresents his product as that of the pursuer, thus causing actual or potential damage to the pursuer's business. There is little difficulty if the exact device is used: but an action of passing off will lie even where there are differences provided there is likelihood of confusion among a substantial number of the pursuer's customers or potential customers. If there is no likelihood of confusion, then there is no passing off even if, for example, the same name is used.[3] Thus in *Dunlop Pneumatic Tyre Co v Dunlop Motor Co*[4] it was held that the pursuers, a large manufacturer of tyres, would not be confused with a small family-owned garage of a similar name in Kilmarnock. There is less likelihood of confusion where the products do not belong to a 'common field of activity'. In *Scottish Milk Marketing Board v Dryborough & Co Ltd*,[5] for example, the pursuer, who marketed 'Scottish Pride' butter, failed to interdict the defender from selling 'Scottish Pride' lager since it was unlikely that the products – being so different – would be confused. Although confusion is more likely to be established where there is a common field of activity, a common field of activity is not essential where the device to be protected is, for example, a household name.[6] If there is sufficient likelihood of confusion, it may not be permissible for the defender to use his own name.[7]

In *John Haig & Co Ltd v Forth Blending Co Ltd*[8] the pursuers established that a particular type of bottle (Dimple) was distinctive to their product's get up and successfully interdicted a rival from using a similarly shaped bottle in spite of its having a different label and stopper. The court was satisfied that when in use in a bar, there was a sufficient degree of likelihood of confusion to constitute passing off.

It has been held that manufacturers of Scotch whisky may interdict persons from exporting Scotch whisky which they know will be mixed with local spirit abroad and passed off in the foreign country as the genuine article.[9] Similarly, passing off actions will lie where a spirit not distilled in Scotland is marketed as Scotch.[10] In *Lang Bros Ltd v Goldwell Ltd*[11] the defender manufactured 'Wee McGlen', a whisky Mac, a blend of Scotch whisky and ginger wine which was made in England. This get up consisted of various words and phrases as well as a caricature of a betartaned Scotsman. The Lord Ordinary (Wheatley), a well-known teetotaller, held that the action was relevant. The get up could mislead the public into thinking that the whole product, ie the ginger wine as well as the whisky, was made in Scotland. This misrepresentation as to the origin of the ginger wine could endanger the reputation and goodwill which attaches to Scotch whisky because of its origins. This decision seems to push the wrong to its limits since the defender was not misrepresenting his product as Scotch whisky, nor was the get up proved to be part of the exclusive goodwill of the pursuer.[12]

At one time it was thought that passing off was simply a particular aspect of the delict of fraud. This is no longer thought to be sound – at least if the only remedy sought is interdict as opposed to damages. Although the misrepresentation which constitutes passing off must be 'calculated to injure' the pursuer's business or goodwill, it is enough if this is a reasonably foreseeable consequence of the misrepresentation.[13] In other words, the 'calculated to injure' element is objectively ascertained.

The primary remedy is interdict. Damages may be restricted to cases of actual fraud. It is extremely difficult to assess and quantify damages in respect of loss of custom, potential custom and goodwill.[14]

1 [1979] AC 731 at 742, [1979] 2 All ER 927, HL. This approach was applied by the Second Division of the Inner House of the Court of Session in *Lang Bros Ltd v Goldwell Ltd* 1980 SC 237, 1982 SLT 309.

2 For a slightly different formulation, see also the speech of Lord Fraser of Tullybelton in *Erven Warnink BV v J Townend & Sons (Hull) Ltd* [1979] AC 731 at 755 and 756, [1979] 2 All ER 927, HL.

3 *Harrods Ltd v Harrodian School* [1996] RPC 697, (1996) *Times*, 3 April 1996, CA.

4 1907 SC (HL) 15, 15 SLT 362. But in *Property Care Ltd v White Thomson Preservation Ltd* [2008] CSIH 44, 2008 GWD 28–440, Extra Div, the similarity in trade, in trading area and names between the parties was held sufficient to cause confusion among customers.

5 1985 SLT 253, OH.
6 In *Lego System A/S v Lego M Lemelstrich Ltd* [1983] FSR 155, a toy manufacturer successfully obtained an injunction preventing the manufacturers of irrigation equipment from using the name 'Lego' on the basis that their goodwill might be affected if they entered the same type of business as the defendant some time in the future.
7 *Parker-Knoll Ltd v Knoll International* [1962] RPC 265, HL.
8 1954 SC 35, 1954 SLT 2, OH.
9 *John Walker & Sons Ltd v Douglas Laing & Co* 1993 SLT 156, OH.
10 *John Walker & Sons Ltd v Douglas McGibbon & Co Ltd* 1972 SLT 128, OH; *John Walker & Sons Ltd v Henry Ost & Co Ltd* [1970] 2 All ER 106, [1971] 1 WLR 917. Nevertheless, the author has noted that 'House of Lords' whisky, which used to be sold in the Crush Bar at Covent Garden was manufactured in England!
11 1980 SC 237, 1982 SLT 309.
12 See, further, H L MacQueen 'Wee McGlen and the Action of Passing Off' 1982 SLT (News) 225.
13 *Erven Warnink BV v J Townend & Sons (Hull) Ltd* [1979] AC 731 at 742 per Lord Diplock.
14 On passing off generally, see 18 *Stair Memorial Encyclopaedia* paras 1451–1500.

(d) Confidential information

1.19   Information can be very valuable. However, the law has not yet been prepared to regard information per se as a form of property.[1] Nevertheless, it is now clear that Scots law recognises a general obligation arising *ex lege* not to divulge information given in confidence.[2] But what is not clear is whether this obligation is delictual *stricto sensu* or whether, given the influence of equitable principles on the development of the obligation in English law,[3] it is better treated as an obligation *sui generis*. In these circumstances, only a basic outline of the law will be discussed in this section.[4]

The essence of the obligation is the duty not to disclose information given in confidence. There is generally no limit on the type of information which is protected; it is the fact that it is given in confidence which is important.[5] Information which has been protected includes sensitive government intelligence, trade secrets and personal information as to a person's sexual activities.

At first the obligation not to disclose information given in confidence arose from a contractual relationship between the parties. The classic example is, of course, employer and employee. In *Duke of Argyll v Duchess of Argyll*,[6] the Duke of Argyll obtained an injunction [interdict] to prevent the Duchess divulging information as to his private life which he had given to her when they were married. While there is, of course, a contractual nexus between husband and wife, the obligation is also recognised where there is no contract between the parties but the relationship is clearly one of confidence, for example, doctor and patient, priest and parishioner, cohabitees whether heterosexual or homosexual, or simply friends.[7] At one time confidentiality did not attach to all acts of physical, ie sexual, intimacy: the degree of intimacy, the nature of the relationship of the parties and the effect of disclosure on third parties, for example children, were all relevant factors.[8] In particular the transitory relationship between a prostitute and a customer in a brothel was not confidential and the fact that sexual activity had taken place did not per se create a relationship of confidentiality.[9] But as a result of the increasing influence of Article 8(1) of the European Convention on Human Rights, the right to respect for a person's private and family life [sic], it appears that engaging in sex with prostitutes can now of itself generate a relationship of confidence between the parties provided the parties are genuinely consenting and there is no significant breach of the criminal law.[10]

1 *Grant v Allan* 1987 JC 71, 1988 SLT 11.
2 *Lord Advocate v Scotsman Publications Ltd* 1988 SLT 490 at 502–503 per Lord Justice Clerk (Ross), at 508–509 per Lord Dunpark and at 514 per Lord McDonald; 1989 SLT 705, HL at 708 per Lord Keith of Kinkel.
3 The view has been taken that the substance of the law is the same in both Scotland and England: *Lord Advocate v Scotsman Publications Ltd* 1989 SLT 705, HL at 708 per Lord Keith. It has been observed that this is a developing area of Scots law and could evolve differently from the law in England: *Quilty v Windsor* 1999 SLT 346 at 356 per the Lord Ordinary (Kingarth).
4 For a full account, see R Goldberg SULI *Delict* Chapter 12.
5 An employee may use information given in confidence by a former employer provided it is not a trade secret and there is no valid restrictive covenant: *Faccenda Chicken Ltd v Fowler* [1987] Ch 117, [1986] 1 All ER 617, CA.
6 [1967] Ch 302, [1965] 1 All ER 611.
7 *Stephens v Avery* [1988] Ch 449, [1988] 2 All ER 477; *Barrymore v News Group Newspapers Ltd* [1997] FSR 600, Ch D.
8 *A v B plc* [2003] QB 195 (married professional footballer's adulterous affairs with two women not confidential).
9 *Theakston v MGN Ltd* [2002] EWHC 137 (QB), [2002] EMLR 398 137.
10 *Mosley v News Group Newspapers Ltd* [2008] EWHC 1777 (QB), [2008] All ER (D) 322 (Jul), QBD (the claimant and all the participants acknowledged the code of discretion on the S and M scene): see Elspeth Reid 'No Sex Please, We're European' 2009 13 Edin LR 116. In *McKennitt v Ash* [2008] QB 73 it was observed by the Court of Appeal that Article 8 constitutes the very content of breach of confidence.

1.20 It is therefore clear that if A gives information to B, where there is a confidential relationship between the parties, then even if there is no contract between A and B, B is under an obligation not to divulge the information. If B divulges the information to C, the question then arises whether C owes an obligation to A not to disclose the information. At first, the Scottish courts were reluctant to impose an obligation on C unless there was an agreement between A and C that the information was given in confidence.[1] It is now settled that C does owe an obligation to A if C knows or ought to have known that the information was confidential.[2] In *Douglas v Hello! Ltd (No 5)*[3] for example, the defendant knew that the plaintiffs had agreed that another magazine had an exclusive right to publish the plaintiffs' wedding photographs. A paparazzo managed to evade the security at the wedding and took unauthorised photographs which the defendant published. The photographic representation of the wedding was held to have the necessary quality of confidence and could be protected as a trade secret. Given that the defendant knew about the arrangements for the exclusive right to publish the wedding photographs, as a reasonable person he must have known that the paparazzo's photographs constituted a breach of confidence, so that the defendant's publication of those photographs was in turn a breach of confidence. The test would appear to be that an obligation arises if a reasonable person would have realised in all the circumstances that he/she was bound to treat the information as confidential. The 'reasonable person' test explains not only why, in the example above, C owes an obligation to A not to disclose the information but also why B owes a similar obligation to A. For where there is an agreement between A and B not to disclose the information, or where there is a confidential relationship with or without a contractual nexus, a reasonable person in B's position would realise that the information is given in confidence.

In *Campbell v MGN*,[4] the House of Lords decided that in respect of private information the wrong should be called misuse of private information. Information was private and therefore confidential if the *claimant* had a reasonable expectation of privacy or the person publishing the material knew or ought to have known that the *claimant* had a reasonable expectation that the information would be kept confidential.[5] Thus photographs of Miss Campbell leaving a drug addiction clinic were regarded as private as the publisher ought to have know that *she* had a reasonable expectation that her attendance at the clinic would be kept confidential. Other examples would be love letters or intimate photographs or photographs of a celebrity's child when the publisher knew that the parents would object.[6]

Nevertheless it is submitted that there should only be one test for determining whether a person owes an obligation not to disclose information, ie whether in all the circumstances a reasonable person in that position would have realised that the information was confidential. The factors to be considered is the nature of the information itself for example, private information or government information; the relationship between the parties, for example employer and employee or lovers; whether or not there is an express statement as to confidentiality[7] or an implied term as to confidentiality between the parties; whether or not the information was obtained by illegal or improper means, for example industrial espionage or computer 'hacking'.[8] If the 'reasonable person' test is satisfied, then the obligation not to divulge the information arises.

1 *Roxburgh v Seven Seas Engineering Ltd* 1980 SLT (Notes) 49, OH.
2 *Lord Advocate v Scotsman Publications Ltd* 1988 SLT 490, affd 1989 SLT 705, HL.
3 [2003] EWHC 786 (Ch), [2003] 3 All ER 996.
4 [2004] UKHL 22, [2004] 2 AC 457, [2004] 2 WLR 1232, [2004] UKHRR 648, HL.
5 Ibid per Lord Nicholls at para 14, per Lord Hope at para 85 and Baroness Hale at para 134.
6 This was so even though the photographs were taken of the child in a public place: *Murray v Big Pictures (UK) Ltd* [2008] EWCA Civ 446, [2008] 2 FLR 599, [2008] 3 FCR 661, CA (the child was the child of JK Rowling). By accepting that private property could consist of photographs of a child of a celebrity going about in public, the Court of Appeal appears to be embracing the approach of the European Court of Human Rights in *von Hannover v Germany* (2005) 40 EHHR 1 (photographs of Princess Caroline in a public place). Cf *von Hannover v Germany No 2* (2012) 55 EHRR 15 where the publication of the photographs contributed, at least to some degree, to a debate of general interest.
7 The fact that the parties considered themselves to be under an obligation of confidence is important but not decisive. The test is ultimately objective: *De Maudsley v Palumbo* [1996] FSR 447, (1995) *Times*, 19 December 1995, Ch D.
8 See further 'Breach of Confidence' (SLC no 90; Cmnd 9385 (1984)) p 64.

1.21 The obligation not to disclose information only continues if the information remains confidential. But merely because the information is known to some other people, for example specialists in a scientific field, does not prevent the information being confidential. In *Exchange Telegraph Co Ltd v Giulianotti*,[1] the pursuer transmitted the results of races to subscribers. It was held that the information was still confidential even though the spectators at the event knew the result. But if the information is clearly in the public domain, it is no longer confidential and the obligation ceases to exist.[2] Thus, if A gives confidential information to B, and A later divulges the information to the world, B's obligation not to disclose the information comes to an end.[3] This principle has also been extended to the following situation: A gives information in confidence to B and B gives the information to C in circumstances where C as a reasonable person would realise it is confidential; if B divulges the information to the world, then C's obligation comes to an end. A will, of course, have a remedy in damages against B for breach of confidence.[4] That said, in *Douglas v Hello! (No 8)*,[5] a majority[6] of the House of Lords held that the authorised photographs of the wedding remained protected by the obligation of confidence in spite of the publication of the unauthorised photographs since the complainant magazine had bought the rights from the Douglases to be the only source of publication of their wedding.

Although it has been held in England that there can be liability for unintentional breach of confidence,[7] it is thought that a pursuer would be unlikely to obtain damages in Scots law unless the defender intended to breach the confidence.[8]

1 1959 SC 19, 1959 SLT 293, OH.
2 *Attorney-General v Guardian Newspapers Ltd (No 2)* [1990] 1 AC 109, [1988] 3 All ER 545, HL. If the information has always been in the public domain, it will never have been confidential: *Author of a Blog v Times Newspapers Ltd* [2009] EWHC 1358.
3 *O Mustad & Son v S Allcock & Co Ltd and Dosen* [1963] 3 All ER 416, [1964] 1 WLR 109, HL.
4 *Attorney-General v Guardian Newspapers Ltd (No 2)* [1990] 1 AC 109, [1988] 3 All ER 545, HL. A could not obtain an interdict against B to prevent further disclosure since the information was no longer confidential.
5 [2008] 1 AC 1.
6 Lord Hoffmann, Baroness Hale, Lord Brown; Lord Nicholls and Lord Walker dissenting.
7 *Seager v Copydex Ltd* [1967] 2 All ER 415, [1967] 1 WLR 923, CA. But the defender must use the information before the principle applies: *Vestergaard Frandsen S/A v Bestnet Europe Ltd* [2013] UKSC 31.
8 Since the test of confidentiality is that of the reasonable person, ie an objective test, it is theoretically possible that a person could breach the obligation when he or she did not subjectively know that the information was confidential, ie because the person had not in fact reached the standard of the reasonable person.

1.22   The obligation not to disclose information given in confidence is not absolute. A defence is available if disclosure was in the public interest. Thus disclosure is justifiable if the information concerned the commission of a crime or a civil wrong.[1] Information disclosed to a public official or agency which could take appropriate action, for example the police, is more likely to provide justification than simple disclosure to the media.[2] The courts must engage in a balancing exercise between the public interest in protecting confidential information and the public interest in access to information which should be known. In *X v Y*[3] a newspaper disclosed the identity of two doctors suffering from AIDS. The newspaper argued that it was in the public interest that patients should know the HIV status of their medical practitioners.

In rejecting this defence, the court took the view that the public interest in maintaining confidentiality prevailed because it encouraged persons suffering from AIDS, including doctors, to seek treatment. In the case of government information, the Crown cannot obtain an interdict merely because the information is confidential: the public interest in open government will justify disclosure.[4] However, the public interest in disclosure will be 'trumped' if the disclosure of the information would be damaging to national security.[5]

In more recent cases, the court has articulated that what is often involved is a balancing exercise between the individual's right to respect for his private and family life under Article 8(1) and the right to freedom of expression under Article 10(1).[6] In *Campbell v MGN*[7] for example, the claimant's right to privacy was held to outweigh the publisher's right to freedom of expression because the publication of Miss Campbell leaving the clinic in addition to the text might undermine her treatment and was offensive. In *Mosely v News Group Newspapers Ltd*,[8] Eady J took the view that the Article 8 right to enjoy sex in privacy would usually outweigh the Article 10 right unless publication disclosed questions of national security, political, social or artistic debate, corruption or mismanagement in the political or commercial sector and crime or other wrongdoing. Nevertheless in *Ferdinand v MGN*,[9] the defendant was allowed to publish an article concerning Ferdinand's alleged relationship with a woman. There was public interest in showing that the image he had previously tried to convey of himself was false and a substantial body of the public would expect higher standards from the England football captain.

The primary remedy for breach of confidence is interdict.[10] Damages are possible though difficult to assess. The person divulging the information may be required to account for any profits made from doing so.[11]

This is an area where the European Convention on Human Rights is playing a particularly significant role. It is difficult to remember that just over ten years ago in *Wainwright v Home Office*[12] the House of Lords held that English law did not have to accept some high-level legal principle of privacy in order to comply with Article 8. But the development of legal protection of confidential information has often had the effect of protecting the privacy of a person's private life.[13]

1 *Initial Services Ltd v Putterill* [1968] 1 QB 396, [1967] 3 All ER 145, CA.

2 *British Steel Corpn v Granada Television Ltd* [1981] AC 1096, [1981] 1 All ER 417, HL.
3 [1988] 2 All ER 648, [1988] RPC 379.
4 *Lord Advocate v Scotsman Publications Ltd* 1988 SLT 490, affd 1989 SLT 705, HL.
5 *Attorney-General v Guardian Newspapers Ltd (No 2)* [1990] 1 AC 109, [1988] 3 All ER 545, HL. Although the information in that case was prima facie damaging to national security, by the time the case reached the House of Lords knowledge of the material was so widespread that an injunction on further serialisation of the information was refused; in other words, the information was no longer confidential.
6 *McKennitt v Ash* [2008] QB 73. In the balancing act between Articles 8 and 10, the jurisprudence of the European Court of Human Rights can be followed.
7 [2004] UKHL 22, [2004] 2 AC 457, [2004] 2 WLR 1232, [2004] UKHRR 648, HL.
8 [2008] EWHC 1777 (QB), [2008] All ER (D) 322 (Jul), QBD.
9 [2011] EWHC 2454 (QB).
10 The general criteria for granting interdict must, of course, be present: see, for example, *Waste Systems International Inc v Eurocare Environmental Services Ltd* 1999 SLT 198, OH.
11 *Attorney-General v Guardian Newspapers Ltd (No 2)* [1990] 1 AC 109, [1988] 3 All ER 545, HL.
12 [2003] UKHL 53, [2004] 2 AC 406, [2003] 3 WLR 137, [2003] 4 All ER 969, HL.
13 *Douglas v Hello! Ltd (No 5)* [2003] EWHC 786 (Ch), [2003] 3 All ER 996.

1.23 It should also be remembered that where there is a breach of Article 8, a claimant might be entitled to damages under the Human Rights Act 1998, even though the defender's conduct does not amount to a breach of confidence. In *Peck v United Kingdom*[1] the applicant had been filmed on CCTV walking around his home town carrying a knife; he intended to kill himself. The police were alerted and he was saved. The local council allowed the footage to be used by the media to promote the utility of CCTV. The material was not defamatory and its publication did not constitute a breach of confidential information. Nevertheless the European Court of Human Rights held that there had been a breach of Article 8(1) as the disclosure of the footage could not be justified as being in the public interest since the applicant had not been engaged in the commission of a crime. The applicant was awarded damages against the government.

This case illustrates how an action for damages may lie when there is a breach of the Convention even though the defender's conduct which constituted the breach would not be regarded as delictual under Scots law. This issue arose again in *Martin v McGuiness*.[2] The pursuer claimed that the conduct of the defender's private investigator in pretending to be a former army colleague when questioning his wife in their home, causing her distress, constituted a breach of his rights under Article 8(1). The court held that while the investigator's conduct could amount to an infringement of the pursuer's Article 8(1) right, nevertheless it was open to the defender to argue that it was a reasonable and proportionate step to take to preserve his rights in accordance with Article 8(2) (no unlawful interference with a person's Article 8(1) right if the infringement is for the protection of the rights of others). In these circumstances the court did not have to answer the difficult question of the nature of the pursuer's remedy if there had been a breach. As we have seen,[3] damages under the Human Rights Act 1998 can only be awarded against a public authority and there was no existing delictual remedy apt to provide redress in relation to the infringement of privacy which Martin had suffered.

1 (2003) 36 EHRR 41.
2 2003 SCLR 548.
3 See Introduction above.

CHAPTER 2

The economic wrongs and fraud

A. THE ECONOMIC WRONGS

(1) Introduction – the general principle

2.1 In a free market, competition is regarded as essential and in the public interest. This can result in one business being successful while another goes to the wall. The common law therefore took the view that A was entitled to harm B economically provided A used lawful means, for example undercutting the price of his product, in order to do so. Towards the end of the nineteenth century and during the twentieth century, the courts recognised a range of actionable wrongs which set parameters beyond which parties could not wield their economic and social power.[1] Since then, important statutory provisions and principles of EU law have been introduced directly to regulate competition, for example the Office of Fair Trading. Competition law is outwith the scope of this book. Nevertheless the economic wrongs remain important. The theoretical nature of these wrongs was radically redrawn by the House of Lords in *OBG v Allan*[2] (*OBG*) and *Customs and Excise Commissioners v Total Network SL*[3] (*Total*). This chapter proceeds on the principles laid down in these cases and will not discuss the earlier, now discredited, law.[4]

The basic principle is still that laid down by the House of Lords in *Allen v Flood*.[5] In this case boilermakers objected to the practice of employing shipwrights to repair ironwork on board ships. The plaintiffs were shipwrights who were employed to repair woodwork on certain ships. Members of the boilermakers' union discovered that they had previously been employed by another employer to repair ironwork on ships. Incensed, a trade union representative approached the current employer of the shipwrights and informed him that unless he dismissed the plaintiffs, his other employees would strike. This was done maliciously, to punish the plaintiffs. The employer dismissed the plaintiffs who brought the action against the trade union representative.

Three points should be noticed. First, the case proceeded on the basis that there was no conspiracy, ie no agreement among the boilermakers that they would strike; it was simply the individual trade unionist who said that there would be a strike. Second, if there had been a strike, the employees would have terminated their contracts of employment lawfully. Third, when the employer dismissed the plaintiffs he did so by lawfully terminating their contracts. In other words, the individual trade unionist used lawful means (the threat of a lawful strike) to compel the employer to use lawful means (the lawful dismissal) to harm the plaintiffs economically (the loss of their employment). In these circumstances, the House of Lords held that no wrong was committed even though the defendant had acted maliciously.

Accordingly, *Allen v Flood* is authority that an individual, A, can wield economic pressure to force B to act to his own or another's economic harm provided the means used by A are lawful. If, as in this case, the means used are lawful, no wrong is committed even if A acts maliciously to harm B or another person rather than to further A's economic interests. This result, while harsh, is an inevitable consequence of a free market economy. But if the means used are *not* lawful, delictual liability may be incurred. It is to these circumstances that we shall now turn.

1 For an excellent account of these wrongs, see Greg Gordon, SULI *Delict*, Chapter 15.
2 [2008] 1 AC 1.
3 [2008] 1 AC 1174.
4 For the previous law, see the 3rd edn of this book, Chapter 2.
5 [1898] AC 1, HL.

(2) Inducing breach of contract

2.2 If A induces B to break his contract with C, C can sue B for breach of contract. Alternatively, C may be able to sue A in *delict* for inducing B to break his contract with C. This actionable wrong was recognised as part of Scots law in *British Motor Trade Association v Gray*.[1] There Lord Russell approved counsel's concession that:

'by the law of Scotland an actionable wrong is committed by one who intentionally and without lawful justification induces or procures someone to break a contract made by him with another, if damage has resulted to that other, provided the contract creates contractual relations recognised by law'.[2]

In *OBG* the House of Lords emphasised that inducement of breach of contract is an example of accessory liability in the sense that A is only liable if B breaks his contract with C as a consequence of A's acts: A's liability in *delict* for inducement of breach of contract is therefore *accessory* to B's breach of his contract with C.

The wrong can be represented by the following diagram.

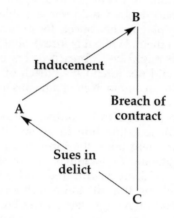

1 1951 SC 586, 1951 SLT 247.
2 1951 SC 586 at 603.

2.3   In *Global Resources Group v MacKay*[1] Lord Hodge, following the analysis in *OBG*, said that inducement of breach of contract has five characteristics:

(1) B must *breach* the contract with C: interference with B's performance of the contract which does not result in a breach of contract by B will not suffice.

(2) A must *know* that his acts will result in B breaching his contract with C. Therefore, A must be aware of the existence of the contract between B and C. It is not enough that A was reckless as to whether or not a contract existed between B and C.[2] But if A consciously decided not to inquire into the terms of the contract between B and C in the knowledge of the existence of the contract and that his actions were likely to induce a breach of that contract, that knowledge and the deliberate turning of a blind eye would probably be sufficient.

(3) A must *intend to induce the breach of contract* either as an end in itself or as the means by which he achieves some further end.[3] There is no need for A to intend to harm C. If for example A induces B to break his contract of hire with C and come to work for A at a bigger fee, A is liable even if A did not intend to harm C; the breach of contract was the means by which A achieved his objective of obtaining B's services. However there is no liability merely because it is reasonably foreseeable that A's acts might cause B to break his contract with C. If A, an artiste, under a contract to sing for an impresario, B, cancels the concert, she would not be liable to the musicians B has hired to play at the concert for inducing B to break his contracts with them. While it is foreseeable that by cancelling the concert, B might be in breach of his contracts with the musicians, A did not intend B's breach of contract with the musicians to be an end in itself or a means to an end when she cancelled the concert.[4]

(4) A must *in fact induce* B to break the contract by persuading, encouraging or assisting him to do so.[5] It is not necessary that A's inducement takes the form of unlawful means, for example threatening to assault B: A will still be liable to C if the means used are lawful and, indeed, beneficial to B, for example giving B a gift to break his contract with C. If A stands by and knowingly lets parties break their contracts this is not inducement even if it was in A's economic interests that they should do so.[6] C must suffer loss as a result of the inducement but proof of specific damage is not required and once inducement of the breach is established, some damage will readily be inferred by the court.[7]

(5) A will have a defence if the inducement of the breach is justified, for example inducing female artistes to break their contracts of employment to obtain better wages so that they do not have to resort to prostitution.[8]

---

1 2008 SLT 104 at 106–107.
2 *Rossleigh Ltd v Leader Cars Ltd* 1987 SLT 355, OH. Cf the position in England where constructive knowledge is sufficient, ie turning a blind eye: *Emerald Construction Co Ltd v Lowthian* [1966] 1 All ER 1013, [1966] 1 WLR 691, CA; *Inshore Services (International) v NFFO Services* [2001] EWCA Civ 1722.
3 *BGC Capital Markets (Switzerland) LLC v Rees* [2011] EWHC 2009 (QB). (Defendants only engaged a broker when they believed that it was lawful to employ him. In fact broker was in breach of his contract with his former employer when he did so. No liability, as defendant did not intend to cause a breach of contract.)
4 In *OBG* the House of Lords held that the decision of the Court of Appeal in *Millar v Bassey* [1994] EMLR 44 was wrong.

5 The inducement must be directed at B, the person in the contractual relationship with the victim, C: *Middlebrook Mushrooms Ltd v Transport and General Workers' Union* [1993] ICR 612, CA.
6 'Failing to stop a breach is not enough': *Calor Gas Ltd v Express Fuels (Sc) Ltd* 2008 SLT 123 per Lord Malcolm at 135.
7 *British Motor Trade Association v Gray* 1951 SC 586, 1951 SLT 247.
8 *Brimelow v Casson* [1924] 1 Ch 302.

(3) Intentional infliction of harm by unlawful means

2.4 In *OBG* the House of Lords recognised the existence of an actionable wrong of causing loss by unlawful means. The classic form of this wrong involves three parties. A with the intention of harming C uses unlawful means against B in order to cause economic harm to C.[1] In this situation, A's delictual liability is primary: it is not dependent on B committing a wrong, such as a breach of contract, against C. Consider the following examples:

(i) A steals B's tools which prevents B fulfilling a contract with C. A is not liable to C for inducing B to break his contract with C as A has not induced the breach but has prevented B's performance. But B has used unlawful means, ie theft against B and will therefore be liable for causing loss to C by unlawful means provided it can be established that A intended to harm C.
(ii) A breaks his contract with B. As a consequence, B is unable to perform his contract with C. A is not liable to C for inducing B to break his contract with C as A has not induced the breach but has prevented B's performance. But A has used unlawful means ie his own breach of contract with B and will therefore be liable to C for causing loss to C by unlawful means provided that it can be established that A intended to harm C.
(iii) A induces B to break his contract with C. As a consequence C is unable to fulfil his contract with D. A is liable to C for inducing B to break his contract with C whether or not he intended to harm C. But A has used unlawful means, ie inducing a breach of contract between B and C and will therefore be liable to D for causing loss to D by unlawful means provided it can be established that A intended to harm D.
(iv) A threatens to break his contract with B unless B ceases to trade with C. B yields to the threat and stops trading with C. As a consequence C sustains a loss. C has no redress against B as it is lawful to cease trading with a customer. But A's threat to break his contract with B is a threat to use unlawful means against B: this is intimidation and amounts to unlawful means. Therefore A has used unlawful means, intimidation of B, and

will therefore be liable to C for causing loss to C by unlawful means provided it can be established that A intended to harm C.[2]

1 See *Global Resources v McKay* 2009 SLT 104.
2 Before *OBG*, intimidation was treated as a separate actionable wrong: on intimidation see the 3rd edn of this book at pp 44–46.

2.5   The characteristics of the actionable wrong are:

(1)   A must use *unlawful means* against B. In *OBG* Lord Hoffmann[1] held that unlawful means were restricted to conduct which amounted to a civil wrong against B and which affected B's freedom to deal with the claimant, C. Thus the theft in: (i) qualifies, as B can sue A for restitution of his tools and/or recompense and the absence of his tools interfered with his freedom to perform his contract with C; in (ii) A's breach of contract with B qualifies, as it is actionable by B and interfered with his freedom to perform his contract with C; in (iii) A's inducement of a breach of contract between B and C qualifies, as it is actionable in delict by C and interfered with C's freedom to perform his contract with D. In (iv) B cannot sue A because he has sustained no loss. However in *OBG*, Lord Hoffmann held that A's conduct would be treated as unlawful means if absence of loss was the only reason B could not sue. So in (iv) A's threat to breach his contract with B qualifies as B could have sued A for breach of contract if he had not succumbed to the intimidation and the threat interfered with his freedom to trade with C. But if C had an exclusive license from B to use B's intellectual property and A infringed B's intellectual property rights, while this is a criminal offence and will cause economic loss to C the infringement would not constitute unlawful means because it does not interfere with B's freedom to deal with C.[2]

On the other hand, Lord Nicholls thought that unlawful means should embrace all acts which a person is not permitted to do whether by civil or criminal law provided the acts against B were instrumental in causing economic harm to C.[3] As we shall see, there has been support for Lord Nicholls' test in the context of unlawful means conspiracy[4] but it is thought that Lord Hoffmann's concept of unlawful means is more likely to ensure that the scope of this actionable wrong is kept within reasonable bounds.

(2) A must *intend* to harm C. The intention appears to be subjective. Harm to C does not have to be A's predominant intention. It is enough that A intentionally causes harm to C as a means to protect or promote his own economic interests. As in the case of inducement of breach of contract, there is no liability if economic harm to C is merely a foreseeable consequence of A's conduct but was not intended by A to further A's ends. So if A, a singer, cancels a concert in breach of her contract with an impresario, B, she would not be liable for any loss sustained by the musicians B had hired: but if A cancelled because she thought that the musicians had been insufficiently deferential to her during rehearsals and that they should be taught a lesson, then there would be liability.

(3) While there is no authority directly in point, it appears that a defence of justification might be possible.

We have been considering the classic three-party situation, where A uses unlawful means against B in order to cause economic harm to C. There are *dicta* that the wrong may take a two-party form, *viz* A uses unlawful means against B in order to harm B.[5] It is difficult to see how this form of the wrong can arise other than in the context of intimidation, ie where A threatens B with unlawful means unless B causes himself economic harm. In the present writer's view, however, there is no wrong of two-party intimidation because it is unnecessary. If A threatens B with violence that is itself an assault and B can sue in delict. If A threatens B with breach of contract by A, that is an anticipatory breach of contract and B can sue A in contract. If A threatens B with other delictual conduct, B must be robust and wait until the threat is carried out and then sue in delict; B cannot sue for an 'anticipatory' delict since he has not yet suffered any loss.

1 [2008] 1 AC 1 at para 45. Lord Brown and Baroness Hale agreed with Lord Hoffmann.

2 This was the result reached in *RCA v Pollard* [1983] Ch 335. In *McLeod v Rooney* [2009] CSOH 158 the defender (A) ran a company's business (B) in such a way that the company's value was greatly reduced resulting in the shareholders (C) selling their shares to A at a low price. Even though B had suffered economic loss by A's breach of contract, C could not sue A for intentional harm inflicted by unlawful means as A's conduct did not interfere with B's freedom to deal with C while they were shareholders. C might have had a claim for damages on the ground of an unlawful means conspiracy: see para 2.8 beyond.

3 [2008] 1 AC 1 at para 162. Lord Nicholls' test has difficulty in accommodating bootlegger cases such as *RCA v Pollard* [1983] Ch 335. Lord Walker did not support Lord Nicholls preferring an 'incremental approach' to unlawful means: *OBG* at para 270.

4 See para 2.8 beyond.

5 See *OBG* per Lord Hoffmann at para 61; per Lord Nicholls at para 161.

(4) Conspiracy

2.6   *Allen v Flood*[1] was concerned with the situation where A uses lawful means to harm B economically. There it was held that A was not liable in delict to B, even if his predominant motive or intention was to harm B rather than further A's legitimate business interests. Only three years later, in *Quinn v Leathem*,[2] the House of Lords held that if A and B combine together with the intention to harm C, then A and B are liable in delict for harm caused to C as a result of their combination or conspiracy against him. The rationale of the wrong of conspiracy is that while a person can be expected to withstand the harmful but lawful acts of another, he cannot be expected to withstand the harm caused by a combination or conspiracy of persons to harm him.[3] This rationalisation has been doubted, for a multinational conglomerate or oil company may exercise far greater economic power than a combination of small businesses.[4]

The essence of conspiracy is therefore a combination of persons, who come together with the intention of harming the pursuer economically. There are two types of conspiracy: (a) where the means used by the conspirators are lawful in the sense that they would not be actionable if carried out by one person alone (lawful means conspiracy); (b) where the means used by the conspirators are unlawful in the sense that *either* they would be actionable if carried out by one person alone, for example if the means constitute a delict or breach of contract, *or* they involve a crime or a breach of statute which does not provide a civil remedy for breach (unlawful means conspiracy).

1 [1898] AC 1, HL. Discussed at para 2.1 above.
2 [1901] AC 495, HL.
3 *Mogul Steamship Co Ltd v McGregor, Gow & Co* (1889) 23 QBD 598, CA, at 616 per Bowen LJ.
4 *Lonrho Ltd v Shell Petroleum Co Ltd (No 2)* [1982] AC 173, [1981] 2 All ER 456, HL, at 464 per Lord Diplock; see also *Crofter Hand Woven Harris Tweed Co Ltd v Veitch* 1942 SC (HL) 1 at 8 per Viscount Simon LC.

(a) Lawful means conspiracy

2.7   A combination of persons will be liable in conspiracy if they come together with the predominant motive or intention of harming the pursuer rather than furthering their own legitimate interests. Thus, if A and B come together with the predominant motive or intention to harm C, A and B are liable in conspiracy even if their actions, for example undercutting C's prices, would not be actionable in delict if carried out by A or B alone. It is the *combination* of A and B together *and* their predominant motive or intention of harming C which renders their conspiracy wrongful. If the predominant motive or intention of A and B is not to harm C but to further their own legitimate interests, the conspiracy is not wrongful even though C suffers economic loss as a result of the actions of A and B, always provided these actions are lawful. Where lawful means are used, a conspiracy is wrongful only if the predominant motive or intention of the conspirators is to harm the pursuer.

These principles were laid down in the leading case of *Crofter Hand Woven Harris Tweed Co Ltd v Veitch*.[1] Mill owners on the Island of Lewis who made and sold tweed cloth from yarn spun on the island were unable to agree a 100 per cent union membership agreement (closed shop) with the TGWU because of competition from rival producers on the island (the pursuers) who obtained cheaper yarn from the mainland, wove it into cloth and sold it at a lower price than the mill owners. The TGWU and the mill owners came together. They instructed the members of the TGWU who were employed at the port to refuse to handle the yarn being imported by the pursuers to the island from the mainland. The case proceeded on the basis that the dockers were not in breach of their contracts of employment with the port authority in refusing to handle the imported yarn because they were never asked by their employer to do so. The question was whether the combination amounted to an actionable conspiracy. This complex factual situation can be shown thus:

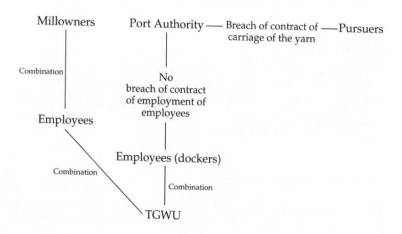

The House of Lords held that since no unlawful means were used because the dockers were not in breach of their contracts of employment, ie there was no conduct which would be actionable if done by one person alone, the conspiracy would be wrongful only if the pursuers could establish that the predominant motive or intention of the conspirators was to harm the pursuers. In this case, the predominant motive or intention was to further the union's legitimate interests, ie 100 per cent union membership. Harm to the pursuers was not their primary intention: it was only incidental to achieving their goal. Accordingly, the defenders were not liable.

It can, of course, be a very difficult issue of fact to establish whether the predominant purpose of the conspiracy is to harm the pursuer or whether the damage done to the pursuer is simply incidental to the furtherance of the conspirators' legitimate interests, be they commercial[2] or trade union interests as in the *Crofter* case. In *Scala Ballroom (Wolverhampton) Ltd v Ratcliffe*[3] it was held to be legitimate for trade union officials to organise a boycott among their members from playing at a dance hall which operated a colour bar; although this objective did not bring any financial benefits to the members of the union, it was genuinely thought by them to be in the interests of the union.

To summarise: when the combination uses lawful means, ie means which would not be actionable if done by one person alone, then the conspiracy is not delictual unless the predominant motive or intention of the conspirators is to injure the pursuer. The onus rests on the pursuer to prove that the predominant purpose of the conspiracy was to harm the pursuer economically. Moreover, the pursuer must prove economic loss.[4]

1 1942 SC (HL) 1, 1943 SLT 2.
2 As in *Mogul Steamship Co Ltd v McGregor, Gow & Co* (1889) 23 QBD 598, CA.
3 [1958] 3 All ER 220, [1958] 1 WLR 1057, CA.
4 In *Lonrho plc v Fayed (No 5)* [1994] 1 All ER 188, [1993] 1 WLR 1489, CA, the Court of Appeal accepted that the defendants could be liable in conspiracy even if the statements they had made about the plaintiff were true, ie when they would have had a defence to an action of defamation. Since the means were lawful, their predominant motive would have had to have been harm to the plaintiff. Only damages for patrimonial loss would be recoverable; cf loss of reputation. On defamation, see Chapter 15 below.

(b) Unlawful means conspiracy

2.8 In considering unlawful means conspiracy, two situations have to be discussed. First is the case where the means used are unlawful in the sense that they would be actionable as a breach of contract or delict if committed by one person alone. So, for example, if the boycotting of the imported yarn in the *Crofter* case had involved a breach of the dockers' contracts of employment (unlawful means), the union would have been liable to the pursuers for inducement of a breach of their contract with the port authority to carry the imported yarn. Where the means are delictual or amount to a breach of contract, the pursuer will usually sue on the substantive delict or breach of contract without relying on the conspiracy.

Second, the means may be unlawful but not actionable as a breach of contract or a delict if committed by one person alone. This will usually arise where the means used involve a breach of a statutory provision.[1] While breach of some statutes gives rise to an action in delict,[2] not all breaches of statute give a person who suffers harm as a result the right to sue in delict. In particular, the pursuer will not generally have title to sue in delict unless the statute was specifically designed to protect the interests of a class of persons to which the pursuer belongs.[3] In this situation, since the means used do not constitute a substantive delict, conspiracy may be the only form of redress.

The criteria for an actionable unlawful means conspiracy were the subject of two decisions of the House of Lords concerned with Lonrho. The first is *Lonrho Ltd v Shell Petroleum Co Ltd (No 2)*.[4] Lonrho owned a pipeline running from Beira in Mozambique to a refinery in Southern Rhodesia. The pipeline was operated under an agreement between Lonrho and oil companies including Shell. When Southern Rhodesia declared unilateral independence, the British government made a sanctions order under the Southern Rhodesia Act 1965. As a result of the sanctions order, oil was no longer shipped to Beira, the pipeline ceased to be used and Lonrho lost profits. Before unilateral independence was declared, the oil companies gave assurances to the Rhodesian government that they would supply petroleum products to Rhodesia through South Africa. After independence had been declared, the defendants supplied the oil to Rhodesia in breach of the sanctions order. In an action of conspiracy against the defendants, Lonrho argued that the breach of the sanctions order enabled unilateral independence to last longer and thereby led to a loss of its revenue as a result of the prolonged non-use of its pipeline.

While the supply of the oil was a breach of the sanctions order, this was simply a criminal offence. In other words, the sanction order was not imposed for the benefit of persons like Lonrho who had traded with Rhodesia before independence. There was therefore no substantive delict arising from the defendants' breach of the order. The only delictual claim had to be based on conspiracy. Both the Court of Appeal and the House of Lords held that the conspiracy was not actionable because Lonrho had failed to establish that the defendants had *intended* to harm Lonrho when they breached the sanctions order. In the course of his speech in the House of Lords, Lord Diplock expressed the view that he did not wish to extend the wrong of conspiracy beyond its existing limits.[5] Since the previous cases had been concerned with lawful means conspiracy where there is no liability unless the predominant motive or intention of the conspirators was to harm the pursuer, Lord Diplock's *dicta* were subsequently taken as authority that there was also no liability for an unlawful means conspiracy unless the primary aim of the combination was to harm the pursuer.[6]

The issue was purportedly clarified by the House of Lords in the second Lonrho case, *Lonrho plc v Fayed*.[7] Here Lonrho argued that the defendants had committed an unlawful means conspiracy against them, an alleged fraudulent misrepresentation to the Secretary of State constituting unlawful means. The House of Lords held that Lord Diplock's analysis in *Lonrho Ltd v Shell Petroleum Co Ltd (No 2)*[8] was not intended as a definitive account of the law relating to unlawful means conspiracy.[9] While accepting that a lawful means conspiracy was wrongful only if the predominant motive or intention of the conspirators was to harm the pursuer, an unlawful means conspiracy was actionable if the pursuer could establish that the conspirators had *an* intention to harm the pursuer even though that was not their *predominant* motive or intention. This intention could not be proved merely by showing that the defenders had used unlawful means: otherwise, Lonrho should have succeeded in the *Shell Petroleum* case.

In the *Total* case[10] the House of Lords unanimously rejected the argument that the concept of unlawful means should be the same for the purpose of unlawful means conspiracy as for intentional infliction of harm by unlawful means. While it might be necessary to restrict unlawful means to actionable civil wrongs to limit the scope of the latter wrong, criminal conduct which was not actionable as a substantive delict could nevertheless amount to unlawful means for the purpose of unlawful means conspiracy. It should be noticed that *Total* only involved two parties, the Revenue and the conspirators: a third party was not involved.

It remains to be seen whether the narrower concept of unlawful means would be used if the conspirators had acted against a third party in order to further their ends against the pursuer. For the present, *Total* confirms that if the conspirators have an intention to harm the pursuer, an unlawful means conspiracy is an actionable wrong even if the unlawful means used would not be actionable if done by one person alone.

To summarise: if the means used are lawful, a conspiracy is actionable only if the *predominant* motive or intention of the conspirators is to harm the pursuer; if the means used are unlawful, a conspiracy is actionable if *an* intention of the conspirators was to harm the pursuer even though that was not their primary purpose. Unlawful means include means which are delictual if done by one person alone or which constitute a breach of contract or amount to a breach of criminal law even though this would not give rise to a delictual action if done by one person alone.

1 But in the leading case of *Customs and Excise Commissioners v Total Network SL* [2008] 1AC 1174 the wrongful means was the common law crime of cheating the public revenue.
2 See Chapter 11 below.
3 *RCA Corpn v Pollard* [1983] Ch 135, [1982] 3 All ER 771, CA.
4 [1982] AC 173, [1981] 2 All ER 456, HL.
5 [1981] 2 All ER 456 at 464.
6 *Allied Arab Bank Ltd v Hajjar (No 2)* [1988] QB 944, [1988] 3 All ER 103; *Metall und Rohstoff AG v Donaldson Lufkin and Jenrette Inc* [1990] 1 QB 391, [1989] 3 All ER 14, CA.
7 [1991] 3 All ER 303, HL.
8 [1982] AC 173, [1981] 2 All ER 456, HL.
9 *Lonrho plc v Fayed* [1992] 1 AC 448, [1991] 3 All ER 303 at 312 per Lord Bridge; Lord Bridge had been a member of the House of Lords in *Lonrho Ltd v Shell Petroleum Co Ltd (No 2)* [1982] AC 173, [1981] 2 All ER 456, HL.
10 [2008] 1 AC 1174. See also *Croesus Financial Services v Bradshaw* [2013] EWHC 3685 (QB).

(5) Postscript

2.9 The economic wrongs were developed in the context of industrial conflict between employers and trade unions. Most forms of effective industrial action will involve the commission of one or more of the economic wrongs. In order to obtain a balance between the power of capital and labour for the purpose of collective bargaining, legislation has been passed to give immunity to trade unions and trade unionists from civil liability in respect of some, at least, of these wrongs. Immunity arises only if the acts which prima facie constitute an economic wrong are carried out in contemplation or furtherance of a trade dispute. There are now stringent balloting requirements of the members of a trade union which must be satisfied before the statutory defences are applicable; and the defences do not apply to some forms of secondary industrial action. The law has now been consolidated in the Trade Union and Labour Relations (Consolidation) Act 1992 (as amended) and the reader seeking an account of the law relating to industrial action is referred to the textbooks on labour law.

B. FRAUD

2.10   Fraud is the paradigm of an intentional delict in Scots law. It has been defined as 'a machination or contrivance to deceive'.[1] Fraud will usually cause pure economic loss to the pursuer. As we shall see, this provides a stark contrast to the situation where unintentional conduct results in pure economic loss; there the courts have traditionally been unwilling to allow damages in negligence for pure economic loss. But fraud is not restricted to economic loss. If A lies to B when A tells B that B's wife and children have been seriously injured, with the result that B suffers distress or a psychiatric disorder, B can recover damages from A for fraud.[2]

Much confusion has arisen in this area because the fraudulent conduct will often take the form of a misrepresentation which induces the misrepresentee to enter into a contract with the misrepresentor. In these circumstances, the misrepresentee may have two sets of remedies, ie contractual and delictual. If the fraudulent misrepresentation prevented the formation of the contract, the contract is null;[3] if, however, a contract is concluded but the misrepresentee was induced by the fraudulent misrepresentation to contract under essential error, the contract may be reduced provided *restitutio in integrum* is possible.[4] But, in addition, the misrepresentee can sue in *delict* for damages. Thus, if A lies to B to induce B to enter a contract with A, B will have contractual remedies against A, for example reduction, and the right to sue A for damages in delict. If A lies to B who as a result enters into a contract with C, B will have no contractual remedies against C (unless A was acting as C's agent) but B will be able to sue A in delict.

Although the institutional writers had a flexible view of the concept of fraud, as a result of developments in the nineteenth century fraud as a wrong was confined to a relatively narrow range of situations where the defender *intended* to harm the pursuer. In effect, the Scots wrong of fraud was equated with the English tort of deceit.[5]

Before delictual liability arises for fraud, there must be a positive act by the defender which causes loss to the pursuer. This will often take the form of a misrepresentation by words. But positive conduct can amount to a fraudulent misrepresentation, for example supplying reconditioned as opposed to new cash registers[6] or selling reproduction furniture 'got up' to look like antiques.[7] As a general rule, non-disclosure does not amount to a misrepresentation unless there is a fiduciary relationship between the parties or the contract is a contract *uberrimae fidei*.[8]

Before there is liability for fraud, the pursuer must establish that the defender had the requisite mental element, *mens rea*. In other words, the pursuer has to show that at the time of the misrepresentation the defender's state of mind was such that he did not, or could not, believe his statement was true. It is, of course, extremely difficult to prove this mental element. In *Zurich v Gray and Kellas*[9] Lord Brodie observed[10] 'Fraud is not something to be lightly inferred. Nor should it be lightly averred. It is for the party alleging fraud to prove it and, in order to do so, to set out in specific terms the basis upon which the court will be invited to infer that the party against whom fraud is alleged did not honestly believe that the representation was true.' Consequently, the law has developed liability for negligent – as opposed to fraudulent – misrepresentation where the defender's conduct can be tested objectively.[11]

What, then, will constitute the *mens rea* of fraud? The first situation is where the defender makes a statement which he knows is false. For example, A tells B there is a gold seam in A's garden when A knows that no seam is there. In these circumstances, A is lying. The second situation is where the defender makes a statement which he does not positively *know* is false but which he positively *believes* to be false. For example, A tells B there is a gold seam in A's garden; A has not dug up his garden and therefore does not know that there is no gold seam but A believes no gold seam is there. If in fact there is no gold seam, then A can be sued by B for fraud. B will have great difficulty in proving that A believed his statement was false if A maintains he believed it was true. However, the court will infer fraud if the statement was destitute of all reasonable grounds for believing it was true or the least inquiry would immediately correct.[12]

The final situation is where the defender makes a statement which he does not positively know is false and does not positively believe is false but is recklessly indifferent to whether it is true or false. If the matter is of no importance to speaker and listener, this is not dishonesty. But if it is a matter of importance between them, it is fraud since the speaker has attempted to induce a belief in the listener, ie that the statement is true, which the speaker does not actually entertain.[13] For example, A tells B there is a gold seam in A's garden. A has done tests which establish that the strata are not inconsistent with a gold seam but A, nevertheless, has serious doubts whether a gold seam is actually there. Assuming B has an interest in the statement, although A does not positively know that the statement is false and does not positively believe that it is false, if he does not care whether it is true or false, he is liable in fraud to B if in fact there is no gold seam in the garden.[14] Proof of the requisite *mens rea* in this situation will be difficult but again will be inferred if the statement was destitute of all reasonable grounds for believing it was true or the least inquiry would immediately correct.

To summarise,[15] *mens rea* for the purposes of fraud arises if the misrepresentor:

(1)   positively knows the statement is false;[16] or
(2)   positively believes the statement is false even though he does not positively know it is false: liability if in fact untrue;
(3)   does not positively believe the statement is true even though he does not positively know or believe it is false: liability if in fact untrue, provided both parties have an interest in what has been said.

There can, therefore, be no liability in fraud if the defender positively believes that the statement is true. In these circumstances, if he did not take reasonable care in making the statement, there may be liability for negligent misrepresentation.[17]

Because fraud is an intentional delict, the pursuer is entitled to recover damages for all the losses directly arising from the fraud – even if the losses are not reasonably foreseeable by the defender. Suppose, for example, A bought shares from B for £100K. A was induced by B to purchase the shares as a result of B's fraudulent misrepresentation as to the value of the shares. In fact their value is only £80K. However, unknown to A and B, at the time of the transaction the shares were in fact overvalued at £80K because of a fraud by C. When C's fraud is subsequently discovered, the shares fall in value to £30K. A can recover the full extent of his loss, ie £70K as opposed to £20K, from B since A has been the victim of a fraudulent misrepresentation: B is liable for all A's losses directly arising from B's fraud, even though they were unforeseeable and,

indeed, the result of the actions of a third party. In other words,
A is put back into the position he would have been if he had not
entered the transaction.[18] It is not possible to exclude liability for
fraud by an exemption clause.[19]

1 Erskine *Institute* III, 1, 16.
2 *Wilkinson v Downtown* [1897] 2 QB 57; *Wainwright v Home Office* [2003] UKHL 53,
  [2004] 2 AC 406, [2003] 3 WLR 1137, [2003] 4 All ER 969, HL. Cf *Powell v Boladz*
  [1998] Lloyd's Rep Med 116, CA (defendant had no intention to harm plaintiff
  by falsifying medical records). Similarly if A obtained sexual intercourse with B
  as a result of fraudulent misrepresentation.
3 *Morrisson v Robertson* 1908 SC 332, 15 SLT 697; *Shogun Finance Ltd v Hudson*
  [2004] 1 All ER 215.
4 *Spence v Crawford* 1939 SC (HL) 52, 1939 SLT 305; *MacLeod v Kerr* 1965 SC 253,
  1965 SLT 358. See generally MacQueen and Thomson *Contract Law in Scotland*
  (3rd edn 2012), Chapter 4.
5 On these developments see, generally, 11 *Stair Memorial Encyclopaedia* paras
  701–789.
6 *Gibson v National Cash Register Co Ltd* 1925 SC 500, 1925 SLT 377.
7 *Patterson v H Landsberg & Son* (1905) 7 F 675, 13 SLT 62.
8 For example, a contract of insurance.
9 [2007] CSOH 91.
10 At para 24. See also *Grant Estates Ltd v Royal Bank of Scotland* [2012] CSOH 133
   per Lord Hodge at paras 85 ff. In *The Royal Bank of Scotland v Holmes* 1999 SLT
   563, Lord Macfadyen stated at 569 that it was essential to have clear and specific
   averments on three matters, *viz*: the act or representation founded upon, the
   occasion on which the act was committed or the representation made, and the
   circumstances relied on as yielding the inference that that act or representation
   was fraudulent.
11 On these developments, see paras 4.10 ff below.
12 *Western Bank of Scotland v Addie* (1867) 5 M (HL) 80.
13 *Lees v Tod* (1882) 9 R 807.
14 *H & J M Bennet (Potatoes) Ltd v Secretary of State for Scotland* 1986 SLT 665, OH
   (revsd on another point 1988 SLT 390).
15 The *locus classicus* is to be found in *Derry v Peek* (1889) 14 App Cas 337, HL, at
   374 per Lord Herschell.
16 See, for example, *Henry Ansbacher & Co Ltd v Binks Stern* [1998] Lloyd's Rep
   Bank 1, (1997) *Times*, 26 June 1997, CA.
17 However, where a solicitor discovers that his client was engaged in fraudulent
   dealings, he will be liable as an accessory of his client's fraud if he does not
   dissociate himself from the fraud and alert his client's potential victim. Liability
   for being an accessory to fraud does not require subjective dishonesty, but
   rests on the solicitor's failure to come up to the objective standard of honest
   behaviour which the law requires, ie because the solicitor is in bad faith. See
   Frank Houlgate Investment Company Ltd v Biggart Baillie LLP [2013] CSOH 80.
18 *Smith New Court Securities Ltd v Scrimgeour Vickers (Asset Management) Ltd* [1997]
   AC 254, [1996] 4 All ER 769, HL. The House of Lords indicated that B would
   not be liable for all A's losses if C's fraud had occurred after the transaction
   on the basis that the causative influence of B's fraud on A's losses vis-à-vis C's
   fraud had faded: *sed quaere?* In *Barry v Sutherland* 2002 SLT 413, the pursuers
   bought a pub as a result of the seller's fraudulent misrepresentation concerning
   the business accounts. The Lord Ordinary (Eassie) held that the pursuers were
   able to recover damages for trading losses they had incurred when running

the business: they were not restricted to compensation for the difference in the price paid as opposed to the true price of the pub. In other words, they were entitled to recover for the losses which directly flowed from entering into the sale and running the business.

19 Hence the necessity to plead fraud in *H & J M Bennet (Potatoes) Ltd v Secretary of State for Scotland* 1986 SLT 665, OH.

Part II

UNINTENTIONAL DELICT – GENERAL PRINCIPLES OF LIABILITY

CHAPTER 3

The duty of care

A. INTRODUCTION

3.1 In the first part of this book we examined the intentional wrongs. *Culpa* or fault is the basis of delictual liability and is present in those delicts because the defender intended to carry out the wrongful actions. Moreover, and this is important, the range of potential pursuers in those delicts is automatically restricted to those persons whom the defender intended to harm or to be affected by his conduct. In Scots law the concept of *culpa* also covers conduct which is merely careless, ie where the defender causes harm to the pursuer *unintentionally*. Immediately a difficulty arises. If A acts in a careless manner, ie his conduct fails to meet the standard of care demanded by society of a person in his position, then prima facie A is liable to anyone who suffers harm as a result of such conduct.[1] In order to *limit* A's potential liability in delict to an indeterminate class of persons, the law has had to develop devices which restrict the number of persons who can claim damages for harm incurred by A's unintentional, but careless, conduct.

While there are many ways to restrict A's potential liability,[2] modern Scots law has accepted as a general principle that A will be liable for careless conduct only if he owed a duty of care to the person harmed by his actions. This duty of care must pre-exist the careless conduct. Whether a duty of care is owed by A to a particular person or class of persons is ultimately a question of law to be determined by the courts. In deciding whether or not to recognise the existence of a duty of care in particular circumstances, the courts are influenced by issues of policy as well as legal principle. By recognising – or refusing to recognise – the existence of a duty of care, the courts in effect set the parameters of delictual liability for unintentional, but careless, conduct.

1 Cardozo J's phrase 'liability in an indeterminate amount for an indeterminate time, to an indeterminate class' elegantly summarises the point: *Ultramares Corpn v Touche* (1931) 255 NY 170 at 179.
2 For example by developing a doctrine of proximate causation before A will be liable.

B. *DONOGHUE v STEVENSON*: THE NEIGHBOURHOOD PRINCIPLE

3.2 The starting point of any discussion of the duty of care in Scots law is the famous case of *Donoghue v Stevenson*.[1] One Sunday evening Mrs Donoghue went to visit a friend in Paisley.[2] They went to Wellmeadow Café at Wellmeadow Place, Paisley. The café was owned by Mr Minchella. They decided to have 'iced drinks', ie ice cream over which was poured lemonade. Mrs Donoghue's friend bought the ice cream and a bottle of 'ginger'.[3] The case proceeded on the assumption that Mrs Donoghue's friend had in fact bought ginger beer which would have been contained in an opaque bottle. The friend poured some of the ginger beer over Mrs Donoghue's ice cream; but when, later in the evening, the friend poured the rest of the ginger beer over Mrs Donoghue's melting ice, out floated the decomposing remains of a snail. The sight of the snail and her consumption of the snail-tainted iced drink resulted in Mrs Donoghue becoming ill. Mrs Donoghue sued Stevenson, the manufacturer of the ginger beer, in delict. The question before the courts was whether the manufacturer was liable to Mrs Donoghue in delict even if she could prove the facts alleged and Stevenson had, in fact, been careless.

A most important point to notice is that there was no contractual nexus between Mrs Donoghue and Stevenson. The facts of the case can be shown thus:

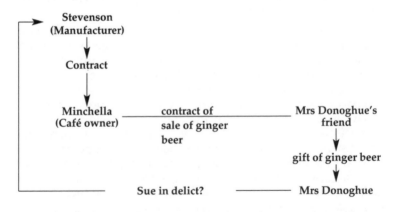

Mrs Donoghue's friend could sue Minchella for breach of the contract of sale on the grounds that the ginger beer was not of merchantable (ie satisfactory) quality. However, the friend's damages would be minimal since the friend did not suffer any ill-effects.[4] Mrs Donoghue could not sue Minchella because she was not a party to the contract. Minchella could also have sued Stevenson in contract if he had suffered any loss. But Mrs Donoghue had no contractual remedy. Therefore the issue before the House of Lords was whether *in the absence* of any contractual nexus between them, Mrs Donoghue, the ultimate consumer of the product, could sue the manufacturer in delict.

1 1932 SC (HL) 31, 1932 SLT 317. The literature on this case is voluminous, but see in particular A F Rodger 'Mrs Donoghue and Alfenus Varus' (1998) 41 CLP 1.
2 The sex of the friend changes as the case proceeds through the courts!
3 In the parlance of the West Coast of Scotland at the time, 'ginger' was a generic term covering all kinds of aerated drinks.
4 For that reason it would have been pointless for the friend to have assigned his or her rights under the contract to Mrs Donoghue.

3.3 It was held by a majority of the House of Lords[1] that Mrs Donoghue was entitled to sue Stevenson in delict because he owed her a duty of care: if he had *in fact* broken his duty towards her by his careless conduct and she had suffered harm, then she would succeed.[2] In other words, the relationship between the pursuer and defender was sufficiently proximate that the majority was prepared to hold that Stevenson owed Mrs Donoghue a duty of care for the purpose of liability in delict. Lord Atkin concluded:[3]

' … a manufacturer of products, which he sells in such a form as to show that he intends them to reach the ultimate consumer in the form in which they left him, with no reasonable possibility of intermediate examination, and with the knowledge that the absence of reasonable care in the preparation or putting up of the product will result in an injury to the consumer's life or property, owes a duty to the consumer to take that reasonable care'.

Lord Macmillan had

'no hesitation in affirming that a person, who for gain engages in the business of manufacturing articles of food and drink intended for consumption by members of the public in the form which he issues them, is under a duty to take care in the manufacture of these articles. That duty, in my opinion, he owes to those whom he intends to consume his produce … '[4]

At its most specific level *Donoghue v Stevenson* is authority that a manufacturer of food and drink which he intends to be used by the ultimate consumer without the opportunity of inspection or interference before use owes a duty of care to the ultimate consumer to prevent him sustaining harm to his person or property as a result of the manufacturer's carelessness when manufacturing the product. In other words, the relationship between manufacturer and ultimate consumer was sufficiently proximate in these circumstances that the court was prepared to impose a duty of care on the manufacturer towards the ultimate consumer. Four years later, the Privy Council refused to interpret *Donoghue v Stevenson* in such a narrow way and held that the manufacturer of underpants owed a duty of care to the ultimate consumer even though the product was not for internal consumption, the underpants had been removed by the retailer from packets in which they had been delivered and they could have been – but had not been – washed by the ultimate consumer before use.[5] *Donoghue v Stevenson* thus becomes authority for the more general principle that a manufacturer of *any* product owes a duty of care to the ultimate consumer not to cause harm to his person or property as a result of a latent defect in a product which could not be discovered by inspection before use and was intended by the manufacturer to be used by the ultimate consumer in the same condition as it left the manufacturer. If by his careless conduct the manufacturer breaches this duty, causing harm to the ultimate consumer's person or property, then he is liable in delict to make reparation for the harm sustained by the consumer.

1 Lord Atkin, Lord Thankerton and Lord Macmillan; Lord Buckmaster and Lord Tomlin dissented.
2 After the decision of the House of Lords on the relevancy point, the case was settled and did not go to proof.
3 1932 SC (HL) 31 at 57.
4 1932 SC (HL) 31 at 71. On the genesis of Lord Macmillan's speech, see A F Rodger (1992) 168 LQR 236.
5 *Grant v Australian Knitting Mills Ltd* [1936] AC 85, PC. The plaintiff suffered dermatitis because free sulphites used in the manufacturing process had not been washed out of the garments before they were marketed. The fact that, unlike Mrs Donoghue, the plaintiff could have sued the retailer for breach of contract did not prevent recovery against the manufacturer in delict.

3.4   Even at this more general level, there are two important limitations on the extent of the duty of care laid down in *Donoghue*:

(1) The duty only extends to *latent* defects; the bottle of ginger beer was opaque and the snail could not be seen before the contents were used.[1] If the defect is patent, ie obvious, and the consumer chooses to use it, the manufacturer may escape liability because the chain of causation is broken[2] or the damages will be reduced by the ultimate consumer's contributory negligence.[3]

(2) The duty is to prevent harm to the ultimate consumer's person or property. If A is physically injured by a defective product,

carelessly manufactured by B, A can sue B for damages for pain and suffering (solatium). A can also sue B for economic loss which derives from his injuries (derivative or parasitic economic loss), for example loss of wages when in hospital, loss of wages in the future if A is permanently incapacitated and so forth.[4] If A's property is damaged by a defective product carelessly manufactured by B, then A can recover damages from B in respect of the damage to his property: for example if A's dog dies as a result of contaminated dog food or a defective vacuum cleaner damages A's carpet. But A is not able to sue B in delict if the only property damaged is the defective product itself. A cannot sue B in delict for the cost of repairing a defective car or for replacing a defective vacuum cleaner which blew up without harming A's person or damaging any property other than the vacuum cleaner itself. In these situations, A has suffered *pure*, as opposed to derivative or parasitic, economic loss, ie the cost of repair or replacement or the difference in value between the property with and without the defect. As we shall see, the courts are reluctant to allow a person to recover damages for pure economic loss in *delict*; A's remedy lies in *contract* against the person who sold him the goods, not the manufacturer.[5] Similarly, if the defect is discovered before there has been any harm done to A's person or property, the cost of repairing the defect is pure economic loss and cannot be recovered in delict.[6]

1 Similarly, the defect in the underpants in *Grant* was latent.
2 On causation, see Chapter 6 below. Where the defect was originally latent, the chain of causation is not necessarily broken if the defect later comes to the attention of the consumer or the fact that a third party had the opportunity or indeed an obligation to inspect the product. In the latter circumstances, the manufacturer and the third party can be jointly and severally liable: see *Grunwald v Hughes* 1964 SLT 94, OH, 1965 SLT 209; *Clay v A J Crump & Sons Ltd* [1964] 1 QB 533, [1963] 3 All ER 687, CA.
3 On contributory negligence, see paras 6.12–6.13 below.
4 On damages generally, see Chapter 16 below.
5 Of course A may not have a contract; for example if the goods were a gift. But the purchaser could assign his contractual rights against the seller to A.
6 On economic loss, see further paras 4.10 ff below. There is no such restriction in the case of the intentional delicts.

3.5 *Donoghue* is therefore an important decision in relation to product liability. But what makes the case remarkable is that two of the judges attempted to lay down criteria to determine the existence of a duty of care which would be applicable whenever an action for reparation as a result of unintentional, but careless, conduct arose. Lord Macmillan sets the scene:[1]

'The law takes no cognisance of carelessness in the abstract. It concerns itself with carelessness only where there is a duty to take care and where failure in that duty has caused *damage*.[2] In such circumstances carelessness assumes the legal quality of negligence and entails the consequences in law of negligence. What then are the circumstances which give rise to this duty to take care? In the daily contacts of social and business life, human beings are thrown into, or place themselves in, an infinite variety of relations with their fellows; and *the law can refer only to the standards of the reasonable man in order to determine whether any particular relationship gives rise to a duty to take care as between those who stand in relation to each other.* The grounds of action may be as various and manifold as human errancy; and the conception of legal responsibility may develop in adaption to altering social conditions and the changing circumstances of life. *The categories of negligence are never closed.* The cardinal principle of liability is that the party complained of should owe to the party complaining a duty to take care, and that the party complaining should be able to prove that he has suffered damage in consequence of a breach of that duty.'

Lord Macmillan is arguing that given changes in society, the courts, using as a yardstick the values of the reasonable man, may consider that new relationships are sufficiently proximate to impose a duty of care, breach of which gives rise to delictual liability for unintentional, but careless, conduct. *Donoghue v Stevenson* thus introduces a dynamic into the law which can extend the parameters within which there is delictual liability for careless conduct; this is done by the court deciding that a duty of care exists between parties in new social or economic relationships. Conversely, the court can refuse to extend the boundaries of delictual liability for careless conduct by deciding that a duty of care does not exist between parties in the circumstances of the case. In determining whether or not to impose a duty of care, the courts will clearly be influenced by policy considerations as well as legal principle.

It cannot be emphasised enough that in Scots law there is no delictual liability unless a breach of a duty of care has caused harm to the person to whom the duty is owed: *damnum injuria datum*. Harm is a constituent, as well as a consequence, of negligence. We can owe a duty of care and be careless, but there is no liability unless our carelessness has caused harm to the pursuer.[2] In other words the breach of the duty of care must result in the pursuer sustaining ' constituent' harm.

1 *Donoghue v Stevenson* 1932 SC (HL) 31 at 70 (italics added).
2 *Rothwell v Chemical and Insulating Co Ltd* [2007] UKHL 39, [2008] 1 AC 281. This case is discussed in detail at para 5.2 beyond.

3.6 In *Donoghue v Stevenson* Lord Atkin attempted to provide a criterion for the existence of a duty of care which, at first sight, appears to be more objective. In a famous passage, he said:[1]

'The liability for negligence, whether you style it such or treat it as in other systems as a species of *"culpa"*, is no doubt based upon a general public sentiment of moral wrongdoing for which the offender must pay. But acts or omissions which any moral code would censure cannot, in a practical world, be treated so as to give a right to every person injured by them to demand relief. *In this way rules of law arise which limit the range of complaints, and the extent of their remedy.* The rule that you are to love your neighbour becomes in law, you must not injure your neighbour; and the lawyer's question, Who is my neighbour? receives a *restricted* reply. You must take reasonable care to avoid acts or omissions which you can *reasonably foresee* would be likely to injure your neighbour. Who, then, in law, is my neighbour? The answer seems to be – persons who are so *closely and directly* affected by my act that I ought reasonably to have them in contemplation when I am directing my mind to the acts or omissions which are called in question.'

For Lord Atkin a duty of care arises when it is reasonably foreseeable by the defender that a person in the position of the pursuer would be closely and directly affected by the defender's acts or omissions. This neighbourhood principle can explain why a duty of care arises in many situations. A driver owes a duty of care to other road users because it is reasonably foreseeable that if he drives carelessly he may harm other road users. The occupier of property owes a duty of care to those who enter her property because it is reasonably foreseeable that they may be injured if the occupier is careless in the way she maintains the property. An employer owes a duty of care to his employee because it is reasonably foreseeable that if he is careless in the way he runs his system of working the employee may be harmed. A manufacturer of a product owes a duty of care to the ultimate consumer because it is reasonably foreseeable that the ultimate consumer may be injured or his property may be damaged if the product is defective.

1 1932 SC (HL) 31 at 44 (italics added).

3.7 It will be noticed that in these examples the duty of care is to prevent *physical* harm to the pursuer or physical damage to his property and will enable the pursuer only to recover economic loss which is *derivative* from the injuries or damage sustained. But in situations where the pursuer does not suffer physical harm or damage to property, for example pure economic loss, the courts tend to be reluctant to impose a duty of care even though the loss to the pursuer would have been reasonably foreseeable by a person in the position of the defender. In other words, the reasonable foreseeability criterion, while a necessary condition for the existence of a duty of care, might not be sufficient to persuade the court to impose a duty of care in areas where no precedent for such a duty exists. Initially, in relation to recovery in delict for pure economic loss,[1] the House of Lords refused to impose a duty of care simply because the loss was reasonably foreseeable: in *Caparo Industries plc v Dickman*,[2] their Lordships held that not only had loss to the pursuer to be reasonably foreseeable but, in addition, there had to be a close degree of proximity between the parties *and* it had to be 'fair, just and reasonable' to impose a duty of care.

This tripartite test, the *Caparo* criteria, was applied to a case of *physical* damage to property by the House of Lords in *Marc Rich & Co AG v Bishop Rock Marine Co Ltd, The Nicholas H*.[3] A surveyor (the defendant) advised the owner of a damaged vessel to continue on her voyage. The vessel sank and the cargo was lost. It was held that the surveyor did not owe a duty of care to the owner of the *cargo* (the plaintiff) to avoid damage to his property.

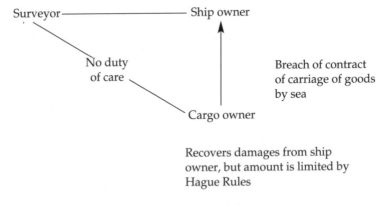

Although it was reasonably foreseeable that the surveyor's careless advice could result in *physical* harm to the plaintiff's property, nevertheless no duty of care arose since the relationship between the parties was not sufficiently proximate and it would have been unfair, unjust and unreasonable to hold otherwise. To have imposed a duty of care in this case would have disturbed 'the intricate blend' of internationally accepted rules of shipping law under which the owner of the cargo has a remedy against the owner of the ship in *contract* but the amount of compensation is limited.[4]

1 For full discussion, see paras 4.10 ff below.
2 [1990] 2 AC 605, HL, at 616–618 per Lord Bridge, at 628 per Lord Roskill, and at 633–634 per Lord Oliver.
3 [1996] AC 211, [1995] 3 All ER 307, HL.
4 When a passenger was injured in an aircraft, it was held that a safety inspector owed him a duty of care on the basis of reasonable foreseeability of harm per se, without having to resort to the tripartite test. This was because it was not a novel situation and it concerned personal injuries: *Perrett v Collins* [1998] 2 Lloyd's Rep 255, (1998) *Times*, 23 June 1998, CA.

3.8 The tripartite test has now been transplanted into Scots law to determine the existence of a duty of care in novel situations not governed by existing precedent. In *Coleridge v Miller Construction Ltd*,[1] for example, the defender cut an electric cable supplying power to the pursuer's factory. The absence of electricity caused damage to the pursuer's furnace and to the glass being manufactured. Although the pursuer had sustained physical damage to his property, the Lord Ordinary (MacLean) held that the defender did not owe the pursuer a duty of care. His reasoning was that although damage was reasonably foreseeable and there was sufficient proximity between the parties, it was not fair, just and reasonable to impose a duty of care because this would upset the well-established liabilities of the parties' insurers.[2] The tripartite test has also been adopted where the pursuer has suffered personal injuries,[3] although it is accepted that in these circumstances 'it is self-evident that a civilised system of law should hold that a duty of care has been broken'.[4]

Put shortly, where the courts are being asked to extend delictual liability into hitherto uncharted waters, under the guise of determining whether or not there is a sufficient degree of proximity for the imposition of a duty of care and whether it is fair, just and reasonable to do so, the courts are undoubtedly influenced by policy considerations. In doing so they are governed by their concept of a fair distribution of risk in contemporary society – allowing the loss to be compensated in some areas, letting the risk lie where it has fallen in others.

To summarise: Lord Atkin's neighbourhood principle, based on reasonable foreseeability of harm, undoubtedly explains why a duty of care arises in many situations where there is the risk of physical harm to the pursuer or physical damage to the pursuer's property. But at the parameters of the field of existing delictual liability, the courts, for policy reasons, may refuse to extend the frontiers even though loss to the pursuer is reasonably foreseeable. On the other hand, there may be other factors present – as well as reasonable foreseeability of harm – which will persuade the courts that a duty of care should be imposed in the particular circumstances.

1   1997 SLT 485, OH. Cf *Tartan American Machinery Corp v Swan & Co* 2003 SLT 1246 (packer of goods on ship owed duty of care to the owner of the goods to prevent them being damaged during the voyage: *Caparo* criteria used). In *Burnett v Grampian Fire and Rescue Service* 2007 SCLR 192, the pursuer's flat was damaged in a fire which had originated in the flat below and which had continued to smoulder in the void between the two flats to reignite a day after the defender had appeared to have extinguished it. Lord Macphail held that the defender owed the pursuer a duty of care. The defender had entered the pursuer's flat to check that the original fire had not spread upwards. Given that the defender was therefore aware of the potential danger to the pursuer's property if the fire should reignite, there was sufficient proximity between the parties and it was fair just and reasonable to impose a duty of care on the defender to protect the pursuer's flat and its contents. See also *Marshall v North Ayrshire Council* 2006 SCLR 143. In *Santander v Keeper of the Registers of Scotland* [2013] CSOH 24 the court held that it was not fair just and reasonable that the Keeper should owe a duty of care to the bank to prevent them sustaining economic loss when the Keeper registered a forged discharge of a standard security in the bank's favour. It has been held that it is not fair just and reasonable to impose a duty of care on a social worker to prevent him causing a client mental harm by having a consensual affair with her: *Shields v Crossroads (Orkney)* [2013] CSOH 144. The social worker's behaviour was unprofessional and he was disqualified, but was not liable to pay his 'victim' damages on the grounds of negligence.
2   See also *British Telecommunications plc v James Thomson & Sons (Engineers) Ltd* 1999 SC (HL) 9. The House of Lords, reversing the Second Division of the Court of Session, held that a domestic sub-contractor did owe a duty of care to an employer whose insurance covered only nominated sub-contractors. Lord Mackay of Clashfern accepted that the tripartite test was appropriate: 1999 SC (HL) 9 at 12.
3   *Gibson v Orr* 1999 SC 420, OH discussed beyond para 11.7; *ICL Tech Ltd v Johnston Oils Ltd* [2013] CSOH 159 (the suppliers of gas did not owe a duty of care to workers who were injured in an explosion caused by the failure of their employer to maintain the gas pipes). Nevertheless the simple *Donoghue v Stevenson* reasonable foreseeability of physical harm test is still used: *Heary v Phinn* 2013 SLT (Sh Ct) 145 (owner of a breakers yard owed a duty of care to any person who was invited into the yard, to ensure that the invitee was not locked in the yard since it was reasonably foreseeable that he might be injured when he tried to escape).
4   *Marc Rich & Co AG v Bishop Rock Marine Co Ltd, The Nicholas H* [1996] AC 211 at 235 per Lord Steyn.

3.9   Although *Donoghue v Stevenson*[1] was a milestone in the development of the law of negligence, Lord Atkin's neighbourhood principle based on reasonable foreseeability of harm is no longer adequate as the touchstone for the imposition of a duty of care. The *Caparo* criteria – the three elements of reasonable foreseeability, proximity and the 'fair, just and reasonable' criterion – has overtaken it in novel situations, ie those not governed by existing precedent. In *Gibson v Orr*, in the course of his judgment, the Lord Ordinary (Hamilton) said:[2]

'Although there is no authority directly binding on me, the three element test now falls ... to be applied in Scotland in personal injury actions based on a duty of care as well as in other actions of damages so based. The more traditional approach in Scotland has been to apply the test laid down by Lord Atkin in *Donoghue v Stevenson*.[3] In *Dorset Yacht Co Ltd v Home Office* Lord Reid said that *Donoghue v Stevenson* might "be regarded as a milestone".[4] A milestone is an object encountered in the course of a journey. The relevant journey did not end in 1932 but went on, albeit not perhaps in a straight line ... to the present day. Progress on that journey does not mean that milestones passed are no longer relevant; they remain important stages in the development of the law. However, I see no logical justification in modern circumstances and as the law has developed for applying a different test for the existence of a duty of care in respect of personal injury from that applicable relative to physical damage to property or to economic loss.'

That the *Caparo* three-fold test is to be used in novel cases of physical harm as well as economic loss was put beyond doubt in *Mitchell v Glasgow City Council*[5] where Lord Hope said:[6]

'But I see no good reason why, as a general guide to what is required, it should not be regarded as part of Scots law. It is really no more than an expression of the idea that lies at the heart of every judgment about legal policy. If liability is to attach, it should be in situations where this is readily understandable because, looking at both sides of the argument, it is fair and reasonable that there should be liability....There is no principle of Scots law that contradicts it, and the fact that the law of liability for negligence has developed on common lines both north and south of the Border provides powerful support for the defender's argument that it should be applied in this case.'

In *Matthews v Hunter and Robertson*[7] when applying the *Caparo* criteria to determine whether or not to impose a duty of care to prevent pure economic loss in a novel situation, the Lord Ordinary (Brodie) observed:

'I have characterised the three part foreseeability; proximity; fair, just and reasonable criteria set out in *Caparo* as potentially exclusionary in effect. The party, such as the pursuer here, who claims to have sustained an economic loss for which he seeks to be compensated by reason of what he says was a duty of care owed to him by another party in respect of that kind of loss must satisfy the court that he can surmount each of the three hurdles placed in his way. Putting it slightly differently, the court armed with this threefold test, is able to appraise, in a relatively systematic way, any supposed duty of care with a view to preventing it extending liability beyond what is pragmatically acceptable. The categories rather shade one into the other but the court, by finding any one of the tests not to have been met, negatives the duty of care.'

In *Sutradhar (FC) v National Environmental Research Council*[8] the defendant carried out tests on ground water systems in Bangladesh for the purpose of discovering whether the water might contain toxic trace elements. At the time standard procedures for testing ground water did not include tests for arsenic. The defendant was not asked and did not test for arsenic. Their report made it clear that they had not done so. Four million shallow hand pumped wells were installed to supply drinking water. The water was contaminated with arsenic. The claimant was one of the thousands to suffer from arsenic poisoning. The House of Lords held that the defendant did not owe the claimant a duty of care on the ground that there was no proximity between the parties. In the course of his opinion, Lord Hoffmann opined of the *Caparo* three fold test:[9]

'It has often been remarked that the boundaries between these three concepts are somewhat porous but they are probably none the worse for that. In particular, the requirement that the imposition of a duty should be fair, just and reasonable may sometimes inform the decision as to whether the parties should be considered to be in a relationship of proximity and may sometimes provide a special reason as to why no duty should exist, notwithstanding that the relationship would ordinarily qualify as proximate. In these proceedings the defendant does not allege any such special reason but the concept of fairness and justice obviously looms large in the question whether it is fair, just and reasonable that the author of a geological survey should be treated as having a relationship of proximity to the population of Bangladesh.'

The 'fair, just and reasonable' criterion expressly recognises that ultimately the imposition of a duty of care is an issue of policy and that any extension of delictual liability will occur on an incremental basis. In certain situations the *Caparo* tripartite test has itself been overtaken by other criteria for the imposition of a duty of care. In the next chapter we shall consider some important examples of this process. The important point is that the concept of a duty of care is used as a *threshold* device, enabling the courts to extend the scope of delictual liability or to refuse to do so, depending on policy considerations.[10] The duty of care allows the courts, if they so wish, to give an inch without fear that potential pursuers will take the proverbial mile.

The position has been admirably summarised by the Hon Justice Michael Kirby when he said extra-judicially:[11]

'Novel cases therefore require judges with the responsibility of decision to evaluate the choices they make by reference to considerations of legal policy. Will the imposition of a duty of care for negligence impose indeterminate liability on too many people? Will it expose people unreasonably to liability to others? Will it result in intolerable economic burdens upon citizens? Will it have adverse implications for the availability of liability insurance? Will it offend legitimate freedom of action by people in the position of the defendant? Will it drive some useful participants out of a valuable economic market? Will refusing it leave a vulnerable party without recompense reasonable to the circumstances?'

1 1932 SC (HL) 32, 1932 SLT 317.
2 1999 SC 420, OH, at 431. For full discussion of this case, see para 11.7 below.
3 1932 SC (HL) 31 at 44.
4 *Dorset Yacht Co Ltd v Home Office* [1970] AC 1004 at 1027, [1970] 2 All ER 294 at 297.
5 [2009] UKHL 11; 2009 SLT 247. See also *Aitken v Scottish Ambulance Service* [2011] CSOH 49.
6 Ibid at para 25.
7 [2007] CSOH 88 at para 41.
8 [2006] UKHL 33, [2006] 4 All ER 490, HL.
9 Ibid at para 32.
10 See, for example, *D v East Berkshire Community Health NHS Trust* [2005] 2 AC 373 where the House of Lords held that it was not fair, just and reasonable to impose a duty of care on a local authority towards the parents of a child whom they suspected of being a victim of child abuse: but it was fair, just and reasonable that a duty of care was owed to the *child* in relation to their investigations.
11 'Judicial Activism' (2004) 55 Hamlyn Lectures.

CHAPTER 4

Duty of care as a threshold device

We shall now consider four examples of how the existence or non-existence of a duty of care has been used to extend or limit liability in delict for careless acts or omissions.[1]

A. PURE OMISSIONS

4.1 It is a fundamental principle of the law of delict that A is not liable to B in delict simply because A did not confer a benefit on B. This includes the benefit of A preventing B from sustaining harm. As Stevens has said,[2] 'If in acting I fail to confer a benefit on you, which includes the failure to prevent harm, as I have made you no worse by my actions there is prima facie no liability'. Merely because it is reasonably foreseeable to A that harm will happen to B does not of itself generate a duty on A to act to prevent B suffering that harm. Consider the following example:

A, a professor of law, is standing in the quadrangle of the university. He sees B, another professor, who is very shortsighted, walking with a white stick across the quadrangle. There is a banana skin lying in B's path. Instead of warning B, A merely stands and watches. B slips on the banana skin. A walks away, giggling. Is A liable to B in delict for A's failure to warn B about the banana skin? The answer is no. Why? In spite of the fact that it is reasonably foreseeable by A that B may slip on the banana skin if A does not warn him, this does not generate a duty of care as A is not obliged to provide a benefit to B. As a matter of policy, the law does not compel us to be good Samaritans.[3]

But there may be additional factors present which create a closer degree of proximity between the parties so that the defender does owe the pursuer a duty of care and will be liable in delict for an omission to act to B's benefit. In particular, there may be a duty of care when the defender has assumed responsibility for the welfare of the pursuer. Thus parents are under a duty to rescue their child provided it is reasonable to do so; this is because they have assumed responsibility for the care of the child. Similarly, when they have assumed responsibility to tend them, a nurse or a doctor owes a duty of care to treat their patients: if they have not done so, a doctor or nurse incurs no liability if he fails to assist a person who is ill or injured. In *Barrett v Minister of Defence*[4] the Court of Appeal held that the Royal Navy did not owe a duty of care to prevent an adult naval airman from becoming drunk off-duty. However, after the deceased had collapsed and was no longer capable of looking after himself, the Royal Navy assumed responsibility for him and it was accepted that the Royal Navy had a duty to provide him with adequate medical care. But unless there is some factor additional to foreseeability of harm, the law does not impose a duty of care on the defender to rescue the pursuer or to act in such a way that the pursuer will avoid an accident.

Returning to the example, it does not follow that B is without remedy. The university, as his employer, owes B a duty to take reasonable care for his safety at work;[5] moreover, as the occupier of the premises,[6] the university owes B a duty to take reasonable care that he is not harmed as a result of the state of the premises. If, of course, A deliberately dropped the banana skin in B's path, A would be liable for assault if A intended that B should slip. If A had carelessly dropped the banana skin, he could be liable since it is reasonably foreseeable that another person in the quadrangle could slip on the skin. But that duty of care is triggered by A's positive act in dropping the banana skin, ie A has created the risk of injury to B; it is no longer a case of a 'pure' omission.[7]

We must be careful to distinguish the cases of 'pure' omission where the law will not impose a duty to act on a person who is not carrying out a relevant activity and the way in which a relevant activity may be conducted. In the latter situation, where there is a preexisting duty of care, the defender can be liable for careless omissions as well as careless acts. In the case of the driver of a vehicle and other road users or the manufacturer of a product and the ultimate consumer, for example, it is irrelevant for the purpose of the law of delict that the carelessness involves an omission to act as opposed to a positive action. Overtaking without first checking in the mirror is just as careless as driving too fast: failing to check whether a product is infested by a snail is just as careless as giving the wrong instructions on how a product is to be used.

Where the defender is under a duty to protect the pursuer, he will be liable if he fails to do so.[8] Moreover where a person has assumed responsibility to protect the pursuer, the duty may be non-delegable. This means that he cannot escape liability by delegating the performance of the obligation to a third party. The circumstances when a non-delegable duty will arise were outlined by Lord Sumption in *Woodland v Essex County Council*.[9] The essence is that when the defender has undertaken a positive duty to protect a vulnerable person,[10] he will be liable for the negligence of a third party to whom he has delegated some function of the positive duty which he assumed.

1 See generally, Brian Pillans, SULI *Delict* Chapter 5.
2 *Torts and Rights* (Oxford, 2007) at p 9.
3 'Reasonable forseeability of physical injury is the standard criterion for determining the duty of care owed by people who undertake an activity which carries a risk of injury to others. But it is insufficient to justify the imposition of liability upon someone who simply does nothing: who neither creates the risk nor undertakes to do anything to avert it': *Gorringe v Calderdale MBC* [2004] UKHL15 at 17, per Lord Hoffmann. See also *Mitchell v Glasgow City Council* [2009] UKHL 11; 2009 SLT 247: 'A legal duty to take positive steps to prevent harm or injury to another requires the presence of some feature, additional to reasonable foreseeability that a failure to do so is likely to result in the person in question suffering harm or injury' per Lord Scott at para 39.
4 [1995] 3 All ER 87.
5 On employers' liability, see Chapter 12 below.
6 On occupiers' liability, see Chapter 10 below.
7 For an interesting discussion of pure omissions, see T B Smith, *A Short Commentary on the Law of Scotland* (W Green, 1962) p 672.
8 *Dorset Yacht Co Ltd v Home Office* [1970] AC 1004; *Reeves v Metropolitan Commissioner of Police* [2000] 1 AC 360.
9 [2013] UKSC 66 at para 23.
10 For example, a patient in hospital, a child at school or a resident in a care home.

B. MENTAL HARM

4.2   The law has long recognised that A can owe a duty of care to B to prevent B suffering mental harm as a result of A's unintentional, but careless, conduct.[1] In order to succeed, the mental harm must amount to a recognised psychiatric disorder, not simply a fright. Initially at least, the duty of care arose only when the pursuer was in danger of suffering potential physical harm as a result of the defender's conduct. Put another way, where it was reasonably foreseeable by the defender that the pursuer could be physically injured as a result of the defender's conduct, it was also reasonably foreseeable that the pursuer might suffer mental harm if the defender's conduct did not actually cause physical injury to the pursuer but the pursuer had been terrified that it might do so. There was therefore a duty of care not to cause a psychiatric disorder to a person who was within the area of risk of physical harm as a result of the defender's careless conduct. In the leading case of *Page v Smith*,[2] the plaintiff was involved in a road accident caused by the defendant's careless driving. The accident was not serious and the plaintiff suffered no physical harm. However, the accident brought on a recurrence of the plaintiff's ME which had been in remission. The House of Lords held[3] that because the plaintiff was within the area of potential physical harm, he was to be regarded as a primary victim of the accident. In these circumstances, the defendant owed him a duty of care to prevent him suffering physical or psychiatric harm. It was irrelevant that he had not suffered physical harm or that a psychiatric disorder was not reasonably foreseeable because a person of ordinary fortitude would not have suffered mental harm in the circumstances. Thus a duty of care to prevent mental harm arises whenever the pursuer is a primary victim, ie when it is reasonably foreseeable that she might suffer physical injury. It does not matter that she did not sustain physical harm or that a psychiatric disorder was unforeseeable.[4]

It is therefore important to determine when a person is a primary victim. Since the decision of the House of Lords in *Frost v Chief Constable of the South Yorkshire Police*,[5] it might appear that the test is simply whether or not he has been exposed to physical danger:[6] in other words, whether or not the victim has been within the area of potential physical harm. Accordingly, persons who witnessed the death of fellow employees have been held not to constitute primary victims when they were not themselves in physical danger at the time of the accident.[7] Similarly, no duty of care is owed to prevent rescuers suffering mental harm unless they are also in potential physical danger.[8] But there can be exceptional cases where a pursuer will be treated as a primary victim even though he was not at risk of physical harm. These have included cases where the pursuer mistakenly thought that he had killed or injured a fellow employee;[9] parents who felt responsible for the sexual abuse of their children by a foster child introduced into their home by the defendant;[10] and parents whose dead children's organs were removed without permission.[11] On the other hand, a doctor or social worker does not owe a duty of care to a parent to prevent the parent from suffering mental harm if they mistakenly diagnose a child as having been abused by that parent.[12] An employee may recover damages for psychiatric disorder when his employer is in breach of his general duty to take reasonable care for the safety of his employees.[13]

1 See, for example, *Dulieu v White & Sons* [1901] 2 KB 669.
2 [1996] AC 155, [1995] 2 All ER 736, HL. In *Simmons v British Steel plc* 2004 SC (HL) 94 it was accepted by the House of Lords that *Page* was authoritative in Scotland. See also *Donachie v Chief Constable of Greater Manchester Police* [2004] EWCA Civ 405, [2004] All ER (D) 126 (Apr).
3 Lords Ackner, Browne-Wilkinson and Lloyd; Lords Keith and Jauncey dissented.
4 In *Rothwell v Chemical and Insulating Co Ltd* [2008] 1 AC 281 the House of Lords held that it was not reasonably foreseeable that an employee would suffer a mental disorder when he discovered that he had pleural plaques and therefore had an increased risk of contracting an asbestos-related illness in the future. The House rejected the argument that because the claimant was within the area of potential physical harm, the mental harm did not have to be reasonably foreseeable. *Page v Smith* was distinguished on the grounds that (i) in *Page* the foreseeable event – the collision – which might cause a physical or psychiatric injury had happened, while here the foreseeable event – contracting an asbestos-related illness – was still to occur, and (ii) in *Page* the psychiatric injury was caused by an event – the collision – which amounted to a breach of the duty, while here the psychiatric injury had been caused by the diagnosis that the claimant had pleural plaques and therefore learning that he had a greater risk of contracting an asbestos-related illness, and not by the employer's breach of duty in exposing him to asbestos in the first place. For further discussion of *Rothwell*, see beyond para 5.2.
5 [1999] 2 AC 455, [1999] 1 All ER 1, Lords Browne-Wilkinson, Steyn and Hoffmann; Lord Goff dissented and Lord Griffiths dissented in part.
6 Or had reasonable grounds to believe that he was in danger: see, for example, *Hunter v British Coal Corpn* [1999] QB 140, [1998] 2 All ER 97, CA.
7 *Robertson v Forth Road Bridge Joint Board* 1995 SC 364, 1996 SLT 263 (pursuer saw fellow employee blown off lorry on Forth Road Bridge); *McFarlane v EE Caledonia Ltd* [1994] 2 All ER 1 (plaintiff witnessed Piper Alpha explosion from a supply ship); *Campbell v North Lanarkshire Council* 2000 SLCR 373 (proof before answer allowed to determine whether pursuer was in personal danger).
8 *Frost v Chief Constable of the South Yorkshire Police* [1999] 1 All ER 1, [1999] 2 AC 455. Cf *Chadwick v British Transport Commission* [1967] 1 WLR 912, where the plaintiff was within the area of potential physical harm and *Cullin v London Fire and Civil Defence Authority* (31 March 1999, unreported), QB.
9 *Dooley v Cammell Laird & Co Ltd* [1951] 1 Lloyd's Rep 271; *Salter v U B Frozen & Chilled Foods Ltd* 2003 SLT 1011 (pursuer actively involved in the accident which caused the death of a fellow employee for which the pursuer was blameless).
10 *W v Essex CC* [2001] 2 AC 592. See also *McLoughlin v Jones* [2002] 2 WLR 1279 (plaintiff suffered a nervous breakdown having been wrongfully imprisoned as a consequence of his solicitor's negligence in preparing his defence. Plaintiff was treated as a primary victim in his claim against the solicitor for negligence).
11 *Stevens v Yorkhill NHS Trust* 2006 SLT 887; *AB v Leeds Teaching Hospital NHS Trust* [2004] EWHC 644 (QB), [2004] 2 FLR 365, [2004] 3 FCR 324, 77 BMLR 145.
12 *D v East Berkshire Community Health NHS Trust* [2005] AC 373. In *Fairlie v Perth and Kinross Healthcare NHS Trust* 2004 SLT 1200 the Lord Ordinary (Kingarth) considered that the parent in such a case might have a remedy in defamation or breach of his Article 8 right to respect for private life.
13 For employers' liability for psychiatric disorder, in particular as a consequence of stress at work, see discussion beyond at para 12.3.

4.3 Where a person sustains mental harm as a consequence of witnessing or learning of an accident to a third party (the primary victim), she is known as a secondary victim. For a long time, it was trite law that a defender did not owe a duty of care to a secondary victim to prevent her suffering a psychiatric disorder. The leading case in Scots law is *Bourhill v Young*.[1] Young was a motorcyclist. Driving too fast, he overtook a stationary tramcar on its near side. He then crashed into a car which was turning right into a side street some 50 feet from the tramcar. Young was killed. It was accepted that the accident was caused by Young's careless driving. At the time of the accident the pursuer, Mrs Bourhill, a fishwife, was on the far side of the tramcar, putting her creel on her back. She therefore did not see the collision but she heard the crash and, after Young's body was removed, saw the blood on the road. She maintained that as a result of the accident she suffered a 'nervous shock' which had caused her to miscarry. She sued Young's executor in delict. The complex factual situation can be shown as follows:

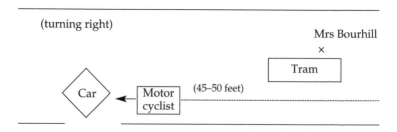

At the time of the accident Mrs Bourhill was 45–50 feet from the collision and on the far side of the tramcar. She was not within the area of risk of potential physical harm and – as we would say today – was therefore not a primary victim. In those circumstances, the House of Lords held that Young did not owe the pursuer a duty of care to prevent her suffering mental harm as a result of his careless driving. It was accepted that a driver owes a duty of care to other road users or persons in premises adjoining the highway, but only when they were 'so placed' that they could reasonably be expected to be physically harmed by the defender's failure to take care.[2] Lord Macmillan stated that:[3]

'The duty to take care is the duty to avoid doing or omitting to do anything the doing or omitting to do which may have as its reasonable and probable consequence injury to others, and the duty is owed to those to whom injury may reasonably and probably be anticipated if the duty is not observed.'

But while Young owed such a duty to the occupants of the motor car, he did not owe it to Mrs Bourhill because she was outwith the area of risk of potential physical harm. As Lord Wright observed,[4] she 'was completely outside the range of the collision. She merely heard a noise which upset her ... She saw nothing of the actual accident, or indeed any marks of blood until later'. Lord Porter expressly articulated the policy considerations involved:[5]

'In the case of a civil action there is no such thing as negligence in the abstract. There must be neglect of the use of care towards a person towards whom the defendant owes the duty of observing care ... The driver of a car or vehicle, even though careless, is entitled to assume that the ordinary frequenter of the streets has sufficient fortitude to endure such incidents as may from time to time be expected to occur in them, including the noise of a collision and the sight of injury to others, and is not to be considered negligent towards the one who does not possess the customary phlegm.'

Thus, as a general rule, there was no duty of care to prevent secondary victims from suffering mental harm; liability only extended to primary victims, ie persons who were placed in physical danger or reasonably in fear of such danger as a result of the defender's careless conduct.

1 1942 SC (HL) 78, 1943 SLT 105. For a discussion of this case, see W W McBryde 'Bourhill v Young: the Case of the Pregnant Fishwife' in *Comparative and Historical Essays in Scots law* (Butterworths, 1992) pp 66 ff.
2 1942 SC (HL) 78 at 86 per Lord Russell of Killowen.
3 Ibid at 88.
4 Ibid at 93.
5 Ibid at 98.

4.4 In *McLoughlin v O'Brian*[1] the House of Lords was persuaded to widen the scope of potential delictual liability for psychiatric disorder. In this case, the plaintiff's husband and three children were involved in a road accident at 4 pm. They were taken to hospital where it was discovered that one child was dead. The plaintiff was told of the accident at 6 pm and went to the hospital where she saw the victims. She later suffered a psychiatric disorder. The Court of Appeal took the view that while it was reasonably foreseeable that a wife and mother might sustain mental harm in these circumstances, the defendant did not owe the plaintiff a duty of care because she was not present at the accident. In other words, she was not a primary but a secondary victim. The House of Lords rejected this argument and held that a duty of care existed in spite of the fact that the plaintiff had not been directly involved in the accident. While it was reasonably foreseeable that the spouse and mother of persons injured in an accident might suffer mental harm this in itself was not sufficient to create a duty of care. However, there were additional factors present in the case which provided the necessary degree of proximity between the parties from which a duty of care could be inferred. First, the plaintiff was with the victims shortly after the accident; accordingly, she had witnessed the aftermath of the accident. Second, she had personally *seen* the effects of the accident on her family and had not simply learned of the accident by letter or on television or from a third party.[2] It follows from *McLoughlin* that before a duty of care is owed to a secondary victim, not only must the risk of a psychiatric disorder to the pursuer be reasonably foreseeable but other factors must be present which show a sufficient degree of proximity between the parties. If these additional factors are *not* present, the court will not impose a duty of care.

These issues were further explored by the House of Lords in *Alcock v Chief Constable of South Yorkshire Police*.[3] Friends and relations of persons crushed to death at Hillsborough football ground brought claims for mental harm. The House of Lords held that before a duty of care arose, it had to be reasonably foreseeable that the plaintiffs would suffer a psychiatric disorder. The criterion could not be satisfied unless there was a close tie of love and affection between the plaintiff and the victim. This would be presumed if they were spouses or parent and child, but merely because they were related in some way would not per se be sufficient. Conversely, if they were not related, a plaintiff might still succeed if it could be shown that the requisite degree of love and affection *in fact* existed between the plaintiff and the victim.[4] Their Lordships then maintained that reasonable foreseeability was not sufficient and two *extra* factors for proximity had also to exist. The plaintiff had to witness the calamity or its aftermath (for example, by being at the stadium); identifying a dead relative or friend eight hours after the event was not enough. Secondly, the plaintiff must have seen or heard the accident: watching the event on television did not suffice since the defendant knew that it was the policy of the television company in such circumstances to ensure that no specific person who was injured could be identified.

1 [1983] 1 AC 410, [1982] 2 All ER 298, HL. For an earlier example of liability to a secondary victim, see *Hambrook v Stokes Bros* [1925] 1 KB 141, CA.
2 *McLoughlin v O'Brian* [1983] AC 410 at 421–423 per Lord Wilberforce.
3 [1992] 1 AC 310, [1991] 4 All ER 707, HL.
4 In *Alcock*, the House suggested that in exceptionally horrific circumstances a duty of care might arise even though the secondary victim did not fulfil the 'love and affection' criterion. This is doubtful. In *Robertson v Forth Road Bridge Joint*

Board 1994 SC 364, for example, the fact that the pursuer who had witnessed his fellow employee being blown off the Forth Road Bridge had been a friend of the deceased and had socialised with him for many years was held not to be sufficient to constitute the necessary degree of 'love and affection'. The same kind of reasoning was applied in *McFarlane v EE Caledonia Ltd* [1994] 2 All ER 1, where the plaintiff had witnessed the Piper Alpha explosion. So, in this respect, *Alcock* has never been followed – what could have been more horrific than the accidents in *Robertson* and *McFarlane*?

4.5   To summarise: a duty of care to prevent mental harm to a secondary victim will only arise if:

(1) there is a tie of love and affection between the secondary victim and the primary victim;
(2) the secondary victim was present at the accident or at its immediate aftermath; and
(3) the psychiatric disorder was caused by direct perception of the accident or its immediate aftermath: it is not enough merely to have been informed of the accident.

The *Alcock* criteria for the imposition of a duty of care in relation to secondary victims were reaffirmed by the House of Lords in *Frost v Chief Constable South Yorkshire Police*.[1]

The law now appears to be settled, but its application can lead to arbitrary results. In *Vernon v Bosley (No 1)*,[2] for example, two children were drowned when the car their nanny was driving drove into a river. Their father was called to the scene and saw the unsuccessful attempts to rescue his children trapped in the car. The father's claim for damages for a psychiatric disorder was successful. The defendant owed him a duty of care because:

(1) he was the father of the primary victims; and
(2) he witnessed the aftermath; and
(3) his psychiatric illness arose from direct perception of the failed rescue attempt.

But if for example, he had not been able to be present at the rescue but was simply informed of his daughters' deaths by telephone, no duty of care would have arisen because of the absence of reasons (2) and (3). Similarly, Mrs Bourhill would still fail in her claim since there was no tie of love and affection between her and Young's primary victims.[3]

There is authority that there is no breach of a duty to prevent mental harm unless it has been induced by a nervous shock, ie the 'sudden appreciation by sight or sound of a horrifying event, which violently agitates the mind'.[4] Claims have therefore been refused where a psychiatric disorder has been caused by a gradual process, for example nursing a dying child.[5]

1 [1999] 2 AC 455 where the police constables could not establish a sufficient tie of love and affection with the primary victims they were attempting to rescue: therefore the constables' claims as secondary victims failed. They were not within the area of potential physical harm and therefore could not be regarded as primary victims. See also *Keen v Tayside Contracts* 2003 SLT 500 (employee treated as secondary victim where he sustained mental harm by witnessing an accident and not being allowed to leave the scene by his supervisor: discussed beyond para 12.3).

2 [1997] 1 All ER 577. See also *Galli-Atkinson v Seghal* [2003] EWCA 697, [2003] All ER (D) 341 (Mar) where a mother visited a hospital mortuary to see her child whom she refused to believe was dead: this was regarded by the Court of Appeal as part of the aftermath of the accident. Cf *Taylor v A Novo* [2013] EWCA Civ 194 where a daughter whose mother died unexpectedly in hospital weeks after an accident at work could not establish sufficient proximity in an action against her mother's employer, as she had not witnessed the accident or its aftermath even though she had been present at her mother's death.

3 But could she have sued if she had been related to Young who was killed in the accident as a result of his own negligence? It is submitted that she could. Cf *Greatorex v Greatorex* [2000] 4 All ER 769 (father claimed damages for a psychiatric disorder sustained when he rescued his son from a car crash. The *Alcock* criteria were satisfied. However, the claim was refused on policy grounds as the son was solely responsible for his own injuries and the court could not countenance a parent suing his own child in such circumstances. *Sed quaere?*).

4 *Alcock v Chief Constable of South Yorkshire Police* [1992] 1 AC 310 per Lord Ackner at 401.

5 *Sion v Hampstead Health Authority* [1994] 5 Med LR 170, CA. Damages may be awarded if there is a sudden realisation of the danger to the primary victim within a continuing process: *Walters v North Glamorgan NHS Trust* [2002] EWHC 321 (QB), [2003] PIQR P2, [2002] All ER (D) 65 (Mar).

4.6   We must distinguish these cases from the situation where the defender has been in breach of his duty to take reasonable care to prevent the pursuer suffering physical harm and the pursuer suffers a mental disorder as well as physical harm. Whether damages can be awarded for the mental as well as physical harm is an issue of remoteness of losses[1]. In *Simmons v British Steel plc*[2] the House of Lords confirmed that because the defender must take the pursuer as he finds him – the thin skull rule – where there has been a breach of duty to prevent physical harm, damages can be awarded for losses arising from an unforeseeable mental disorder caused by the physical harm the victim has suffered.[3] Where the defender is in breach of his duty to take reasonable care to prevent damage to the pursuer's property, any mental harm suffered by the owner from the loss or damage to his property will be too remote unless in the circumstances mental harm to the owner was reasonably foreseeable.[4] In *Yearworth v North Bristol NHS*

Trust[5] the claimants were told that they might become sterile as a result of chemotherapy. Before the treatment, they agreed that the defendant could store samples of their semen for future use. Owing to the negligence of the defendant, the semen thawed and the sperms perished irretrievably. The Court held that the sperms were the property of the men. Provided that the owner's mental disorder was a reasonably foreseeable consequence of learning that his sperms had been destroyed and could not be used for fertilisation, the mental harm would not be too remote and damages would be recoverable.[6]

The law in this area is considered to be unsatisfactory and the Scottish Law Commission has made recommendations for reform.[7]

1 On remoteness of losses see beyond paras 16.1 ff.
2 2004 SC (HL) 94.
3 *Page v Smith* [1996] AC 155 is not, of course, a remoteness case as the defender did *not* cause the plaintiff any physical harm which led to a mental disorder.
4 *Attia v British Gas* [1988] 1 QB 304 (the owner of a house recovered damages for mental harm suffered from witnessing her house burning down as a result of the defendant's negligence. In the circumstances the owner's mental harm was reasonably foreseeable and therefore not too remote).
5 [2009] EWCA Civ 37.
6 In this case the damages were likely to be small as happily the men had not become permanently sterile as a consequence of the chemotherapy.
7 See Report on Damages for Psychiatric Injury (Scot Law Com No 196).

C. WRONGFUL LIFE, WRONGFUL BIRTH AND WRONGFUL CONCEPTION

(1) Wrongful life

4.7 It is generally accepted that a person owes a duty of care not to harm a foetus, ie a child *in utero*. Where a foetus is injured in its mother's womb, if the child is subsequently born alive, the *child* can sue the defender in delict in respect of its physical harm even though the injuries were sustained when the child was a foetus. In *McKay v Essex Area Health Authority*[1] a mother contracted rubella (German measles) during her pregnancy. When the child was born, the baby was badly deformed as a result of the mother's illness. The mother alleged that owing to the hospital's carelessness, she had not been informed that her baby might be born with deformities. Since no tests had been carried out, the mother had been denied the opportunity of a lawful termination of her pregnancy. The Court of Appeal held that the hospital may have been in breach of a duty of care towards the *mother* which would entitle her to damages for having to bring up a deformed child. But the hospital did not owe a duty of care towards the *child* to allow the child's mother the opportunity to terminate the pregnancy. A child has no right to be born whole or not at all. This denial of the existence of a duty of care towards a foetus to terminate the pregnancy if the foetus is deformed is clearly based on principles of public policy.[2] Accordingly the law has refused to recognise wrongful life actions by denying the existence of a duty of care: again, we see the duty of care being used as a threshold device.

1 [1982] QB 1166, [1982] 2 All ER 771, CA.
2 Moreover, even if such a duty existed, the child's deformities were not caused by the careless conduct of the hospital but by the rubella; on the necessity for causation, see Chapter 6. Of course, if the hospital had caused the child's deformities, it *would* have been liable to the child, if born alive; see discussion beyond.

(2) Wrongful birth

4.8   While there will be no duty of care towards a foetus to terminate the pregnancy because it might be born deformed, the Court of Appeal emphasised that the defendant could have been in breach of its duty towards the *mother* in not allowing her the opportunity of a termination. This is known as a wrongful birth action. In *McLelland v Greater Glasgow Health Board*[1] an Extra Division accepted that wrongful birth actions can be pursued in Scots law. Thus a hospital owes a duty of care to the parents of a child to provide the mother with an opportunity to terminate her pregnancy if her child is likely to be born physically or mentally handicapped. While both parents can recover solatium for the distress of having a handicapped child and the mother can recover solatium in respect of the pregnancy and birth, the basic economic cost of maintaining the child cannot be recovered: but any additional costs stemming from the special needs of a handicapped child can be recovered.[2]

1 2002 SLT 446.
2 For full discussion, see beyond para 16.6.

(3) Wrongful conception

4.9   In *McFarlane v Tayside Health Board*,[1] the pursuers sought damages for the birth of a healthy child who had been born as a result of a failed sterilisation on the father. The Lord Ordinary (Gill) admitted that the defenders owed a duty of care to the pursuers who were their patients but denied the pursuers' action of damages. Lord Gill argued that the parents had not sustained any reparable loss. He refused to classify pregnancy and labour as physical injury to the mother and he did not regard the cost of rearing the child as economic loss since such loss was outweighed by the inestimable benefits of being the parents of a healthy child. This decision was reversed by the Second Division.[2] There it was held that the parents' right not to have a child had been infringed, ie that the unplanned conception constituted the harm (*damnum*). This was a reparable interest in modern Scots law.[3] Consequently in a wrongful conception action the mother could recover damages for pain and suffering caused by the pregnancy and birth; and both parents could recover compensation for the economic costs of bringing up the child whose birth had not been planned. Moreover, their damages would not be reduced because the mother had refused to terminate the pregnancy.

This decision was in turn appealed to the House of Lords. There it was accepted that a doctor does owe a duty of care to a man or a woman who undergoes sterilisation and if as a result of medical negligence an unplanned conception occurs then there is a breach of that duty of care. The House agreed that the mother could recover solatium for pain and suffering caused by the pregnancy and birth as well as any derivative economic loss of earnings during that period. But their Lordships held that it was contrary to contemporary values of distributive justice that the parents should be able to recover for the economic cost of maintaining a healthy and normal child.[4] The principle of non-recoverability for the cost of bringing up a normal and healthy child was reaffirmed by the House of Lords in *Rees v Darlington Memorial Hospital NHS Trust*.[5] However, a majority of their Lordships felt that an award of solatium did not adequately recognise the wrongful infringement of the mother's freedom to limit the size of her family and made her a conventional non-compensatory award of £15,000 to afford some measure of recognition of the wrongful conception of her child.

1 1997 SLT 211, OH, 2000 SC (HL) 1.
2 2000 SC (HL) 1.
3 In England, wrongful conception actions had been recognised for a long time. See, for examples, *Thake v Maurice* [1986] QB 644, [1984] 2 All ER 513; *Gold v Haringey Health Authority* [1987] 2 All ER 888, CA. In *Goodwill v British Pregnancy Advisory Service* [1996] 2 All ER 161, CA, the Court of Appeal held that the duty of care did not extend to advising the future sexual partners of male patients that their vasectomy could undergo a spontaneous reversal. *Sed quaere?*
4 For further discussion on the damages issues, see para 16.6. See also Joe Thomson 'Abandoning the Law of Delict' 2000 SLT (News) 43.
5 [2004] 1 AC 309, [2003] 4 All ER 987. *McFarlane* was followed even although the mother in *Rees* was blind.

D. PURE ECONOMIC LOSS

4.10   It is in the area of liability in delict for pure economic loss that the concept of a duty of care has been extensively used by the courts as a threshold device. *Donoghue v Stevenson*[1] is authority for the principle that a duty of care arises when it is reasonably foreseeable by the defender that his careless conduct would cause physical harm to the pursuer or physical damage to the pursuer's property. The pursuer can recover damages for economic loss which derives from the pursuer's injuries or the physical damage to his property, for example loss of earnings while in hospital and loss of earnings in the future when the pursuer is unable to work.[2] This is known as *derivative* or *parasitic* economic loss, ie economic loss which derives from or is parasitic upon the pursuer's physical injuries or the physical damage to the pursuer's property. However, the law does not, as a general rule, allow recovery in *delict* where the pursuer only sustains economic loss as a result of the defender's careless conduct.[3] In the case of a defective product, for example, which has not physically harmed the pursuer or damaged other property belonging to the pursuer, the cost of repair or the difference in value between a defective and a non-defective product is not recoverable in *delict*. The pursuer has sustained pure economic loss and the courts have refused to impose a duty of care on the manufacturer in respect of such losses even though such a loss is reasonably foreseeable. Where the pursuer has bought the product, she, of course, can sue the retailer for breach of contract on the ground that the goods are not of satisfactory quality. The reluctance to allow recovery in delict for pure economic loss is to protect the defender from potentially indeterminate liability.[4]

Although reasonable foreseeability of pure economic loss is not sufficient for the imposition of a duty of care, the courts have, in certain situations, been prepared to hold that a duty of care does exist. But there must be factors *in addition* to reasonable foreseeability of pure economic loss which demonstrate that there is a sufficient degree of proximity between the parties so that it is fair, just and reasonable for a duty of care to be inferred. These additional requirements are simply a rationalisation by the courts of why they are, or are not, prepared to extend the parameters of liability in delict. It is the paradigm of the duty of care being used as a threshold device.

We shall now examine these developments in detail.

1 1932 SC (HL) 31.
2 On damages generally, see Chapter 16 below. Derivative economic losses may not be recoverable if they are too remote: see paras 16.1–16.4 below.

3 Where the defender has intended to cause economic loss, for example by fraud or by wrongful occupation of property, Scots law does provide compensation: see, for example, *Saeed v Waheed* 1996 SLT (Ch Ct) 39, 1995 SCLR 504. The reasoning in *Saeed* is controversial because the Sheriff Principal (Nicholson) relied on English cases concerned with liability for pure economic loss arising from negligence. It is thought that the pursuer should have been awarded violent profits: see para 1.13 above.

4 So when a Scottish football team supporter claimed damages against FIFA and the SFA for economic loss incurred as a result of the delay to a World Cup match between Scotland and Estonia, it was held that the SFA and FIFA did not owe the pursuer a duty of care to ensure that the match took place as scheduled: *Macdonald v Fédération Internationale des Football Associations* 1999 SCLR 59, OH.

(1) Careless misrepresentation

4.11 A may make a statement to B which causes B physical harm or damage to B's property: for example A tells B that it is safe to drink contaminated water. A will owe B a duty of care if it is reasonably foreseeable that B will suffer physical harm or damage to his property if A's statement is made carelessly. This is a simple application of the *Donoghue* neighbourhood principle.[1] But A may make a statement to B which causes B pure economic loss. For example, A tells B that B should enter into a contract with C. Relying on A's advice, B enters into the contract with C. As a result, B loses money. Can B sue A in delict for the pure economic loss B has sustained, if A's statement was made carelessly?[2] The answer depends on whether A owes a duty of care to B not to make careless statements which cause B pure economic loss.

The criteria for the existence of such a duty were laid down by the House of Lords in *Hedley Byrne & Co Ltd v Heller & Partners Ltd*.[3] The plaintiffs through their bankers asked E's bankers, the defendants, whether E was a respectably constituted company. E's bankers replied that E was. On reliance of this statement, the plaintiffs became E's advertising agents. E later went into liquidation. As a result, the plaintiffs suffered pure economic loss. The facts of the case can be shown as follows:

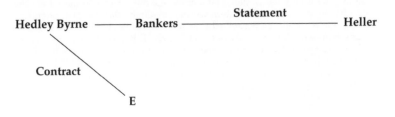

It will be clear that there was no contract between Hedley Byrne and Heller. The question was whether the plaintiffs could sue the defendants in delict. The House of Lords held that the defendants owed a duty of care to the plaintiffs if the defendants had undertaken responsibility for the accuracy of the statement and knew or ought to have known that the plaintiffs would rely on that statement. If the duty was broken as a result of the statement being made carelessly, the defendants could be liable for the plaintiffs' pure economic loss. In the course of his speech, Lord Devlin stated[4] that before there was liability, the plaintiffs had to show that the defendants owed the plaintiffs 'a special duty' to take care. The categories of relationships where this duty arose included not only contractual relationships (ie where there was a contract between the parties) or fiduciary relationships (for example, principal and agent, trustee and beneficiary), but also relationships which were the 'equivalent to contract'. One example of this would be where the defender had voluntarily assumed responsibility for the accuracy of the statement and knew or ought to have known that the pursuer would rely on the information. The paradigm situation is where the defender is a professional businessman, for example a banker, solicitor or accountant, who in the absence of a contract between them, gives advice to the pursuer in the course of the defender's business, knowing that it will be relied on by the pursuer.

It is important to note that reasonable foreseeability of loss to the pursuer is not per se sufficient to establish a duty of care. There must be additional factors present from which the courts will infer the necessary proximity of relationship between the parties. These factors include the defender's knowledge of the identity of the pursuer, either as an individual or as a member of an identifiable class; and the defender's knowledge that the information will be communicated to and used by the pursuer in connection with a particular transaction or transactions of a particular kind.

1 In *United Central Bakeries Ltd v Spooner* [2012] CSOH 111 Lord Hodge accepted the distinction between a misrepresentation causing personal injury or damage to property and a misrepresentation causing pure economic loss. He considered that in determining the existence and ambit of a duty of care in the former the court has to assess (i) the context in which A made the statement or statements (ii) the foreseeability of B's reliance on the statements and (iii) the meaning of any representation. No duty of care will arise if B's relationship to A is not sufficiently proximate at the time the representation is made: *Sutradhar (FC) v Natural Environment Research Council* [2006] UKHL 33, [2006] 4 All ER 490, HL.

2 Cf if A made the statement fraudulently, when, of course, A is liable for fraud. On fraud, see para 2.10 above.

3 [1964] AC 465, [1963] 2 All ER 575, HL.

4 [1963] 2 All ER 575 at 610.

4.12 These limitations on *Hedley Byrne v Heller* liability were recognised by the House of Lords in *Caparo Industries plc v Dickman*.[1] The auditor of a company carelessly carried out an audit showing that the company was in a better financial position than was in fact the case. It was reasonably foreseeable (a) that potential investors in reliance on the audit would invest in the company to their loss; and (b) that existing shareholders, in reliance on the audit, would purchase more shares in the company to their loss. This, in fact, happened. Although the auditor had a contract with the company, he did not have a contract with existing and potential shareholders. Although the losses which had been incurred were reasonably foreseeable, the House of Lords held that the auditor did not owe a duty of care to the shareholders or potential shareholders to prevent them suffering pure economic loss as a result of the careless audit. The reasons were that their relationships were not sufficiently proximate and that it was not fair, just and reasonable to impose a duty of care. In other words, the factors additional to reasonable foreseeability did not exist in this case. Lord Bridge explained:[2]

'The salient feature of all these cases [ie where a *Hedley Byrne v Heller* duty of care was recognised] is that the defendant giving advice or information was fully aware of the nature of the transaction which the plaintiff had in contemplation, knew that the advice or information would be communicated to him directly or indirectly and knew that it was very likely that the plaintiff would rely on that advice or information in deciding whether or not to engage in the transaction in contemplation. In these circumstances the defendant could clearly be expected … specifically to anticipate that the plaintiff would rely on the advice or information given by the defendant for the very purpose for which he did in the event rely on it. So also the plaintiff … would in that situation reasonably suppose that he was entitled to rely on the advice or information communicated to him for the very purpose for which he required it. The situation is entirely different where a statement is put into more or less general circulation and may foreseeably be relied on by strangers to the maker of the statement for any one of a variety of different purposes which the speaker has no specific reason to anticipate. To hold the maker of the statement to be under a duty of care in respect of the accuracy of the statement to all and sundry for any purpose for which they may choose to rely on it is not only to subject him, in the classic words of Cardozo CJ to "liability in an indeterminate amount for an indeterminate time to an indeterminate class",[3] it is also to confer on the world at large a quite unwarranted entitlement to appropriate for their own purposes the benefit of the expert knowledge or professional expertise attributed to the maker of the statement.'

Accordingly, the House of Lords held that an auditor did not owe a duty of care to a member of the public at large who relied on the audit to purchase shares or increase an existing shareholding in the company: such a duty would arise only if the auditor knew that his statement would be communicated to the plaintiff and relied upon by the plaintiff in a particular transaction of a particular kind.[4]

1　[1990] 2 AC 605, [1990] 1 All ER 568, HL.
2　[1990] 1 All ER 568 at 576.
3　*Ultramares Corpn v Touche* (1931) 255 NY 170 at 179.
4　In *Nordic Oil Services Ltd v Berman* 1993 SLT 1164, OH, the Lord Ordinary (Osborne) held that directors of a company did not owe a duty of care to creditors of the company to prevent them suffering economic loss as a result of the acts or omissions of the company. In *Reeman v Department of Transport* [1997] 2 Lloyd's Rep 648, CA, it was held by the Court of Appeal that before a duty of care could arise by virtue of *Caparo*, the defendant's statement had to be plaintiff-specific, purpose-specific and transaction-specific. Thus if an auditor is aware that a particular identified bidder or lender would rely on the audited accounts and the auditor intends that the bidder or lender should rely on them, he owes that party a duty of care: *Galoo Ltd (in liquidation) v Bright Grahame Murray* [1994] 1 WLR 1360, [1995] 1 All ER 16, CA; *Royal Bank of Scotland v Bannerman Johnstone Maclay* 2003 SC 125.

4.13　*Hedley Byrne v Heller* was an English case. The principle has been accepted as part of Scots law.[1] In *Grant Estates Ltd v The Royal Bank of Scotland*,[2] Lord Hodge considered[3] that the following factors were relevant in determining whether or not there is a duty of care to prevent financial loss when giving financial advice:

(1)　It is not sufficient to set up a duty of care to assert the existence of an advisory relationship. There is a clear distinction between giving advice and assuming legal responsibility for that advice.

(2)　The absence of any written advisory agreement is a significant pointer against the existence of an advisory obligation.

(3)　The contractual terms the parties have agreed can define the parties' relationship in a way that no assumption of responsibility can be inferred.

(4)　The contractual delineation of responsibility and allocation of risk may preclude a party from founding on what has actually occurred if he has contracted to accept a particular state of affairs.

(5)　The approach in (4) extends to any retrospective agreement in relation to past events.

1　*John Kenway Ltd v Orcantic Ltd* 1979 SC 422, 1980 SLT 46, OH; *Eastern Marine Services (and Supplies) Ltd v Dickson Motors Ltd* 1981 SC 355, OH; *Twomax Ltd v Dickson, McFarlane and Robinson* 1982 SC 113, 1983 SLT 98, OH. The last decision must now be read in the light of the limitations laid down in *Caparo Industries plc v Dickman* [1990] 2 AC 605, [1990] 1 All ER 568, HL. See also *Cramaso LLP v Reidhaven Trs* [2011] CSIH 81.
2　[2012] CSOH 133.
3　Ibid at para 73.

4.14   Another area where it has been applied is in relation to the liability of surveyors. Consider the following example. A wishes to purchase a house from B. He approaches a bank for a loan. Before it can give the loan the bank must obtain a report on the value of the property from a surveyor. It is a term of A's contract with the bank that A will pay the surveyor's fee. Instead of obtaining an independent survey, A relies on the valuation report commissioned for the bank and goes ahead with the purchase. The house turns out to have faulty foundations which will cost £20,000 to repair. The facts of the case can be shown as follows.

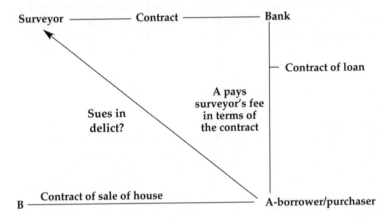

Since A has not been physically harmed and the faulty foundations have not caused physical damage to any other property owned by A, A has suffered only pure economic loss. This is either the cost of repairs or the difference in value between the house with faulty foundations and the house if the foundations were sound. Although A has a contract of sale with B, the seller of heritage does not usually warrant that a house built on the land conveyed is sound. Therefore, A has no *contractual* remedy against B. Moreover, although A paid for the survey, he has no contract with the surveyor: the surveyor's contract is with the bank. However, it has been held that the surveyor owes a duty of care to A, if the surveyor knows that the report will be used by A and will be relied upon by A to purchase the house.[1] As well as reasonable foreseeability of loss to A, the surveyor's knowledge of A and the particular transaction, A's reliance on the report, and the fact that A paid for the report, provide the additional factors which create a sufficient degree of proximity between A and the surveyor for a *Hedley Byrne v Heller* duty of care to arise. Accordingly, if the report was made carelessly,

A can recover damages for pure economic loss from the surveyor. If, however, A later sold the house to C and C relied on the valuation report rather than commission a new survey, the surveyor would not owe a duty of care to C. For although it is reasonably foreseeable that the report would be relied on by a subsequent purchaser of the house, since the surveyor did not know the identity of C at the time of the survey and C did not pay the fee, the additional factors are not present and the duty of care does not arise.[2]

Although the existence of a duty of care to prevent pure economic loss to the plaintiff was recognised in *Hedley Byrne & Co Ltd v Heller & Partners Ltd*,[3] in fact the plaintiff did not obtain damages in that case. When they provided the information, the defendants expressly stated that it was given 'without responsibility on the part of the bank'. The House of Lords held that this disclaimer was effective to protect the defendants from liability. After their potential delictual liability towards purchasers of property was established, surveyors started to insert a similar disclaimer in their valuation reports or in the bank's contract with the borrower/purchaser. Provided the disclaimer came to the notice of the purchaser before the purchaser entered into the contract of sale,[4] for a time these disclaimers were effective to protect the surveyor from liability in delict.[5] However, where the disclaimer is a term of the purchaser's contract with the bank,[6] it cannot be relied on unless it satisfies the requirement of reasonableness under the Unfair Contract Terms Act 1977 (UCTA 1977).[7] Moreover, the controls in UCTA 1977 also extend to disclaimers which are not contractual terms.[8] This includes any disclaimers in the surveyor's valuation report. Consequently, a surveyor cannot escape delictual liability by relying on a disclaimer unless it satisfies the requirement of reasonableness. In *Smith v Eric S Bush; Harris v Wyre Forest District Council*,[9] the House of Lords, applying the parallel English provisions of UCTA 1977, held that a disclaimer was not reasonable when the purchaser was of limited means and buying domestic property. If the purchaser was wealthy or the property bought was commercial, then a surveyor might be able to establish that the disclaimer was reasonable.[10] A similar view has been taken by the courts in Scotland.[11]

---

1   *Martin v Bell-Ingram* 1986 SC 208, 1986 SLT 575; *Smith v Eric S Bush; Harris v Wyre Forest District Council* [1990] 1 AC 831, [1989] 2 WLR 790. See also *Smith v Carter* 1994 SCLR 539, 1995 SLT 295, OH, where the survey was commissioned by A acting as the undisclosed agent of B. It was held that a duty of care was owed to B because it is not uncommon for one person to commission a report on behalf of joint purchasers.

2   This would follow from the ratio of *Caparo Industries plc v Dickman* [1990] 2 AC 605, [1990] 1 All ER 568, HL. Similarly, the absence of such additional factors prevented the surveyor owing a duty of care to the owner of the lost cargo in

Marc Rich & Co AG v Bishop Rock Marine Co Ltd, The Nicholas H [1994] 3 All ER 686,
[1994] 1 WLR 1071, CA (affd [1995] 3 All ER 307, HL), discussed at para 3.7 above.
3 [1964] AC 465, [1963] 2 All ER 575, HL.
4 If it did not come to the purchaser's notice before the contract of sale was agreed,
the disclaimer was not effective: *Martin v Bell-Ingram* 1986 SC 208, 1986 SLT 575.
5 *Robbie v Graham and Sibbald* 1989 SCLR 578, 1989 SLT 870, OH.
6 *Melrose v Davidson and Robertson* 1993 SC 288, 1993 SLT 611.
7 Unfair Contract Terms Act 1977, ss 16 and 25(5). See *Melrose v Davidson and Robertson* 1993 SC 288, 1993 SLT 611.
8 Law Reform (Miscellaneous Provisions) (Scotland) Act 1990, s 68.
9 [1990] 1 AC 831, [1989] 2 All ER 514, HL.
10 As happened, for example, in *Omega Trust Co Ltd v Wright Son & Pepper (No 1)* [1997] 1 EGLR 120, CA.
11 *Bank of Scotland v Fuller Peiser* 2002 SLT 574. In *Smith v Eric S Bush; Harris v Wyre Forest District Council* [1990] 1 AC 831, [1989] 2 All ER 514, HL, the House of Lords also rejected the argument that the disclaimer prevented a duty of care arising in the first place. Instead, it held that the duty of care existed in spite of the disclaimer and that the disclaimer was therefore an exemption clause purporting to exclude liability. The matter is academic: by UCTA 1977, s 25(5) any clause which purports to prevent a duty of care from arising is also subject to the requirement of reasonableness before it can be effective. Where the disclaimer satisfies the requirement of reasonableness, no duty of care arises: *McCullagh v Lane Fox and Partners* [1996] 1 EGLR 35, (1995) *Times*, 22 December 1995, CA; *Bank of Scotland v Fuller Peiser* 2002 SLT 574.

4.15 The classic example of *Hedley Byrne v Heller* liability is where A makes a misrepresentation to B which B relies on to enter a contract with C. A owes B a duty of care which enables B to sue A in *delict* for pure economic loss. Does A owe B a *Hedley Byrne v Heller* duty of care when A makes a misrepresentation to B which induces B to enter a contract with A? For many years, as a result of the decision in *Manners v Whitehead*,[1] B was denied a remedy in delict against A unless A's misrepresentation was fraudulent.[2] The rule in *Manners v Whitehead* has been abolished.[3] Accordingly, provided the *Hedley Byrne v Heller* criteria are established,[4] A will owe B a duty of care so that B can sue A in *delict* if the misrepresentation was made carelessly and caused B pure economic loss. In addition or as an alternative, B will have contractual remedies, for example reduction, arising from the misrepresentation.[5] In *Hamilton v Allied Domecq plc*,[6] the first reported decision in Scotland where an action for negligent misrepresentation in delict was successfully brought against the other party to the contract,[7] the effect of s 10 appears to have been misunderstood. The Lord Ordinary (Carloway) suggested that s 10 equated a negligent misrepresentation with a fraudulent misrepresentation and therefore there was no need to establish a special relationship between the parties before a duty of care arose. With respect, it is thought that this is wrong.[8] The function of s 10 was merely to abolish the rule in *Manners v Whitehead* and allow the courts to develop negligent misrepresentation untrammelled by that rule. It is submitted, therefore, that the pursuer must establish a special relationship between the defender and himself, though, as in *Hamilton* itself, this should not be too difficult given that *ex hypothesi* they are parties to the same contract.[9] Nevertheless, in *BSA International SA v Irvine*,[10] the Lord Ordinary (Glennie) followed the approach of Lord Carloway in *Hamilton*. In Lord Glennie's view there was no reason to import into the pre-existing relationship of intending contractual parties concepts that have developed in the law of delict to identify other situations in which a party may owe a duty of care as regards the accuracy of statements made by him.[11]

However, in *Cramaso LLP v Ogilvie Grant, Earl of Seafield and others*[12] the Supreme Court upheld the author's view on the correct interpretation of s 10. Lord Reed explained:[13]

'Section 10(1) is drafted in a negative form. It does not provide that a party to a contract who has been induced to enter into it by a negligent misrepresentation made by or on behalf of another party to the contract is entitled to recover damages: it provides that such a person shall not be disentitled by reason only that the misrepresentation is not fraudulent, and that any rule that such damages cannot be recovered unless fraud is proved shall cease to have effect. Whether such a person is entitled to damages therefore depends on the common law ... The consequence is that entitlement to damages depends upon establishing the breach of a duty of care, since at common law it is the breach of a duty of care which renders a negligent misrepresentation wrongful.'

Lord Reed is also recognised[14] that 'it has long been accepted that the relationship between the parties to contractual negotiations may give rise to such a duty in respect of representations which the representor can reasonably foresee are likely to induce the other party to enter into the contract unless circumstances negativing the existence of such a duty ... are present'.[15]

1 (1898) 1 F 171.
2 On fraud, see para 2.10 above.
3 Law Reform (Miscellaneous Provisions) (Scotland) Act 1985, s 10.
4 And it is submitted that in this situation they usually are.
5 These are the same as the contractual remedies available after a fraudulent misrepresentation, discussed at para 2.10 above.
6 [2007] UKHL 33, 2008 SCLR 69, HL; 2006 SC 221 (IH 2 Div); 2001 SC 829.
7 An attempt failed in *Palmer v Beck* 1993 SLT 485, OH, on the ground that s 10 of the Law Reform (Miscellaneous Provisions) (Scotland) Act 1985 was not retrospective. See also *Clelland v Morton Fraser Milligan* 1997 SLT (Sh Ct) 57, where an action under s 10 failed because it was not brought against the other party to the pursuer's contract.
8 For full discussion see Joe Thomson, 'Misrepresentation' 2001 SLT (News) 279.
9 The pursuer's claim for damages in *Hamilton* ultimately failed because it could not be established that the defender had in fact made a misrepresentation to the pursuer: *Hamilton v Allied Domecq plc* 2006 SC 221(IH) app [2007] UKHL 33.

10 [2010] CSOH 78.
11 Ibid at para 15.
12 [2014] UKSC 9.
13 Ibid at para 36.
14 Ibid at para 42.
15 In *Cramaso*, a businessman incorporated a company as a vehicle to enter into the lease of a grouse moor on the defender's estate. The defender's misrepresentation was made to the businessman in negotiations before the company was incorporated. After incorporation the company entered into the lease with the defender. The Supreme Court held that the company could rely on the misrepresentation because it had a continuing effect from the time it was made until the conclusion of the lease.

(2) *Henderson v Merrett* – A general duty of care to prevent pure economic loss?

4.16 An attempt to rationalise the law on delictual liability for pure economic loss was made by the House of Lords in *Henderson v Merrett Syndicates Ltd.*[1] Actions for damages were brought by Lloyd's 'names' against Lloyd's members' agents and managing agents of syndicates. The 'names' alleged that they had suffered losses as a result of the negligence of the agents. Under contracts with their members' agents, the names gave the agents the exclusive right to undertake risks and reinsurance on their behalf. This was done directly through the members' agents or indirectly by the members' agents delegating the tasks to managing agents through a sub-agency contract. This can be illustrated as follows:

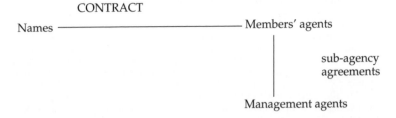

The obvious remedy was for the names to sue the members' agents for breach of contract. Unfortunately, this action was time-barred. So an action against them and the management agents could lie only in tort/delict. The question before the House of Lords was whether the management agents and the members' agents owed a duty of care to the names. Their Lordships held that they did. Why?

Lord Goff of Chieveley maintained that a duty of care arises to prevent the plaintiff sustaining pure economic loss when the defendant has voluntarily assumed responsibility for the economic interests of the plaintiff with the knowledge that the plaintiff is relying on the defendant's expertise. This assumption of responsibility covers the provision of services as well as information; careless omissions as well as careless actions. When the parties are linked directly or indirectly by contracts, the terms of the contracts may exclude liability in delict but to be effective any such exemption clauses or disclaimers will have to satisfy the requirements of reasonableness under the UCTA 1977.

Like Lord Atkin with his neighbourhood principle,[2] Lord Goff was laying down a general duty of care: if the two criteria are satisfied, ie voluntary assumption of responsibility and concomitant reliance, then a duty of care exists and it is not necessary to consider whether or not it is fair, just and reasonable to impose a duty of care, ie the *Caparo* tripartite criteria are irrelevant.[3]

To summarise: in Lord Goff's opinion a general duty of care to prevent pure economic loss would arise if:

(1) the defender has voluntarily assumed responsibility for the economic interests of the pursuer;

(2) the defender knows that the pursuer is relying on the defender's professional expertise; and

(3) the terms of any contract linking the pursuer and defender do not negative delictual liability.

1 [1995] 2 AC 145, [1994] 3 All ER 506, HL.

2 See *Donoghue v Stevenson* 1932 SC (HL) 31, 1932, SLT 317.

3 The general nature of the duty was emphasised by the House of Lords in *Williams v Natural Life Health Foods Ltd* [1998] 2 All ER 577, HL, at 581 per Lord Steyn. A director of a company was held not to owe a duty of care to the plaintiff in this case because he had not assumed personal responsibility for the plaintiff's financial interests: the company was, of course, liable. This decision is of vital significance in company law where a creditor's limited resource to the assets of the company as opposed to the personal assets of the director/shareholder is a fundamental reason for incorporation: *Salomon v A Salomon & Co Ltd* [1897] AC 22, HL. But a managing director (as well as the company) is personally liable for a *fraudulent* misrepresentation: *Standard Chartered Bank v Pakistan Shipping Corpn (No 2)* [2003] 1 All ER 173.

4.17 Whether or not the defender has voluntarily assumed responsibility for the pursuer's economic interests is objectively ascertained from all the circumstances of the case. The absence of an exemption clause or disclaimer is thus indicative that the defender undertook such responsibility.[1] Where there is such a clause, it must satisfy the requirement of reasonableness under the UCTA 1977 before it will be effective to prevent the duty of care from arising. In *Bank of Scotland v Fuller Peiser*,[2] for example, the defender provided the purchaser of a hotel with a valuation of the property. The valuation report stated that the defender accepted 'no responsibility' for anyone other than the purchaser. The pursuer relied on the report when they lent money to the purchaser. When the purchaser defaulted, the pursuer sought damages in delict from the defender. The Lord Ordinary (Eassie) held that the disclaimer satisfied the requirement of reasonableness under the UCTA 1977 because both parties were of equal bargaining power and could equally bear the loss. The disclaimer was therefore effective to prevent a duty of care from arising as the defender had *not* voluntarily assumed responsibility for the pursuer's economic interests.[3] Moreover, the defender must know that the pursuer does or will rely on his expertise. The necessity for 'concomitant reliance' by the pursuer, which is known to the defender, provides an element of mutuality between the parties which restricts the defender's potential delictual liability.[4]

The *Henderson v Merrett* criteria provide a rationale for the liability for negligent misrepresentations discussed in the previous section. They also explain other situations where delictual liability for pure economic loss has been recognised. In *Spring v Guardian Assurance plc*,[5] for example, the House of Lords held that an employer owed a duty of care to a former employee when providing a reference for him. Because of the defendant's carelessness, the plaintiff had been unable to obtain a job. By agreeing to provide a reference, the employer had voluntarily assumed responsibility for Spring's financial interests, knowing that he would rely on the employer to prepare the reference carefully.[6]

1 *Royal Bank of Scotland v Bannerman Johnstone Maclay* 2003 SC 125. See also *Realstone v J & E Shepherd* [2008] CSOH 31, which concerned a contractual chain between A and B and C. In deciding whether C could owe a *Henderson v Merrett* duty of care to A the Lord Ordinary (Hodge) emphasised that it was important to analyse the particular circumstances of the case including the contractual arrangements between A and B and C.

2 2002 SLT 574. See J Thomson 'A General Duty to Prevent Pure Economic Loss' 2002 SLT (News) 225.

3 Cf *Smith v Eric S Bush; Harris v Wyre Forest District Council* [1990] 1 AC 831, [1989] 2 All ER 514, HL, discussed above.

4 It is enough that the defender knows that the pursuer will rely on his expertise; there is no need to show that the defender intended the pursuer to do so. See *Royal Bank of Scotland v Bannerman Johnstone Maclay* 2003 SC 125.

5 [1995] 2 AC 296, [1994] 3 All ER 129, HL.

6 See also *Donlon v Colonial Mutual Group (UK Holdings) Ltd* 1998 SC 244, 1997 SCLR 1088 (failure by employer to exercise reasonable care in ensuring that facts communicated to third parties were accurate). In *Durkin v DSG Retail Ltd* [2014] UKSC 21, the Supreme Court held that where Durkin asserted that his credit agreement with the defender had been rescinded, the defender was under a duty to investigate that assertion in order reasonably to satisfy itself that the credit agreement remained enforceable before reporting in the credit reference agencies that Durkin was in default: ibid per Lord Hodge at para 33.

4.18   The present writer took the view that the concepts of voluntary assumption of responsibility and concomitant reliance could provide the basis for a general duty of care to prevent pure economic loss. As a result of the defender's carelessness, the pursuer is prevented from entering into prospective contracts[1] or induced to enter an uneconomic contract or an existing contract becomes less profitable. We can call this interference with the pursuer's contracts 'relational economic loss'. The defender's liability arises from his assumption of responsibility *and* his knowledge of the pursuer's reliance – which provides the necessary proximity. In addition Scottish courts had also begun to accept the *Henderson v Merrett* criteria as giving rise to a general duty of care to prevent pure economic loss.[2] But at the same time it had to be recognised that there was an air of artificiality in the *Henderson v Merrett* test. In particular it was difficult to accept that a person had in fact voluntarily assumed responsibility when he had clearly intended not to do so by inserting an exemption clause in a contract or issuing a non-contractual disclaimer. To argue that the assumption of responsibility should be assessed 'objectively' involves imposing a duty rather than inferring a duty from the defender's voluntary conduct.

In *Customs and Excise Commissioners v Barclays Bank*[3] after reviewing the authorities, the House of Lords held that the *Henderson v Merrett* test did not provide a 'single touchstone' for the existence of a duty of care to prevent economic loss. While it could be useful when there had in fact been an assumption of responsibility, when this was not the case the court would have to fall back on the *Caparo* tripartite criteria and in particular, the 'fair, just and reasonable' criterion. Lord Hoffmann took the view that where there had in fact been an assumption of responsibility it would be fair, just and reasonable to impose the duty *because of the relationship:* but it could be fair, just and reasonable to impose a duty in the absence of such an assumption. On the latter, Lord Hoffmann observed,[4] 'Questions of fairness and policy will enter into the decision and it maybe more useful to try to identify these questions than simply to bandy terms like "assumption of responsibility" and "fair ,just and reasonable"'. Lord Rodger was equally sceptical:[5]

'Part of the function of appeal courts is to try to assist judges and practitioners by boiling down a mass of case law and distilling some shorter statement of the applicable law. The temptation to try to identify some compact underlying rule which can then be applied to solve all future cases is obvious. [Counsel] submitted that in this area the House had identified such a rule in the need to find that the defendant had voluntarily assumed responsibility. But the unhappy experience with the rule so elegantly formulated by Lord

Wilberforce in *Anns v Merton LBC* … suggests that appellate judges should follow the philosopher's advice to "Seek simplicity, and distrust it".[6]

In the circumstances, the House held that the bank did not owe the Customs and Excise a duty to take reasonable care to ensure that those of their customers who owed VAT did not remove funds from their accounts. The irony is that the key factor why their Lordships concluded that it would not be fair, just or reasonable to do so was that the bank had not voluntarily assumed any responsibility for the economic interests of the Commissioners!

1 As in *Spring v Guardian Assurance plc* [1995] 2 AC 296, [1994] 3 All ER 129, HL.
2 *Bank of Scotland v Fuller Peiser* 2002 SLT 574; *Royal Bank of Scotland v Bannerman Johnstone Maclay* 2003 SC 125. But the *Caparo* tripartite test was still being used: *Weir v National Westminster Bank plc* 1994 SLT 1251 (extending bank's liability to detect and report forged signatures to include the agent of a disclosed principal who under a power of attorney was the sole signatory on the account).
3 [2007] 1 AC 181.
4 Ibid at para 36. His Lordship did concede that the *Henderson v Merrett* test had the merit of emphasising that a duty of care is usually generated by what the defender has decided to *do* and not by mere omissions: ibid at para 38.
5 Ibid at para 51.
6 On Lord Wilberforce's elegant formulation see beyond para 4.24: it is believed that the philosopher is Whitehead.

(3) Liability arising from defective performance of a contract

4.19   A enters a contract with B. In order to fulfil his contract with A, B enters into a contract with C. C's performance of his contract with B is carried out carelessly. As a result, A suffers pure economic loss. The facts can be represented as follows:

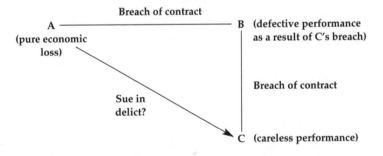

A's obvious remedy is to sue B for breach of contract. But if this is not possible (for example if there is an exemption clause in A's contract with B) or not desirable (for example if B is bankrupt) can A sue C in delict?

If C's careless performance of his contract with B had caused physical harm to A or physical damage to A's property, C would owe A a duty of care provided A's injury or the damage to A's property was reasonably foreseeable: ie the *Donoghue v Stevenson* neighbourhood principle would apply.[1] Since A suffers only pure economic loss, reasonable foreseeability of such loss is not sufficient to give rise to a duty of care. But A, B and C are connected by a series of contracts. If C had broken his contract with B with the intention of harming A, A can sue C in *delict* for intentional infliction of harm by unlawful means and can recover for pure economic loss.[2] In this case, however, C has not broken his contract with B in order to harm A. Instead, C has by his *careless* conduct broken his contract with B with the result that B's performance of his contract with A is defective, causing A economic loss. In these circumstances, does C owe a duty of care to A not to perform his contract with B in a careless manner if it will cause A economic loss to do so?

In *Junior Books Ltd v Veitchi Co Ltd*,[3] the House of Lords held that such a duty of care could exist. The pursuers entered into a contract with Ogilvie (Builders) Ltd (the main contractor) for the construction of a factory. The pursuers' architects nominated Veitchi, a floor specialist, to lay a floor in the factory. In other words, Veitchi was a nominated sub-contractor. However, Veitchi's contract to lay the floor was with the main contractor, not Junior Books. The floor laid was seriously defective and had to be replaced by the pursuers. There was no averment that the floor laid was dangerous so as to be likely to cause physical harm to any persons in the factory or any damage to the pursuers' property. The pursuers sought damages from the defenders for the cost of replacing the floor. This complex factual situation can be illustrated as follows:

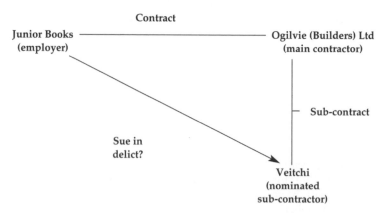

Although nominated by Junior Books' architect, Veitchi had no contractual relationship with Junior Books. Although Junior Books could have sued the main contractor for breach of contract, they chose not to do so. Their only remedy against Veitchi, therefore, lay in delict. Since there was no danger of any physical harm to persons in the factory or damage to the pursuer's property, the case fell outside the neighbourhood principle of reasonable foreseeability of harm laid down in *Donoghue v Stevenson*.[4] In other words, the case was concerned with the recovery of pure economic loss, ie the cost of replacing the defective floor. Nevertheless, the House of Lords held[5] that in the circumstances there was sufficient proximity between the parties for a duty of care to arise: the defenders were under a duty to prevent loss to the pursuers as a result of the defenders' careless performance of their contract with Ogilvie (Builders) Ltd.

Lord Roskill identified eight factors from which the requisite proximity for a duty of care could be inferred:[6]

'(1) The appellants [Veitchi] were nominated sub-contractors. (2) The appellants were specialists in flooring. (3) The appellants knew what products were required by the respondents [Junior Books] and their main contractors and specialised in the production of those products. (4) The appellants alone were responsible for the composition and construction of the flooring. (5) The respondents relied upon the appellants' skill and experience. (6) The appellants as nominated sub-contractors must have known that the respondents relied upon their skill and experience. (7) The relationship between the parties was as close as it could be, short of actual privity of contract. (8) The appellants must be taken to have known that if they did the work negligently (as it must be assumed that they did) the resulting defects would at some time require remedying by the respondents expending money upon the remedial measures as a consequence of which the respondents would suffer financial or economic loss.'

1 *Donoghue v Stevenson* 1932 SC (HL) 31, 1932 SLT 317.
2 On the delict, see paras 2.4–2.5 above.
3 1982 SC (HL) 244, 1982 SLT 492.
4 Lord Keith of Kinkel took the view (1982 SC (HL) 244 at 267) that if such a danger was present, the neighbourhood principle in *Donoghue* was wide enough to cover the cost of averting such a danger. This is doubtful after the decision of the House of Lords in *Murphy v Brentwood District Council* [1991] 1 AC 398, [1990] 2 All ER 908, HL, discussed at para 4.24 below.
5 Lords Fraser of Tullybelton, Russell of Killowen, Keith of Kinkel and Roskill; Lord Brandon dissented.
6 *Junior Books Ltd v Veitchi Co Ltd* 1982 SC (HL) 244 at 277.

4.20 Several points should be noted. First, the defender and the pursuer are connected by a series of contracts which are subsisting at the time of the defenders' careless acts (ie the installation of the defective floor). Second, Veitchi had been nominated by the pursuers' architect. This is important because as a nominated sub-contractor, Veitchi must have known the identity of the employer, Junior Books, who was contracting with the main contractor, Ogilvie (Builders) Ltd. Third, because Veitchi knew that Junior Books required their services, knew that Junior Books relied upon their expertise, and knew that careless performance of their contract would require the floor to be repaired by Junior Books, Veitchi must have *known* that careless performance by them of their contract with Ogilvie (Builders) Ltd would cause *economic* loss to the pursuer.

Thus, for a *Junior Books* duty of care to arise, the pursuer A and defender C must be connected by a series of contracts: A–B–C.[1] In addition to reasonable foreseeability of loss as a result of his careless acts, C must know the identity of the pursuer A, know that A has a contract with B and know that A will suffer economic loss as a result of C's careless performance of his contract with B, since this will, in turn, render defective B's performance of his contract with A. In establishing this degree of knowledge, the fact that C is a nominated sub-contractor is important but not necessary.[2] A's reliance on C's expertise etc is important. It provides *evidence* that C knows that his careless performance will cause A economic loss. The crucial point is that C must know that the careless performance of his contract with B will cause A economic loss as a result of B's consequent defective performance of his contract with A.[3]

It is the present writer's submission that *Junior Books* liability could be seen as an extension of the economic delict of intentional infliction of harm by unlawful means. If in the above example, C broke his contract with B with the result that B renders defective performance of his contract with A, it is long settled that A can sue C in delict for pure economic loss if C broke his contract with B *with the intention* of harming A. *Junior Books* goes a step further by providing that A can sue C in delict where C carelessly performs his contract with B with the result that B renders defective performance of his contract with A, provided C *knew* that his careless performance of his contract with B would cause economic loss to A, ie C owes a duty of care to A not to perform his contract with B in a careless manner.

1 *Comex Houlder Diving Ltd v Colne Fishing Co Ltd (No 2)* 1992 SLT 89, OH; *Scott Lithgow Ltd v GEC Electrical Products Ltd* 1989 SC 412, 1992 SLT 244, OH; *Strathford East Kilbride Ltd v HLM Design Ltd* 1999 SLT 121.
2 In *Scott Lithgow Ltd v GEC Electrical Products Ltd* 1989 SC 412, 1992 SLT 244, OH, the Lord Ordinary (Clyde) thought at 250 ff that it would be enough if the defender had been approved by the pursuer.
3 On the other hand, if A's reliance on C's expertise is held to be necessary and given that C must know that A will suffer economic loss by C's careless

performance of the contract, it could be argued that *Junior Books* liability is simply an example of the general *Henderson v Merrett* duty of care to prevent relational economic loss.

4.21 Read this way, the duty of care held to exist in *Junior Books* is kept within the narrowest of limits. First, it only applies where the parties are connected by contracts which are existing at the time of the defender's careless acts. In *D & F Estates Ltd v Church Commissioners for England*,[1] for example, the Church Commissioners owned a block of flats built by the main contractors. The main contractors sub-contracted the plaster work to sub-contractors. The plaster was defective but was not a source of danger. *After* the flats were built, a flat was leased to the plaintiffs. The plaintiffs sued *inter alios* the main contractors in delict for the cost of repairing the plaster work. The House of Lords held that the main contractors and the sub-contractors were not under a duty of care to prevent economic loss to the plaintiffs as a result of the defective plaster.[2] In the present writer's view, there was also no possibility of a *Junior Books* duty of care in this case because there was no contractual nexus between the plaintiffs and the main contractor or sub-contractor at the time of the careless act, as illustrated below.

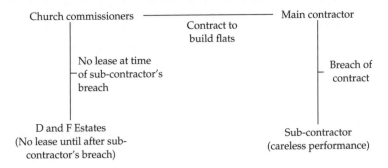

Second, even if there is an existing contractual nexus, no *Junior Books* duty of care will arise unless the defender knows the identity of the pursuer; this will therefore prevent such a duty of care arising in most cases involving mass production. For example, if A manufactures components for B who uses them to produce products which he sells to C, a distributor, who sells them to X, Y and Z etc, A does not owe a *Junior Books* duty of care to X, Y or Z to prevent *economic loss*[3] due to A's careless performance of his contract with B in supplying B with defective components. This is because A will generally not know of the contracts between C and X, Y and Z:

No *Junior Books* liability if A
does not know of C's contracts
with X, Y and Z.

Third, even if there is an existing contractual nexus and the
defender knows the identity of the pursuer, the terms of the
contracts between the parties, for example exemption or
indemnity clauses, may indicate that the parties intended to
exclude potential liability in delict.[4] In those circumstances, the
court is unlikely to find the existence of a *Junior Books* duty of care.
Finally, the defender must anticipate loss to the particular pursuer
as a result of the defender's defective performance.[5]

The limitations which are inherent in the *Junior Books* duty of care
are therefore sufficient to keep potential liability for pure economic
loss within relatively narrow parameters. Once again we see the
duty of care operating as a threshold device.

1   [1989] AC 177, [1988] 2 All ER 992, HL. See also *Strathford East Kilbride Ltd v HLM Design Ltd* 1999 SLT 121.
2   For discussion of the absence of a duty of care to prevent economic loss arising from a defective building, see paras 4.24 ff below.
3   Of course, A may owe a *Donoghue v Stevenson* duty of care to X, Y and Z to prevent them suffering physical injury or damage to their property as a result of A's careless manufacture of the components.
4   Cf *British Telecommunications plc v James Thomson & Sons (Engineering) Ltd* 1999 SC (HL) 9 when the contractual relationships between the parties were taken into account to determine whether or not there was a duty of care on the defender to prevent the pursuer sustaining damage to his property.
5   *Simaan General Contracting Co v Pilkington Glass Ltd (No 2)* [1988] QB 758, [1988] 1 All ER 791, CA.

4.22   If it is accepted that the *Junior Books* duty of care is simply
an extension of the wrong of intentional infliction of harm
by unlawful means so as to trigger liability as a result of the
defender's careless conduct as well as conduct intended to harm
the pursuer, then it is thought that there is a future for *Junior
Books* liability. Nevertheless, *Junior Books Ltd v Veitchi Co Ltd*[1] has
been consistently distinguished in cases south of the border. In *D
& F Estates Ltd v Church Commissioners for England*,[2] Lord Bridge
opined[3] of *Junior Books*:

'The consensus of judicial opinion, with which I concur, seems to be that
the decision of the majority is so far dependent on the unique, albeit non-
contractual, relationship between the pursuer and the defender in that

case and the unique scope of the duty of care owed by the defender to the pursuer arising from that relationship that the decision cannot be regarded as laying down any principle of general application in the law of tort or delict.'

The reason for this scepticism is that *Junior Books* has *not* been regarded as a case which is only concerned with defective performance of the pursuer's existing contracts (ie recovery of relational economic loss). Instead, it has been read as laying down potential liability for economic loss arising from the careless manufacture of a defective product which is not dangerous in the sense of causing physical harm to the pursuer or damage to her property (ie non-relational economic loss). If this were the case, then there would, indeed, be cause for concern. But if analysed as above, *Junior Books* liability does not have this potential. Within its relatively narrow sphere, *Junior Books* is both an important and principled decision. That said, in *Realstone v J & E Shepherd* the Lord Ordinary (Hodge) took the view that 'The risk of introducing uncertainty into complex commercial transactions justifies the retreat from *Junior Books*. That retreat having occurred, I consider that *Junior Books* does not provide a basis for the existence of an established duty of care.'[4]

1 1982 SC (HL) 244, 1982 SLT 492.
2 [1989] AC 177, [1988] 2 All ER 992, HL.
3 [1988] 2 All ER 992 at 1003.
4 [2008] CSOH 31 at para 22. *Junior Books* has however been approved by the Court of Appeal in Singapore! See *RSP Architects Planners and Engineers v Ocean Front Pte Ltd* (1998) 14 Const LJ 139, CA (Sing).

(4) Liability arising from defective products and buildings

4.23 A owes a duty of care to B when it is reasonably foreseeable that B will sustain physical harm or physical damage to his property as a result of A's careless conduct. In *Donoghue v Stevenson*[1] it was held that the manufacturer of a product owed a duty of care to the ultimate consumer to prevent the consumer suffering personal harm or physical damage to his property as a result of a defect in the product caused by the manufacturer's carelessness. The consumer is entitled to damages not only for pain and suffering but also for economic loss which *derives* from his personal injuries or the damage to his property, ie derivative economic loss.

There is an important limitation on the scope of *Donoghue v Stevenson* liability. The duty of care extends only to the pursuer's physical injuries or damage to his property which was caused by the defective product. The damage must be done to property other than the defective product itself. For example, if a defective vacuum cleaner explodes and burns the pursuer or burns the pursuer's carpet there is *Donoghue v Stevenson* liability. But if the defective vacuum simply does not work or it explodes and does not physically harm the pursuer or does not damage any other property of the pursuer there is no *Donoghue v Stevenson* liability. Why? In these circumstances, the pursuer has sustained only *pure* economic loss, ie the cost of repairing the vacuum cleaner or the difference in value between a defective and a non-defective cleaner. The courts have consistently refused to allow the pursuer to recover compensation in *delict* for such losses. Instead, the pursuer must resort to the law of contract to obtain compensation:

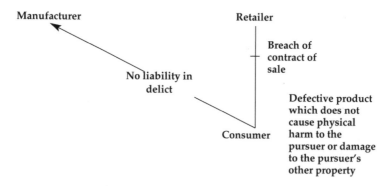

The consumer cannot sue the manufacturer in delict because the consumer has suffered only pure economic loss. The consumer must sue the retailer for *breach of contract* to recover any loss suffered as a result of the product being defective. If the ultimate consumer does not have a contract with the retailer, for example where the defective product was a gift from a third party, the consumer prima facie has no remedy. But the third party could assign the rights under *his* contract with the retailer to the consumer thus enabling the consumer to recover damages for breach of contract.

It should also be noticed that there will generally be no possibility of *Junior Books* liability in this situation. This is for two reasons: (1) no contractual chain or nexus exists between the manufacturer and the consumer at the time of the careless act since the consumer will only enter into a contract with the retailer *after* the product has been manufactured; and (2) the manufacturer will not know the identity of the consumer.[2] Similarly, there is no *Henderson v Merrett* duty of care[3] to prevent relational economic loss because the defender manufacturer does not voluntarily assume responsibility for the ultimate consumer's financial interests and there is no concomitant reliance on the consumer's part.

This principle of non-liability for economic loss also applies to the provision of services. In *D & F Estates Ltd v Church Commissioners for England*[4] the plaintiffs incurred expense in repairing defective plasterwork. The defective plasterwork was not a danger to the plaintiffs' person or property. The House of Lords held that the plaintiffs could not sue the defendants who were responsible for the defective plasterwork in *delict* because they had only suffered pure economic loss, ie the cost of repair. The plaintiffs' only remedy would be in contract.

1 1932 SC (HL) 31, 1932 SLT 317.
2 It might, of course, be different in both respects if the manufacturer were supplying a product specifically designed for the consumer.
3 *Henderson v Merrett Syndicates Ltd* [1995] 2 AC 145, [1994] 3 All ER 506, HL.
4 [1989] AC 177, [1988] 2 All ER 992, HL. There was no *Junior Books* liability in this case. See also *Strathford East Kilbride Ltd v HLM Design Ltd* 1999 SLT 121.

4.24   At one time there appeared to be an exception in respect of defective buildings. Local authorities are under a duty to ensure that buildings conform to building regulations and bye-laws: this is done by a local authority engineer approving the plans and the design of the proposed building. In *Anns v Merton London Borough Council*[1] the defendants approved the design of the foundations of a building. After it was built, the foundations were discovered to be defective. The House of Lords held that the local authority owed the owner[2] of the house a duty of care in this situation and that damages could include the cost of repair. It was also decided that the builder owed a similar duty of care to the owner of the property. The fact that the plaintiff had only suffered pure economic loss appeared to be irrelevant. The concept of the duty of care was clearly being used as a threshold device significantly to extend the parameters of delictual liability for pure economic loss. In a famous passage, Lord Wilberforce explained:[3]

'The position has now been reached that in order to establish that a duty of care arises in a particular situation, it is not necessary to bring the facts of that situation within those of previous situations in which a duty of care has been held to exist. Rather the question has to be approached in two stages. First one has to ask whether, as between the alleged wrongdoer and the person who has suffered damage there is a sufficient relationship of proximity or neighbourhood such that, in the reasonable contemplation of the former, carelessness on his part may be likely to cause damage to the latter, in which case a prima facie duty of care arises. Secondly, if the first question is answered affirmatively, it is necessary to consider whether there are any considerations which ought to negative, or to reduce or limit the scope of the duty or the class of person to whom it is owed or the damages to which a breach of it may give rise.'

Applying these principles, Lord Wilberforce held that a local authority owed a duty of care to the owner of a building which was subject to latent defects in construction when the plans had been inspected and approved by the local authority. The fact that the owner may suffer only pure economic loss was not sufficient to deny the existence of the duty on policy grounds since the class of potential plaintiffs was restricted to the owners or lessees of the property.

This was to prove to be the high-water mark of the extension of the parameters of delictual liability for defective buildings. The courts thereafter refused to use Lord Wilberforce's two-stage test further to extend the scope of liability. At length, *Anns* itself came to be doubted and was ultimately overruled in *Murphy v Brentwood District Council*.[4] In this case, a builder laid foundations of a house in accordance with designs approved by the local authority. The foundations proved to be defective. The owner could not afford the £45,000 required for repairs; instead he sold the house for £35,000 less than its market value would have been if the foundations had been sound. The owner sued the local authority for the loss of the value of the house. The House of Lords held that *Anns* was wrongly decided. Neither a local authority nor a builder owes the owner of a house a duty of care in respect of pure economic loss arising from the defective construction of the property; and pure economic loss includes the cost of repairs or the loss of the property's value.

1 [1978] AC 728, [1977] 2 All ER 492, HL.
2 Technically, the plaintiff in this case was a lessee of the property.
3 [1978] AC 728 at 751–752.
4 [1991] 1 AC 398, [1990] 2 All ER 908, HL. The House of Lords doubted the value of Lord Wilberforce's two-stage test for the existence of a duty of care. Instead, a duty should only be imposed by analogy with earlier precedents, ie it is an incremental process. In this respect, *Murphy* has been followed in Scotland. '[I]n determining the existence and scope of a duty of care in a context in which a claim is made for economic loss, the court must have particular regard to the traditional categorisation of situations in which duties may or may not have been recognised in particular circumstances': *Nordic Oil Services Ltd v Berman* 1993 SLT 1164 at 1171 per the Lord Ordinary (Osborne). *Murphy* has not been followed in Australia or New Zealand: see *Bryan v Maloney* (1995) 11 Const LJ 274, HC (Aus); *Invercargill City Council v Hamlin* [1996] AC 624, [1996] 1 All ER 756, PC.

4.25   The House of Lords was also sceptical of what is known as the 'complex structure' doctrine. It can be argued that the foundations should be regarded as separate from the rest of the house. If they are defective and cause physical damage to another part of the house, for example by cracks in the walls, this is damage to 'other' property and falls within the *Donoghue v Stevenson* duty of care. The view was taken that this approach is unrealistic:[1]

'The reality is that the structural elements in any building form a single indivisible unit of which the different parts are essentially interdependent. To the extent that there is any defect in one part of the structure it must to a greater or lesser degree necessarily affect all other parts of the structure. Therefore any defect in the structure is a defect in the quality of the whole and it is quite artificial, in order to impose a legal liability which the law would not otherwise impose, to treat a defect in an integral structure, so far as it weakens the structure, as a dangerous defect liable to cause damage to "other property".'

But where a distinct item, such as a central heating boiler, is incorporated into the structure of a building there can be *Donoghue v Stevenson* liability if, as a result of a defect, it causes damage to the house. The owner in these circumstances could sue the manufacturer of the boiler for physical damage to his 'other' property, ie his house.

It is important to examine the implications of *Murphy* for purchasers of heritable property. Consider the following example. A, a company, enters into a contract with B to build a block of flats. After the flats are completed, A sells the flats to various purchasers including C. After a few years, cracks appear in C's flat. It is discovered that the foundations are unsound and that it will cost approximately £20,000 to have them repaired:

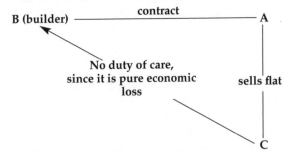

As a result of *Murphy*, C has no delictual remedy against B because C has suffered only pure economic loss; ie B does not owe C a duty of care in respect of the cost of repairs.[2] Although there is a contractual relationship between A and C, this will not help C because a seller of a flat (land) does not warrant the quality of the buildings sold. Moreover, B does not owe C a *Junior Books* duty of care.[3] This is because there is no contractual nexus between B and C at the time of the careless act since C only purchases the property *after* it is built. Even if C had an option from A to purchase a flat while it was being built, a *Junior Books* duty of care will not arise unless B knows the identity of the purchaser, C. Similarly, there is no *Henderson v Merrett* duty of care to prevent relational economic loss because there is no voluntary assumption of responsibility and concomitant reliance.

Because of the absence of a delictual claim against B or a contractual claim against A, in order to protect his interests C should obtain an independent survey *before* purchasing the property. If, as a result of the surveyor's carelessness, the defects are not discovered, C can sue the surveyor for breach of contract. And, as we have seen,[4] even if C relied upon a survey carried out on behalf of C's bank for the purpose of obtaining a loan, C may be able to sue the surveyor in delict on the ground of careless misrepresentation where damages for pure economic loss are recoverable.

1 *Murphy v Brentwood District Council* [1990] 2 All ER 908 at 928 per Lord Bridge.
2 If C was physically injured or any property of C's other than the house was damaged, C can sue B in delict as B owes C a duty of care under the *Donoghue v Stevenson* neighbourhood principle.
3 *Strathford East Kilbride Ltd v HLM Design Ltd* 1999 SLT 121.
4 See para 4.14 above.

(5) Non-liability for secondary economic loss

4.26   We have been considering the situation where the defender has directly caused pure economic loss to the pursuer. However, there is a second situation where pure economic loss can arise. This is where the defender has caused physical harm to A or A's property and as a result B suffers pure economic loss. This will most often arise where B has a contract with A and as a consequence of the defender's wrongful conduct A can no longer perform the contract or the contract becomes less profitable. This is known as secondary economic loss.

In *Reavis v Clan Line Steamers Ltd,*[1] Mrs Reavis and her orchestra were involved in a collision at sea which was caused *inter alia* by the fault of the defender, the owner of the ship in which they were sailing. Some members of the orchestra drowned while others were injured and the orchestra had to be disbanded. Mrs Reavis claimed that the services of the players had been secured by contracts of employment and she sought damages from the defender for the loss of profits she had sustained as a result of having to disband the orchestra. The court held that she was not entitled to recover. An employer is not entitled to sue in delict in respect of secondary economic loss sustained as a result of the death or personal injury of an employee caused by the negligence of a third party. In other words, the defender did not owe Mrs Reavis a duty of care to prevent her sustaining pure economic loss as a result of her employees being no longer able to perform their contracts of employment with her. If Mrs Reavis had been physically harmed, she could, of course, recover for derivative economic loss arising from her *own* injuries – but she could not sue in respect of the death or injury of her employees. (The injured employees and the families of the deceased employees, would, of course, have separate claims in delict against the defender.)

Accordingly, where a person is physically harmed or property is damaged, prima facie it is only the injured person or the owner of the property who has title to sue. Third parties who suffer economic loss as a result of the personal injuries or damage to the property are not entitled to sue for secondary economic loss because the defender does not owe them a duty of care. For example, in *Dynamco Ltd v Holland and Hannen and Cubitts (Scotland) Ltd*[2] the defender's excavator damaged an underground electric supply cable owned by the South of Scotland Electricity Board. As a result, there was a power cut at the pursuer's factory which lasted for 15½ hours. The pursuer sued for the loss of profits while the factory was closed. The court held that although the defender owed a duty of care to the electricity board not to damage its property, ie the cable, the defender did not owe a duty to the pursuer in respect of secondary economic loss, even though such loss was reasonably foreseeable. In *Coleridge v Miller Construction Ltd*,[3] the power cut physically damaged the glass that the pursuer manufactured in his factory. The Lord Ordinary (MacLean) held that the test for the existence of a duty of care should be the same whether or not the pursuer suffered physical damage to his property or pure economic loss. In the absence of averments that the defender knew that the pursuer required a continuous supply of electricity, it was not reasonably foreseeable that the pursuer would suffer damage to his products if an electric cable were cut. Moreover, even if damage had been reasonably foreseeable it was not fair, just and reasonable to impose a duty of care in these circumstances because the pursuer should have insurance to cover any losses arising from power cuts howsoever caused. Thus secondary physical damage is irrecoverable, as well as secondary economic loss.[4]

1 1925 SC 725, 1925 SLT 386, OH.
2 1971 SC 257, 1972 SLT 38.
3 1997 SLT 485, OH.
4 In *Skerries Salmon Ltd v The Braer Corpn* 1999 SLT 1196, the Lord Ordinary (Gill) held that the defender did not owe the pursuers a duty of care to prevent them from

having to sell their salmon at low prices. The pursuers alleged that this was caused by a loss of public confidence in the quality of Shetland salmon after the *Braer* oil tanker had run aground. In the absence of any evidence that the pursuers' fish had been contaminated with oil, this was a case of secondary economic loss and no duty was owed. In *Landcatch Ltd v The Braer Corpn; Landcatch Ltd v International Oil Pollution Compensation Fund* 1999 SLT 1208 the pursuers were unable to supply fish farmers in Shetland with salmon smolt because salmon farming had been banned in designated areas contaminated by oil from the *Braer*. There were no contracts subsisting between the fish farmers and the pursuers at the time. This was held to be secondary economic loss and no duty of care arose.

4.27   In the important case of *Nacap Ltd v Moffat Plant Ltd*,[1] the pursuers entered into a contract with British Gas to lay a pipeline owned by British Gas in the North Sea. During the work, the defenders damaged the pipeline. As a result, Nacap were unable to complete the work in the time agreed in their contract with British Gas and consequently suffered economic loss. The Inner House held that the pursuers had no title to sue because they were not the owners of the pipeline. In other words, they could not sue in delict for the secondary economic loss they had sustained as a result of the damage to property owned by a third party, ie British Gas.

This approach has been followed in England. In *Candlewood Navigation Corpn Ltd v Mitsui OSK Lines Ltd, The Mineral Transporter*[2] the plaintiffs time-chartered a vessel from the owners of the ship. The vessel was damaged by the defendants. The Privy Council held that the plaintiffs could not recover damages for the hire charges they had to continue to pay and the loss of profits they had incurred while the ship underwent repairs. The defendants did not owe a duty of care to the plaintiffs in respect of the secondary economic loss they had suffered as a result of their contract with the owners becoming less profitable:

Owner of ship ◄───────────── Defendants damage ship

Charterparty

Plaintiffs – contract becomes less profitable

In this and the previous cases, a *Junior Books* duty of care does not arise because there is no contractual nexus between the parties. Even if in *Dynamco Ltd v Holland and Hannen and Cubitts (Scotland) Ltd*,[3] the defender had been engaged on a contract with the electricity board, who had, of course, a contract with its customer,

Dynamco, *Junior Books* liability would still not have arisen because the defender would not have known the identity of the pursuer. Similarly, no *Henderson v Merrett* duty of care arises because in none of these cases did the defender voluntarily assume responsibility for the financial interests of the pursuers.

1 1987 SLT 221, reversing 1986 SLT 326.
2 [1986] AC 1, [1985] 2 All ER 935, PC.
3 1971 SC 257, 1972 SLT 38.

4.28 Nevertheless, in other circumstances it is thought that there could be sufficient proximity between the parties for a *Junior Books* or *Henderson v Merrett* duty to arise. In *Leigh and Sillavan Ltd v Aliakmon Shipping Co Ltd, The Aliakmon*,[1] the plaintiff (the buyers) entered into a cost and freight (c & f) contract for the purchase of steel coils. Under a c & f contract the seller arranges for the shipping of the goods and obtains a bill of lading from the shipper. The bill of lading is the contract of carriage of the goods. The buyer becomes the owner of the goods when the bill of lading is indorsed by the seller and delivered to the buyer against payment by the buyer of the price. On indorsement, the buyer 'steps into the shoes' of the seller in relation to the bill of lading issued by the shipper. Accordingly, if the goods are damaged in transit, the buyer can sue the shipper for breach of contract. This did not happen in this case because the c & f contract was varied by the parties with the effect that the seller remained owner even though the risk of damage to the goods passed to the buyers. The bill of lading was not indorsed, so that the buyers did not have title to sue the shippers for breach of contract. When they eventually became the owners of the goods, the plaintiff attempted to sue the shippers in delict. The complex facts can be shown thus:

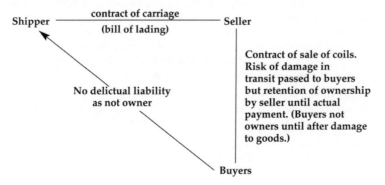

Because the buyers assumed the risk under the contract of sale, they had no right to sue the seller for breach of contract when the goods were damaged. As a result of the variation, the buyers could not use the usual remedy in a c & f situation of suing the shipper for breach of contract. The House of Lords held that the buyers could not sue the shipper in delict because they were not the owners of the goods at the time the goods were damaged. *Junior Books Ltd v Veitchi & Co Ltd*[2] was distinguished on the ground that the pursuer in that case was the owner of the floor when it was carelessly laid.[3]

In the *Aliakmon* case,[4] an attempt was made to circumvent the principle of non-recovery in delict for secondary economic loss by invoking the doctrine of 'transferred loss'. In the Court of Appeal, Goff LJ as he then was formulated the doctrine thus:[5]

'Where A owes a duty of care in tort [delict] not to cause physical damage to B's property, and commits a breach of that duty in circumstances in which the loss of or physical damage to property will ordinarily fall on B but (as is reasonably foreseeable by A) such loss or damage, by reason of a contractual relationship falls on C, then C will be entitled, subject to the terms of any contract restricting A's liability to B, to bring an action in tort against A in respect of such loss or damage to the extent that it falls on him, C.'

This would have enabled the plaintiff to succeed in *Aliakmon* provided such loss was reasonably foreseeable by the defendant; it is submitted that it would have been reasonably foreseeable as in a normal c & f contract the buyer would have had an action to sue on the bill of lading if the goods were damaged in transit. Similarly, in *Nacap Ltd v Moffat Plant Ltd*[6] the pursuer could have relied on this doctrine, although it might have been more difficult to establish that the loss suffered as a result of the contract with British Gas was reasonably foreseeable.[7] However, the introduction of the principle of transferred loss into English law was vigorously rejected when the *Aliakmon* case was appealed to the House of Lords.[8] It is thought that, after *Nacap*, the principle would not fare any better north of the border.

1 [1986] AC 785, [1986] 2 All ER 145, HL, affirming [1985] 2 All ER 44, CA. The contractual position has now been overtaken by the Carriage of Goods by Sea Act 1992 which makes it easier for the buyer who undertakes the risk to sue the shipper for breach of contract.
2 1982 SC (HL) 244, 1982 SLT 492.
3 For similar reasons, it would be unlikely that the shipper had voluntarily assumed responsibility for the financial interests of the buyers. But if in *Reavis v Clan Line Steamers Ltd* 1925 SC 725, 1925 SLT 386, OH, Mrs Reavis had been killed or injured with the result that her employees suffered economic loss, it is

submitted that there would now be a possibility of their recovering damages for economic loss under *Junior Books* if the defender, who had a contract of carriage with Mrs Reavis, had known the identity of her employees and the existence of the contracts of employment.

4 See *Leigh and Sillavan Ltd v Aliakmon Shipping Co Ltd, The Aliakmon* [1986] AC 785, [1986] 2 All ER 145, HL, affirming [1985] 2 All ER 44, CA.
5 [1985] 2 All ER 44 at 77.
6 1987 SLT 221, discussed at para 4.27 above.
7 Goff LJ expressly stated ([1985] 2 All ER 44 at 77) that the doctrine would not have helped the plaintiff in *Candlewood Navigation Corpn Ltd v Mitsui OSK Lines Ltd, The Mineral Transporter* [1986] AC 1, [1985] 2 All ER 935, PC; the present writer would have thought that loss to a time-charterer from a collision would be reasonably foreseeable by a shipowner: see para 4.27 above.
8 [1986] 2 All ER 145 at 157 per Lord Brandon.

4.29 It therefore appears that the courts have set their face against recovery in delict for secondary economic loss by restricting title to sue to the person who has been physically harmed or the owner of the damaged property. But where a person has a possessory title to the property, he may be able to sue. For example, if A pledges his watch worth £500 to B in return for a loan of £300, B, the pledgee, has a possessory title to the watch. If the watch is damaged by C, B can sue C in delict to the extent of his interest in the watch, ie up to £300.

Cases of possessory title apart, it is clear from *Nacap* that merely to have lawful possession of the property is not sufficient; the pursuers in that case had lawful possession of the pipeline which they were laying but title to sue in delict was denied. In *North Scottish Helicopters Ltd v United Technologies Corpn Inc (No 2)*,[1] however, the pursuers were allowed to sue in respect of economic loss sustained as a result of damage to a helicopter which they leased but did not own. Under the lease agreement with the owner, a finance company, the second pursuer had to maintain the helicopter, indemnify the finance company if the helicopter was damaged or destroyed and replace or repair the helicopter at the pursuer's expense. It was agreed with the finance company that the helicopter could be flown by the first pursuer, a subsidiary company of the second pursuer. The finance company had no obligation to provide a replacement if the helicopter was not operational. Owing to a fault in the manufacturing process, the helicopter went on fire and was destroyed. The pursuers sought damages for the economic loss sustained in indemnifying the finance company in terms of the lease and loss of profits sustained due to the absence of a helicopter. The complex facts can be shown thus:

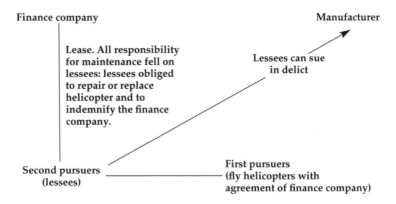

Finance company

Manufacturer

Lease. All responsibility
for maintenance fell on
lessees: lessees obliged
to repair or replace
helicopter and to
indemnify the finance
company.

Lessees can sue
in delict

Second pursuers
(lessees)

First pursuers
(fly helicopters with
agreement of finance company)

The Lord Ordinary (Davidson) held that because of the onerous terms of the lease and the fact that the finance company had agreed that the helicopter could be flown by the first pursuers, the second pursuers were 'owners' of the helicopter as a matter of substance even if, technically, the finance company was the owner as a matter of law. In other words, the pursuers had far more than lawful possession of the helicopter and this gave them title to sue in spite of not being the legal owner of the property. Thus it appears that there can be exceptional circumstances when a non-owner has title to sue.

It was assumed in this case that the manufacturer owed a duty of care to the pursuer. It should be noticed, however, that the destruction of the helicopter was pure economic loss: the defective product did not cause physical harm to the pursuers or damage to any other property owned by the pursuers – it only destroyed itself! The manufacturer's duty of care could therefore not have arisen by virtue of the *Donoghue v Stevenson* neighbourhood principle. Nor could there be a *Junior Books* duty of care[2] owing to the absence of a contractual nexus between the pursuer and defender at the time of the fault in the manufacturing process. The action could therefore have been defended on the ground that the defender did not owe a duty of care to prevent pure economic loss arising to the pursuers and, indeed, the finance company, rather than the absence of the pursuers' title to sue for secondary economic loss.

In the cases we have been discussing, the only remedy available to a person who has sustained secondary economic loss is to obtain an assignation of the owner's rights against the defender. In Scots law, delictual rights as well as contractual rights can be assigned. For example in *Nacap Ltd v Moffat Plant Ltd*,[3] British Gas could have assigned to the pursuer its rights as owner of the pipeline to sue the defender in delict. The difficulty here is that British Gas's loss arising from damage to its pipeline is not the same as the losses incurred by Nacap in being unable to perform their contract on time. But where, as in *Aliakmon*,[4] the owner has a contractual remedy against the defender, the assignation of the contractual rights to the pursuer will provide a just solution provided, of course, the owner is prepared to assign his rights.

1 1988 SLT 778n, OH.
2 *Junior Books Ltd v Veitchi Co Ltd* 1982 SC (HL) 244, 1982 SLT 492.
3 1987 SLT 221.
4 *Leigh and Sillavan Ltd v Aliakmon Shipping Co Ltd, The Aliakmon* [1986] AC 785, [1986] 2 All ER 145, HL.

(6) Conclusion

4.30 The law on delictual liability for pure economic loss has been an area of extensive judicial activity where the concept of the duty of care has been used to mark the boundaries of liability. These have shifted from time to time and the current position remains controversial as well as conceptually difficult and, indeed, uncertain. Why this is so has been summarised admirably by Mummery LJ in *The Rebecca Elaine*:[1]

'The judicial line has not been drawn arbitrarily; it is explicable by rational and pragmatic considerations, some more potent than others, some more often articulated than others: the disproportionate burden of imposing indeterminate liability of the kind envisaged by Judge Cardozo in the *Ultramares* case; the evidential difficulties in establishing causation and delimiting remoteness; the relative cost and practicability of obtaining insurance cover for risks of pure financial loss suffered to an unlimited degree by an amorphous class of claimants; the apprehension of a deluge, in an already overstretched legal system, of litigation by an indefinite number of claimants with multiple claims arising out of a single incident … the dubious and lethal colonisation by the tort [delict] of negligence of the conceptual territory of contract; the perception that financial loss occupies a significantly lower place than physical injury to person and property in the scale of contemporary social and ethical values; and the inevitability (and acceptability) of widespread and uncompensatable financial loss in a free market economy, in which even intentional infliction of substantial financial loss (eg by one trade competitor on another) does not normally attract legal liability.'

1 *The Rebecca Elaine* [1999] 2 Lloyd's Rep 1 at 8.

CHAPTER 5

Breach of a duty of care

A. INTRODUCTION

5.1 We have been considering situations where an action in delict fails at the outset because there is no duty of care owed by the defender to prevent harm as a result of the defender's unintentional, but careless, conduct. This is done by the courts utilising the concept of duty of care as a threshold device, and the decision whether or not to recognise the existence of a duty of care in particular circumstances ultimately involves issues of policy.

Even where it is recognised that the defender owes the pursuer a duty of care, a pursuer is not entitled to succeed unless it can be shown that the harm sustained by the pursuer arose as a result of a *breach* by the defender of the duty of care which he owed to the pursuer. In this chapter we shall examine the criteria which must be satisfied before the defender's conduct will constitute a *breach* of the duty of care which, *ex hypothesi*, the defender owes to the pursuer. Only when these criteria are satisfied, ie when there is a breach by the defender of the duty of care he owes to the pursuer, will the defender be liable to make reparation to the pursuer for harm sustained as a result of the defender's breach of duty.[1]

1 In this chapter, I owe an immense debt to W A Wilson 'The Analysis of Negligence' in *Introductory Essays on Scots Law* (2nd edn, 1984) pp 126–148.

5 2 But even though there has been a breach of the duty of care, it is important to appreciate that the delict is only completed and delictual liability is only incurred when *harm* is sustained by the pursuer.[1] There must be a concurrence of *damnum* (harm sustained) and *injuria* (breach of the duty of care) before delictual liability arises (*damnum injuria datum*).[2] If the pursuer does not suffer harm as a result of the defender's breach of a duty of care which he owes to the pursuer then there is no delictual liability. Harm to the pursuer is a constituent of, as well as a consequence of, negligence.

This point was emphasised by the House of Lords in *Rothwell v Chemical and Insulating Co Ltd*.[3] The claimants had been negligently exposed to asbestos. Fibres had entered their lungs. They had developed pleural plaques. These are fibrous thickening of the pleural membrane which surrounds the lungs. Apart from exceptional cases – which did not arise in these claims – pleural plaques are asymptomatic, ie do not cause any symptoms, do not cause asbestosis, mesothelioma or lung cancer in the future: but the risk of contracting asbestos-related illnesses is significantly higher in persons with plaques than persons who have been exposed to asbestos but have not developed plaques. Because of the increased risk of future asbestos-related illness, persons diagnosed as having plaques become anxious about the possibility of the risk materialising. Because pleural plaques are benign and asymptomatic and do not cause any future asbestos-related disease, their Lordships held that the development of pleural plaques could not be characterised as harm or material damage. Accordingly the claimants had no delictual cause of action and were not entitled to any compensation from the defendants. Two points should be noticed. The claimants could not simply sue for the anxiety caused by the increased risk of contracting asbestos-related illnesses, because in *Gregg v Scott*[4] the House of Lords had held that the *risk* of contracting an illness in the future (and any related anxiety) does not per se constitute reparable harm. Second, the claimants could sue if and when they contracted an asbestos-related illness because the illness would constitute material harm and a delict would then have been committed.

While the reasoning in *Rothwell* is a paradigm of orthodoxy, the decision has been controversial. Before it, Scottish courts were prepared to make awards of provisional damages[5] if pursuers were diagnosed as having pleural plaques: this would provide compensation for their anxiety about their future health while enabling them to claim further compensation, should they develop an asbestos-related disease. Once pleural plaques were held not to constitute material harm, this was no longer possible as no delict had been committed. For this reason the Scottish Parliament decided to reverse *Rothwell* and pass legislation under which pleural plaques are to constitute material harm for the purposes of the law of delict.[6] Pleural plaques apart, the law of delict does not provide compensation for the anxious healthy, ie hypochondriacs.

To summarise, unless the pursuer sustains the harm which the defender was under a duty of care to prevent, there is no liability. We shall refer to this as constituent harm. We shall now consider the criteria which determine whether or not there has been a breach of the duty of care.

1 *Watson v Fram Reinforced Concrete Co (Scotland) Ltd and Winget Ltd* 1960 SC (HL) 92, 1960 SLT 321.
2 Thus, for example, the prescriptive period will only begin to run from the date that the pursuer suffers harm, not the date of the breach of duty: for example, when Mrs Donoghue became ill, not when Stevenson manufactured the ginger beer carelessly.
3 [2008] 1 AC 281.
4 [2005] AC 176.
5 On provisional damages see beyond paras 16.18–16.19.
6 Damages (Asbestos-related Conditions) (Scotland) Act 2009. The validity of the 2009 Act was challenged on the basis that it was outside the legislative competence of the Scottish Parliament. The Supreme Court has held that the 2009 Act is valid: *Axa General Insurance Ltd v Lord Advocate* [2011] UKSC 46.

B. THE CRITERIA USED TO ESTABLISH A BREACH OF A DUTY OF CARE

(1) Voluntary act or omission of the defender

5.3 Before there is a breach by the defender of a duty of care owed to the pursuer, the relevant act or omission must be voluntary on the part of the defender. In *Waugh v James K Allan Ltd*[1] a lorry driver, Gemmell, suffered symptoms consistent with a gastric attack. When he felt he had recovered, he drove the lorry. In fact the symptoms were the onset of thrombosis and he shortly thereafter died at the wheel. The lorry swerved and seriously injured a pedestrian. Although the lorry driver clearly owed the pursuer a duty of care, it was held that there was no breach of duty in this case. On the medical evidence, the driver had no reason to anticipate the onset of the thrombosis and had therefore acted reasonably in driving the lorry after he felt better. Accordingly, the driver's act which injured the pursuer, ie his death, was involuntary and there was therefore no breach of the duty of care. If, however, the driver should have realised that he was seriously ill, then the act of driving while unfit to do so would have been a voluntary act which could have amounted to a breach of duty. But, in the circumstances, Lord Reid observed:[2]

'I am therefore of opinion that the appellant [the pursuer] has failed to prove that Gemmell acted rashly or negligently in driving off so soon after his illness, and no other fault can be imputed to him. One must have great sympathy with the appellant who has suffered so severely through no fault of his own, but I find it impossible to blame Gemmell. Accordingly, I would dismiss this appeal.'

1 1964 SC (HL) 102, 1964 SLT 269. The pursuer was suing the driver's employer
   as vicariously liable for the employee's wrong: on vicarious liability, see paras
   12.5 ff below.
2 1964 SC (HL) 102 at 106.

(2) The defender's act or omission must have as its reasonable and probable consequence constituent harm to the pursuer

5.4   Before there is a breach of a duty of care, constituent harm
to the pursuer must be a reasonable and probable consequence of
the acts or omissions of the defender. The leading case is *Muir v
Glasgow Corpn.*[1] Members of the Milton Free Church were having
a Sunday school picnic in King's Park, Glasgow. Although it was a
June afternoon, it began to rain. Mrs Alexander, the manageress of
a tea room/sweet shop in the park, gave permission to the party to
have their tea in the tea room. Access to the tea room was through
a narrow passage where the sweet shop was situated. Some of the
children were queuing in the passage to purchase sweets from the
shop. When two members of the party carried a tea-urn full of
boiling water through the passage in order to gain entry to the tea
room, the tea-urn dropped, scalding several children. It was never
established how the urn was upset. We can illustrate the case as
follows:

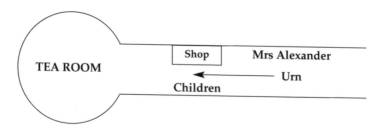

Clearly the persons carrying the urn owed a duty of care to the
scalded children but no action in delict was brought against
them either because of difficulty in establishing the cause of the
accident or, more likely, because they had no assets or insurance.
Instead, an action was brought against the Glasgow Corporation
on the basis that, as Mrs Alexander's employer, the corporation
was vicariously liable for any delicts she committed in the course
of her employment.[2] It was accepted that as manageress of the
tea room Mrs Alexander owed a duty of care to any persons she
allowed to enter the premises. But, in order to succeed, the pursuer

had to show that by allowing the urn to be carried through the passage crowded with children, Mrs Alexander was in breach of the duty of care she undoubtedly owed to them. The House of Lords took the view that Mrs Alexander could only be liable for those consequences of her actions which a reasonable person in her position would have had in contemplation in the circumstances of the case. Lord Thankerton said:[3] '... it has long been held in Scotland that all that a person can be held bound to foresee are the reasonable and probable consequences of the failure to take care, judged by the standard of the ordinary reasonable man [sic]'. Lord Wright considered[4] that:

'It is not, of course, a question of what she [Mrs Alexander] actually thought at the moment, but what the hypothetical reasonable person could have foreseen. That is the standard to determine the scope of her duty. This involves the question: Was the operation of carrying the tea-urn something which a reasonable person in Mrs Alexander's position should have realised would render the place in which it was performed dangerous to the children in the circumstances? This is the crucial issue of fact and the acid test of liability.'

The House of Lords held that the answer to this question was no. Mrs Alexander was entitled to assume that the tea-urn would be carried by responsible persons and that if carried with reasonable care would cause no harm to the children. A reasonable person in her position would not therefore have foreseen as a possibility, let alone a probability, that the urn would slip and the children would be scalded. Thus, because injury to the children could not have been foreseen as a *reasonable* and *probable* consequence of allowing the urn to be carried through the passage, Mrs Alexander had not broken the duty of care she owed the children.[5]

1 1943 SC (HL) 3, 1944 SLT 60.
2 On vicarious liability, see paras 12.5 ff below.
3 1943 SC (HL) 3 at 8.
4 1943 SC (HL) 3 at 15.
5 Lord Wright thought it would have been different if, for example, Mrs Alexander had allowed lions or tigers to be taken through the passage: 1943 SC (HL) 3 at 16.

5.5 *Muir v Glasgow Corpn* is therefore authority that before a breach of a duty of care can arise the defender's conduct must have as their *reasonable* and *probable* consequence injury to the pursuer or damage to the pursuer's property. The test is the reasonable foresight of the hypothetical reasonable person in the position of the defender as opposed to what the particular defender actually foresaw. But since the hypothetical reasonable person is in effect the court, it will be obvious that the scope of the duty of care in a particular case is, to some extent at least, determined by the judges.[1]

Thus, for example, in *Malcolm v Dickson*[2] a painter who was working on a house set the house on fire. A guest who was staying there attempted to save some of the property. As a result of his exertions, the guest collapsed and died. The court held that the painter had not broken the duty of care he owed to the deceased because it could not have been anticipated by a reasonable person in the defender's position that an occupant of the house would die as a result of trying to salvage furniture. As Lord Patrick said:[3]

'It would not occur to the ordinary reasonable man that a reasonable and probable consequence of his being careless in burning paint from a window frame would be that some intervener would suffer a substantial injury through over-exertion, strain and excitement in carrying furniture from the house.'

It is important to note in this case that the deceased died from a heart attack. If he had died as a result of the fire, for example suffocated by smoke, it is submitted that there would have been a breach of the duty of care because it is foreseeable as a reasonable and probable consequence of carelessly setting a house on fire that an occupant might die from the smoke.

Since policy considerations are inevitably involved in determining what the hypothetical reasonable person can be deemed to have foreseen, it should occasion little surprise that, as a general rule, the courts take the view that when a person causes an accident, it is a reasonable and probable consequence of his carelessness that a rescuer may appear on the scene and be injured.[4]

1 In *Mullin v Richards* [1998] 1 All ER 920, CA, the Court of Appeal held that a reasonable 15-year-old schoolgirl could not foresee as a probable consequence of play fighting with plastic rulers that her friend (the plaintiff) could lose her eye as a result of the plastic snapping. See too *McDougall v Strathclyde RC* 1996 SLT 1124 (PE instructor not in breach of his duty to assist a pupil when pupil chose to perform an exercise not previously performed without supervision during teacher's absence to assist another pupil: not reasonably foreseeable as a probable consequence of instructor's absence that pupil would try out the difficult exercise); *Kemp v Secretary of State for Scotland* 2000 SLT 471 (in determining whether a kerb they were obliged to maintain was a hazard to pedestrians, a local authority was not entitled to assume that all pedestrians using the footpath would behave with reasonable care at all times. While they were not bound to foresee every extremity of folly, it was foreseeable, at least in Scotland, that some pedestrians would use the road while under the influence of drink. In these circumstances it was reasonably foreseeable as a probable consequence of failing to light the raised kerb that a pedestrian who had had a drink might fall over it: pursuer held one-third contributorily negligent);

McGinnes v Endeva Service Ltd 2006 SLT 638 where the Lord Ordinary (Emslie) held that the pursuer had failed to establish that it was reasonably foreseeable as a probable result of his employer's failure to operate a double manning system that the pursuer, a field service engineer, would be criminally assaulted by a third party at the place where he was working; *French v Strathclyde Fire Board* [2013] CSOH 3 (reasonably foreseeable by a watch commander that firefighters under his control might suffer personal injuries if a gable collapsed while they were fighting the fire).
2 1951 SC 542, 1951 SLT 357.
3 1951 SC 542 at 556.
4 See, for example, *Steel v Glasgow Iron and Steel Co Ltd* 1944 SC 237, 1945 SLT 70; *Videan v British Transport Commission* [1963] 2 QB 650, [1963] 3 WLR 374, CA.

5.6 In determining whether or not the injury was a reasonable and probable consequence of a careless act or omission, the scientific knowledge available to the hypothetical reasonable person at that time can be crucial. In *Roe v Minister of Health*[1] a patient was given a spinal anaesthetic. As was ordinary practice at the time, the phials containing the anaesthetic were kept in a solution of phenol. Unknown to the hospital, the phials developed invisible cracks and the anaesthetic became impregnated with phenol. As a result of the phenol in the anaesthetic, the patient was paralysed. The court held that the defendant had not broken the duty of care owed to the plaintiff: given the state of scientific knowledge at the time, a reasonable medical practitioner could not have foreseen that paralysis of a patient was a reasonable and probable consequence of storing the phials in phenol.
1 [1954] 2 QB 66, [1954] 2 All ER 131, CA.

5.7 Before there is a breach of the duty of care, the act or omission must have as its reasonable and probable consequence injury to the *pursuer*. In *Bourhill v Young*,[1] for example, even if Young had owed Mrs Bourhill a duty of care, he did not breach that duty in respect of her because a reasonable motor cyclist could not have foreseen as a reasonable and probable consequence of his careless driving that a pedestrian who was 50 feet or so away from the collision, ie outwith the area of potential physical danger, would be harmed. Mrs Bourhill was, of course, a secondary victim. In *Page v Smith*,[2] the House of Lords held that the defender was in breach of his duty of care to a primary victim even though a psychiatric disorder was not reasonably foreseeable as a probable consequence of the defendant's careless driving. This can only be justified on the basis that *physical* harm was reasonably foreseeable, since otherwise the plaintiff would not have been a primary victim. However, when the pursuer is a secondary victim, a psychiatric disorder will only be treated as a reasonably foreseeable, probable consequence of the defender's carelessness if a person of ordinary phlegm would have suffered psychiatric harm in the circumstances.

1 1942 SC (HL) 78, 1943 SLT 105: for full discussion see paras 4.2 ff above.
2 [1996] AC 155, [1995] 2 All ER 736, HL.

5.8 It is not necessary reasonably to foresee the *extent* of the pursuer's injuries; it is enough that the injuries actually sustained by the pursuer are of a *kind* which would be foreseeable as a reasonable and probable consequence of the defender's careless conduct. Nor does every aspect of the accident have to be reasonably foreseeable. These points were settled by the House of Lords in the important decision, *Hughes v Lord Advocate*.[1] In order to work on underground cables, Post Office workers uncovered a manhole. They erected a canvas shelter over the manhole. At 5 pm, when it was dusk, they left the manhole unattended; they also left outside the shelter a ladder, a rope, and paraffin warning lamps. Two boys[2] saw the shelter and decided to explore. They carried the ladder, the rope and a paraffin lamp inside the tarpaulin. One boy tripped over the lamp which fell into the manhole. The paraffin spilled from the lamp, was vaporised by the heat and there was an explosion. There was a rush of flame and one of the lads fell into the manhole and suffered severe burns. It was agreed by expert witnesses that in the circumstances[3] an explosion was not reasonably foreseeable. But it was accepted that the workmen were careless in leaving the manhole unattended.

The House of Lords held that it was foreseeable as a reasonable and probable consequence of leaving the manhole unattended that a child might enter the tent with a lamp, that the paraffin might spill and the child suffer a burn, ie that a boy might be burned by the lamp. This was sufficient to establish a breach of the duty of care which the workmen undoubtedly owed to prevent physical harm to pedestrians by leaving the manhole unattended. The fact that there had been an unforeseeable explosion and that the child's burns were therefore much worse than could have been reasonably anticipated was irrelevant. As Lord Morris of Borth-y-Gest explained:[4]

'The circumstances that an explosion as such could not have been contemplated does not alter the fact that it could reasonably have been foreseen that a boy who played in and about the canvas shelter and played with the things that were thereabouts might get hurt and might in some way burn himself. That is just what happened. The pursuer did burn himself, though his burns were more grave than would have been expected. The fact that the features and developments of an accident may not reasonably have been foreseen does not mean that the accident itself was not foreseeable. The pursuer was, in my view, injured as a result of the type or kind of accident or occurrence that could reasonably have been foreseen.'

Hughes v Lord Advocate is therefore authority that a breach of a duty of care will occur when the pursuer suffers the kind or type of injury which is a reasonable and probable consequence of the defender's careless act or omission;[5] the fact that the injuries sustained are greater than could have been reasonably foreseen and/or that some of the causes of the accident were unforeseeable is irrelevant as long as the type of injury suffered by the pursuer and the fact that an accident could occur as a result of the defender's carelessness are reasonably foreseeable.[6]

1 1963 SC (HL) 31, 1963 SLT 150.
2 The pursuer, aged 8, and his 10-year-old *uncle*!
3 Cf if they had been working on a gas main.
4 *Hughes v Lord Advocate* 1963 SC (HL) 31 at 43–44.
5 One of the difficulties with *Page v Smith* [1996] AC 155, [1995] 2 All ER 736, HL is that foreseeable physical harm is a different type of injury from the unforeseeable psychiatric disorder which in fact occurred.
6 In *Galbraith's Curator ad Litem v Stewart (No 2)* 1998 SLT 1305, the Lord Ordinary (Nimmo Smith) held that it was enough that it was reasonably foreseeable that children would be attracted to pipes left unsecured overnight and that they might suffer personal injuries when playing with them: the precise nature of the accident which had occurred did not have to be reasonably foreseeable. In *Jolley v Sutton London Borough Council* [2000] 3 All ER 409, the House of Lords held that an accident to a child while attempting to repair an abandoned boat left near a block of council flats was reasonably foreseeable. The council had conceded that it was reasonably foreseeable that a child might be injured by falling through rotten planking when playing *on* the boat: but that it was not reasonably foreseeable that a child might be injured by the boat falling on the child who was *underneath* the boat attempting to repair it! Their Lordships held that it was sufficient that it was reasonably foreseeable that children might sustain physical harm by meddling with the boat. See also *Given v James Watt College* 2007 SLT 39 (employer liable to an employee who fell when she was frightened by a malfunctioning drinks dispensing machine even though this was the first time that the machine had emitted a flash).

5.9 Finally, there can be difficulties if a defender has been careless but the harm to the pursuer has been caused as a result of the intervention of a third party. As a general rule, there will be no breach by the defender of his duty of care in these circumstances unless it is foreseeable as a reasonable and probable consequence of the defender's carelessness that a third party would intervene and harm the pursuer. In *Maloco v Littlewoods Organisation Ltd*[1] the defender owned an empty cinema. Vandals broke in and started a fire which damaged neighbouring property. While the defenders owed the pursuers, as neighbouring proprietors, a duty of care not to damage their property, the House of Lords held that there had been no breach of the duty in the circumstances. The defenders did not know that vandals were trespassing on their property and kindling fires there. Accordingly, it was not foreseeable that the defenders' failure to mount a 24-hour guard on the property would have as a reasonable and probable consequence the destruction by fire of neighbouring properties. As Lord Mackay of Clashfern explained:[2]

'While no doubt in this case ... it was probable that children and young persons might attempt to break into the vacated cinema, this by no means establishes that it was a probable consequence of its being vacated with no steps being taken to maintain it lockfast that it would be set on fire with consequent risk of damage to neighbouring properties.'[3]

On the other hand, in *Dorset Yacht Co Ltd v Home Office*[4] borstal boys were working on the Isle of Wight under the custody and control of three borstal officers. The officers went to bed, leaving the boys to their own devices. Seven boys decided to escape. They went on board a yacht moored off the island, which collided and damaged the plaintiff's yacht. The House of Lords held that the borstal officers owed a duty of care to the plaintiff which they had broken in the circumstances. The officers were responsible for the boys and were under a duty to guard them and prevent them absconding. It was foreseeable as a reasonable and probable consequence of leaving the boys alone that they would try to escape. Since the only means of escape was by sea, it was also reasonably foreseeable as a probable consequence that they would steal a yacht and, being inexperienced mariners, collide with another vessel.[5] If there had not been a special relationship between the officers and the third party who caused the damage, ie the boys, there would have been no liability.[6]

As a general rule a landlord is not responsible for the wrongs of his tenant.[7] Thus if tenant A causes harm to a neighbour, tenant B, their landlord is not liable because the landlord does not owe A a duty of care to prevent B causing harm to A. A's remedy is to obtain an interdict against B to prevent his conduct or sue B for damages in delict if the harm has been sustained. It would only be in the exceptional circumstances where the landlord assumed responsibility for A's safety from B, that a duty of care could arise and even then the landlord would only be liable for B's wrong against A if it was a reasonably probable consequence of the breach. But in the absence of such an assumption of responsibility, a landlord is not liable in delict for damage caused by the deliberate acts of third parties.[8]

1 1987 SC (HL) 37, 1987 SCLR 489, 1987 SLT 425: discussed in the context of delictual liability of owners of heritage at para 10.2 below.
2 1987 SLT 425 at 431.
3 Cf *Nolan v Iceland Frozen Foods* (3 December 1997, unreported), CC (Liverpool), where a supermarket was held liable for damage caused by children misusing abandoned trolleys – not an unusual occurrence.
4 [1970] AC 1004, [1970] 2 All ER 294, HL.
5 It is important to note that the duty was owed to the plaintiff only because it was reasonably foreseeable that damage might be caused to his yacht because the only method of effecting escape was by sea. If the boys had broken into a shop to steal food and drink, it is unlikely the court would have imposed a duty of care on the officers towards a member of the general public who suffered damage as a result of the acts of an absconding criminal.
6 See also, for example, *Reeves v Metropolitan Commissioner* [2000] 1 AC 360 (prison officers under a duty to prevent a prisoner from harming himself while in confinement).
7 *Mitchell v Glasgow City Council* [2009] UKHL 11; 2009 SLT 205.
8 *Modbury Triangle v Anzil* (2000) 205 CLR 254 (owner of a car park not liable for the assault on the plaintiff carried out by a third party when the car park was unlit).

(3) The standard of care – negligence

5.10 Before a defender is in breach of a duty of care, it must be established that the careless act or omission which caused harm to the pursuer constituted *culpa*. In modem terminology, the careless conduct must amount to *negligence*. What the law requires is that the defender's conduct should not fall below the standard of the reasonable person in the position of the defender. If the defender's act or omission does not fall below the standard of the reasonable person, there is no breach of duty even though damage to the pursuer was foreseeable as a reasonable and probable consequence of the defender's conduct. But when the defender's conduct has not met the standards of the reasonable person in the position of the defender, the defender is negligent and the law demands reparation. The law does not expect the defender to go beyond the standards of the reasonable person. The defender is only obliged to take reasonable care: he is not expected to ensure that his acts or omissions never harm the pursuer. This point was forcibly made in *Muir v Glasgow Corpn*,[1] where the House of Lords held that the duty of the manageress was only to take reasonable care and not to prevent any accident occurring on the premises.

How then do we determine the standard of care of a reasonable person in any particular circumstance? Once again, since the standard of care is that of the hypothetical reasonable person in the position of the defender, the issue is ultimately a question for the court. What the judges do is to consider a number of relevant factors and then determine what steps a reasonable person would have taken to prevent a foreseeable risk of harm to the pursuer. If the defender did not take these steps – or their equivalent – then she has been negligent and has broken the duty of care which she owed to the pursuer, always provided that harm to the pursuer is a reasonable and probable consequence of her failure to do so.

This involves a balancing process. The relevant factors to be considered include the probability of injury, the seriousness of the injury, the practicability of precautions, the cost of the precautions and the utility of the defender's activities. The practice of other persons in the same type of business or profession as the defender can also be important. The court then balances the costs of preventing harm to the pursuer against the risk of injury to the pursuer. By such a calculus of risk, there emerges the standard of the reasonable person in the position of the defender. If the defender's conduct has *in fact* not reached that standard, she has been negligent and therefore in breach of the duty of care owed to the pursuer.

Considering the factors in more detail:

1 1943 SC (HL) 3, 1944 SLT 60, discussed at paras 6.12–6.13 ff above.

(a) Probability of injury to the pursuer

5.11   Even if harm to the pursuer is foreseeable, a defender who causes such an injury is not negligent in failing to take precautions to avoid it if the risk of such an injury is so improbable that a reasonable person in the position of the defender would not have taken any precautions. Thus, for example, in *Bolton v Stone*[1] the plaintiff was injured by a cricket ball which had been hit out of a cricket ground. This had happened on six occasions in the previous 30 years and no one had been injured. The House of Lords held that the defendants had not been negligent in failing to take precautions since the risk of injury was so slight in the circumstances that a reasonable person in the position of the defendants would not have taken any precautions. Lord Reid explained:[2]

'In my judgment, the test to be applied here is whether the risk of damage to a person on the road was so small that a reasonable man in the position of the appellants [the defendants], considering the matter from the point of view of safety, would have thought it right to refrain from taking steps to prevent the damage. In considering the matter I think that it would be right to take into account, not only how remote is the chance that a person might be struck, but also how serious the consequences are likely to be if a person is struck, but I do not think that it would be right to take into account the difficulty of remedial measures. If cricket cannot be played on a ground without creating a substantial risk, then it should not be played there at all.'

In *Gillon v Chief Constable of Strathclyde Police*,[3] it was held that the risk of a police officer being injured by a player at a football match was so small that a reasonable employer – and the football club – were not required to take any precautions.

In *McTear v Imperial Tobacco Ltd*[4] the Lord Ordinary (Nimmo Smith) held that when a consumer is harmed by a defender's product, in this case tobacco, there is no breach of a duty of care if the consumer knew of the product's potential for causing harm prior to consumption. It was enough that the manufacturer had supplied him with such information as a normally intelligent person would include in his assessment of how he wishes to conduct his life and therefore being capable of making an informed choice of whether or not to smoke and run the risk of contracting lung cancer. Of course, there could be liability if the manufacturer's product contained a substance other than that which the public would expect ie when the tobacco was subject to a latent defect.

1 [1951] AC 850, [1951] 1 All ER 1078, HL.
2 [1951] 1 All ER 1078 at 1086. See in relation to golf balls 'driven' off course where the pursuer succeeded: *Whitefield v Barton* 1987 SCLR 259, Sh Ct.
3 1997 SLT 1218, (1996) *Times*, 22 November 1996, OH.
4 2005 2 SC 1.

(b) Seriousness of injury to potential pursuer

5.12 As Lord Reid indicated in the passage cited above, the seriousness of the consequences for a person if he is injured is a relevant factor. In *Paris v Stepney Borough Council*,[1] a mechanic who had the use of only one eye was not supplied with goggles. When he was removing a rusty bolt from a car with a hammer, a chip of metal flew into his good eye and as a result he became totally blind. The employer had known that the plaintiff had only one eye. It was accepted that it was not the practice in the industry to supply goggles to workers engaged on the plaintiff's tasks. The question, however, was whether the employer had been negligent in failing to provide goggles for an employee whom they knew was already partially sighted. In the Court of Appeal,[2] the plaintiff's claim failed. Asquith LJ took the view that while the greater risk of injury was a relevant factor, the risk of greater injury was not. The House of Lords[3] held, however, that the seriousness of the consequences of an injury for a particular plaintiff was a relevant consideration. Since the consequences of an eye injury for an already partially sighted person could be total blindness, the court held that the employer had been negligent in failing to provide him with goggles. It was irrelevant that the defendants might not have been negligent in failing to provide goggles to two-eyed workers. Lord Normand observed:[4]

'The court's task of deciding what precautions a reasonable and prudent man would take in the circumstances of a particular case may not be easy. Nevertheless, the judgment of the reasonable and prudent man should be allowed its common every day scope, and it should not be restrained from considering the foreseeable consequences of an accident and their seriousness for the person to whom the duty of care is owed ... the seriousness of the injury or damage risked and the likelihood of its being in fact caused may not be the only relevant factors. For example Asquith LJ in *Daborn v Bath Tramways Motor Co Ltd and Smithey*[5] pointed out that it is sometimes necessary to take account of the consequences of not assuming a risk.'

1 [1951] AC 367, [1951] 1 All ER 42, HL.
2 [1949] 2 All ER 843, CA.
3 [1951] AC 367, [1951] 1 All ER 42, HL.
4 [1951] 1 All ER 42 at 49.
5 [1946] 2 All ER 333, CA.

(c) Utility of the activity

5.13   *Daborn v Bath Tramways Motor Co Ltd and Smithey*[1] concerned an ambulance with a left-hand drive which was used during World War II. The plaintiff had put a sign at the back of the vehicle which said, 'Caution – Left hand drive – No signals'. When she was turning to the right, having given a hand signal, she collided with a bus which she could not see was trying to overtake her. The plaintiff was injured. The defendant argued that the plaintiff, as well as the bus driver, had been negligent and that her damages should be reduced on the grounds of her contributory negligence.[2] The Court of Appeal held that the plaintiff had not been negligent. In the course of his judgment Asquith LJ said:[3]

'I think that the plaintiff did all that in the circumstances she could reasonably be required to do if you include in those circumstances, as I think you should: (i) the necessity in time of national emergency of employing all transport resources which were available and (ii) the inherent limitations and incapacities of this particular form of transport. In considering whether reasonable care has been observed, one must balance the risk against the consequences of not assuming that risk, and in the present instance that calculation seems to me to work out in favour of the plaintiff.'

Thus, the social utility of the activities which it is foreseeable may cause injury must be taken into account. In *Watt v Hertfordshire County Council*[4] a woman was trapped under a vehicle. The fire service sent a lorry with a jack. During the attempt to rescue the woman, the jack slipped and a fireman was injured. He claimed that the defendants, his employers, were negligent in not using a specially adapted lorry. The court held that given the emergency the employers were justified in using the vehicle which was available, ie a reasonable employer would have used the vehicle. They had not therefore fallen below the standard of the reasonable person in their position and therefore had not broken the duty of care which they owed to their employee. In *French v Strathclyde Fire Board*[5] it was observed that when fighting a fire, it might be reasonable to take a risk to save a life which would not be reasonable to prevent damage to property.

There can also be a social value in not taking steps to prevent a foreseeable accident. In *Tomlinson v Congleton Borough Council,*[6] the House of Lords held that a local authority was not under an obligation to take steps to reduce or eliminate the dangers of swimming in a lake. It was enough that they had provided warning notices. To do more would hinder the general public from enjoying the amenities of the lakeside:

'The majority of people who went to the beaches to sunbathe, paddle and play with their children were enjoying themselves in a way which gave them pleasure and caused no risk to themselves or anyone else. This must be something to be taken into account in deciding whether it was reasonable to expect the council to destroy the beaches.'[7]

Conversely, if there is no social value in the defender's failure to take reasonable steps to eliminate or reduce a risk, the defender's omission to do so will be negligent.[8]

1 [1946] 2 All ER 333, CA.
2 On contributory negligence, see paras 6.12–6.13 below.
3 [1946] 2 All ER 333 at 336.
4 [1954] 2 All ER 368, [1954] 1 WLR 208, CA.
5 [2013] CSOH 3.
6 [2004] 1 AC 46.
7 [2004] 1 AC 46 per Lord Hoffmann at 84. His speech at 82–86 provides an excellent example of the calculus of risk. Lord Hoffmann also considered that as a general rule the owner or occupier of property did not owe a duty of care to prevent persons engaging in activities on their land such as swimming or mountaineering, which involved an inherent risk of personal harm: [2004] 1 AC 46 at 84.
8 *Jolley v Sutton Borough Council* [2000] 3 All ER 409 (no social value in failing to remove a rotting boat from a council estate!).

(d) Practicality of precautions

5.14   The hypothetical reasonable person in the position of the defender will – indeed, can – only take such precautions as are practicable to avoid the risk of harm. In *Quinn v Cameron and Roberton Ltd*,[1] for example, the pursuer developed pneumoconiosis as a result of prolonged exposure to silica dust where he was working. His case against his employers failed on the basis that since the danger to employees from silica dust in iron foundries was not appreciated during the period when the pursuer was working for the employer (nine years prior to 1951), the defenders were not in breach of their duty of care by not providing precautions. Another reason why they had not been negligent was that effective dust-extraction appliances were not available to the employers until 1950. The Lord President (Clyde) explained:[2]

'The Lord Ordinary has held it proved that the provision of dust extraction appliances at plough buffs was not general practice between 1946 and 1951, and the expert evidence is really unanimously in favour of this conclusion. Indeed any apparatus to cope with the dangerous dust only seems to have come into the market in 1950, and went into general practice thereafter.'

1 1956 SC 224, 1957 SLT 2. See also *Smith v P & O Bulk Shipping Ltd* [1998] 2 Lloyd's Rep 81, QBD (employer could not have known about danger from asbestos when plaintiff was employee).
2 1956 SC 224 at 233.

(e) Cost of precautions

5.15   The hypothetical reasonable person in the position of the defender will take into account the cost of precautions and balance this against the probability of risk of harm and the seriousness of any injuries likely to be sustained. The defender's duty is not to be negligent; it is not to act to eliminate all risks of injury to the pursuer. Thus, for example, in *Latimer v AEC Ltd*[1] a factory floor became slippery as a result of a phenomenal rainstorm. In an attempt to avoid accidents, the employer spread three tons of sawdust on the floor. Nevertheless, an employee slipped and was injured on a part of the floor *not* covered by sawdust.[2] The plaintiff argued that the employer should have closed down the factory while the floor was properly cleaned, thus eliminating the risk of employees slipping. This would, of course, have involved loss of production. The House of Lords held that the employer did all that a reasonable person would have done and was therefore not negligent. For Lord Tucker[3] the only question was:

'Has it been proved that the floor was so slippery that, remedial steps not being possible, a reasonably prudent employer would have closed down the factory rather than allow his employees to run the risks involved in continuing work? ... The absence of any evidence that anyone in the factory during the afternoon or night shift, other than the appellant, slipped, or experienced any difficulty, or that any complaint was made by or on behalf of the workers, all points to the conclusion that the danger was, in fact, not such as to impose on a reasonable employer the obligation [to close down the factory].'

In *Charlton v Forrest Printing Ink Co Ltd*[4] it was one of the tasks of a group of employees to collect the wages for the workforce from a bank and take them to the factory. The employer had warned them of the possibility of being robbed and advised them to vary the times – and the transport used – when they went to collect the wages. Nevertheless, there was a robbery and the plaintiff was blinded by acid which had been thrown in his face. The Court of Appeal held that the employer had taken reasonable precautions and had not been negligent in failing to use the services of Securicor to uplift the wages, which could have been done at a very modest cost. On the other hand, if a risk can be eliminated or reduced at little cost, then the defender's failure to do so will be negligent.[5] In *Napier v Scottish Ministers*,[6] on the other hand, it was held that the defenders were in breach of their duty to take reasonable care for the health and safety of the pursuer who was in prison and still had to slop out. The cost of the improvements necessary to eliminate the need for slopping out did not prevent liability arising.

1 [1953] AC 643, [1953] 2 All ER 449, HL.
2 In spite of using three tons, some areas were left uncovered!
3 [1953] 2 All ER 449 at 455.
4 [1980] IRLR 331, CA. The case was concerned with an employer's *contractual* duty to take reasonable care for the safety of employees; but the point is also applicable in respect of the employer's *delictual* duty of care towards his employees.
5 *Jolley v Sutton Borough Council* [2000] 3 All ER 409. It should be noted that in *Tomlinson v Congleton Borough Council* [2004] 1 AC 46, Lord Hoffmann at 83 did not regard the cost of destroying the lakeside as an important factor as opposed to the loss of social utility which that would have involved.
6 2005 1 SC 229. There was also a breach of the pursuer's right under Article 3 not to suffer torture or inhuman or degrading treatment or punishment.

(f) Practice of other persons in the same business, trade or profession as the defender

5.16 The standard to be reached is that of the hypothetical reasonable person in the position of the defender. The practice of other persons in the same business, trade or profession as the defender will be at least an indication of the standard expected by a reasonable person in that situation. This was recognised by the Lord President (Dunedin) in *Morton v Wm Dixon Ltd.*[1] There a miner sued his employer on the basis that the employer had been negligent in failing to provide a 'shielding contrivance' to prevent coal falling between a cage and the side of the mine shaft. In determining whether the employer was negligent and in breach of his duty of care, Lord Dunedin said:[2]

'I look upon this matter as one of great importance not merely for this particular case, but for cases of this sort generally. Where the negligence of an employer consists of what I may call a fault of omission, I think that it is absolutely necessary that the proof of fault of omission should be one of two kinds, either – to shew that the thing which he did not do was a thing which was commonly done by other persons in like circumstances, or – to shew that it was a thing which was so obviously wanted that it would be folly in anyone not to provide it.'

While the determination whether the particular defender has fallen below the requisite standard is a question of fact, the standard of care demanded is that of the hypothetical reasonable person and is ultimately the standard which the court decides is appropriate in a particular situation. If, for example, an employer does not take certain precautions, the court may still take the view that he did not reach the standard of care of the reasonable person in that situation even though he was following the usual practice in his trade or business in not taking the precautions. In *Cavanagh v Ulster Weaving Co Ltd*[3] an employee who was wearing rubber boots slipped off a roof ladder while carrying cement. No handrail was provided on the ladder. There was evidence that it was not the practice in the building trade to provide a handrail in these circumstances. The House of Lords held that evidence of the practice, while important, was not conclusive in establishing the requisite standard of care: that remained the standard of the reasonable person in the defendant's position. Given the circumstances of this case, including the fact that the employee's boots were two sizes larger than they should have been, a reasonable employer would have supplied a handrail and therefore the defendant was negligent. Lord Dunedin's formula in *Morton v Wm Dixon Ltd,*[4] while important, was not 'intended to depart from or modify the fundamental principle that an employer is bound to take reasonable care for the safety of his workmen'.[5]

Conversely, where the defender has not followed the usual practice in his trade or profession, he may nevertheless have taken reasonable care. In *Brown v Rolls Royce Ltd*[6] it was common practice in the defenders' industry to supply workers in the position of the pursuer with a barrier cream. The defenders considered that barrier cream was ineffective and instead took other precautions advised by a medical officer. The pursuer contracted dermatitis. The House of Lords held that while the defenders' failure to follow the usual practice was prima facie evidence of negligence, it was not conclusive. Because the defenders had taken other precautions against the risk of their employees suffering dermatitis, the defenders had not failed to take reasonable care. In relation to Lord Dunedin's formula, Lord Keith of Avonholm observed:[7]

'As has been said before in this House, Lord Dunedin was laying down no proposition of law; nor did he say that, if a practice was averred and proved which might have avoided the accident, this was necessarily conclusive of negligence on the part of an employer who had not followed the practice. The ultimate test is lack of reasonable care for the safety of the workman in all the circumstances of the case.'

The standard of care required of professional men and women, such as members of the medical and legal professions, is discussed later in the book.[8]

1 1909 SC 807, 1909 1 SLT 346.
2 1909 SC 807 at 809. This *dictum* still remains authoritative: see for example *Pratt v Scottish Ministers* 2013 SLT 590; *Shields v Crossroads (Orkney)* [2013] CSOH 144.
3 [1960] AC 145, [1959] 2 All ER 745, HL.
4 1909 SC 807 at 809.
5 *Cavanagh v Ulster Weaving Co Ltd* [1959] 2 All ER 745 at 751 per Lord Keith of Avonholm.
6 1960 SC (HL) 22, 1960 SLT 119.
7 1960 SC (HL) 22 at 26.
8 See Chapter 7.

(4) Remoteness of injury

5.17 In some earlier Scottish cases, delictual liability has been rejected on the ground that the harm suffered by the pursuer was 'too remote'. In *Reavis v Clan Line Steamers Ltd*,[1] for example, the court denied Mrs Reavis compensation for the loss of her orchestra on the simple basis that this loss was 'too remote'. It is submitted that the better analysis is that the defender did not owe her a duty of care to prevent her suffering secondary economic loss. Similarly, in *Bourhill v Young*,[2] it was argued by some of the judges that the pursuer could not sue in delict because the mental harm she sustained was too remote. Again it is submitted that Mrs Bourhill's claim failed because Young did not owe her a duty of care in respect of inflicting mental harm because she was a secondary victim. Conversely, *Hughes v Lord Advocate*[3] has been treated as a case where the pursuer's injuries were not regarded as too remote. But it is thought that that decision is better analysed as an example of how a breach of duty occurs. In other words, since physical harm to the pursuer was foreseeable as a reasonable and probable consequence of the defender's carelessness, there was a breach of duty even though the extent of the pursuer's injuries could not have been reasonably foreseen. It is thought that the concept of remoteness of injury has no part to play in determining the existence of a duty of care or the breach of such a duty in the modern Scots law of delict.

Remoteness of injury must not be confused with remoteness of losses. Where there has been a breach of a duty of care and the pursuer has suffered harm, the pursuer may not be able to recover for all the losses suffered as a result of the defender's negligence. Some losses may be considered by the court to be too remote. For example, if A injures B as a result of negligent driving, B is entitled to damages for pain and suffering and derivative economic loss, such as loss of wages, loss of future earnings etc. But when as a result of the accident B was unable to post his football coupon, could he recover damages from A for the fortune he would have won if the coupon had been sent? In other words, is the loss of the winnings too remote to be compensated by A? This is a question of remoteness of losses and is discussed later in the book.[4]

1 1925 SC 725.
2 1942 SC (HL) 78, 1943 SLT 105.
3 1963 SC (HL) 31, 1963 SLT 150.
4 See beyond paras 16.1 ff.

C. CONCLUSION

5.18   In this chapter we have been discussing when a breach of a duty of care arises. The defender's act or omission must be voluntary; constituent harm to the pursuer must be foreseeable as a reasonable and probable consequence of the defender's act or omission; and, finally, the act or omission must amount to negligence, ie the defender must have failed to reach the standard of care of the hypothetical reasonable person in the position of the defender. Where those criteria are satisfied, there is a breach of the duty of care owed to the pursuer and a delict is committed when the pursuer sustains constituent harm as a result of the defender's breach of the duty of care.

CHAPTER 6

Causation and related issues

Before there is liability in delict, the pursuer must prove on the balance of probabilities that the defender's breach of her duty of care was the cause of the harm sustained by the pursuer. The concept of causation is a complex and difficult subject raising fundamental philosophical as well as legal issues. In a work of the present compass, only an outline of the relevant issues is given.[1]

1 For a superb account of the subject, see Hart and Honoré *Causation and the Law* (2nd edn, 1985). The book is an excellent example of the constructive use to which linguistic philosophy can be put in the context of law. See also B Pillans SULI *Delict* Chapter 7.

A. FACTUAL CAUSATION

6.1 The first essential is that the defender's acts or omissions are a cause of the harm suffered by the pursuer. This is a question of fact. If the defender's conduct is not a factual cause of the harm, there is no liability even if the defender has broken a duty of care which he owed to the pursuer. To use Latin terminology, the defender's breach of duty must be a *causa sine qua non* of the pursuer's material harm. In other words, 'but for' the defender's conduct, the pursuer would not have sustained the harm. If the pursuer would have suffered the same harm notwithstanding the defender's breach of duty, then the defender's conduct is not a factual cause of the harm, ie it is not a *causa sine qua non*. Accordingly, to determine whether the defender's breach of duty is a factual cause of the harm suffered by the pursuer, we must ask ourselves whether 'but for' the breach of duty, the harm would have occurred. If it would *not* have occurred, the defender's conduct is a factual cause of the pursuer's harm:[1] if it would still have occurred, the defender's conduct is *not* a factual cause of the pursuer's harm. The onus of satisfying the 'but for' test on the balance of probabilities rests on the pursuer:[2] it is not for the defender to provide an alternative explanation.[3]

In *Barnett v Chelsea and Kensington Hospital Management Committee*,[4] for example, the plaintiff's husband drank a cup of tea and became violently ill because the tea had been poisoned. The hospital doctor refused to treat the husband telling him to see his own doctor. The husband died. It was held that although the defendant may have been in breach of a duty of care, the hospital was not liable because the husband would still have died of the poison even if he had been treated by the hospital doctor, ie the husband did not die 'but for' the hospital's negligence. Accordingly, the breach of duty was not a *causa sine qua non* of the husband's death and the plaintiff's action failed.

In *Kay's Tutor v Ayrshire and Arran Health Board*[5] a child was brought into hospital suffering from meningitis. He was given a massive overdose of penicillin.[6] The child thereupon suffered severe convulsions but, as a result of treatment, recovered. However, the child was left deaf. In an action against the hospital, the defenders admitted that they were in breach of their duty of care in administering the overdose of penicillin but denied that this breach of duty had caused the child's deafness. The House of Lords held that the onus lay on the pursuer (the child's father) to prove that 'but for' the overdose the child would not be deaf. In the absence of evidence to show that an overdose of penicillin caused deafness in a patient and given that deafness is common in patients who suffer meningitis, the pursuer failed to establish that 'but for' the breach of duty deafness would not have occurred. The breach was therefore not a *causa sine qua non* of the child's deafness and the pursuer's action failed.

1 It is enough if it can be shown that 'but for' the defender's act or omission it was probable that the injury would not have occurred: *Porter v Strathclyde Regional Council* 1991 SLT 446.

2 See, for example, *Dingley v Chief Constable of Strathclyde Police (No 1)* 1998 SC 548, OH (pursuer failed to establish on the balance of probabilities that a whiplash injury sustained in a road accident had triggered the onset of symptomatic multiple sclerosis); *Pickford v ICI plc* [1998] ICR 673, [1998] 3 All ER 462, HL (onus was on plaintiff to prove that her condition had an organic cause: the employer's failure to prove that the condition was psychogenic was no more than a relevant factor in determining whether or not the plaintiff had discharged the burden of proof. In the circumstances the plaintiff had failed to do so); *Thomson v Kvaerner Govan Ltd* 2004 SLT 24 (pursuer failed to establish that plank supplied by the defender was not of adequate strength and caused him to fall when he stepped on it); *McTear v Imperial Tobacco Ltd* 2005 2 SC 1 (pursuer failed to establish that her husband would not have died of lung cancer if he had not smoked the defender's cigarettes); *McGinnes v Endeva Service Ltd* 2006 SLT 638 (pursuer could not establish that he would not have been assaulted by a third party if a second employee had accompanied him to the *locus* where he was working); *Clough v First Choice Holidays and Flights Ltd* [2006] EWCA Civ 15, [2006] PIQR

P22 (the claimant could not establish that he would not have fallen off a wall into a swimming pool if the wall had been painted with non-slip paint: 'The judge remained unpersuaded that the claimant's slip was caused, or materially contributed to, by the absence of non-slip paint on the surface of the wall. Non-slip paint would have made the surface less slippery, but not non-slippery, nor removed altogether *the risk* of a slip by someone walking on the top of the wall with wet feet' per President of the Queen's Bench Division (Sir Igor Judge) at para 47); *McGlinchey v General Motors UK Ltd* [2012] CSIH 91 (pursuer failed to establish that an accident in which she was crushed by her car was caused by its handbrake being defective).

3   *Thomson v Kvaerner Govan Ltd* 2004 SLT 24. In *Drake v Harbour* [2008] EWCA Civ 25, 121 Con LR 18, [2008] NPC 11, [2008] All ER (D) 283 (Jan), CA. Toulson LJ observed at para 28: ' … where a claimant proves both that a defendant was negligent and that loss ensued which was of a kind likely to have resulted from such negligence, this will ordinarily be enough to enable a court to infer that it was probably so caused, even if the claimant is unable to prove positively the precise mechanism. That is not a principle of law nor does it involve an alteration in the burden of proof; rather, it is a matter of common sense. The court must consider any alternative theories of causation advanced by the defendant before reaching its conclusion about where the probability lies. If it concludes that the only alternative suggestions put forward by the defendant are on balance improbable, that is likely to fortify the court's conclusion that it is legitimate to infer that the loss was caused by the proven negligence.'

4   [1969] 1 QB 428, [1968] 1 All ER 1068.

5   1987 SC (HL) 145, 1987 SLT 577, HL, affirming 1986 SLT 435.

6   30 times the prescribed amount.

6.2   This concept was taken a stage further by the House of Lords in *Bolitho v City and Hackney Health Authority*.[1] It was accepted that a doctor had been in breach of her duty of care by failing to attend her patient, a child. The child died. It was also accepted that the only way in which the child's life could have been saved was by intubation. However, evidence was led that a responsible body of medical opinion would not have intubated in the circumstances. In other words, if the doctor had attended her patient, she would not have been negligent if she had not attempted to save the child's life by intubating her. Consequently, the child would still have died even if the doctor had attended her. The logic appears strained but it is nevertheless compelling. Since the patient would still have died even if she had received reasonable care, ie no intubation, the doctor's negligence in failing to attend her was not a factual cause of her death.[2]

Where the treatment of a patient would have had less than a 50 per cent chance of success, the failure to treat is not regarded as the cause of the pursuer's injuries or illness: in other words, the chances of success must be more than 50 per cent.[3] In *Gregg v Scott*[4] owing to the negligence of his GP, the treatment of the claimant's cancer was delayed by nine months. He argued that had he been referred to hospital when he first saw his GP there would have been a high likelihood of cure, whereas by the time treatment commenced his chances of recovery had fallen to below 50 per cent. Chances of recovery were defined as surviving for a period of ten years. At the trial it was established that even if he had been diagnosed and treated promptly, his chances of surviving for ten years would have been only 42 per cent: now they were only 25 per cent. Because his chances of surviving ten years were never 50 per cent or more, the trial judge held that on a balance of probability the complainant would not have survived for ten years even if treated promptly; and therefore he had failed to establish that the negligent misdiagnosis would cause him to die prematurely. A majority of the House of Lords agreed. The claimant had to establish that the clinical negligence was the cause of the adverse consequences which had befallen him. Since the claimant would only have had a 42% chance of surviving had he been treated immediately, he was unable to prove on the balance of probabilities that the failure to survive for ten years was the result of the negligent misdiagnosis rather than the cancer. The majority of their Lordships also held that the reduction in his chances of a cure – from 42 per cent to 25 per cent – was not a recoverable head of damage. Put another way, their Lordships refused to award damages for the increased risk of suffering harm in the future as opposed to the lost chance of avoiding a result which has in fact occurred.

Another striking example of the 'but for' test is *McWilliams v Sir William Arrol & Co and Lithgows Ltd*.[5] The pursuer's husband, a steel erector, was killed. It was held that the defenders were in breach of their duty of care towards McWilliams in failing to provide him with a safety belt. But it was also established that even if they had provided him with a safety belt, McWilliams would not have worn it. In these circumstances, the pursuer failed to prove that 'but for' the defenders' breach of duty the accident would not have occurred. The defenders' breach was not a *causa sine qua non* of McWilliams' death and the pursuer's action failed.

Where the pursuer suffers harm which he would have suffered anyway, but as a result of the defender's breach of duty he suffers the harm at an earlier date, the Scottish courts have held that the 'but for' test is satisfied and an action will lie in delict.[6] Conversely, where a pursuer is injured as a result of the defender's breach of duty but later suffers an accident or disease unrelated to the defender's conduct, the fact that he would have been debilitated by the later accident or disease is taken into account in assessing the pursuer's loss.[7]

The 'but for' test also applies when the pursuer's claim is for pure economic loss. For example, D provides P with information about C which P uses to decide whether or not to enter into a transaction with C. P sustains economic loss as a consequence of the transaction with C. In an action to recover the loss from D, P must prove that he would not have entered into the transaction with C 'but for' D's misrepresentation in respect of C. If P would have entered into the transaction with C in the absence of D's advice, the action will fail for lack of factual causation.[8]

1 [1998] AC 232, [1997] 4 All ER 771, HL.
2 It would still be very difficult to explain to the child's parents why their action failed given the doctor's admitted negligence in not attending their child.
3 See *Kenyon v Bell* 1953 SC 125, 1952 SLT (Notes) 79, OH; *Hotson v East Berkshire Area Health Authority* [1987] 2 All ER 909, HL.
4 [2005] 2 AC 178.
5 1962 SC (HL) 70, 1962 SLT 121.
6 *Sutherland v North British Steel Group Ltd* 1986 SLT (Sh Ct) 29 (accelerated hernia operation).
7 See *Jobling v Associated Dairies Ltd* [1982] AC 794, [1981] 2 All ER 752, HL.
8 *Leeds & Holbeck Building Society v Alex Morison & Co (No 2)* 2001 SCLR 41.

6.3   Difficulties arise where there is more than one potential cause of the pursuer's injuries, ie the defender's breach of a duty of care and another source of danger which is not the responsibility of the defender. The starting point of the discussion is *Wardlaw v Bonnington Castings Ltd.*[1] A workman contracted pneumoconiosis from breathing dust in the atmosphere of his workplace. Some of the dust was caused by a hammer in relation to which there were no known or available precautions which could be taken to prevent the employee breathing contaminated air. Therefore the defender was not in breach of the duty of care owed to the pursuer in respect of the dust caused by the hammer. However, there were other machines in the workshop which also produced dust for which adequate extraction plant was available and the employers were held responsible for not adequately maintaining the extracting plant.[2]

There were therefore two possible sources of the dust which had caused the pursuer's illness for only one of which the defender was delictually liable, ie the dust from the other machines. The House of Lords held that the onus lay on the pursuer to show that on the balance of probabilities the dust from the machines was a *causa sine qua non* of his illness. In the situation of two potential sources of danger, the pursuer would discharge the onus if he could show that the source for which the defender was responsible had materially contributed to his injury. Lord Reid observed:[3]

'It appears to me that the source of his [the pursuer's] disease was the dust from both sources, and the real question is whether the dust from the swing grinders [the other machines] materially contributed to the disease. What is a material contribution must be a question of degree. A contribution which comes within the exception *de minimis non curat lex* is not material but I think that any contribution which does not fall within that exception must be material.'

In this case, the dust from the machines did materially contribute to the pursuer's illness and the pursuer was successful. Thus, where there are two or more sources of harm to the pursuer which operate concurrently, the source for which the defender is responsible will be regarded as a *causa sine qua non* of the pursuer's injury if it materially contributed to the injury.

1 1956 SC (HL) 26, 1956 SLT 135.
2 This was a breach by the employer of their statutory duty under the Grinding of Metals (Miscellaneous Industries) Regulations 1925, SR & O 1925/904. On breach of statutory duty, see Chapter 11 below.
3 *Wardlaw v Bonnington Castings Ltd* 1956 SC (HL) 26 at 32.

6.4   The concept of factual causation was taken a considerable step further in *McGhee v National Coal Board*.[1] The pursuer worked all day in a hot and dusty kiln. He had to cycle home unwashed because the defender failed to provide on-site washing facilities. After several days, the pursuer contracted dermatitis. It was admitted that the dermatitis was attributable to the work the pursuer did in the brick kiln but the defender was not in breach of a duty of care in allowing the pursuer to work there. The breach of duty was the failure to provide on-site washing facilities. This omission only resulted in the pursuer cycling home unwashed: clearly, it did not relate to the hours he spent working in the kiln. Common sense would suggest that it was far more likely that the dermatitis was contracted when he was working in the kiln, for which the employer was not delictually liable, rather than during the short time he cycled home. But the expert evidence could not establish how dermatitis was actually contracted. *Wardlaw v Bonnington Castings Ltd*[2] could therefore not provide a solution since it could not be proven that the additional exposure to injury caused by cycling home unwashed had materially contributed to his injury. *Wardlaw v Bonnington Castings Ltd* is concerned with two sources of danger operating *concurrently*; but *McGhee v National Coal Board* is concerned with two sources of danger operating *consecutively* where the defender was responsible only for the later one. Therefore it can be argued that the pursuer in *McGhee* would have to prove – which on the evidence he could not – that the later source of danger had caused, or at least materially contributed to, his dermatitis.

However, the House of Lords was prepared to take a broader view of causation. The medical evidence suggested that the fact that the pursuer had to cycle home caked with grime and sweat added materially to *the risk* that the disease might develop, although it could not explain why this was so. In the view of the House, materially to increase the risk of the pursuer's injuries was to be regarded as a material contribution to the injury. Lord Reid opined:[3]

'But it has often been said that the legal concept of causation is not based on logic or philosophy. It is based on the practical way in which the ordinary man's mind works in the every-day affairs of life. From a broad and practical viewpoint I can see no substantial difference between saying that what the defender did materially increased the risk of injury to the pursuer and saying that what the defender did made a material contribution to his injury.'

Lord Salmon observed:[4]

'In the circumstances of the present case,[5] the possibility of a distinction existing between (a) having materially increased the risk of contracting the disease and (b) having materially contributed to causing the disease may no doubt be a fruitful source of interesting academic discussions between students of philosophy. Such a distinction is, however, far too unreal to be recognised by the common law'!

Thus, where there are two or more sources of danger for only one of which the defender is delictually liable, factual causation will be established if the pursuer can prove on the balance of probabilities *either* that the defender's breach of duty materially contributed to his injury *or* that the defender's breach of duty materially increased the risk of the pursuer sustaining injury. It does not matter if the sources of danger operate concurrently or consecutively.[6]

1 1973 SC (HL) 37, 1973 SLT 14; see Lord Hope of Craighead 'James McGhee – A Second Mrs Donoghue?' [2003] CLJ 587.
2 1956 SC (HL) 26, 1956 SLT 135.
3 *McGhee v National Coal Board* 1973 SC (HL) 37 at 53–54.
4 1973 SC (HL) 37 at 62.
5 Given the defender's admitted breach of a duty of care.
6 The implications of *McGhee* are remarkable. For example, suppose A has smoked cigarettes for 30 years. B, her employer, allows C and D, fellow employees, to smoke in a room occupied by A. A contracts lung cancer a week later. Since A's passive smoking of C and D's cigarette smoke materially increases the risk of A contracting lung cancer, C and D's smoking (and B's allowing them to smoke) could be treated as the cause of A contracting the disease. But common sense would suggest that A contracted the disease as a result of her own smoking habit. A would, of course, be contributorily negligent: see paras 6.12–6.13 ff below.

6.5   *McGhee v National Coal Board* was approved and extended by
the House of Lords in *Fairchild v Glenhaven Funeral Services Ltd*.[1]
F was employed by E1 and E2 at different times and for different
periods. Both E1 and E2 were in breach of a duty of care to F by
allowing him to breathe asbestos dust. F contracted cancer. The
medical evidence established that the disease was contracted by
breathing asbestos dust but, because of the limits of scientific
knowledge, it could not be established that the cancer was the
result of inhaling asbestos dust during his employment with E1 or
E2 or both employers. But it was also proven that once the disease
had been contracted, F's condition would not deteriorate as a
consequence of further exposure to asbestos dust. Thus causation
could not be established on the basis of a material contribution
to F's illness. On the other hand, it was accepted that the *risk* of
contracting the cancer increased in relation to the total exposure
to asbestos dust. In these circumstances, their Lordships took the
view that the normal 'but for' test should be suspended. Lord
Nicholls considered that the plaintiff should succeed as 'any
other outcome would be deeply offensive to instinctive notions of
what justice requires and fairness demands'.[2] Since both E1 and
E2 were in breach of the duty of care they owed to F and these
breaches had materially increased the risk of F contracting cancer,
McGhee was applicable and the causal requirement was satisfied.[3]
It should be noted that in *McGhee*, the pursuer sustained harm as
a consequence of the defender's breach of duty or the defender's
non-delictual conduct, both of which materially increased the risk
of his contracting dermatitis: even if the illness was not contracted
as a result of the defender's breach of duty, it was nevertheless
caused by the defender's conduct – albeit conduct that might not
have been negligent. *Fairchild* goes further in that by increasing the
risk of the pursuer sustaining harm as a result of the defender's
breach of duty, the defender may be held to have caused the
pursuer's illness when it was in fact caused by the negligence of
another person.

In *Sienkiewicz v Grief (UK) Ltd*[4] the defendant's negligent exposure
of the plaintiff to asbestos over her working life at their premises
increased her risk of contracting mesothelioma by only 18 per cent.
Although this case only involved one defendant, the Supreme
Court nevertheless held that the *Fairchild* exception applied
and the plaintiff was entitled to succeed as the defendant had
materially increased the risk of her contracting the disease. There
was no need for her to prove that the defendant's negligence had
doubled the risk of her contracting mesothelioma.[5]

There are, however, important limitations. First, as the Supreme Court re-emphasised in *Sienkiewicz*, the principle in *McGhee* and *Fairchild* only applies when it is impossible to establish scientifically the cause of the pursuer's injury. Second, while the *sources* of danger may be different, it must be established that each source could have in fact been the cause of the pursuer's injuries. In *Wardlaw, McGhee* and *Fairchild* it was clear that dust caused the pursuers' diseases: the only question was whether the defenders' breach of duty had materially contributed to, or increased the risk of, the pursuers' illnesses. By way of contrast, in *Kay's Tutor v Ayrshire and Arran Health Board*,[6] there was no evidence that the defender's breach of duty in giving the overdose of penicillin could in fact have caused the child's deafness. In these circumstances, *Wardlaw, McGhee* and *Fairchild* are irrelevant. As Lord Griffiths explained:[7]

'The principle in *McGhee* would only fall for consideration if it was first proved that it was an accepted medical fact that penicillin in some cases caused or aggravated deafness. The question would then arise whether when there are two competing causes of deafness, namely meningitis and penicillin, the law should presume in favour of the plaintiff [sic] that the tortious [sic] [delictual] cause was responsible for the damage.'

Moreover, the departure from the ordinary 'but for' rule only applies when there are two or more sources of the *same* noxious agent which caused the pursuer's illness or injuries: if there is more than one noxious agent which could have caused the pursuer's injuries or illness, the threshold 'but for' test of causal connection will not be relaxed. In *Wilsher v Essex Area Health Authority*,[8] a baby's medical condition could have been caused by a noxious agent (a) which arose as a consequence of the defendant's breach of duty: but there were another four different noxious agents – for which the defendant was not responsible – each of which could equally have harmed the child. The fact that the defendant's negligence materially increased the risk of the child from being harmed by noxious agent (a) was held not to be a sufficient causative link when the child's condition could have been caused by noxious agents (b), (c), (d) or (e).

As we have seen[9] in *Chester v Afshar*[10] the House of Lords was prepared to suspend the normal operation of the 'but for' test in order to ensure that a doctor's obligation to inform a patient of the risks inherent in a medical procedure would not be undermined. The purpose of the obligation was to enable a patient to make an informed decision on whether or not to agree to the procedure. This duty would be rendered almost obsolete if only those patients who would not have agreed to the procedure were able to sue when their doctor was in breach of this duty.

1   [2003] 1 AC 32, [2002] 3 All ER 305. See Joe Thomson 'The Raising of Lazarus: The Resurrection of *McGhee v National Coal Board*' (2003) 7 Edin LR 80.
2   [2002] 3 All ER 305 at 336. See also Lord Bingham at 312 and Lord Hoffmann at 341.
3   If *in fact* F had contracted cancer while in the employment of E1, it is difficult to see how the exposure to asbestos dust while in the employment of E2 materially increased the risk of F contracting cancer!
4   [2011] UKSC 10.
5   The pursuer will fail if the increase in the risk of contracting the disease as a result of the defender's negligence is minimal: *Garner v Salford City Council* [2013] EWHC 1573.
6   1987 SC (HL) 145, 1987 SLT 577. Discussed at para 6.1 above.
7   1987 SLT 577 at 581.
8   [1988] 1 All ER 871, HL, approved by the House of Lords in *Fairchild*.
9   Above para 1.4.
10 [2005] 1 AC 134.

B. LEGAL CAUSATION

6.6   For the purpose of liability in delict, it is not enough that the defender's breach of duty is a factual cause or *causa sine qua non* of the pursuer's harm. While factual causation is a necessary condition of delictual liability, it is not sufficient. In addition, the defender's breach of duty must be the legal cause of the pursuer's harm. To use Latin terminology, it must be the *causa causans*. Various terms are used to describe legal causation: these include the direct, decisive, proximate, real, dominant, efficient, effective and substantial cause of the pursuer's loss or harm.

For example, A drops a brick on B's foot, breaking his toe. B is taken to hospital in an ambulance. The ambulance is driven carelessly and B is killed in a road accident. A's breach of duty is a *causa sine qua non* of B's death since 'but for' A's dropping the brick on his toe, B would not have been in the ambulance in which he died. But should A be delictually liable for B's death which was caused by the ambulance driver's careless driving? The answer is no. A's breach of duty, although a *causa sine qua non* of B's death, is not treated as the legal cause, ie it is not the *causa causans*. The *causa causans* is the ambulance driver's careless driving. We can say that the chain of causation between A's breach of duty and B's death has been broken as a result of the careless act of the ambulance driver, which prevents A's breach of duty from being the legal cause of B's death. To use legal terminology, the ambulance driver's conduct is a *novus actus interveniens* which

breaks the chain of causation so that A is not delictually liable for
B's death, although A remains liable for B's broken toe.

In this example, the *novus actus interveniens* was the conduct of a
third party: the ambulance driver. But the conduct of the victim
may also break the chain of causation. So, for example, if A drops
a brick on B's foot, breaking his toe, whereupon B cuts his own
throat to put himself out of pain, A will not be delictually liable
for B's death. B's action has broken the chain of causation and, as
a result, A's breach of duty is not regarded as the legal cause, the
causa causans, of B's death.[1]

When, then, will an act of a third party or the act of the victim
constitute *a novus actus interveniens*, breaking the chain of
causation? Since we are concerned with determining legal
causation, this is ultimately a question for the courts: the judges
will *evaluate* whether or not in the circumstances it is fair to relieve
the defender of his delictual liability. At one time, this was a crucial
decision where the victim had contributed to his own injuries: for
if the court decided that the pursuer's conduct was a *novus actus
interveniens* so that the defender's breach of duty was not the *causa
causans*, the pursuer was denied any compensation. However, as
a result of the Law Reform (Contributory Negligence) Act 1945,
the court now has the power to reduce the damages awarded to
the pursuer in proportion to the pursuer's responsibility for her
own injuries.[2] Although the 1945 Act has, in so far as the pursuer's
conduct is concerned, reduced the importance of determining a
single cause or *causa causans*, the court still retains the power of
limiting a defender's delictual liability for breach of a duty of care.
It does this by deciding that the breach is not the legal cause of
the pursuer's injuries, for example because of the intervention
of a third party. Therefore, the determination of legal causation
remains important.

The decision as to whether or not a breach of duty constitutes the
causa causans of the pursuer's injuries 'must be dealt with broadly
and upon common sense principles as a jury would probably deal
with it'.[3] Two factors are important, as we shall now see.

1 The victim's suicide will not break the chain of causation if the purpose of
   the defender's duty of care was to look after the victim (*Reeves v Metropolitan
   Commissioner* [2001] 1 AC 360) or the defender's conduct caused the victim
   physical harm which led to depression which led to the victim's suicide (*Corr v
   IBC Vehicles* [2008] 1 AC 884).
2 On contributory negligence, see paras 6.12–6.13 below.
3 *Admiralty Comrs v SS Volute* [1922] AC 129, HL, at 144 per Birkenhead LC;
   Galoo Ltd (in liquidation) v Bright Grahame Murray [1995] 1 All ER 16, CA at 29

per Glidewell LJ, quoting an Australian decision: 'The answer in the end is "By the application of the court's common sense"'; *Simmons v British Steel plc* 2003 SLT 62 per the Lord Justice-Clerk (Gill) at 65: 'This is a case where the question of causation can be decided straightforwardly on a common sense view of the whole evidence.'

(1) Foreseeability

6.7   Where there has been a breach of duty by the defender, the act of a third party or the victim will not generally break the chain of causation if it was reasonably foreseeable that the subsequent act would take place. In *Sayers v Harlow Urban District Council,*[1] for example, the plaintiff entered a cubicle in a public lavatory maintained by the defendant. Owing to a fault in the lock, she could not reopen the door. She banged on the door and put her hand out of the window in unsuccessful attempts to attract attention. After 15 minutes, she tried to escape through the space between the top of the door and the roof. She put her left foot on the lavatory seat, her right foot on the toilet roll holder, one hand on the lavatory cistern and the other hand on the top of the door. When she found it impossible to squeeze through the space, she proceeded to come down but, because of her weight, the toilet roll holder rotated, she lost her balance and fell. The court held that it was reasonably foreseeable that a person in Mrs Sayers' position would try to escape and that this was not a hazardous enterprise. Accordingly, her attempted escape was not a *novus actus interveniens* and the defendant's breach of duty was the *causa causans* of the accident. However, when she found she could not escape, she was careless in putting so much weight on the toilet roll holder: although this did not break the chain of causation, it did constitute contributory negligence and her damages were reduced by 25 per cent.[2]

Even if the subsequent act of a third party or the pursuer is reasonably foreseeable, it may break the chain of causation if it was hazardous for the third party or the pursuer to act in such a way. In *McKew v Holland and Hannen and Cubitts (Scotland) Ltd,*[3] the pursuer injured his ankle as a result of the defender's breach of duty. Because of the fracture, his leg was liable to 'give way' from time to time. After the accident, the pursuer went to see a flat. The stairway leading to the fiat had no handrail. Although he knew that his leg was likely to give way at any time, after visiting the flat the pursuer went down the stairs in a normal manner ie he did not go down slowly so that he could sit on a step if his leg 'gave way'. His leg gave way and in panic the pursuer jumped down ten steps and was injured. The court held that the defender was not liable for the second injury. Although it was reasonably foreseeable that the pursuer might climb stairs which had no handrail, he had acted in a hazardous manner in walking down the stairs in the normal way without assistance. The defender's breach of duty which had caused the injury to the pursuer's ankle was not the *causa causans* of the pursuer's second injury. Instead, the pursuer's carelessness in walking down the stairs without assistance constituted hazardous conduct on the pursuer's part which broke the chain of causation between the defender's breach of duty and the pursuer's second injuries.

McKew was distinguished in *Spencer v Wincanton Holdings Ltd (Wincanton Logisitics Ltd)*.[4] Here the defendant admitted liability for the injuries the plaintiff had suffered from an accident at work which led to the amputation of his leg. Eight months after the amputation, he tripped and fell when he was filling his car at a garage without summoning help or steadying himself using his sticks or his prosthesis. As a result of this fall he was confined to a wheelchair. The Court of Appeal held that the second accident was an unexpected but real consequence of the first accident. Whether an intervening event should be treated as breaking the chain of causation was ultimately a question of fairness ie whether it was fair to relieve the defendant of liability for the subsequent event. The plaintiff's act of filling his car without any help fell far below the unreasonableness of the pursuer's behaviour in *McKew*. The defendant was therefore liable with a reduction of a third to reflect the plaintiff's contributory negligence. This case illustrates how legal causation is ultimately an evaluative judgment by the court on the extent of the defender's liability and whether or not it is fair that he should be liable for the full extent of the pursuer's injuries.[5]

In *Sabri-Tabrizi v Lothian Health Board*,[6] the pursuer became pregnant as a result of a failed sterilisation. She had a termination. Knowing that she was fertile, she had sexual intercourse with her husband on several occasions. She fell pregnant again. Although the defenders admitted liability for the first pregnancy, they denied liability for the second. The Lord Ordinary (Nimmo Smith) agreed:[7]

'The alleged negligence resulted in the pursuer's being still fertile, just as she would have been had the failed sterilisation operation never been carried out. The pursuer knew this, and consequently knew that there was a risk of her becoming pregnant if she had sexual intercourse with her husband ... She avers that she took precautions, but in so far as there remained a residual risk, in a question between her and the defenders I think that it is unreasonable of her to expose herself to that risk. Accordingly I regard her decision to have sexual intercourse in the knowledge that she was not sterile as constituting a *novus actus interveniens*, breaking the chain of causation, with the result that the defenders cannot be held liable for the second pregnancy and the consequences thereof.'

1 [1958] 2 All ER 342, [1958] 1 WLR 623, CA.
2 On contributory negligence, see paras 6.12–6.13 below.
3 1970 SC (HL) 20, 1970 SLT 68.
4 [2009] EWCA Civ 1404.
5 See also *Chubb Fire Ltd v Vicar of Spalding* [2010] EWCA Civ 981 (any liability of the defendant was broken as a result of the intervening acts of vandals).
6 1998 SC 373, 1998 SLT 607.
7 1998 SC 373, at 378.

(2) The order of events

6.8   The order of events may be important in determining whether or not the defender's breach of duty is the *causa causans* of the pursuer's injuries. In *Donaghy v National Coal Board*,[1] the defender broke the duty of care which was owed to the pursuer by leaving a detonator lying around the workplace. The pursuer took the detonator home and hit it with a hammer. As a result, he was injured. The court held that the pursuer's conduct amounted to a *novus actus interveniens*: it was unforeseeable, unreasonable, ie hazardous, and was the last act which had led to the accident. On the other hand, in *Davidson v City of Glasgow District Council*,[2] the second defender supplied the pursuer's employer, the first defender, with planks which were too short for a particular task. The employer rejected the planks but owing to the employer's alleged carelessness one of the short planks was not rejected. As a result of the plank being too short, there was an accident and the pursuer was injured. The pursuer sued the employer (first defender) and the supplier (the second defender). The second defender argued that the employer's failure to reject all the planks constituted a *novus actus interveniens*. The court held that merely because the employer's conduct was the 'last act' that led to the accident, this did not necessarily mean that it amounted to a *novus actus interveniens*:

'Even although there was in effect an intermediate inspection, and assuming in the alternative that the first defenders [the employer] failed to discover that one of the planks remained and was inadvertently used, it does not follow that that was negligence or that it broke the chain of causation and was the sole cause of the accident.'[3]

Thus, where an accident is caused to A as a result of a breach of duty by B *and* a breach of duty by C, the mere fact that B's breach of duty arose after C's breach of duty will not necessarily break the chain of causation to exonerate C from delictual liability. In *Grant v Sun Shipping Co Ltd*,[4] ship repairers working on a ship left hatches uncovered. By doing so, they were in breach of a duty of care owed to dock labourers on the ship. The ship owners also failed to ensure that the hatches were covered and did not provide an adequate system of lighting: this also constituted a breach of their duty of care to dock labourers on the ship. The pursuer, a dock labourer, fell through an unlit hatch. The House of Lords held that the shipowner's breach of duty did not constitute a *novus actus interveniens* breaking the chain of causation between the accident and the ship repairers' breach of duty of care towards the pursuer by leaving the hatches uncovered. Instead, both the ship owners and the ship repairers were jointly liable in delict.[5] Where there is joint liability, under s 3 of the Law Reform (Miscellaneous Provisions) (Scotland) Act 1940 the court has the power to apportion the damages between the defenders.[6]

1 1957 SLT (Notes) 35.
2 1993 SLT 479, OH.
3 1993 SLT 479 at 482 per Judge D B Robertson QC.
4 1948 SC (HL) 73, 1949 SLT 25.
5 See also *Davidson v City of Glasgow District Council* 1993 SLT 479, OH, above.
6 On joint liability, see para 6.14 below.

(3) Conclusion

6.9 Where A's breach of a duty of care is a *causa sine qua non* of B's injuries, the courts appear unwilling to be persuaded that a subsequent act – even if careless – constitutes a *novus actus interveniens* unless it is so unusual or unexpected that it could not have been reasonably foreseeable, or so hazardous on the part of B, that it would be unreasonable to hold A liable. If the subsequent act is that of a third party, C, and constitutes a breach of duty owed by C to B, A and C will be held jointly liable in delict to B. If the subsequent act is that of B, A remains liable, ie B's act will not break the chain of causation but instead it will lead to a reduction of damages on the grounds of contributory negligence. Although this will be the usual result, there can, of course, still be exceptional cases where the chain of causation is broken and A's breach of duty is not treated as the *causa causans* of B's injuries. So, for example, if A injured B's foot and B suffered an infection in hospital, the chain of causation would not be broken as it is reasonably foreseeable that B might get an infection in hospital. But if the surgeon in the hospital is careless and amputates B's uninjured foot, the chain of causation is broken since the surgeon's conduct is so unusual and unexpected that it is not reasonably foreseeable and therefore it constitutes a *novus actus interveniens*. This exonerates A from delictual liability in respect of the amputation, but not, of course, in respect of the original injury to B's foot.

The chain of causation is not broken by an act of a third party where the defender's duty of care was to prevent the third party from causing injury or damage to the pursuer.[1] But as a general rule, A does not owe B a duty of care to prevent B from being injured as a result of the deliberate conduct of a third party, C.[2] Here, of course, it is the absence of a duty of care which prevents A from being liable to B in delict.

1 *Dorset Yacht Co Ltd v Home Office* [1970] AC 1004, [1970] 2 All ER 294, HL; *Mitchell v Glasgow City Council* 2008 SLT 368, discussed above at para 5.9.
2 *Modbury Triangle Shopping Centre v Anzil* (2000) 205 CLR 254; *Chubb Fire Ltd v Vicar of Spalding* [2010] EWCA Civ 981. There are, of course, exceptions. See, for example, *Empress Car Co (Abertillery) Ltd v National Rivers Authority* [1998] 1 All ER 481, HL (a person causes a pollutant to enter controlled waters even if a necessary condition of the actual escape of the pollutant is the act of a third party, provided the third party's conduct is an act of normal life, eg vandalism, and not extraordinary).

C. RELATED MATTERS

(1) *Volenti non fit injuria*

6.10   The chain of causation will be broken if the pursuer has voluntarily undertaken the risk of harm created by the defender's breach of duty. This is the doctrine of *volenti non fit injuria*. Because the chain of causation is broken and the defender's breach of duty is no longer the *causa causans* of the pursuer's injuries, the doctrine of *volenti* provides the defender with a complete defence to an action in delict. The theoretical basis of *volenti* is that by knowing acceptance of the risk, the pursuer has absolved the defender of the consequences of the defender's breach of the duty of care owed to the pursuer. In other words, the defender still owes the pursuer a duty of care but the chain of causation is broken by the pursuer voluntarily undertaking the risk.[1]

Before the defender will succeed in the defence of *volenti non fit injuria* the defender must prove that before or at the same time as the negligent conduct,[2] the pursuer knowingly and willingly undertook the risk of the danger created by the defender's breach of duty. In *Titchener v British Railways Board*[3] the defender failed to maintain a fence made of sleepers which was positioned along a railway track. A 15-year-old girl climbed through the fence and went up the embankment to take a short cut across the railway line to a piece of waste ground where she intended to have a kiss and cuddle with her boyfriend. She was injured by a train when she was crossing the line. As we shall see,[4] the House of Lords held that in the circumstances the defender did not owe the pursuer a duty of care. But the House indicated that even if a duty of care had been owed and there had been a breach of duty, the defender would have had the defence of *volenti* since the pursuer knew and accepted the risk of being injured by a train when she crossed the line.

Because the pursuer must have knowledge of, and be *willing* to accept, the risk, the courts are unlikely to accept a plea of *volenti* in an action between employee and employer. Nevertheless, the defence succeeded in *ICI v Shatwell*.[5] Contrary to their employer's instructions, the plaintiff and his brother, who were experienced shotfirers, agreed to test their detonators without first returning to a safety shelter. There was an explosion; the plaintiff was injured and his brother was killed. It was held that the employer had not been in breach of a duty of care towards the plaintiff.[6] However, the plaintiff sued the employer as vicariously liable for his brother's careless act in testing the detonator.[7] The House of Lords held that since the plaintiff had agreed with his brother to run the risk of injury by testing the detonators without first returning to a place of safety, the employer could successfully plead the defence of *volenti*.

1 *Winnik v Dick* 1984 SC 48, 1984 SLT 185.
2 *Sabri-Tabrizi v Lothian Health Board* 1998 SC 373, 1998 SLT 607. A person who chooses to smoke cigarettes is not *volens* since the manufacturer is *not* negligent in manufacturing them: *McTear v Imperial Tobacco Ltd* 2005 SC 1 per the Lord Ordinary (Nimmo Smith) at paras 7.204 ff.
3 1984 SC (HL) 34, 1984 SLT 192. See also *Devlin v Strathclyde Regional Council* 1993 SLT 699, OH.
4 Para 16.11 below.
5 [1965] AC 656, [1964] 2 All ER 999.
6 Or in breach of any statutory duty.
7 On vicarious liability, see paras 12.5 ff below.

6.11 The defence of *volenti* does not apply in the case of a rescuer. By virtue of s 149 of the Road Traffic Act 1988, the defence of *volenti* does not apply to a claim by a passenger against the driver of a vehicle which has compulsory third-party insurance. And so where a passenger accepts a lift from a drunken driver and the car has compulsory third-party insurance, the driver cannot plead *volenti* if the passenger is injured as a result of the driver's breach of duty. The passenger's damages could be reduced on the ground of contributory negligence.

Where the duty of care is to *prevent* the defender from acting in a particular way, it would make nonsense of the existence of the duty if *volenti* could be used when the defender does the act the pursuer should have prevented. For example, the police owe a duty of care to prevent prisoners from harming themselves while on remand: if, in breach of their duty, a prisoner is able to injure or kill himself, the defence of *volenti* cannot be used.[1]

It is sometimes argued that the reason why a spectator at a dangerous sport, such as motor racing, cannot sue a participant who injures him by crashing into the crowd at high speed is that the spectator is *volens* of the risk of harm inherent in the sport. However, it is thought that the better way to analyse the situation is to argue that in the circumstances the participant does not owe the spectator a duty of care to avoid the possibility of such an accident. The organiser of the event may owe the spectator a duty of care, if, for example, the circuit was not suitable for racing or the safety precautions were inadequate; the spectator will not be *volens* of these risks simply by attending the event.[2] Where a participant in a dangerous sport is injured by another participant, again it is thought the reason an action in delict will not be successful is not that the pursuer was *volens*, but that the defender does not owe a duty of care to the pursuer to protect him from injuries the risk of which are inherent in the sport, for example being bruised when tackled at rugby football.[3] If the injury arises from conduct which is contrary to the rules of the game, the pursuer's remedy lies in assault rather than in a breach of a duty of care.

1 *Reeves v Metropolitan Commissioner* [2001] 1 AC 360.
2 See *Wooldridge v Sumner* [1963] 2 QB 43, [1962] 2 All ER 978, CA; *Lewis v Buckpool Golf Club* 1993 SLT (Sh Ct) 43.
3 *Cf Sharp v Highland and Islands Fire Board* 2005 SLT 855 which proceeded on the basis that players in a football match do owe each other a duty of care which will be breached if the injury was caused by an error going beyond what might reasonably be regarded as excusable. In the present writer's view where such an error occurs, the defender has been reckless and is liable for assault. However, a referee owes a duty of care to the players. When the referee has been negligent, an injured player is not *volens* merely by participating in the game: *Smoldon v Whitworth* [1997] PIQR P133, (1996) *Times*, 18 December 1996, CA.

(2) Contributory negligence

6.12   As we have seen, where the defender's breach of duty to the pursuer is a *causa sine qua non* of the pursuer's injuries, the courts are reluctant to accept that the pursuer's subsequent conduct is a *novus actus interveniens* or amounts to *volenti* so that the defender is exonerated from delictual liability. This is particularly the case where the pursuer has acted in the 'agony of the moment' ie reacts carelessly in a situation caused by the defender's breach of duty, for example jumps out of a window to escape a fire caused by the defender's negligence. Instead, the court will hold that the pursuer's conduct was a contributory cause of the injury. The effect of a finding of contributory negligence is to reduce the damages which would otherwise have been awarded to the pursuer, to reflect the pursuer's responsibility for the damage or injury sustained. Section 1(1) of the Law Reform (Contributory Negligence) Act 1945 provides:

'Where any person suffers *damage as the result partly of his own fault* and *partly due to the fault of any other person or persons*, a claim in respect of that damage shall not be defeated by reason of the fault of the person suffering the damage, but the *damages recoverable* in respect thereof *shall be reduced* to such an extent as the *court thinks just and equitable* having regard to the *claimant's share in the responsibility* for the damage.' [Emphasis added]

Before the 1945 Act applies, the pursuer must have suffered damage partly as a result of his own *fault*.[1] Fault covers the pursuer's deliberate as well as negligent actions.[2] In relation to the latter, the pursuer's act must fall below the standard of the reasonable person in the pursuer's position. In *McGowan v W&JR Watson Ltd*[3] it was observed that a momentary lapse caused by human fallibility would not fall below that standard when the pursuer had been injured as a consequence of a breach by his employer of an absolute statutory duty. The onus rests on the defender to prove that the pursuer was at fault. Although, for example, a passenger injured in a motor accident will usually be at fault if he or she fails to wear a seat belt, in *Mackay v Borthwick*[4] the pursuer was held not to be contributorily negligent for failing to wear a seat belt since it was uncomfortable for her to wear it because she was suffering from a hiatus hernia. In *Pace v Culley*[5] the pursuer, who was a taxi driver, failed to wear a seat belt because he had been advised by the police not to do so in the event that he might be attacked by his passengers. Although he accepted that failure to wear a seat belt could amount to contributory negligence, the Lord Ordinary (Weir) thought that the driver's conduct in this case was a misjudgment rather than a failure to take care for his own safety.[6] In *Blackhall v MacInnes*,[7] the pursuer was injured while she was changing the offside wheel of her motor car. She was held to be 20 per cent contributorily negligent because – contrary to the Highway Code – she had made no attempt to get the vehicle off the road although it was practicable to drive on the verge.

The defender must also prove that the pursuer's fault contributed to the harm sustained, ie 'but for' the pursuer's fault, the injuries or damage suffered would not have been as bad as actually occurred. In other words, the defender must establish that the pursuer's fault was a factual cause, a *causa sine qua non*, of the harm sustained. Thus contributory negligence was established when the defender proved, on the balance of probabilities, that the pursuer would have suffered less severe neck injuries if she had worn a seat belt.[8]

1 'Fault' is defined in s 5(a) of the Law Reform (Contributory Negligence) Act 1945 as: 'wrongful act, breach of statutory duty or negligent act or omission which gives rise to liability in damages … '.
2 *Reeves v Metropolitan Commissioner* [2000] 1 AC 360 (prisoner killed himself: family's damages reduced by 50 per cent as a result of his suicide); *Corr v IBC Vehicles Ltd* [2008] 1 AC 884 (employee killed himself as a consequence of a mental disorder caused by a physical injury for which his employer was responsible: inappropriate to reduce for contributory negligence in absence of satisfactory material upon which to make a reduction).
3 2007 SLT 169.
4 1982 SLT 265, OH.
5 1992 SLT 1073, OH.
6 The contributory negligence, if any, would have been *de minimis* in respect of the total claim and could therefore be ignored.
7 1997 SLT 649, OH.
8 *Hanlon v Cuthbertson* 1981 SLT (Notes) 57, OH. Cf *Neil v Docherty and Akram* (23 May 1996, unreported), HC, where the plaintiff's injuries were sustained on initial impact, ie before she was ejected from the taxi because she was not wearing a seat belt.

6.13   But before a reduction can be made it must be established that the pursuer's conduct was a potent cause of the harm he has suffered. In *St George v The Home Office*[1] the complainant was a prisoner. He was a drug addict and an alcoholic. In his cell, he was put in a top bunk. He suffered a withdrawal seizure and fell out of the bunk and sustained head injuries. While accepting that he might have been at fault in becoming addicted to drugs and alcohol, the Court of Appeal held that his addiction had no causal potency in relation to the defendant's negligent conduct which had led to his head injuries *viz* being put in a top bunk. In the same way, a patient who has suffered harm as a consequence of medical negligence is not contributorily negligent merely because her lifestyle choices, for example smoking or drinking, have led her to seek medical treatment. There is, of course, causal potency where the claimant's drug or alcohol induced state is closely connected in time and place to, or is mixed up with, the negligent conduct of the defender. This would arise where, for example, the pursuer was drunk as he was walking along a road when he was knocked down by the defender and the accident was attributable to a combination of their negligence.

When contributory negligence is established, the proportion to be deducted from the damages is a matter for the discretion of the judge, ie what the judge considers just and equitable having regard to the pursuer's share in the responsibility for the damage. In *St George v The Home Office*[2] the Court of Appeal held that even if the prisoner's addiction had amounted to contributory negligence, in the circumstances it would not have been just and equitable to make any deduction. But in most cases if the pursuer is found contributorily negligent, some deduction will be made.

This can vary from as little as 5 per cent in 'agony of the moment' cases to as much as 80 per cent.[3] It is submitted that 100 per cent deduction is not possible under the Law Reform (Contributory Negligence) Act 1945 since in those circumstances the pursuer would be solely responsible and not 'share in the responsibility for the damage'.[4] A drunken pedestrian run down by a careless driver has had his damages reduced by 50 per cent as a result of contributory negligence.[5] Similarly, a guest injured at a party has had his damages reduced by 50 per cent because he had been drinking heavily.[6]

Damages for pure economic loss can be reduced on the grounds of the pursuer's contributory negligence.[7] However, in a case of fraudulent – as opposed to negligent – misrepresentation, the defender cannot seek to have the pursuer's damages reduced on the ground of the pursuer's contributory negligence.[8]

As a matter of public policy, if the pursuer is participating in a criminal activity at the time he is injured, he may be barred from obtaining reparation: for example if A and B steal a car and A is injured as a result of B's careless driving or a thief is shot by the owner of a house in the course of a burglary.[9] These are examples of the principle that a cause of action does not arise from a wrong committed by the pursuer: *ex turpi causa non oritur actio*. In *Gray v Thames Trains Ltd*[10] the plaintiff suffered post traumatic stress disorder after being injured in a train crash caused by the defendant's negligence. As a result of his psychological problems, he killed a man. He was convicted of manslaughter on the grounds of diminished responsibility and detained in a mental hospital. The House of Lords held that the plaintiff could not obtain compensation for loss of earnings for the time he was compulsorily detained as that loss had arisen from the plaintiff's criminal act, ie the manslaughter.[11] Where the injuries have not been caused by the pursuer's criminal acts the defence will fail,[12] unless the pursuer and defender were engaged in joint criminal activity.[13]

However, as the doctrine is a matter of public policy, the bar is not automatic and depends on the circumstances. In *Weir v Wyper*[14] the pursuer was not barred when she was injured in a car crash even though she knew that the driver had only a provisional licence. When the action is not barred, the pursuer's damages could, of course, be reduced on the ground of contributory negligence.[15]

1 [2008] EWCA Civ 1068.
2 [2008] EWCA Civ 1068.
3 *Uddin v Associated Portland Cement Manufacturers Ltd* [1965] 2 QB 582, [1965] 2 All ER 213, CA.
4 If the pursuer is solely responsible, the defender will escape liability because either his breach of duty is not the *causa causans* or the pursuer is *volens*: see *ICI v Shatwell* [1965] AC 656. Cf *McEwan v Lothian Buses* 2006 SCLR 592 where the Lord Ordinary (Emslie) considered at para 32 that there was no logical reason why there could not be 100 per cent contributory negligence if the degree of fault on the part of the defender was regarded as too small to warrant an apportionment.
5 *Malcolm v Fair* 1993 SLT 342, OH. See also *Kemp v Secretary of State for Scotland* 2000 SLT 471 (pursuer's damages reduced by one-third because he was drunk at the time of the accident). In *Gilfillan v Barbour* 2003 SC 1127 in cross actions arising from a collision, both parties had their damages reduced by 50 per cent as both had been careless. See also *Robb v Salamis (M and I) Ltd* 2007 SLT 158 (pursuer held to be 50 per cent contributorily negligent when he was injured when descending from a top bunk due to an unsuitable ladder: he knew that the ladders were often removed and not properly replaced: *sed quaere?*); *Wallace v Glasgow City Council* [2011] CSIH 57 (pursuer sustained foot injuries when opening a window in the staff toilet: damages reduced by 50 per cent as it was a deliberate act which she knew was dangerous); *Cowan v Hopetoun House Preservation Trust* [2013] CSOH 9 (pursuer who was attending a guided 'bat walk' at night at a stately home fell over a ha-ha on taking a short cut back to the car park: contributory negligence assessed as 75 per cent).
6 *Brannan v Airtours* Times, 1 February 1999, CA. Although there is no duty to prevent an adult from becoming drunk, there may be a duty to look after the drunk person if she becomes incapable of looking after herself. When there is such a duty and it is broken, the plaintiff's damages can be reduced on the grounds that she got inebriated: *Barrett v Ministry of Defence* [1995] 3 All ER 87, CA (two-thirds contributorily negligent).
7 *Platform Home Loans Ltd v Oyston Shipways Ltd* [1999] 1 All ER 833, HL. For further discussion, see beyond para 16.9.

8 *Standard Chartered Bank v Pakistan National Shipping Corpn* [2003] 1 All ER 173, HL.

9 *Duncan v Ross Harper & Murphy* 1993 SLT 105n, OH.

10 [2009] UKHL 33.

11 See also *Stone & Rolls Ltd v Moore Stevens* [2009] UKHL 39 (where a 'one man-company' deliberately engaged in serious fraud, the *ex turpi causa* principle prevented the company suing its auditors in failing to detect the fraud).

12 *McLaughlin v Morrison* [2013] CSOH 163.

13 *Andersen v Hameed* [2010] CSOH 99 (a passenger in a car involved in an accident who had allowed himself to be driven while knowing the car had been taken without the owner's consent was participating in a joint criminal activity and was therefore not entitled to recover damages from the driver).

14 1992 SCLR 483, 1992 SLT 579, OH.

15 *Taylor v Leslie* 1998 SLT 1248, 1998 Rep LR 110, OH (defender drove car while unlicensed, uninsured and underage. Passenger killed. Conduct not regarded as reprehensible by the community of Shapinsay, a remote island. The deceased had encouraged the defender to speed. Damages reduced by 50 per cent).

(3) Joint fault

6.14 Joint fault arises where harm is caused to the pursuer as a result of the conduct of more than one defender. This is known as joint liability if the harm has been caused as a result of a breach by each defender of a duty of care owed to the pursuer; in the case of other delicts, it is known as joint wrongdoing. Before there can be joint liability, each breach of duty must have materially contributed to, or materially increased the risk of, the *same* delict to the pursuer. In *Anderson v St Andrew's Ambulance Association*[1] a passenger in a bus was injured in a collision between the bus and an ambulance. The bus driver had failed to observe a 'slow' sign; the ambulance driver had failed to observe a 'halt' sign. The court held that this was a case of joint liability, for both drivers were responsible for the same wrong suffered by the pursuer. Conversely, in *Fleming v McGillivray*[2] the court held that it was not a case of joint liability where an injured pursuer sued a van driver for careless driving and the owner of the van for failing to have compulsory third-party insurance: the driver was being sued for breach of his duty of care (delict 1), while the owner was being sued for breach of statutory duty in not having insurance (delict 2). Since they were not responsible for the same delict, this was not a case of joint liability or joint wrongdoing.

If A and B are jointly liable, the pursuer may sue A or B or both. If the pursuer sues only A and obtains a decree, if A pays the damages the pursuer cannot then sue B; but if A does not pay the damages, the pursuer can sue B. If the pursuer successfully sues both A and B, he will be awarded a joint and several decree. This entitles the pursuer to obtain *all* the damages from either A or B. In *Barker v Corus*[3] the House of Lords held[4] that where the defendants' liability had only been established by relying on the *Fairchild* exception to 'but for' causation,[5] liability was not joint and several but should be apportioned between the defendants. This would mean that the complainant might not obtain all his damages if one or more of the defendants were insolvent and uninsured. *Barker* has now been reversed by retrospective legislation[6] but only in respect of cases, such as *Barker* itself, involving mesothelioma. The extent to which *Barker* will be followed in non-mesothelioma cases remains to be seen but it will only apply if resort has had to be made to the *Fairchild* exception. In *Stoddard v Wright*,[7] however, the Lord Ordinary (Uist) chose to follow the orthodox reasoning of Lord Rodger in *Barker* rejecting apportionment.

Where there is joint and several liability and A has paid all the damages, the court can apportion the damages between A and B; and if B was not sued in the original action, A can, nevertheless, recover from B the proportion of the damages which the court deems attributable to B's conduct.[8] Where the pursuer is contributorily negligent, the total damages to be paid by A or B will be reduced to reflect the pursuer's responsibility for the injury or harm suffered.

1 1943 SC 248, 1943 SLT 258.
2 1946 SC 1, 1945 SLT 301.
3 [2006] 2 AC 572.
4 Lord Rodger dissenting.
5 Discussed above at para 6.5.
6 Compensation Act 2006, s 3.
7 [2007] CSOH 138.
8 Law Reform (Miscellaneous Provisions) (Scotland) Act 1940, s 3. The proportions *inter se* the defenders are what the court, or jury, considers just in the circumstances: see, for example, *BOC v Groves* 1993 SLT 360, OH (75 per cent and 25 per cent); *Phee v Gordon* 2013 SLT 439. (Pursuer was injured by a stray golf ball. The golfer who hit the shot was 20 per cent liable and the golf club 80 per cent liable in view of the hazardous layout of the course.)

Part III

DELICTUAL LIABILITY IN SPECIFIC SOCIAL AND ECONOMIC CONTEXTS

INTRODUCTION

Having discussed the general principles of delictual liability, it is now proposed to examine the law of delict as it operates in certain specific social and economic contexts. As we shall see, the general principle of delictual liability for harm caused to the pursuer as a result of the defender's *culpa* is often supplemented by other common law principles, for example, nuisance and vicarious liability. More importantly, perhaps, in certain areas common law delictual liability has been supplemented or supplanted by statutory liability. It is thought that these developments are better understood if discussed in the context of the particular social and economic relationships in which they occur.

CHAPTER 7

Professional liability

7.1 The general principles of the law of delict apply where a person causes harm to another in the course of his trade, business or profession.[1] Often of course, the person harmed will be a client or a customer of the defender; if this is so, the pursuer's primary remedy will be to sue the defender in contract. Almost inevitably, the defender will have assumed responsibility for the interests of the client or customer and the customer or client will have relied on the defender's expertise. Accordingly, unless the terms of their contract expressly negative delictual liability, the defender will also owe the pursuer a *Henderson v Merrett*[2] duty of care to prevent economic loss arising from the defender's negligence. Put another way, where the client and professional are directly linked by contract, concurrent liability in contract and delict can arise. If there is no direct contractual relationship between the parties, liability can lie only in delict.

Where the pursuer suffers physical harm or damage to his property, the defender will be liable in delict if the damage or harm was caused intentionally or as a result of a breach of a duty of care owed by the defender to the pursuer. The existence of such a duty of care will be determined by the *Donoghue v Stevenson* neighbourhood principle.[3] Where the pursuer has suffered pure economic loss, liability will lie in delict if the defender intended to harm the pursuer or if a *Henderson v Merrett* duty of care exists. A duty of care could also arise if the *Caparo* tripartite test is satisfied.[4]

In determining whether or not there has been a breach of a duty of care, the defender's conduct is judged by the standard of care expected in his or her profession. Put another way, in order to establish that the defender was negligent the pursuer must prove that the defender's conduct fell below that of the reasonable accountant, architect, lawyer, medical practitioner or surveyor etc. While ultimately a question of law,[5] the usual practice of persons in the same trade, business or profession as the defender will be a significant factor in determining whether or not the defender was negligent.

1 On professional negligence, see Kenneth Norrie, SULI *Delict* Chapter 19.
2 See *Henderson v Merrett Syndicates Ltd* [1995] 2 AC 145, [1994] 3 All ER 506, HL, discussed at paras 4.16 ff above.
3 See *Donoghue v Stevenson* 1932 SC (HL) 31, 1932 SLT 317.
4 *Caparo Industries plc v Dickman* [1990] 2 AC 605, [1990] 1 All ER 568, HL. See, for example, *Weir v National Westminster Bank plc* 1993 SC 515, 1994 SLT 1251; *Matthews v Hunter & Robertson* [2007] CSOH 88.
5 *Bolitho v City and Hackney Health Authority* [1998] AC 232, [1997] 4 All ER 771, HL.

7.2   It can be particularly difficult to establish negligence where the defender's conduct involves an exercise of professional judgment. Often there will be several courses of action open to the defender. In these circumstances, the defender will *not* be negligent if she adopted a course of action which resulted in harm to the pursuer unless no reasonable professional person in her position would have chosen that option. Nor does it matter that the course of action chosen was *not* the normal practice in the profession. In the leading case of *Hunter v Hanley*[1] the pursuer alleged that the defender, a doctor, was negligent in using a needle which was unsuitable for treating the patient. In discussing the standard of care appropriate to a doctor, the Lord President (Clyde) observed:[2]

'... in regard to deviation from ordinary professional practice ... such deviation is not necessarily evidence of negligence. Indeed it would be disastrous if this were so, for all inducement to progress in medical science would then be destroyed. Even a substantial deviation from normal practice may be warranted by the particular circumstances. To establish liability by a doctor where deviation from normal practice is alleged, three facts require to be established. First of all it must be proved that there is a normal practice; secondly it must be proved that the defender has not adopted that practice; and thirdly (and this is of crucial importance) it must be established that the course which the doctor adopted is one which no professional man of ordinary skill would have taken if he had been acting with ordinary care.'

Thus it is not enough that the defender's conduct deviated from normal practice: it must be demonstrated that no professional man of ordinary skill would have followed the course taken by the defender. However, a pursuer will not fail merely because she cannot establish that there was a normal practice which the defender did not follow: the crucial issue is the third *viz* that the course that the defender followed was one no professional man of ordinary skill would have taken if acting with ordinary care.[3] Even if the pursuer can establish that a responsible body of medical opinion regards the defender's decision or conduct as wrong, the defender will not be regarded as having been negligent if there is also a responsible body of medical opinion which regards the defender's decision or conduct as reasonable in the circumstances.[4] This test applies not only to medical treatment[5] but also to diagnosis[6] and advice.[7]

1 1955 SC 200, 1955 SLT 213.
2 1955 SC 200 at 206. Lord Clyde's approach was approved by McNair J in the leading English case, *Bolam v Friern Hospital Management Committee* [1957] 2 All ER 118, [1957] 1 WLR 582.
3 *Gerrard v Royal Infirmary of Edinburgh NHS Trust* 2005 SC 192. In *Atwal Enterprises Ltd v Toner t/a Donal Toner Associates* 2006 SLT 537, the Lord Ordinary (Emslie) observed at 547 that it was well settled that liability for professional negligence could only arise where, on the evidence, no ordinarily competent and careful member of the profession could have been guilty of the particular failure alleged against the defender. This case concerned an architect.
4 *Maynard v West Midlands Regional Health Authority* [1985] 1 All ER 635, [1984] 1 WLR 634, HL. The number of specialist doctors who accept the defender's practices need not be substantial provided they are responsible: *Defreitas v O'Brien* [1995] 6 Med LR 108. If there is no recognised standard practice, the court must determine whether or not the defender took reasonable care in all the circumstances: *AB v Tameside and Glossop Health Authority* [1997] 8 Med LR 91, CA (defendant sent a secret letter to patients informing them that a health worker who had treated them was HIV positive: defendant not negligent simply because they sent a standard letter rather than organising face-to-face disclosure of the tiny risk of infection).
5 *Whitehouse v Jordan* [1981] 1 All ER 267, [1981] 1 WLR 246, HL.
6 *Maynard v West Midlands Regional Health Authority* [1985] 1 All ER 635, [1984] 1 WLR 634, HL.
7 *Gold v Haringey Health Authority* [1987] QB 481, [1987] 2 All ER 888, CA. The same criteria apply to the duty to inform a patient of risks inherent in a medical procedure even if it is carried out properly: *Sidaway v Bethlem Royal Hospital Board of Governors* [1985] AC 871, [1985] 1 All ER 643, HL.

7.3 *Gordon v Wilson*[1] provides an illustration of the formidable difficulties facing a pursuer in an action of medical negligence. In that case, the pursuer argued that a doctor was negligent in delaying to refer a patient to a specialist.[2] Although the pursuer established that there was a responsible body of medical opinion which took the view that a reasonable doctor would have referred the patient to a specialist at an earlier stage, the court held that the defender was not negligent because the defender could show that there was also a responsible body of medical opinion to the effect that a reasonable doctor would not have referred the patient to a specialist until the defender had done so. Accordingly, the pursuer's action failed. Professional negligence cannot be established by preferring one body of professional opinion to another; instead the pursuer must prove that no reasonable doctor exercising his ordinary clinical skills would have taken the defender's course of action in the circumstances of the particular case.[3]

The law was summarised by Lord Hodge in *Honisz v Lothian Health Board*:[4]

'First, as a general rule, where there are two opposing schools of thought among the relevant group of responsible medical practitioners as to the appropriateness of a particular practice, it is not the function of the court to prefer one school over the other ... Secondly, however, the court does not defer to the opinion of the relevant professionals to the extent that, if a defender lead evidence that other responsible professionals among the relevant group of medical practitioners would have done what the impugned medical practitioner did, the judge must in all cases conclude that there has been no negligence. This is because, thirdly, in exceptional cases the court may conclude that a practice which responsible medical practitioners have perpetuated does not stand up to rational analysis ... Where the judge is satisfied that the body of professional opinion, on which the defender relies, is not reasonable or responsible he may find the medical practitioner guilty of negligence, despite that body of opinion sanctioning his conduct. This will rarely occur as the assessment and balancing of risks and benefits are matters of clinical judgment. Thus it will normally require compelling expert evidence to demonstrate that an opinion of another medical expert is one which that other expert could not have held if he had taken care to examine the basis of the practice. Where experts have applied their minds to the comparative risks and benefits of a course of action and have reached a defensible conclusion, the court will have no basis for rejecting their view and concluding that the pursuer has proved negligence in terms of the *Hunter v Hanley* test. As Lord Browne-Wilkinson said in *Bolitho* (at p 243D–E) "it is only where the judge can be satisfied that the body of expert opinion cannot logically be supported at all that such opinion will not provide the benchmark by which the defendant's conduct falls to be assessed".'

These cases were concerned with the medical profession. But as indicated above, the test for establishing the requisite standard of care is applicable in relation to other professions where an exercise of professional judgment is involved.[5]

1 1992 SLT 849 n, See also, for example, *Hannigan v Lanarkshire Acute Hospitals NHS Trust* [2012] CSOH 152; *M's Guardian v Lanarkshire Health Board* [2013] CSIH 3.

2 It should also be remembered that in order to establish causation the pursuer must prove that 'but for' the doctor's omission the treatment would have had more than a 50 per cent chance of success: *Kenyon v Bell* 1953 SC 125; *Hotson v East Berkshire Area Health Authority* [1987] AC 750; *Gregg v Scott* [2005] 2 AC 176.

3 In *Bolitho v City and Hackney Health Authority* [1998] AC 232 it was stressed by the House of Lords that the body of medical opinion must be reasonable and responsible. In other words, there must be a logical basis for the opinion the experts support. Although this is ultimately a question of law, it would only be in rare cases that the court would reject the medical experts' views as unreasonable.

4 [2006] CSOH 24 at para 39. Lord Hodge's summary has been approved in many subsequent cases.

5 See, for example, *Campbell v Borders Health Board* [2012] CSIH 49; *Coyle v Lanarkshire Health Board* [2013] CSOH 167 (midwives); *Henderson v Merrett Syndicates Ltd (No 2)* [1997] LRLR 265, QBD (Comm Ct) (underwriting agents); *Sneesby v Goldings* [1995] 2 EGLR 102, CA (surveyors); *Scott v Lothian Regional Council* 1999 Rep LR 15 (guidance teachers); *Leeds & Holbeck Building Society v Alex Morison & Co (No 2)* 2001 SCLR 41; *McCrindle v Maclay, Murray & Spens* [2013] CSOH 72 (lawyers); *Gilfillan v Barbour* 2003 SLT 1127 (police); *Atwal Enterprise Ltd v Toner t/a Donal Toner Associates* 2006 SLT 537 (architects); *WTL International Ltd Retirement Benefits Scheme Trustees v Edwards* [2010] CSOH 34 (actuaries).

7.4 The position of the legal professions requires further treatment. Where a solicitor takes instructions from her client, liability can arise in contract and delict. The contract may stipulate a higher standard of care than that required by the law of negligence, ie strict liability rather than a failure to take reasonable care.[1] As a general rule, the solicitor owes a duty of care to her client: she does not owe a duty of care to a third party, for example a person who would benefit from an *inter vivos* transaction.[2] However, where a solicitor gives advice or information to a person who is not a client, ie who does not have a contractual relationship with the solicitor, the solicitor may be liable in delict provided the *Henderson v Merrett* (or Caparo tripartite) criteria for a duty of care exist.[3] In other words, there must be voluntary assumption of responsibility by the solicitor and concomitant reliance on the third party's part or it must be fair, just and reasonable to impose the duty .Where such a duty exists, the pursuer will only succeed if it can be established that the solicitor was negligent in giving the advice, ie that a reasonable solicitor would not have given that advice in the circumstances.[4]

1 *Mortgage Corporation Ltd v Mitchells Roberton* 1997 SLT 1305, OH.
2 *Tait v Brown & McRae* 1997 SLT (Sh Ct) 63.
3 *Newcastle Building Society v Paterson Robertson and Graham* 2001 SC 734 (pursuer lent money to borrower. It was a condition of the loan that the defenders, the borrower's solicitors, confirm certain matters in a report. The report was inaccurate. Held that the defenders owed a duty of care to the pursuer since the loan would not have gone ahead if the report had been accurate). A proof before answer will usually be necessary *Northern Rock (Asset Management) Plc v Steel* [2014] CSOH 40.
4 When the client is an experienced businessman and a transaction does not involve any hidden legal pitfalls, a solicitor is not obliged to investigate matters outwith his instructions or warn the client of the commercial risks in the transaction: *Pickergill v Riley* (2004), *Times* 2 March 2004. See also *Keith v Chalmers* 2004 SC 287.

7.5 What of the situation where a solicitor acts on the instructions of a client but as a result of the solicitor's carelessness does not give effect to the client's instructions with the result that a third party suffers loss? Normally, no duty of care is owed to the third party.[1] An important exception exists, however, when the third party is a 'disappointed legatee'. Consider the following problem.

A instructs a solicitor to draw up a will under which B is the principal beneficiary. As a result of the solicitor's carelessness the will is invalid and B does not obtain the legacy. There is no contractual relationship between B and the solicitor. Therefore B's remedy, if any, lies in delict against the solicitor. B has suffered pure economic loss and before there is delictual liability the solicitor must owe B a duty of care to prevent B suffering such loss. Unlike the advice and information situations, B has not relied on the solicitor's expertise: B will probably *not* know the solicitor's identity. Even if the solicitor can be said to have assumed responsibility for B's interests, the *Henderson v Merrett* duty of care will not normally arise because of the absence of concomitant reliance on B's part. We have therefore a situation where the courts must be prepared on policy grounds to impose a duty of care before the solicitor can be liable in delict.[2]

For many years, the Scottish courts refused to recognise such a duty of care.[3] However, in England the issue was fully explored by the House of Lords in *White v Jones*.[4] After a family quarrel, a father struck his daughters out of his will. Later he relented. In spite of the family's attempts to encourage their father's solicitor to fulfil the old man's instructions, the father died before the will was altered in favour of the daughters. By a majority,[5] the House of Lords held that the solicitor owed a duty of care to the disappointed legatees. For Lord Goff and Lord Browne-Wilkinson it was enough that the solicitor had assumed responsibility for the potential beneficiaries: this was implicit when accepting their father's instructions. Concomitant reliance was not necessary to impose a duty of care in the case of disappointed legatees. Lord Nolan found actual reliance since the defender had acted as a solicitor for the family, not merely the father. Lord Mustill dissented owing to the absence of concomitant reliance which he felt was constitutive of a *Henderson v Merrett* duty of care.

1 There are very rare cases where a duty can arise because of exceptional degrees of proximity between the parties and the solicitor has assumed responsibility for the third party: *Mortgage Corporation Ltd v Mitchells Roberton* 1997 SLT 1305, OH.
2 Ie the duty of care is being used as a threshold device: see Chapter 4 above.
3 *Robertson v Fleming* (1861) 23 D (HL) 8, (1861) 4 Macq 167 per Lord Campbell LC at 177; *Weir v J M Hodge & Son* 1990 SLT 266 per the Lord Ordinary (Weir) at 270; *MacDougall v MacDougall's Executors* 1994 SLT 1178.
4 [1995] 2 AC 207, [1995] 1 All ER 691, HL.
5 Lord Goff of Chieveley, Lord Browne-Wilkinson and Lord Nolan; Lords Mustill and Keith of Kinkel dissented.

7.6 It is quite clear that the majority in *White v Jones* felt that a negligent solicitor *should* be liable in this situation. But, although we may be sympathetic to the policy, the reasoning is less than happy. In particular, the absence of the need for reliance makes it impossible to fit *White v Jones* within the *Henderson v Merrett* general duty of care to prevent economic loss. In spite of its difficulties, *White v Jones* has been transplanted into Scots law.[1] Given that the potential pursuer falls into a restricted class, ie the 'legatee' named in the instructions and therefore known to the solicitor, it is thought that a duty of care can be justified in these circumstances.[2] For this reason, Scottish courts have not been prepared to extend *White v Jones* beyond disappointed legatees.[3] In *Fraser v McArthur Stewart*[4] a solicitor advised his client that he could not divide the tenancy of a croft. Acting on that advice, the client nominated an individual as the tenant of the croft. After the client died, it was discovered that the advice was wrong and that the testator could have left the tenancy of the croft to be divided between his residuary legatees. The residuary legatees sued the solicitor in delict. The Lord Ordinary (Brailsford) held that while the solicitor had owed a duty of care to his client, he did not owe a duty of care to the residuary legatees. *White v Jones* should only apply where owing to the negligence of the solicitor the will did not represent the last stated intentions of the testator and the potential beneficiary was left disappointed. In *Matthews v Hunter & Robertson*[5] owing to the negligence of his solicitor, a man failed to evacuate a survivorship destination in favour of his former wife. As a result, when he died his estate was diminished by the value of the property which passed to his wife by virtue of the destination. The Lord Ordinary (Brodie) held that the deceased's executor could not recover damages in respect of the wrong advice given to the deceased because he did not sustain any loss while he was alive and there was therefore no actionable delictual claim which could transmit to the executor. Lord Brodie also considered that it would not be fair, just or reasonable to impose a duty of care on the solicitor vis-à-vis the executor, to take reasonable care to ensure that the estate was not diminished after the death of his client as a result of inaccurate advice that might have been given years before the executor had been nominated let alone confirmed. In *McLeod v Crawford*,[6] a solicitor advised a client to accept a full and final settlement rather than provisional damages. After the client died, his widow and children raised an action against the solicitor for professional negligence in respect of the advice he had given to the deceased. Lord Woolman held that the solicitor did not owe a duty of care to the widow or children. At the time the advice was given, there could have been a conflict of interests between the deceased and his family on the settlement he should choose. The solicitors had never assumed responsibility for the interests of the widow or the family. The necessary proximity was therefore absent and accordingly no duty of care arose. If there had been negligence the deceased's executor would have a remedy as the estate could sue.

1   *Robertson v Watt & Co* (4 July 1995, unreported), a decision of the Second Division; *Holmes v Bank of Scotland* 2002 SLT 544; *McLeod v Crawford* [2010] CSOH 101.
2   A better solution, perhaps, would be to allow the court to rectify the will so that it would correspond to the testator's final intentions, evidence of which would have to be very convincing!
3   *McLeod v Crawford* [2010] CSOH 101. In *McDonald v Sutherland* [2008] CSOH 150, the Lord Ordinary (Matthews) took the view (*obiter*) that *White v Jones* could apply to a disappointed liferenter if the liferent which he had purported to set up failed because of the solicitor's negligence.
4   2009 SLT 31.
5   [2007] CSOH 88.
6   [2010] CSOH 101.

7.7   Where there has been a breach of a duty of care by a solicitor, there may be difficulties in quantifying the pursuer's loss. In *Kyle v P & J Stormonth Darling WS*[1] the defender failed to lodge the pursuer's appeal in time, with the result that the pursuer lost the opportunity to do so. In rejecting the defender's argument that the pursuer was entitled to damages only if it could be established on the balance of probabilities that the appeal would have been successful, the Lord Ordinary (Prosser) said:[2]

'where there has been deprivation of a legal right, that will in itself constitute a completed wrong, and one will be entitled, as a matter of valuation, to take into consideration all reasonable prospects of success, if they exceed nuisance value, even if they fall short of probability.'

In *Arthur J S Hall & Co v Simons*,[3] the House of Lords held that under English law barristers no longer have immunity from being sued for professional negligence in their conduct of civil or criminal cases. In his dissenting speech on the latter point, Lord Hope, a Scottish Lord of Appeal in Ordinary, considered that there should still be immunity in respect of the conduct of criminal proceedings. In *Wright v Paton Farrell*[4] the First Division held that advocates and solicitors continued to have immunity under Scots law in respect of the conduct of criminal cases. The position in relation to the conduct of civil proceedings remains unclear.[5] It has always been accepted that an advocate can be liable for giving negligent advice, for example an opinion on a point of law.[6]

1 1993 SC 57, 1994 SLT 191, affirming 1992 SLT 264, OH; *McCrindle Group Ltd v Maclay Murray & Spens*.[2013] CSOH 72.
2 1992 SLT 264 at 268.
3 [2002] 1 AC 615.
4 2006 SLT 269.
5 The difficulty is that the House of Lords in *Hall* did not overrule *Rondel v Worsley* [1969] 1 AC 191 which had given barristers immunity in respect of both civil and criminal proceedings. *Rondel* has been followed in Scotland. *Hall* is technically not binding on the Scottish courts.
6 *Saif Ali v Sydney Mitchell & Co* [1980] AC 198. In *Jones v Kaney* [2011] UKSC 13, the Supreme Court held that there was no longer any justification for continuing to hold expert witnesses immune from being sued for professional negligence in relation to evidence they gave in court or for the views they expressed in anticipation of court proceedings.

CHAPTER 8

Product liability

A. INTRODUCTION

8.1 The basis of product liability in Scots law[1] was, of course, laid down in *Donoghue v Stevenson*.[2] There it was held that the manufacturer of a product owes a duty of care to the ultimate consumer when a product is manufactured which is intended to reach the ultimate consumer in the form in which it left the manufacturer without the possibility of intermediate examination. If the product was manufactured carelessly with the result that the ultimate consumer suffered injury or harm to his property, the manufacturer is liable in delict. However, the onus lies on the pursuer to prove that there was a breach of duty by the manufacturer, ie that the manufacturer was negligent.[3] If negligence cannot be established, the action fails.

Apart from the difficulty of establishing negligence, other factors could operate to prevent the pursuer from succeeding. Where, for example, a manufacturer has provided an adequate warning that a product is potentially dangerous and this is ignored by the ultimate consumer, then there will be no liability because the pursuer's failure to heed the warning will constitute a *novus actus interveniens* which breaks the chain of causation.[4] Indeed, if it is well known that a product is dangerous, like alcohol or tobacco, if an adult of full age and capacity makes an informed decision to use it, there is no breach of the manufacturer's duty of care in merely making the product.[5] Where the product is a complex structure made up of components manufactured by various persons, an action may fail if the pursuer is unable to identify the person who was responsible for the defect in the product. For example, in *Evans v Triplex Safety Glass Co Ltd*,[6] the plaintiff was injured when the windscreen of his motor car disintegrated. The manufacturer of the car fitted a windscreen made by the defendant. Evans failed to establish whether the accident was the result of the windscreen being fitted carelessly by the manufacturer of the car or whether it was due to a defect in the windscreen caused by the negligence of the defendant. In these circumstances, his action was dismissed. Finally, there is no liability under *Donoghue v Stevenson* if the only loss suffered by the pursuer arises from the fact that the product itself is defective, ie the cost of repair or the difference in value between a defective and a non-defective product. This is pure economic loss and is prima facie not recoverable in delict.[7]

1 On product liability and consumer protection, see Francis McManus, SULI *Delict* Chapter 16.
2 1932 SC (HL) 31, 1932 SLT 317. Discussed at paras 3.2 ff above.
3 If it is established that a product has failed because of a specified defect in the manufacturing process, it is open to a judge to hold that on the balance of probabilities this was due to the manufacturer's negligence: *Carroll v Fearon* [1998] PIQR P416, CA.
4 *Kubach v Hollands* [1937] 3 All ER 907, KB. On causation generally, see Chapter 6 above.
5 *McTear v Imperial Tobacco* 2005 2 SC 1. There could of course be a breach of duty if the alcohol or tobacco was contaminated by a different noxious substance.
6 [1936] 1 All ER 283.
7 For full discussion, see para 4.10 above.

B. STATUTORY REGULATION

8.2   Because of these difficulties, but particularly the fact that the onus of proof of negligence lies on the ultimate consumer, the law has now imposed a statutory regime of strict liability in respect of product liability. What this means is that provided the case falls within the statutory provisions, the defender is liable in delict to compensate the pursuer without the pursuer having to prove that the defender was negligent. The strict liability regime for defective products is to be found in Part I of the Consumer Protection Act 1987. This statute implements EC Directive No 85/374/EEC and it is expressly enacted that it should be interpreted to comply with the Directive.[1] The general idea of the Act is simple: it is to place the primary responsibility for personal injury or damage to property caused by a defective product on the producer and to enable the consumer who has been injured by the defective product or whose property has been damaged by the defective product to obtain compensation from the producer without having to prove fault. However, as we shall see, the provisions of the statute are hideously complex. Before considering them, it should be noted that where the statutory regime is not applicable, common law liability remains[2] and the pursuer may bring an action based on a breach of the *Donoghue v Stevenson* duty of care but will, of course, have to prove negligence if he is to be successful.

The Consumer Protection Act 1987 imposes strict liability on the producer of a product 'where any damage is caused wholly or partly by a defect in a product'.[3] Damage is defined as 'death or personal injury or any loss of or damage to property (including land)'.[4] Thus, if a person is killed or injured by a defective product, or his land or other property is damaged by a defective product, the producer of the product is liable to pay compensation without proof of fault. In other words, the producer is strictly liable.

1 Consumer Protection Act 1987, s 1(1). The Act came into force on 1 March 1988. References in this section are to CPA 1987 unless otherwise stated.
2 CPA 1987, s 2(6).
3 CPA 1987, s 2(1).
4 CPA 1987, s 5(1). 'Personal injury' includes any disease and any other impairment of a person's physical or mental condition: CPA 1987, s 45(1).

(1) Exceptions to strict liability

8.3 Damage to certain types of property is excluded from the statutory regime:

(a) loss or damage to the defective product itself.[1] The cost of repair or the difference in value between a defective and a non-defective product is not recoverable under the Consumer Protection Act 1987. Nor is it recoverable in delict at common law since it is pure economic loss. Where the product is a complex structure, loss or damage to the whole or part of the product caused by a defective component is also excluded. For example, if a motor car (complex product) is damaged as a result of a defective wheel (component), the damage to the car is excluded but not injury to the driver or damage to other property;

(b) property damaged or lost as a result of a defective product where the property *damaged or lost* is not for private use.[2] Property is not for private use if it is not of a description of property ordinarily intended for private use, occupation or consumption *and* it is not intended by the person suffering the loss or damage mainly for his own private use, occupation or consumption. What this means is that before the Act applies and there is strict liability, the property damaged must be 'consumer' property, ie of a kind ordinarily intended for private use which the person suffering the loss or damage intended to be used for private use. For example, if A produces a defective vacuum cleaner, the Act will apply if the cleaner damages the carpet in B's home but not if it damages the carpet in B's office or factory. It is important to note that it is the property which is damaged which must be 'consumer' as opposed to 'business' property. If A produces a defective lorry which is used in B's business, the Act *will* apply if the defective lorry damages C's family motor car but the Act will not apply if the defective lorry damages C's van which he uses for his business. When the Act is excluded because the property damaged is not 'consumer' property, resort will have to be made to delictual liability at common law when negligence will have to be established;

(c) property damaged or lost as a result of a defective product, where the loss or damage does not exceed £275.[3] Where such loss or damage occurs, resort must again be made to delictual liability at common law when negligence will have to be established.[4] It should be noted that this exception only applies to damage to property. If, for example, A cuts his finger as a result of B's defective product, the Act still applies and B is strictly liable even if A's damages are less than £275.

1 CPA 1987, s 5(2).
2 CPA 1987, s 5(3).
3 CPA 1987, s 5(4). This includes interest.
4 Such an action would be brought under the small claims procedure.

(2) Definition of 'product'

8.4 Strict liability applies where damage is caused wholly or partly by a defect in a product. A 'product' is defined[1] as any goods or electricity. It includes – and this is important – components and raw materials which are parts of a complex product. So, if there is a complex product such as a motor car and a component of the car, for example a windscreen, is defective, that component, as well as the motor car, is regarded as a product for the purpose of the Consumer Protection Act 1987. Thus the problem which arose in *Evans v Triplex Safety Glass Co Ltd*[2] will not arise under the Act. 'Goods' also include 'substances, growing crops and things comprised in land by virtue of being attached to it and any ship, aircraft or vehicle'.[3] 'Substance' means any natural or artificial substance, whether in solid, liquid or gaseous form or in the form of vapour and includes substances which are comprised in or mixed with other goods, for example a cylinder of gas. Things comprised in land by virtue of being attached to it include, for example, the window frames of a house, a garden shed or a swing. 'Ship' includes any boat or vessel used for navigation; aircraft includes gliders, balloons and hovercraft; 'vehicle' is not defined. Game and agricultural produce constitute products for the purpose of the Act.[4] Blood used for transfusions has been held to be a product for the purposes of the Act.[5]

1 CPA 1987, s 1(2).
2 [1936] 1 All ER 283.
3 CPA 1987, s 45(1).
4 Initially game and agricultural produce were excluded from the regime: the exclusion was removed by the Consumer Protection Act 1987 (Product Liability) (Modification) (Scotland) Order 2001, SSI 2001/265 in response to the CJD crisis.
5 *A v National Blood Authority (No 1)* [2001] 3 All ER 289.

(3) Parties liable

8.5   As mentioned above, prima facie strict liability is imposed on the producer of the product. A 'producer' is defined as the person who manufactured the product[1] or who won or abstracted the substance.[2] Where a product is not manufactured, won or abstracted but its essential characteristics are attributable to an industrial or other process, the producer is the person who carried out the process: for example, where the product is pasteurised milk, the producer is the person who carried out the pasteurisation process.[3] A person who merely packages goods is not a producer. Any person who puts his own name on a product, or uses a trade mark on a product, is liable under the Consumer Protection Act 1987 if by so doing he holds himself out to be the producer.[4] This provision brings 'own branders' within the strict liability regime. Similarly, any person who imports products from abroad with a view to distributing them within the EU is liable under the Act.[5] This clearly is to protect ultimate consumers in EU Member States from having to sue a producer outwith the EU. The importer may, of course, have a remedy, for example in contract, against the non-EU producer. The producer of a component or of raw materials used in a complex product is prima facie jointly and severally liable with the producer of the complex product if it is defective.

Although strict liability falls on the producer, own brander or importer of a defective product, as a fall back position a supplier of the product may also be liable. Thus all parties in the distribution chain from the producer to the own brander or importer are potentially liable under the Act:

Producer ———— Wholesaler ———— Retailer ———— Purchaser

In this example, the wholesaler and retailer are suppliers within the meaning of the Act. However, a supplier will be liable only if the person who suffered the damage asked the supplier within a reasonable time of the damage being sustained to identify the producer or a supplier further up the chain of distribution and the supplier failed to provide the information within a reasonable time, provided it was not reasonably practicable for the person suffering the damage to identify the producer. In order to escape potential strict liability under the Act, a supplier must therefore keep records of his suppliers or producers.[6]

A supplier will not be strictly liable if the defective goods were not supplied in the course of business.[7] Accordingly, A will not be strictly liable if A sells his washing machine to his neighbour B in a private transaction or if A gives B the washing machine as a birthday present: but A will remain liable for breach of contract or in delict at common law if the washing machine is defective and injures B or damages B's property. Where we are dealing with a producer, own brander or importer, they will escape strict liability under the Act only if the goods were supplied otherwise than with a view to profit.[8] If for example, A makes lemon curd which is *donated* to the local church sale of work, A is not liable, although he is a producer, because the goods were not supplied with a view to A's profit. But if A *sells* the lemon curd to the sale of work, A will remain liable under the Act. In both cases, the church will not be liable under the Act, since the only potential liability is as a supplier and the lemon curd was not sold in the course of a business. The church could, of course, be liable at common law.[9]

1 CPA 1987, s 1(2)(a).
2 CPA 1987, s 1(2)(b).
3 CPA 1987, s 1(2)(c).
4 CPA 1987, s 1(2)(b).
5 CPA 1987, s 1(2)(c).
6 CPA 1987, s 2(3). If the producer has the power to determine when the supplier should put the product on to the market, the supplier may be treated as the producer for the purposes of the CPA 1987: *O'Bryne v Aventis Pasteur MSD Ltd* [2010] UKSC 23.
7 CPA 1987, s 4(1)(c)(i). Where a product was supplied and used for a specific medical service which was financed entirely from public funds, the ECJ held that it was nevertheless supplied for an economic or business purpose and the producer remained strictly liable: *Veedfald v Arhus Amtskommune* [2003] 1 CMLR 41.

8 CPA 1987, s 4(1)(c)(ii).
9 If A supplies a 'free gift' when selling another product, A will be strictly liable under the Act if the gift is given away in the course of A's business.

(4) Meaning of 'defective product'

8.6 In order to attract strict liability the damage must be caused 'wholly or partly' by a *defect* in the product.[1] What then is a defective product? A product is defective 'if the safety of the product is not such as persons are entitled to expect'.[2] For these purposes, 'safety shall include safety in the context of risks of damage to property as well as in the context of risks of death or personal injury'.[3] It will be noted that the test is what the *consumer* is entitled to expect in terms of the safety of the product: if it falls below the *consumer's* expectations then the product is defective. This is in marked contrast to the concept of negligence at common law which is tested by the standards of the hypothetical reasonable person in the position of the manufacturer.[4] In *Abouzaid v Mothercare (UK) Ltd*,[5] for example, as he was seeking to assist with fastening an elasticated strap to a pushchair, the plaintiff lost the sight in one of his eyes when the strap recoiled. The Court of Appeal held that the test of defectiveness hinged upon the expectations of the public at large as to the safety of the product and the fact that the manufacturer had not appreciated that there was any risk of injury arising from the strap was irrelevant. In *A v National Blood Authority (No 1)*,[6] the producer knew that some of his blood products might be infected but at the time there were no practical precautions that could be taken. The court held that the blood product was defective because the public did not know of the risk and were entitled to expect that blood transfused to them would be free from infection.

On the other hand, when the public know there is a risk that a product might fail in its purpose, then the product will not be defective if the risk transpires.[7] Where the risk is obvious, for example that coffee served in a polystyrene cup will be hot to hold, the product is not defective.[8] Although the Consumer Protection Act 1987 is concerned with products which are dangerous because badly manufactured or incompetently designed, it also applies to products which are superbly designed and excellently manufactured but which are inherently dangerous if not used carefully, for example drugs.[9] Such products will be defective if there are inadequate warnings or instructions as to use. Thus tobacco or alcohol could be defective products if the warnings as to the dangers of use or abuse are not adequate.[10]

1 CPA 1987, s 2(1). The onus rests on the pursuer to prove that the product was defective: *Foster v Biosil* (2001) 59 BMLR 178; *McGlinchey v General Motors UK Ltd* [2012] CSIH 91.
2 CPA 1987, s 3(1).
3 CPA 1987, s 3(1).
4 For discussion, see paras 5.10 ff above.
5 [2001] TLR 136.
6 [2001] 3 All ER 289.
7 *Richardson v LRC Products* [2000] PIQR 164 (condom failed but public knew that no form of contraception is 100 per cent effective and the manufacturer never claimed that the product was).
8 *B (a child) v McDonald's Restaurants Ltd* [2002] EWHC 490 (QB).
9 *X v Schering Health Care Ltd* [2002] EWHC 1420 (QB) 70 BMLR 88 (third-generation combined oral contraceptives did not increase the level of risk of thrombosis and not defective).
10 Cf *McTear v Imperial Tobacco* 2005 SC 1 for the position at common law.

8.7   In determining what the consumer is entitled to expect, the court must consider all the circumstances of the case.[1] These include:

(a) The purposes for which the product was marketed, its 'get up', any mark in relation to the product and any instructions or warnings.[2] Instructions or warnings are of particular importance where the product is inherently dangerous. If no warning is given, obviously the product will be defective. But if there is an adequate warning, for example in respect of drug dosage, will that satisfy the consumer's expectation of safety or must the container of the drug be, for example, child proof?

(b) What might reasonably be expected to be done with or in relation to the product.[3] Theoretically, this should be what the *consumer* might *reasonably* expect to be done with the product rather than what the producer expects it to be used for. Ultimately, however, it will be the court's view of reasonable expectation which will prevail. The test is clearly objective. So for example, it is unlikely that a freezer which cannot be opened from within would be held to be defective even though a child climbed into the freezer and could not get out: freezers cannot reasonably be expected to be hiding places for toddlers!

(c) The time when the product was supplied by its producer to another.[4] The relevant time for assessing the standard of safety of a product is the time at which it was supplied by the producer: the fact that products which are put on the market after that date have more safety features does not per se mean that the earlier product was defective at the time it was supplied.

Before there is strict liability under the Act, the pursuer has to show that the damage was '*caused* wholly or partly by a defect in a product'.[5] Therefore, as in the case of delictual liability at common law, the claim may fail unless there is a sufficient causative link between the damage and the defective product.[6] However, provided there are no causation problems, the pursuer who has suffered damage is entitled to compensation from the producer, own brander, importer or supplier without having to establish negligence. In other words, there is strict liability.

1 CPA 1987, s 3(2).
2 CPA 1987, s 3(2)(a). *Worsley v Tambrands Ltd* [2000] PIQR P95 (the manufacturer's warnings of the risk of toxic shock syndrome from the use of tampons were sufficient and the product was not defective).
3 CPA 1987, s 3(2)(b).
4 CPA 1987, s 3(2)(c).
5 CPA 1987, s 2(1) (emphasis added); *Foster v Biosil* (2001) 59 BMLR 178; *McGlinchey v General Motors UK Ltd* [2012] CSIH 91.
6 Although CPA 1987 applies when a defective product causes psychiatric illness, it will probably not apply to secondary victims since their illnesses are caused by their reactions to the injuries of primary victims rather than by the defective product which injured the primary victim concerned. So for example persons who suffer mental harm by witnessing a plane crash caused by a defect in the plane's engines cannot recover damages under the CPA 1967 from the manufacturer of the plane. On delictual liability for mental harm, see paras 4.2 ff above.

(5) Defences to claim of strict liability

8.8 The Consumer Protection Act 1987 provides the defender with the following defences to a claim based on *strict* liability:

(a) The defect in the product is attributable to the defender's compliance with statutory or EU obligations.[1]

(b) The defender did not at any time supply the product to another, for example the product was stolen.[2]

(c) The defect did not exist in the product at the relevant times.[3] In the case of a producer, own brander or importer this will be the time he first supplied the product to another; in the case of a supplier, when the product was last supplied by a producer, an own brander or an importer into the EU. So in the case of the producer etc, he will escape strict liability if the product was not defective when it entered circulation, but subsequently becomes defective.[4] There can, of course, still be delictual liability at common law. The supplier will escape strict liability if the product was not defective when it was last supplied by a producer etc even though the defect was subsequently caused by the supplier himself. For example, if a butcher keeps meat which was edible when he obtained it from the producer but sells it when it has gone off, the retailer will not be liable. This is, to say the least, an odd result but, of course, the retailer will be liable in contract to the purchaser and at common law in delict to the ultimate consumer when negligence will readily be inferred.

(d) The state of scientific and technical knowledge at the relevant time[5] was not such that a producer of products of the same description as the product in question, might have been expected to have discovered the defect if it had existed in his products while they were under his control.[6] This is known as the 'state of the art' defence. It is controversial in that a producer can escape *strict* liability if the defect in his product would not have been known by manufacturers of a similar product, given the state of scientific and technical knowledge at the time. It is important to stress that the defence is not what the producer actually knew but what he would have known if he had consulted those who might be expected to know the state of research and all the available literature etc.[7] It has been held that the defence is not available if the producer knows that his product might have harmful consequences.[8]

This defence is similar to the common law principle that a defender cannot be liable in delict if, as a result of the scientific knowledge available to the hypothetical reasonable person at the time, injury to the pursuer was not a reasonable and probable consequence of the defender's conduct.[9] Moreover, the defence expressly refers to the awareness of producers of similar products. This is similar to the important role that the practice of persons in the same trade, business or profession of the defender plays in establishing a breach of a duty of care at common law.[10] It can therefore be argued that the 'state of the art' defence re-introduces negligence into the regime of strict liability laid down in the Consumer Protection Act 1987.

In many cases, the defence will not be available to the producer simply because, given the state of scientific and technical knowledge at the time, he[11] should have known the product was defective. Where the defence could be used is in the production of drugs whose side effects could not have been discovered given the state of scientific knowledge which existed at the time they were produced; it may take years before the side effects of certain drugs become apparent in patients. In these circumstances, the defence could be used by the defender. It is somewhat ironic that one of the reasons for the move towards a strict liability regime for defective products was to avoid the shortcomings of the law of negligence which became apparent in the thalidomide tragedy. The European Court of Justice has held that the scope of the Consumer Protection Act 1987, s 4(1)(e) is not in conflict with EU law.[12]

(e) If the defective product is a complex product, the producer of a component or of any raw materials contained in the complex product has a defence if the defect in the complex product is wholly attributable to the design of the complex product or to the fact that he complied with the instructions of the producer of the complex product;[13] otherwise both the producer of the complex product and the producer of the component or raw materials are jointly and severally liable.[14]

(f) Contributory negligence.[15] Liability under the Consumer Protection Act 1987 cannot be excluded by an exemption clause.[16]

This discussion of product liability is important because it illustrates how the common law of delictual liability based on the defender's *culpa* was thought to be inadequate to protect the interests of consumers who might be injured or whose property might be damaged by defective products. Accordingly, a regime of strict liability was introduced by statute so that the ultimate consumer would no longer have to prove fault before obtaining compensation. But the Consumer Protection Act 1987 is not comprehensive and on occasions it will still be necessary for a pursuer to resort to delictual liability at common law when negligence will have to be established.

1 CPA 1987, s 4(1)(a).
2 CPA 1987, s 4(1)(b). *Veedfald v Arhus Amtskommune* [2003] 1 CMLR 41 (kidney flushing fluid supplied when it was used to prepare a kidney for transplantation).
3 CPA 1987, s 4(1)(d).
4 *Richardson v LRC Products Ltd* [2000] PIQR 164 (condom became damaged by ozone after it left the factory!).
5 See discussion immediately above.
6 Consumer Protection Act 1987, s 4(1)(e).
7 *Richardson v LRC Products* [2000] PIQR 164. In *Abouzaid v Mothercare (UK) Ltd* [2001] TLR 136 the Court of Appeal doubted whether accident reports constituted 'technical knowledge'.

 8 *A v National Blood Authority* [2001] 3 All ER 289. This case provides a very full discussion of when a product is defective and the nature of the 'state of the art' defence: see in particular pp 334–342.
 9 *Roe v Minister of Health* [1954] 2 QB 66, [1954] 2 All ER 131, CA, discussed at para 5.6 above.
10 See para 5.16 above.
11 Or, technically, producers of similar products.
12 *Commission of the European Communities v United Kingdom* (C300/95) [1997] All ER (EC) 481, ECJ (Fifth Chamber).
13 Consumer Protection Act 1987, s 2(4)(f).
14 See paras 6.12–6.13 above.
15 CPA 1987, s 6(4).
16 CPA 1987, s 7.

CHAPTER 9

Delictual liability for animals

A. DELICTUAL LIABILITY AT COMMON LAW

9.1 Where the defender owes the pursuer a duty of care, the defender can be liable where the pursuer's injuries or damage to property is caused by an animal. In *Henderson v John Stuart (Farms) Ltd*[1] an employee was killed by a bull when cleaning out its box. The employer was held to be negligent in failing to fit the box with baffles or escape gaps. In other words, the employer had broken the duty of care he owed to his employee by failing to provide a safe working environment.[2] While a farmer is not under an absolute obligation to prevent his animals from straying onto the highway, she could be liable for injury to a road user or damage to his property if such harm was reasonably foreseeable as a probable consequence of the animal being there. Unless the animal has strayed before, it is unlikely that harm to a road user would be reasonably foreseeable.[3]

In *Hill v Lovett*[4] an employee of the defenders, who were veterinary surgeons, was bitten by one of their West Highland terriers when she went into the garden to clean the windows of the surgery. As a result, the unfortunate pursuer eventually had to have her leg amputated. The Lord Ordinary (Weir) held that the defenders had broken the duty of care they owed to the pursuer both as employers and occupiers of the garden,[5] in failing to take reasonable care to ensure that the pugnacious dogs were not in the garden when the pursuer was there. On the other hand, in *Welsh v Grady*[6] the pursuer was knocked over by the defender's overfriendly black labrador, Ebony. The Lord Ordinary (Malcolm) held that in the absence of some warning or reason to anticipate that a dog might cause harm it would not usually be negligent to let a large dog off the lead when walking in open fields; but it might be negligent to allow a black labrador to run around in a public place close to young children.[7]

A very unusual case is *Cameron v Hamilton's Auction Marts Ltd.*[8] The defenders were driving cattle along the highway. A cow escaped, climbed the stairway of a property adjoining the road, turned on a tap and fell through the floor into the pursuer's shop, causing flooding and damage. Clearly the defender owed a *Donoghue v Stevenson* duty of care[9] to the pursuer as the owner of property adjacent to the highway. In these circumstances, the sheriff held that the defenders would be liable for breach of their duty of care if the cow had escaped because of their negligence.[10]

These cases, then, are examples of breach of an existing duty of care as a result of the defender's carelessness: the fact that the injuries and damage were caused by an animal is largely irrelevant. They are simply examples of common law delictual liability for negligence. However, at common law, certain animals were regarded as *ferae naturae,* ie as having vicious propensities. These included, for example, lions, tigers and elephants. If such an animal caused injury or damage to a person, the person in charge of the animal was strictly liable, ie there was no need to prove fault. Strict liability applied even though the animal had not shown any vicious propensities before.[11] On the other hand, certain animals were regarded as *domitae naturae,* ie as having no vicious propensities. These included, for example, dogs, cats and cattle, including bulls! If such an animal had *in fact* shown vicious propensities before the pursuer suffered injury or damage, then strict liability would attach to the defender. But as in *Henderson v John Stuart (Farms) Ltd*[12] and *Hill v Lovett,*[13] even where the bull and the dog had not hitherto shown vicious tendencies so that strict liability could not be imposed, the defenders were nevertheless successfully sued in negligence for breach of their duty of care.[14]

1 1963 SC 245, 1963 SLT 22, OH. On delictual liability for animals, see generally Kenneth Norrie, SULI *Delict* Chapter 21.

2 On employers' liability, see Chapter 12 below.

3 *Davidson v McIrvine* 2007 SLT (Sh Ct) 71(driver ran into a bull that had strayed onto the highway from the fields: damage to the motorist's car not reasonably foreseeable).

4 1992 SLT 994, OH.

5 On occupiers' liability, see paras 10.9 ff below.

6 2008 SLT 363.

7 'Walking dogs in the open fields around Wellbank, a village just north of Broughty Ferry, is a popular activity. It allows the human and the canine population fresh air, exercise, and opportunities for social interaction. Villagers meet, chat and walk together for a while, as their dogs play and run around. It would appear that the general practice is to keep dogs on their lead until the open and largely uncultivated fields are reached, when they are allowed to run free': ibid per Lord Malcolm at 364.

8 1955 SLT (Sh Ct) 74, 71 Sh Ct Rep 285.

9 See *Donoghue v Stevenson* 1932 SC (HL) 31, 1932 SLT 317.
10 See also *Swan v Andrew Minto & Son* 1998 Rep LR 42; *Wormald v Walker* 2004 SCLR 733 (farmer could owe a duty of care to a motorist to prevent a road accident caused by a cow escaping from a field through a hole in a hedge).
11 See the English case of *Behrens v Bertram Mills Circus Ltd* [1957] 2 QB 1, [1957] 1 All ER 583, where the defendants were held strictly liable for the injuries caused to a midget by an elephant which had hitherto appeared docile.
12 1963 SC 245, 1963 SLT 22.
13 1992 SLT 994, OH.
14 Special rules applied to dogs under the Dogs Acts 1906–28; damage done by straying cattle was governed by the Winter Herding Act 1686.

B. LIABILITY UNDER THE ANIMALS (SCOTLAND) ACT 1987

(1) Introduction

9.2 The common law on *strict liability* for injuries or damage caused by animals was regarded as unsatisfactory. For injury or damage caused by an animal after 10 June 1987, the common law on *strict* liability has been replaced by the provisions of the Animals (Scotland) Act 1987.[1] However, common law liability for injury or damage caused by an animal as a result of the defender's *negligence* has *not* been replaced by the provisions of the 1987 Act[2] and a pursuer is therefore able to sue on the general principles of *culpa* if his case does not fall within the strict liability regime imposed by the 1987 Act.[3]

Where the Animals (Scotland) Act 1987 applies, the defender's liability is strict, ie the defender is liable without the pursuer having to prove that the defender was negligent. The person who is liable is the *keeper* of the animal 'at the time of the injury or damage complained of'.[4] The keeper of an animal for the purposes of the Act is defined as follows:[5]

(a) the owner of the animal: remains the owner, even if the animal has been abandoned or has escaped, until someone else becomes the owner;[6]
(b) the person with possession of the animal:[7] remains in possession, even if the animal has been abandoned or has escaped, until someone else obtains possession.[8] However, a person is not a keeper of an animal by virtue of possession if he is detaining the animal to prevent it from causing injury or damage on his land[9] or is 'temporarily detaining it for the purpose of protecting it or any other person or other animal

or restoring it as soon as is reasonably practicable to its owner or a possessor of it';[10]

(c) a person with 'actual care and control of a child under the age of 16' who is the owner or has possession of the animal.[11] And so a parent of a child under the age of 16 is regarded as the keeper of any animal owned by the child provided the parent has actual care and control of the child.

Where an animal is owned by A but in the possession of B, A and B can be jointly and severally liable under the Act.

1 Animals (Scotland) Act 1987, s 1(8). References in this section are to the Animals (Scotland) Act 1987 unless otherwise stated.
2 See A(S)A 1987, s 1(8).
3 See for example *Welsh v Brady* 2008 SLT 363.
4 A(S)A 1987, s 1(1).
5 A(S)A 1987, s 5(1)(a).
6 A(S)A 1987, s 5(2)(b). The Crown does not become the owner if an animal is abandoned: A(S)A 1987, s 5(2)(c).
7 A(S)A 1987, s 5(1)(a).
8 A(S)A 1987, s 5(2)(b).
9 A(S)A 1987, s 3.
10 A(S)A 1987, s 5(2)(a).
11 A(S)A 1987, s 5(1)(b).

(2) Meaning of 'animal'

9.3 What animals fall within the Animals (Scotland) Act 1987? For strict liability to apply, s 1(1)(b) of the Animals (Scotland) Act 1987 provides that the animal must be of 'a species whose members generally are by virtue of their physical attributes or habits likely (unless controlled or restrained) to injure severely or kill persons or animals, or damage property to a material extent'. Read literally, this definition is potentially very wide indeed. Although bulls can clearly fall within the definition,[1] it could, for example, include a domestic cat, since a cat by virtue of its physical attributes or habits is likely to injure severely or kill animals like birds or mice! It will ultimately be for the court to decide whether or not a certain species falls within the statutory criteria.

For the purpose of s 1(1)(b), certain animals are deemed by s 1(3)(a) to be likely (unless controlled or restrained) to injure severely or kill persons or animals by biting or otherwise savaging, attacking or harrying. These are dogs and dangerous wild animals within the meaning of s 7(4) of the Dangerous Wild Animals Act 1976.[2] All types of dogs are regarded as animals for the purpose of the 1987 Act where the harm is caused by 'biting or otherwise savaging, attacking or harrying': in these circumstances strict liability is imposed on their keepers even if the dog concerned has never shown any vicious tendencies in the past. If the harm was not caused by 'biting, or otherwise savaging, attacking or harrying' there can be liability at common law if it can be established that the defender was negligent. Thus there was no strict liability under the 1987 Act and no liability at common law when the victims had been knocked down by overly affectionate labradors.[3]

Where an animal is a dangerous wild animal within the meaning of the 1976 Act, by s 1(3)(a) it is also deemed to be a s 1(1)(b) animal. Dangerous wild animals include wild dogs, wolves, jackals, coyotes, foxes (but not the common red fox), cassowaries, Old World monkeys, crocodiles and alligators, emus, poisonous snakes, lions and tigers, cheetahs and panthers, Gila monsters and Mexican bearded lizards, gibbons, orangutans, gorillas and chimpanzees, ostriches and bears.[4] Again, strict liability only arises when the dangerous wild animal has caused the injuries or damage by 'biting or otherwise savaging, attacking or harrying'. In addition, by s 1(3)(b) cattle, horses, asses, mules, hinnies, sheep, pigs, goats and deer *in the course of foraging* are deemed to be likely (unless controlled or restrained) to damage to a material extent land or the produce of land for the purpose of s 1(1)(b) of the 1987 Act.[5]

1 *Foskett v McClymont* 1998 SC 96, 1998 SLT 892, OH. It is a question of fact whether the particular animal fulfils the statutory criteria.
2 A(S)A 1987, s 1(3)(a).
3 *Fairlie v Carruthers* 1996 SLT (Sh Ct) 56; *Welsh v Brady* 2008 SLT 363 (upheld by the Inner House: 2009 SLT 747). In determining if the harm was caused by biting or otherwise savaging, attacking or harrying the court, of course, cannot look into a dog's mind to determine *mens rea*! The test is objective after considering what actually happened. Having found in these cases that the dogs could not be deemed to be s 1(1)(b) animals by virtue of s 1(3)(a), the courts held that there was also no liability for negligence since the defenders had no grounds to believe that their dogs would knock the pursuers over.
4 Dangerous Wild Animals Act 1976, s 7(4) and Sch 3.
5 Animals (Scotland) Act 1987, s 1(3)(b). In *Foskett v McClymont* 1998 SC 96, 1998 SLT 892, OH, the bull was not automatically deemed to be an animal for the purpose of the Act since the damage did not occur in the course of foraging and personal injury as opposed to property damage was involved.

9.4 As a result of these provisions a wide range of species are deemed to be animals for the purpose of the Animals (Scotland) Act 1987. But if an animal is not deemed by s 1(3) to fall within the definition in s 1(1)(b), it is, of course, possible to argue that it is nevertheless of a species which by virtue of the physical attributes or habits of its members is likely to injure severely or kill persons or other animals, or damage property to a material extent. In assessing whether this is so, the age and sex of the animal is relevant.[1] Thus a non-foraging cow is unlikely to fall within the definition in s 1(1)(b), while a non-foraging bull could.[2] In *Welsh v Brady*,[3] Lord Malcolm opined[4] that where a dog was not deemed to be a s 1(1)(b) animal by virtue of s 1(3), 'the Act does seem to leave the door open for the possibility, theoretical or otherwise, that it might be proved that a particular type of dog falls within s 1(1)(b) in situations which are outside the scope of s 1(3). However, it is not easy to envisage to which breed or breeds this might apply, and in any event, in my view it does not extend to black labradors'.

The 1987 Act expressly *excludes* from the definition of 'animal' viruses, bacteria, algae, fungi and protozoa.[5]

Where the animal falls within the definition in s 1(1)(b) or is deemed to do so by virtue of s 1(3)(a) or (b), its keeper is strictly liable, ie liable without establishing *culpa*, for any damage or injury suffered by the pursuer which is directly referable to the animal's dangerous attributes or habits.[6] In other words, the damage or injury sustained must arise from the particular attributes or habits of the species which bring the animal within the definition in s 1(1)(b). So, for example, the keeper of a red setter dog is strictly liable under the 1987 Act if the dog bites the pursuer since the injury is directly referable to a dog's attribute or habit to bite.[7] But if the pursuer's injury is sustained as a result of falling over the red setter dog, the keeper is not strictly liable under the 1987 Act although the keeper could be liable if he owed a duty of care to the pursuer and negligence could be established.

Strict liability does not apply to injury or damage caused by the *mere* fact that the animal in question was present on a road or in any other place.[8] Thus, if a motorist was injured while trying to avoid running over a dog, the keeper is not strictly liable under the Animals (Scotland) Act 1987 but may, of course, be liable at common law if a breach of a duty of care towards the pursuer can be established. The 1987 Act does not apply if the injury caused by the animal consists of a disease which was transmitted by means which were unlikely to cause severe injury other than disease.[9] So for example, if A is savaged by a rabid dog and contracts rabies, the keeper is strictly liable under the 1987 Act because the disease was transmitted by means which were likely to cause severe injury, ie the dog's bites. But if the animal had merely licked the pursuer thereby transmitting the disease, the keeper is not strictly liable under the 1987 Act, since the means, ie the licking, was unlikely to cause severe injury other than the disease. In the latter situation, the keeper could still be liable at common law provided there was a breach of a duty of care owed to the pursuer ie if negligence can be established.

1 A(S)A 1987, s 1(2)(a).
2 *Foskett v McClymont* 1998 SC 96, 1998 SLT 892, OH (insufficient averments to allow the pursuer to lead evidence that the bull in question fell within s 1(1)(b)).
3 2008 SLT 363.
4 Ibid at 368.
5 A(S)A 1987, s 7.
6 A(S)A 1987, s 1(1)(c).
7 So if a domestic cat was a dangerous animal, its keeper would only be liable if, for example, it killed the pursuer's pet bird. In other words, the injury must be referable to the attributes or habits of a domestic cat which bring the cat under the statutory definition.
8 Animals (Scotland) Act 1987, s 1(5). *Davidson v McIrvine* 2007 SLT (Sh Ct) 71 (car damaged when it ran into a bull which had strayed on to the road).
9 A(S)A 1987, s 1(4).

(3) Defences to liability under the Animals (Scotland) Act 1987

9.5 Even where the Animals (Scotland) Act 1987 applies and the keeper is prima facie strictly liable, there are several possible defences:

(a) if the injury or damage was due wholly to the fault of the person sustaining it or, in the case of an injury sustained to another animal, the keeper of that animal.[1] This will cover the situation where, for example, the pursuer has goaded a docile animal which attacks the pursuer in defence;

(b) if the person sustaining the injury or damage, or a keeper of the animal sustaining the injury, willingly accepted the risk of it as his.[2] The classic example is a person who willingly puts his head in a lion's mouth. This defence is a statutory form of *volens non fit injuria;*[3]

(c) if the person who was injured or suffered damage was a trespasser, ie was not authorised to be on the keeper's property.[4] The effect of this provision is only to remove strict liability from the keeper. As we shall see,[5] the keeper of the animal as occupier of property owes a duty of care to any person who enters onto the property, including a trespasser. Consequently, although the keeper is not *strictly* liable under the 1987 Act to the trespasser who has been injured by an animal, the keeper may be liable as occupier of the property if negligence can be established. Strict liability in relation to a trespasser is not removed by s 2(1)(c) if the animal which caused the injury or damage was there for the purpose of protecting persons or property. But the keeper will get the benefit of s 2(1)(c) if it is shown that it was reasonable to keep such an animal there and that the use made of the animal was reasonable.[6] Consider the following example:

(i)   If A, a trespasser, is injured by B's goose,[7] prima facie s 2(1)(c) of the Animals (Scotland) Act 1987 applies and B is not strictly liable. But if the goose was on the land to protect B's warehouse, then s 2(1)(c) is disapplied and B is strictly liable. But if B can show that it is reasonable to have a goose as a 'guardbird', s 2(1)(c) is reapplied and B is not strictly liable. It is thought that B would succeed in this case since it is reasonable to have a goose as opposed to a tiger as a 'watch animal'.[8]

Where the animal concerned is a guard dog, the keeper remains strictly liable to a trespasser, ie s 2(1)(c) of the 1987 Act is disapplied unless the keeper can show that he has complied with the provisions of s 1 of the Guard Dogs Act 1975.[9] Under this section, *either* the dog's handler must be present and have the dog under his control, *or* the dog must be secured so that it is not at liberty to go freely about the premises. In addition, notices of the dog's presence must be displayed at every entrance to the property. Consider the following example:

(ii)   If A, a trespasser, is injured by B's guard dog, prima facie s 2(1)(c) of the Animals (Scotland) Act 1987 does not apply and B remains strictly liable. But if B can show that he complied with the provisions of s 1 of the Guard Dogs Act 1975, then s 2(1)(c) of the 1987 Act is reapplied and B is not strictly liable.

In both examples (i) and (ii), B would be liable to A if he was in breach of the duty of care he owes to A as occupier of the property. To be successful, A would have to prove that B did not take reasonable care to protect him from the danger arising from having the animal on the land,[10] ie that B was negligent.

Where the Animals (Scotland) Act 1987 applies, there is no defence on the ground of *damnum fatale* or, for example, of intervention by a third party which caused the animal to escape. This is because liability is strict. However, the pursuer's damages may be reduced on the grounds of contributory negligence.[11]

In this chapter we have seen how the general principles of delictual liability for negligence apply where harm has been caused by an animal. Even at common law it was thought to be in the interests of society that the owner of a dangerous animal should be liable without proof of fault. These rules were unclear and anachronistic and, in so far as strict liability is concerned, they have been replaced by the regime imposed by the 1987 Act. But where a case does not fall within the statutory regime of strict liability, the keeper may still be liable if he was in breach of a duty of care which he owed to the pursuer, but in these circumstances the onus rests on the pursuer to prove that the keeper was negligent.

1 A(S)A 1987, s 2(1)(a).
2 A(S)A 1987, s 2(1)(b).
3 For discussion of the *volens* doctrine, see paras 6.10–6.11 above.
4 Animals (Scotland) Act 1987, s 2(1)(c). In the case of injury to another animal, if the keeper of that animal was not entitled to have the animal on the land.
5 On occupiers' liability, see paras 10.9 ff below.
6 A(S)A 1987, s 2(2).
7 Assuming, of course, that a goose is an animal for the purpose of A(S)A 1987, s 1(2)(b).
8 A(S)A 1987, s 2(2). In Scotland, geese were traditionally used to guard bonded warehouses!
9 A(S)A 1987, s 2(2).
10 On occupiers' liability, see paras 10.9 ff below.
11 The keeper's statutory liability is treated as fault for the purposes of the Law Reform (Contributory Negligence) Act 1945: Animals (Scotland) Act 1987, s 1(6). On contributory negligence, see paras 6.12–6.13 above.

CHAPTER 10

Delictual liability arising from ownership or occupation of property

A. DELICTUAL LIABILITY AT COMMON LAW

10.1 The owner or occupier of property may be liable under general principles of *culpa* if a person is injured or if property is damaged as a result of the state of the defender's property. In a case of unintentional acts or omissions, it will be necessary for the pursuer to show that the owner or occupier owed him a *Donoghue v Stevenson* duty of care[1] and that the defender was in breach of that duty.[2] In order to establish a breach of duty, it will, of course, be necessary to show that the defender was negligent. So for example, if a slate falls off the defender's roof and injures a pedestrian who is using the highway or damages a motor car, the defender may be liable for breach of a duty of care owed to the pedestrian or the owner of the car[3] if the pursuer can establish negligence.[4]

Although it is clear that the owner of property does not act at his peril, ie is not strictly liable,[5] the court will readily infer negligence if the defender has built a structure on his land which if unsafe would cause serious damage. In *Kerr v Earl of Orkney*,[6] the defender built a dam on his land across a stream on which the pursuer had a mill about half a mile lower down. Four months later, after several days of heavy rain, the dam burst and the pursuer's house and his mill were swept away. The court held that the defender was liable unless he could show that the dam had collapsed as a result of a *damnum fatale*, for example an earthquake as opposed to several days of heavy rain. The fact that the dam had burst shortly after it had been built implied that the defender was at fault. Liability arises either because the *opus manufactum* could not be constructed so as to avoid harm to the neighbouring property, in which case there was fault in building the structure at all, or the work was built negligently.[7] While achieving a similar result in cases such as *Kerr*, Scots law does not accept the English doctrine laid down in *Rylands v Fletcher*[8] that the owner of land is strictly liable for damage caused by the escape of dangerous things brought onto his property as a consequence of the defendant's non-natural use of his land.[9] In *RHM Bakeries (Scotland) Ltd v Strathclyde Regional Council*,[10] Lord Fraser of Tullybelton was adamant that *Rylands v Fletcher* 'has no place in Scots law, and the suggestion that it has, is a heresy which ought to be extirpated'.[11]

1 See *Donoghue v Stevenson* 1932 SC (HL) 31, 1932 SLT 317, and Chapter 3 above.
2 See Chapter 5 above.
3 It is thought that as a general principle the owner or occupier of property adjoining the highway would owe a duty of care to a pedestrian or motorist. A roads authority, as owner of an embankment and associated culverting arrangements, has been held to owe a duty of care to the owners of property 700 metres away, not to cause flooding on their property: *Viewpoint Housing Association v the City of Edinburgh* [2007] CSOH 114.
4 *MacColl v Hoo* 1983 SLT (Sh Ct) 23. See also *Todd v Clapperton* [2009] CSOH 112 (landlord not negligent where it could not be established that the landlord could have discovered by a visual inspection that a pane of glass in a door was defective).
5 *McLaughlan v Craig* 1948 SC 599, 1948 SLT 483.
6 (1857) 20 D 298, 30 SJ 158.
7 *GA Estates Ltd v Caviapen Trustees Ltd (No 1)* 1993 SLT 1037, OH, at 1041 per the Lord Ordinary (Coulsfield).
8 (1868) LR 3 HL 330. The scope of *Rylands v Fletcher* liability was re-examined by the House of Lords in *Cambridge Water Co v Eastern Counties Leather plc* [1994] 2 AC 264, [1994] 1 All ER 53, HL.
9 In Scots law liability does not arise simply because a dangerous thing escapes but from the construction of the *opus manufactum*: see *GA Estates Ltd v Caviapen Trustees Ltd (No 1)* 1993 SLT 1037, OH.
10 1985 SC (HL) 17, 1985 SLT 214, HL.
11 1985 SLT 214 at 217.

10.2   Although reasonable foreseeability of harm to the pursuer or damage to his property is the usual criterion for the imposition of a duty of care on the owner or occupier of property, in two situations at least the duty of care has been used as a threshold device to restrict the potential delictual liability of proprietors.[1] The first is whether the owner or occupier of property owes a duty of care to owners or occupiers of adjacent property to prevent damage to their property as a result of the acts of third parties. For example, does the owner of derelict property owe a duty of care to adjacent proprietors to prevent vandals from entering the derelict property and starting a fire which spreads and damages the adjacent properties? Or does the owner of a flat owe a duty of care to the owner of the shop below the flat, to prevent a thief from entering the flat in order to gain access and steal from the shop?

These difficult issues were explored by the House of Lords in *Maloco v Littlewoods Organisation Ltd.*[2] It was accepted by the court that the owner or occupier of property could owe a duty to proprietors of adjacent property to take reasonable care of his property so that it did not cause them physical harm or damage to their property. But there was no general duty to take reasonable care of property to prevent a *third party* from using the premises to cause physical injury or damage to neighbouring proprietors. Using the duty of care as a threshold device, the House of Lords held that no such duty arose even if it was reasonably foreseeable that a third party could enter the defender's property and cause harm to the adjacent proprietor. While it may be reasonably foreseeable that if a person leaves his flat unlocked a thief may enter the premises and gain access to an adjacent flat or shop, the owner of the flat does not owe a duty to take reasonable care to prevent this occurrence. In these circumstances, the owner of the adjacent flat or shop must seek redress against the thief, ie against the third party.

Lord Goff took the view that this could arise if the owner 'negligently causes or permits a source of danger to be created on his land, and can reasonably foresee that third parties may trespass on his land and, if interfering with the source of danger, may spark it off, thereby causing damage to the person or property'.[3] For example, a duty of care would arise if A kept explosives in his house, told persons that the explosives were there, but took no precautions to prevent trespassers from having access to the premises. Similarly, a duty of care would arise if the owner had allowed his property to become a fire hazard, knew persons had been trespassing on the premises and had already started fires, but did not take reasonable precautions to prevent access.[4] As we have seen,[5] no duty arose in the *Littlewoods* case since the defenders did not know that the derelict cinema had, in fact, become a fire hazard: derelict buildings are not, per se, fire hazards.

Lord Goff doubted[6] whether the owner or occupier of property ever owes a duty of care to adjacent proprietors to prevent a thief from gaining access to their premises:

' ... I do not think that liability can be imposed on an occupier of property in negligence simply because it can be said that it is reasonably foreseeable, or even (having regard, for example, to some particular temptation to thieves in adjacent premises) that it is highly likely that, if he fails to keep his property lockfast, a thief may gain access to his property and thence to the adjacent premises. So to hold must presuppose that the occupier of property is under a general duty to prevent thieves from entering his property to gain access to neighbouring property, where there is a sufficient degree of foresight that this may occur. But there is no general duty to prevent third parties from causing damage to others, even though there is a high degree of foresight that they may do so. The practical effect is that everybody has to take such steps as he thinks fit to protect his own property, whether house or flat or shop, against thieves.'

Although *obiter*, this *dictum* is a remarkable example of the duty of care being used as a threshold device to deny delictual liability for reasons of policy.[7] As a result, the decision of the Inner House in *Squires v Perth and Kinross District Council*[8] must be regarded as unsound. There the pursuers who were jewellers successfully sued building contractors who were working on a flat above their shop for not adequately securing the flat against entry by a thief who gained access to their shop and stole jewellery. In the light of Lord Goff's *dictum*, the case should have been dismissed *in limine* because of the absence of a duty of care.[9]

1 On the duty of care as a threshold device, see Chapter 5 above.
2 1987 SC (HL) 37, 1987 SCLR 489, 1987 SLT 425; for facts, see discussion at para 5.9 above.
3 1987 SLT 425 at 439. Lord Goff's approach was approved by the House of Lords in *Mitchell v Glasgow City Council* [2009] UKHL 11, 2009 SLT 247.
4 *Thomas Graham & Co Ltd v Church of Scotland General Trustees* 1982 SLT (Sh Ct) 26.
5 Para 5.9 above. *Maloco* was followed on this point in *Ferns v Scottish Homes* 2007 SLT (Sh Ct) 27.
6 *Maloco v Littlewoods Organisation Ltd* 1987 SLT 425 at 441.
7 For full discussion, see Chapter 5 above.
8 1986 SLT 30.
9 Even if there was a duty of care it is doubtful whether the defender should have been liable. In his evidence, the thief claimed that although he got the idea of gaining access to the shop via the flat when he saw the defender's scaffolding and the open windows, he in fact entered the flat from the back by going up a drain pipe and entering an open door. The chain of causation between the defender's carelessness and the theft is therefore very fragile – provided, of course, we believe the thief!

10.3 The second situation where the duty of care is used as a threshold device is concerned with the law of landlord and tenant. While a landlord owes a duty of care to his tenant to prevent him suffering harm as a consequence of the state of the leased premises, the landlord does not owe the tenant a duty of care to prevent *a third party* injuring the tenant on the premises. In *Mitchell v Glasgow City Council*[1] for several years Mitchell, a tenant of the defender, had been harassed and threatened by Drummond, his neighbour, who was also a tenant of the defender. After many complaints by Mitchell, eventually the defender had a meeting with Drummond in which he was told that he would be evicted. Drummond returned home and assaulted Mitchell who died from the attack. The House of Lords held that the defender did not owe Mitchell a duty of care to warn him about the meeting with Drummond. In accordance with the fundamental principle that there is no liability for pure omissions[2] their Lordships held that the defender did not owe a duty to prevent the risk of harm being caused to Mitchell by the criminal act of a third party, Drummond, which the defender had not created and had not undertaken to avert. But Lord Hope maintained that a duty might arise if the Council had assumed responsibility for Mitchell's safety. Lord Hope said:[3]

'The situation would have been different if there had been a basis for saying that the defenders had assumed a responsibility to advise the deceased of the steps that they were taking, or in some other way had induced the deceased to rely on them to do so. It would then have been possible to say not only that there was a relationship of proximity but that a duty to warn was within the scope of that relationship … I would also hold, as a general rule, that a duty to warn another person that he is at risk of loss, injury or damage as the result of the criminal act of a third party will arise only where the person who is said to be under that duty has by his words or conduct assumed responsibility for the safety of the person at risk.'

The occupier of property owes the owner a duty of care to prevent damage to the premises. Since there is usually a contract between them, this duty is usually contractual. Nevertheless, it was held in *Fry's Metals Ltd v Durastic Ltd*[4] that the defenders were liable in *delict* for failing to maintain an alarm system after their lease with the pursuer had expired. Their duty of care arose because they had retained the keys and were the only persons who had access to the building to operate the alarm. Moreover, they were liable for the damage caused by vandals who had broken into the premises because, in the circumstances, it was highly probable that this would occur if the alarm system was not working.

1 [2009] UKHL 11, 2009 SLT 247.
2 See above paras 4.1 ff.
3 Ibid at para 29.
4 1991 SLT 689n, OH.

B. THE *ACTIO DE EFFUSIS VEL DEJECTIS* AND THE *ACTIO DE POSITIS VEL SUSPENSIS*

10.4   The owner or occupier of property may be liable in delict on general principles of *culpa* for physical injury or damage caused by the defective state of the property: to be successful the pursuer must establish fault on the part of the defender. In Roman law, however, in two situations actions were available in which an owner or occupier was strictly liable ie where there was no need to establish *culpa*. These were the *actio de effusis vel dejectis* where something was poured or thrown out of a building, causing harm to the victim, and the *actio de positis vel suspensis* where something placed on or suspended from a building fell, causing harm to the victim. Under these *actiones* the owner or occupier was strictly liable for personal injuries or damage to property. Given its civilian background, it has been argued that these *actiones* are part of Scots law.[1] In *McDyer v The Celtic Football and Athletic Club*,[2] however, the First Division held that liability for objects falling from buildings required *culpa* in Scots law.[3]

1 See, for example, D M Walker, *The Law of Delict in Scotland* (2nd edn, 1981, W Green) p 284.
2 2000 SLT 736.
3 Cf *Gray v Dunlop* 1954 SLT (Sh Ct) 75; *MacColl v Hoo* 1983 SLT (Sh Ct) 23. In both cases the argument for liability under the *actiones* was rejected on the ground of absence of fault. In *McDyer* the Lord President (Rodger) pointed out that in his opinion the *actiones* were only concerned with liability for physical harm to the persons who were *outside* the premises: in Scotland liability to persons who were on the premises is now governed by the Occupiers' Liability (Scotland) Act 1960. On the 1960 Act, see beyond.

C. *IN AEMULATIONEM VICINI*

10.5 If the proprietor uses his land in such a way as to interfere with his neighbour's use or enjoyment of his property then the conduct may be actionable *in aemulationem vicini*. Before there is liability, it must be shown that the defender's use of his property was done with the intention of interfering with the neighbour's use or enjoyment of his land. A single incident is sufficient to establish liability. This delict has been fully discussed in the context of the intentional delicts.[1]

1 See para 1.14 above.

D. NUISANCE

10.6 The owner of property[1] must not use his land in such a way as to disturb his neighbour's enjoyment of his property or cause damage to his neighbour's land.[2] If a person does so, he may be liable in nuisance. Nuisance is usually a continuing wrong, ie there is more than one act. But delictual liability for nuisance arises even if the defender did not intend to cause inconvenience to the pursuer's enjoyment of his land or damage to the pursuer's property. The delict can be summarised in the brocard *sic utere tuo ut alienum non laedas*, namely use your own property in such a way that you do not do harm to others.

Common examples of nuisance are noise, smells, the emission of fumes and burst pipes. The existence of a building per se does not constitute a nuisance even if it interferes with another person's enjoyment of her land, for example by causing interference with her television signal.[3] The essence of the delict is that as a result of the defender's actions on his property, the pursuer has suffered more than he could reasonably be expected to tolerate: *plus quam tolerabile*. Whether this has been established is a matter of fact and degree in the particular circumstances of the case. For instance, the smell of dung may be acceptable in the countryside but not in the confines of a city tenement. Regularly to play CDs of Wagner at full blast may be acceptable in a large detached house but not in a two-bedroomed semi-detached. Even if the defender is a professional musician who has to practise an instrument 12 hours a day, if the noise disturbs his neighbour more than the neighbour can be expected to tolerate, it is a nuisance and the fact that it is a normal and familiar use of a musician's home is no defence. Nor can it be argued that the pursuer came to the nuisance.[4] So if in our example the musician's previous neighbour enjoyed hearing him practise, this is no defence to an action of nuisance brought by the new proprietor of the neighbour's house, if the continual practising is driving the pursuer mad!

Noise caused by normal domestic use of a family home does not amount to nuisance provided it would not seriously disturb or substantially inconvenience an average reasonable person living in the locality.[5] To constitute a nuisance, the defender's use must amount to offensive conduct, the effects of which are *intolerable*: it is not enough that they merely cause discomfort to the pursuer.[6]

1 This can include the owner of a servitude right. Persistent use of a servitude right which involves a serious risk of damage to the servient tenement can constitute a nuisance: *Cloy v Adams & Sons* 1999 GWD 19-908. On nuisance, see Gordon Cameron, SULI *Delict* paras 14-1–14.68.
2 *Watt v Jamieson* 1954 SC 56 at 58 per the Lord President (Cooper).
3 *Hunter v Canary Wharf Ltd* [1997] AC 655, [1997] 2 All ER 426, HL. The building must, of course, satisfy planning controls.
4 *Coventry (t/a RDC Promotions) v Lawrence* [2014] UKSC 13.
5 *Davidson v Kerr* 1997 Hous LR 11, 1996 GWD 40-2296, Sh Ct. In *Murdoch v Glacier Metal Co Ltd* [1998] Env LR 732, [1998] EHLR 198, CA, the noise from the defendant's factory did not constitute a nuisance even though it exceeded the maximum level recommended by the World Health Organisation.

6 *Anderson v Dundee City Council* 1999 GWD 1-52. In *Canmore Housing Association v Bairnsfather* 2004 SLT 673 the Lord Ordinary (Brodie) held that a nuisance was not established merely because the defender kept derelict vehicles on his land: the petitioner had to show that there was a material risk of harm to his property and this had not been established even though there had been one incident when vandals had set a fire in a vehicle.

10.7 Where the use of the defender's property is in the public interest, this is no defence if it would otherwise constitute a nuisance. In *Webster v Lord Advocate*[1] the pursuer had bought a flat in Edinburgh near the Castle. As the Edinburgh Festival approached, the enjoyment of her flat was disturbed by the noise of workmen erecting the grandstand for the military tattoo. The court held that this was a prima facie case of nuisance: it was irrelevant that the noise could be reduced if the pursuer closed her windows or installed double glazing. While accepting that the tattoo was a valuable and profitable part of the Festival, the court decided that this 'greater good' argument was not sufficient to prevent it from ordering that the nuisance should cease. Accordingly, the court granted declarator that a nuisance was established and that the defender should take steps to ensure that the grandstand was constructed by using less noisy techniques. It is a defence, however, to an action that the conduct constituting the nuisance was carried out with statutory authority.[2]

Because nuisance usually involves *continuing* acts or omissions, the primary remedy is interdict, ie an order that the defender's act or omission should cease. In determining whether or not to grant interdict, the court is concerned with the position of the pursuer ie whether the pursuer should have to continue to suffer the nuisance. Whether or not the nuisance was caused by conduct which amounted to *culpa* on the part of the defender is largely irrelevant. Thus, in the context of granting interdict, the defender's liability for nuisance is strict ie there is no need to aver or prove fault.

1 1985 SC 173, 1985 SLT 361. Cf *Dennis v Ministry of Defence* [2003] EWHC 793, (QB), [2003] 2 EGLR 121 (noise of aircraft flying from a military base was a nuisance but the plaintiff's private property rights should be subjugated to the public interest. *Sed quaere?* However, as the nuisance was an interference with the plaintiff's right to respect for his home under Article 8(1), he was awarded the equivalent of common law damages under the Human Rights Act 1998). This decision must be doubtful given that the environmental pollution of the noise of night flights from Heathrow has been held not to involve an interference with the Article 8(1) rights of property owners around the airport: *Hatton v UK* [2003] All ER (D) 122, approved by the House of Lords in *Marcic v Thames Water* [2004] 1 All ER 135). See also *Barr v Bifffa Waste Services Ltd* [2012] EWCA Civ 312.
2 A planning authority has no jurisdiction to authorise a nuisance unless it has a statutory power to permit a change in the character of the neighbourhood

and the nuisance was an inevitable consequence of the change: *Wheeler v J J Saunders Ltd* [1995] 2 All ER 697, [1995] 3 WLR 466, CA; *Watson v Croft Promo-Sport Ltd* [2009] EWCA 15 (planning permission to use a former aerodrome for motor racing had not altered the nature and character of the locality which was essentially rural: those motor racing activities which constituted a nuisance would not be allowed).

10.8 However, where the nuisance has caused damage to the pursuer's property, no claim for damages will be successful unless the pursuer avers and proves that the nuisance arose as a result of the defender's *culpa*. This was settled by the House of Lords in *RHM Bakeries (Scotland) Ltd v Strathclyde Regional Council*.[1] The pursuer's premises were flooded as a result of the collapse of a sewer, the maintenance of which was the responsibility of the defender. Food and packing materials stored in the bakery were damaged. Even if the failure to maintain the sewer adequately amounted to nuisance, the House of Lords held that the pursuer's action in damages failed because they had not averred, let alone proved, that the collapse of the sewer was due to the negligence of the defender. Accordingly, before the pursuer can obtain damages for harm caused by nuisance, *culpa* on the part of the defender must be established.

But what constitutes *culpa* in this context? This issue was explored in *Kennedy v Glenbelle Ltd*.[2] The pursuer sought damages for harm sustained to his property as a result of the removal of a wall within the defender's premises. The Lord President (Hope) held[3] that *culpa* would arise if:

(1) the defender deliberately intended to damage the pursuer's property (malice); or
(2) the defender knew that her act or omission would damage the pursuer's property; or
(3) the defender was reckless, ie she had no regard to the question whether or not her conduct might be likely to damage the pursuer's property; or
(4) the defender's conduct had such potentially hazardous consequences for the pursuer's property that knowledge that her conduct would damage the pursuer's property is presumed; or
(5) the defender's acts or omissions were carried out carelessly, ie negligence.

In cases (1) to (4), *culpa* arises because the defender knows (or is deemed to know) that the conduct which constitutes the nuisance will damage the pursuer's property, ie it is intentionally caused harm. It is quite irrelevant that the defender's actions were carried out carefully. The fault lies in the fact that the defender knows (or is deemed to know) that her conduct will harm the pursuer's property. Given that the defender's conduct must satisfy the *plus quam tolerabile* test before it will constitute a nuisance, it is thought that in case (5) damages will lie if the pursuer can show that the defender's conduct fell below the standard of reasonable care: it is not necessary that the defender owed the pursuer a pre-existing duty of care.[4]

Because of the difficulty of proving *culpa*, in *RHM Bakeries* Lord Fraser expressed the view that the court would readily infer *culpa* from the fact that the sewer had collapsed causing serious damage.[5] Although this may be the case where the defender has built a dangerous *opus manufactum* on his property, it is doubtful that negligence will be inferred from the mere fact that the pursuer has sustained harm. In *Argyll and Clyde Health Board v Strathclyde Regional Council*[6] the Lord Ordinary (McCluskey) held that in an action for damages it was not sufficient for the pursuers simply to aver that a pipe running below their field had burst causing damage. Instead, the pursuers had to have specific averments showing why the defenders were at fault: for example that they were negligent in failing to inspect the pipe and carry out regular maintenance. The fact that the pipe had burst causing damage to the pursuers did not have the effect that the onus automatically shifted to the defenders to show that they were not negligent in maintaining the pipe.[7]

Therefore it is now clear that if a nuisance is established an interdict can be granted without proof of fault whereas damages are awarded only on proof of *culpa*. The question arises whether this distinction is sensible. Where, for example, the nuisance is fumes emanating from the defender's factory, the effect of an interdict may mean that the defender has to close the factory while extensive – and expensive – repairs are carried out; yet, in theory at least, the defender may not have been negligent. But given that nuisance is often a continuing wrong the defender still remains obliged to ensure that the nuisance stops ie the defender could be interdicted if it were to continue. It is therefore submitted that where the nuisance has caused damage the defender should not have to meet the *additional obligation* of compensating the pursuer unless *culpa* is established: *culpa* is, after all, the basic tenet of the obligation to make reparation in Scots law.

Finally, the function of the law of nuisance is to protect the pursuer's right in his land. Therefore only a person with a recognised right in heritable property has title to sue.[8] A nuisance may also amount to a breach of Article 8(1) of the European Convention on Human Rights: 'Everyone has the right to respect for his private and family life, his home and his correspondence.' Persons living in the same household as the proprietor but who have no proprietary rights may nevertheless have title to sue for breach of Article 8. In determining compensation for such a person, any award of damages the proprietor has received in respect of nuisance will be taken into account.[9]

Moreover, damages are awarded only to compensate the pursuer for any diminution in the value of her *property* caused by a nuisance. In *Glove (Aberdeen) v North of Scotland Water*[10] an Extra Division held that the owner of a pub could seek damages in nuisance for loss of profits which arose because patrons were deterred from coming to the bar as a consequence of the defender's repairs to a sewer which had taken nine months rather than six weeks! Although the pursuer sought reparation for pure economic loss, it is thought that the loss of profits was a legitimate way of assessing the diminution of the value of the property during that period. Where *personal injuries* are involved, the pursuer, even if she is the owner of the land, must sue either for intentional wrongdoing or in negligence, where the defender will not be liable unless he has breached a pre-existing duty of care which he owed to the pursuer.[11]

1 1985 SC (HL) 17, 1985 SLT 214.

2 1996 SC 95.

3 1996 SC 95 at 100 ff.

4 Nevertheless, it is recognised that there can be an overlap between a claim for damages based on nuisance and a claim based on breach of a duty of care, see for example, *Viewpoint Housing Association v Edinburgh City Council* [2007] CSOH 114.

5 *RHM Bakeries (Scotland) Ltd v Strathclyde Regional Council* 1985 SC (HL) 17 at 45.

6 1988 SCLR 120, 1988 SLT 381, OH.

7 In the *RHM Bakeries* case the House of Lords did not overrule its earlier decision in *Caledonian Rly Co v Greenock Corpn* 1917 SC (HL) 56, 1917 2 SLT 67. In that case, Greenock Corporation had altered the channel of a burn to make a paddling pool. After heavy rainfall, the pursuer's property was flooded. The House of Lords awarded the pursuer damages without the need to prove fault, ie the defender was held to be strictly liable. This decision was distinguished in *RHM Bakeries* on the ground that it was concerned with the alteration of the natural direction of a stream, not with damage caused by 'unnatural' use of property. It is submitted that the distinction is tenuous and that, at the very least, the decision in the *Caledonian Rly* case rests uneasily with the ratio in *RHM Bakeries* where it was held that when a nuisance has damaged property, compensation is available only if *culpa* on the part of the defender can be established. The exception in relation to altering the natural flow of a stream was accepted by the Lord Ordinary (Coulsfield) in *GA Estates Ltd v Caviapen Trustees Ltd (No 1)* 1993 SLT 1037 at 1041.

8 *Harvie v Robertson* (1903) 5 F 338, 10 SLT 581; *Hunter v Canary Wharf Ltd* [1997] AC 655, [1997] 2 All ER 426, HL. See also *Dundee (City of) District Council v Cook* 1995 SCLR 559.

9 *Dobson v Thames Water Utilities Ltd* [2009] EWCA Civ 28. Where a proprietor has received damages for nuisance, this will normally constitute just satisfaction for a breach of Article 8(1).

10 2000 SLT 674.

11 For an authoritative statement of the law of nuisance, see 14 *Stair Memorial Encyclopaedia* paras 2001–2168.

E. OCCUPIERS' LIABILITY

10.9   We have been considering cases where, as a result of acts or omissions on his property, the owner/occupier of property causes harm to persons who are not on his property, for example adjacent proprietors, neighbouring proprietors, pedestrians or motorists on the highway who pass the defender's property. In this section, we shall consider the delictual liability of the occupier of property towards persons who *enter* upon the property.

Scots common law was strongly influenced by English law. As a result of the decision of the House of Lords in *Dumbreck v Robert Addie & Sons*,[1] the duty of care towards a person entering onto property depended on the status of the person who was injured, ie whether he was a licensee, for example a lodger or member of the occupier's family; an invitee, for example a guest; or a trespasser. In the case of a trespasser, liability was restricted to intentional, as opposed to negligently caused, harm. However, as a matter of law, these classifications were swept away by the Occupiers' Liability (Scotland) Act 1960.[2]

The general thrust of the Act is that occupiers of property owe a duty to take such care in respect of persons entering their land or premises as is reasonable in all the circumstances of the case. The statutory obligation rests on the person 'occupying or having control of land or other premises' who is referred to in the Act as the 'occupier of premises'.[3] Where the owner of the property is also the occupier of the premises, the statutory obligation lies with him. If the owner is not the occupier, he will not be liable under the 1960 Act but may incur liability under the general duty of care incumbent on owners of property provided *culpa* is established.[4] A person occupies the land or other premises if he is in possession of the property, for example he is a tenant. But he will also be treated as the occupier if he has control of the land or other premises. A person has 'control' if he is entitled to take the steps in relation to the land or property which the statute requires in order to fulfil the duty of taking reasonable care of the premises. So, for example, the owner of derelict property who is not *in fact* in possession is nevertheless the occupier because he has control of the premises. The determination whether a defender has sufficient possession or control to be an occupier is one of fact and degree in the light of the circumstances of the particular case.[5]

While 'land' is self-explanatory, 'premises' are not defined in the 1960 Act. They would include houses, flats, sheds, garages, shops etc; land would include gardens. Moreover, the statutory obligation to take such care as is reasonable in all the circumstances expressly applies to occupiers of 'any fixed or moveable structure, including any vessel, vehicle or aircraft'.[6] Thus the 1960 Act applies to a wide range of property: for example ships, barges, oil rigs, buses, caravans, cars, tractors, helicopters, planes and hovercraft. It is *not* therefore restricted to heritable property.

1 1929 SC (HL) 51, 1929 SLT 242. See T B Smith 'Full Circle: The Law of Occupiers' Liability in Scotland' in *Studies Critical and Comparative* (1962, W Green) p 154. On occupiers' liability, see Angus McAllister, SULI *Delict* Chapter 17.
2 In this section, references are to the Occupiers' Liability (Scotland) Act 1960 unless otherwise stated.
3 OL(S)A 1960, s 1(1). The common law rules for determining whether or not a person is an occupier for these purposes is expressly reserved in the Act: s 1(2).
4 See paras 10.1–10.3 above.
5 *Feely v Co-operative Wholesale Society* 1990 SCLR 356, 1990 SLT 547, OH. On the difficulties of determining who is the relevant occupier when the property is in multi-occupation, see *Gallacher v Kleinwort Benson (Trustee) Ltd* 2003 SCLR 384.
6 OL(S)A 1960, s 1(3)(a).

10.10 Section 2(1) of the Occupiers' Liability (Scotland) Act 1960 lays down the nature and extent of the statutory duty:

'The care which an occupier of premises is required, by reason of his occupation or control of the premises, to show towards a person entering thereon in respect of dangers which are due to the state of the premises or to anything done or omitted to be done on them and for which the occupier is in law responsible shall ... be such care as in all the circumstances of the case is reasonable to see that that person will not suffer injury or damage by reason of any such danger.'

It will be noted that the 1960 Act imposes a positive duty on the occupier to take such care as is reasonable in all the circumstances to ensure that a person entering the premises will not suffer injury or damage by reason of any danger on the premises. Nevertheless, the onus lies on the pursuer to show that the occupier did not take the care that was reasonable in the circumstances: it is not enough simply to aver that there was a danger and that the pursuer suffered injury or damage as a result.[1] In *McGuffie v Forth Valley Health*

Board,[2] for example, the pursuer slipped on snow on the defender's premises which had not been removed by the defender. The pursuer's action failed because she had not specified the period in which it would have been reasonable for the defender to have removed the snow or instructed its employees to do so. On the other hand, in *Porter v Strathclyde Regional Council*,[3] the pursuer slipped on food which had been spilled on the floor of a nursery under the control of the defender. She was able to establish that the defender did not have a system of working whereby an employee would mop up the mess soon after it was spilled. The failure to have such a system was held to be a breach of the occupier's statutory duty to take reasonable care to prevent the pursuer from slipping on the floor as it was probable that the accident would not have occurred if such a system had been in operation.[4]

The Occupiers' Liability (Scotland) Act 1960 applies where the injury or damage arose from dangers 'which are due to the state of the premises *or* to anything done or omitted to be done on them'.[5] Dangers 'due to the state of the premises' clearly covers dangers such as dry rot arising from dilapidated buildings. It would also include uneven roads,[6] a sunken gulley beside a cycle path,[7] a haha[8] slippery floors and unsafe furniture or plenishings.[9] In *Taylor v Glasgow Corpn*,[10] where a child died as a result of eating poisonous berries which were growing in the Glasgow Botanic Gardens, the poisonous berries constituted a danger due to the state of the premises. But the statutory duty also applies to dangers which are due to anything done or omitted to be done on the premises. Thus the 1960 Act would apply to dangers caused by the occupier's failure to provide adequate lighting or to secure a fence, as well as by his positively creating a hazard. As we have seen, the failure to ensure that a pursuer would not enter a garden to clean windows while pugnacious West Highland terriers were also there has been held to be a breach of the 1960 Act.[11] But it is submitted that in the usual case there will be no breach of the 1960 Act where the pursuer sustains physical harm as a consequence of the criminal acts of a third party carried out on the defender's property.[12] In *Honeybourne v Burgess*[13] it was held that hiring a bouncer who violently ejected a patron did not constitute a danger due to anything done or omitted to be done on the premises.

---

1 *Wallace v City of Glasgow District Council* 1985 SLT 23; *Leonard v Loch Lomond and the Trossachs National Park Authority* [2014] CSOH 38. However, the pursuer may be able to rely on the *res ipsa loquitur* principle: *McDyer v Celtic Football and Athletic Co Ltd* 2000 SLT 736.

2 1991 SLT 231.

3 1991 SLT 446.

4 However, the pursuer's damages were reduced by 50 per cent as a result of her contributory negligence.
5 Occupiers' Liability (Scotland) Act 1960, s 2(1) (italics added).
6 *Beggs v Motherwell Bridge Fabricators Ltd* 1998 SLT 1215, 1997 SCLR 1019, OH.
7 *Anderson v Scottish Ministers* [2009] CSOH 92.
8 *Cowan v Hopetoun House Preservation Trust* [2013] CSOH 9.
9 *Kerr v East Ayrshire Council* 2005 SLT (Sh Ct) 67 (glass pane in front door held to be a danger); *Bell v North Ayrshire Council* [2007] CSOH 144 (window that stuck held not to be a danger).
10 1922 SC (HL) 1, 1921 2 SLT 254. This was, of course, a case before the 1960 Act.
11 *Hill v Lovett* 1992 SLT 994, OH, discussed in the context of liability for animals, para 9.1 above.
12 This is for the same policy reasons discussed at para 5.9 above. See *Modbury Triangle v Anzil* (2000) 205 CLR 254 (no breach of duty where plaintiff assaulted by a third party in an unlit car park owned by the defendant).
13 2006 SLT 585.

10.11 It is important to appreciate that the occupier's statutory obligation is only to take such care as is reasonable in all the circumstances to prevent injury or damage from such dangers: it is not to eliminate the risk that an accident might happen. Accordingly, in determining whether or not the occupier has taken reasonable care, the calculus of risk is relevant. The court will consider such factors as the nature of the danger, the occupier's knowledge of the danger,[1] the extent of the injury or harm, the probability of the injury or harm arising, the age of the person injured, whether or not the pursuer was permitted onto the premises and the cost of eliminating the danger. Thus, in *McGlone v British Railways Board*,[2] the defender was held to have taken reasonable care in respect of the danger of a 12-year-old child being burnt by a transformer. The defender had put up warnings and surrounded the transformer with a barbed wire fence which had proved not to be impenetrable. Nevertheless, the House of Lords held that to provide an impenetrable and unclimbable fence went beyond what was reasonable in the circumstances, given that a 12-year-old child should have realised the danger he would incur if he climbed through the barbed wire. In the circumstances, the defender had discharged its duty of reasonable care by erecting an obstacle which a 12-year-old would take some trouble to overcome before he would be in danger. If the fence could have been penetrated by a 3-year-old, then there might well have been a breach of the duty to take reasonable care in respect of a child of that age. The fact that the pursuer was a trespasser was also held to be a relevant factor in assessing whether or not reasonable care had been taken.[3]

A similar approach can be discerned in *Titchener v British Railways Board*.[4] A young man was killed by a train and his 15-year-old girlfriend was seriously injured. The couple had taken a short cut over the line to have a 'kiss and a cuddle' in a derelict brickworks. The defender had provided a fence made of sleepers but there were gaps in the fence through which it was possible for persons to reach the railway line. It was argued that the Board had been in breach of its duty of reasonable care in failing to maintain the fence and thus ensure that there were no gaps providing access to the railway. The House of Lords held that the statutory duty was owed to the particular pursuer, ie a 15-year-old girl who knew the danger involved in crossing a railway line. Accordingly, in determining whether or not the defender had taken reasonable care, the pursuer's age and knowledge were relevant factors. In these circumstances, the fence – even with gaps – gave adequate warning to a girl of 15 who knew the danger of crossing the line. Indeed, Lord Fraser thought[5] that the defender would have taken reasonable care in respect of the pursuer if there had been no fence at all! It would therefore appear that the more obvious and greater the danger, the *less* by way of warning is required for the average person; conversely, *more* is required if the pursuer is, for example, a young child.

1   It would appear that the defender must know of the danger: *Keane v Walker Contracts (Scotland) Ltd* 1999 GWD 9-410. *Sed quaere*? It is surely enough that the defender ought reasonably to have known of the danger. In *Duff v East Dunbartonshire Council* 2002 Rep LR 98, the First Division held that the owner of land will be presumed to know any physical features which might constitute a danger and should be fenced (drop of six feet from embankment to rocks by river bed: need for fence or at least warning notices). In *Kirkham v Link Housing Group* [2012] CSIH 58, the court observed at para 33: 'the Occupiers' Liability (Scotland) Act 1960 does not impose a duty of insurance on the defenders. The defenders must have knowledge, actual or deemed of any danger before they can be found liable in terms of the Act.'
2   1966 SC (HL) 1, 1966 SLT 2.
3   In *Platt v Liverpool City Council* CCRTF 97/0072/C, CA the court described as 'absurd' the contention that the defendant had not taken reasonable care to prevent children from entering dangerous premises, when it had put an eight-foot-high corrugated metal fence around the property.
4   1984 SC (HL) 34, 1984 SLT 192. See also *Devlin v Strathclyde Regional Council* 1993 SLT 699, OH (no breach of duty in respect of injuries to a 14-year-old child deliberately jumping on a skylight cover on a roof: the child was also a trespasser).
5   1984 SLT 192 at 195.

10.12   It has been held that any duty on occupiers to fence off dangers does not apply to dangers inherent in the ordinary and familiar features of the landscape whether natural or man made, for example a loch or reservoir.[1] This was recognised a century ago:

'in a town, as well as in the country, there are physical features which may be productive of injury to careless persons or to young children against which it is impossible to guard by protective measures. The situation of a town on the banks of a river is a familiar feature; and whether the stream be sluggish like the Clyde at Glasgow, or swift and variable like the Ness at Inverness, or the Tay at Perth, there is always danger to the individual who may be so unfortunate as to fall into the stream. But in none of these places has it been found necessary to fence the river to prevent children or careless persons from falling into the water.'[2]

In *Tomlinson v Congleton BC*[3] the House of Lords reaffirmed the principle 'that it is contrary to common sense, and therefore not sound law, to expect [the occupier] to provide protection against an obvious danger on his land arising from a natural feature such as a lake or a cliff and to impose a duty on him to do so'.[4] Moreover, it was thought that it would be extremely rare for an occupier to be under a duty to prevent people taking risks inherent in the activities they chose to undertake on the occupier's land, for example swimming or mountaineering.[5] It was not the policy of the law 'to require the protection of the foolhardy or reckless few to deprive, or interfere with, the enjoyment by the remainder of society of the liberties and amenities to which they are rightly entitled'.[6] In other words, an individual should be allowed to engage in dangerous but otherwise harmless pastimes at her own risk, enabling the rest of society fully to enjoy the pleasures of the countryside and saving the occupier considerable expense.

The defence of *volenti non fit injuria* can be used by the defender.[7] Thus, if there had been a breach of duty in *Titchener,* the House of Lords indicated that *volenti* would have been a defence.[8] Damages may be reduced on the ground of contributory negligence. The parties are free to vary the statutory duty by *agreement.*[9] This enables the occupier to undertake a more onerous or less onerous obligation. Where the premises are used for business, any exemption clause excluding or limiting the occupier's liability for death or personal injuries is void and any clause restricting liability for other kinds of damage is unenforceable unless it satisfies the requirement of reasonableness.[10]

By s 3 of the Occupiers' Liability (Scotland) Act 1960, a landlord who is responsible for the maintenance or repair of premises which have been let owes a similar obligation to persons who enter the premises in respect of dangers arising from the landlord's failure to maintain or repair the property. The statutory obligation extends to anyone lawfully on the premises, such as the tenant's child.[11] The landlord is not obliged to *improve* the premises.[12]

1 *Graham v East of Scotland Water Authority* 2002 SCLR 340; *Fegan v Highland Council* 2007 SC 723. However, in *Cowan v Hopetoun House Preservation Trust* [2013] CSOH 9 the Lord Ordinary (Bracadale) held at para 36 that a 'ha-ha falls to be distinguished from natural features such as riverbanks and cliffs and from man-made features such as canals, railway embankments and jetties. It is an unusual feature of a concealed nature, particularly in the dark. While the ha-ha was a permanent feature of the landscape at Hopetoun House, it is an unusual feature about which someone crossing the lawn in the dark would be likely to be unaware.'
2 *Stevenson v Corpn of Glasgow* 1908 SC 1034 per Lord McLaren at 1039.
3 [2004] 1 AC 46 (young man broke his neck when diving in a lake where swimming was prohibited).
4 Ibid per Lord Hutton at 89.
5 Ibid per Lord Hoffmann at 84.
6 Ibid per Lord Hobhouse at 96.
7 Occupiers' Liability (Scotland) Act 1960, s 2(1).
8 *Volenti* would also have been a defence in *Devlin v Strathclyde Regional Council* 1993 SLT 699, OH.
9 OL(S)A 1960, s 2(1). A non-contractual notice is therefore ineffective.
10 Unfair Contract Terms Act 1977, s 16.
11 *Guy v Strathkelvin District Council* 1997 SCLR 405, OH.
12 *Scott v Glasgow City Council* 1997 Hous LR 107, Sh Ct.

CHAPTER 11

Breach of statutory duty and public law issues

A. BREACH OF STATUTORY DUTY

11.1 The common law principles of delictual liability may be supplemented or supplanted by delictual liability for breach of a statutory duty.[1] Provided the pursuer can establish that he was harmed or suffered damage to his property as a result of the defender's breach of statutory duty, the pursuer will obtain reparation: it is not necessary for the pursuer to establish delictual liability at common law. The statutory duty may be similar to the common law standard of reasonable care as, for example, in the case of the Occupiers' Liability (Scotland) Act 1960.[2] More often, however, the statute may impose a standard which is higher than that expected of the reasonable person at common law, ie the statute imposes strict liability on the defender. We have seen examples of this in Part I of the Consumer Protection Act 1987[3] and in the Animals (Scotland) Act 1987.[4] These statutes expressly stipulate that breach of the statutory duty gives rise to a civil remedy in delict for reparation. Conversely, some statutes expressly stipulate that a breach of statutory duty does not give rise to a civil remedy for reparation even if a person sustains harm as a result.[5]

But there are many statutes which are silent on whether or not a person is entitled to seek reparation in a civil action if he or she suffers personal injury or damage as a result of a breach of statutory duty. Yet it has long been recognised that even where a statute is silent on the matter, a person who has suffered loss may still be able to seek reparation in a delictual action for breach of statutory duty. Thus, for example, where an employee was injured at work and the injury arose as a result of a breach of the employer's statutory duty to maintain machinery, the court held that the employer was liable to compensate the employee for breach of statutory duty even though the statute provided criminal sanctions for breach.[6]

What criteria are used by the courts to determine whether or not a breach of statutory duty gives rise to a civil action in delict where the statute is silent on the matter? The answer appears to be that it is a question of construction of the particular statute to discover whether Parliament intended to confer on the pursuer the right to obtain reparation for breach of statutory duty. This gives the courts considerable discretion albeit within the confines of the language of the statute. And, like the use of the duty of care as a threshold device,[7] the decision whether or not to allow the pursuer an action for breach of statutory duty will ultimately turn on policy considerations, ie whether or not such an action makes social or economic sense. That said, there are certain presumptions which are used by the courts when construing a statute in order to determine whether a civil remedy lies for breach of statutory duty and these will now be briefly considered.

1 On breach of statutory duty see Eleanor Russell, SULI *Delict* chapter 6.
2 Discussed in Chapter 10 above.
3 Discussed in Chapter 8 above.
4 Discussed in Chapter 9 above.
5 For example the Health and Safety at Work etc Act 1974, s 47.
6 *Groves v Lord Wimborne* [1898] 2 QB 402, CA.
7 For further discussion, see Chapter 4 above.

11.2   As a general principle, where a statute provides a specific mode of enforcement of the statutory duties, the presumption is that Parliament did not intend that a civil action for damages in delict was necessary as an *additional* sanction if the statutory obligation is breached. For example, in *Morrison Sports Ltd v Scottish Power*,[1] after construing the legislation on the supply of electricity to the public, Lord Rodger observed (at para 37):

'Looked at as a whole, therefore, the scheme of the legislation with its carefully worked out provisions for various forms of enforcement on behalf of the public, points against individuals having a private right of action for damages for contravention of regulations made under it.'

Conversely, if the statute does not provide a specific mode of enforcement of the statutory duties, then there is a presumption that Parliament did intend that a civil action for damages would lie. So, for example, in *Dawson v Bingley Urban District Council*,[2] the defendant's breach of statutory duty in failing to provide a notice indicating the position of a fire plug, with the result that there was a delay in putting out a fire at the plaintiff's premises, was held to be actionable by the plaintiff in a civil action. The statute did not provide a penalty or other remedy for breach of the statutory obligations.

Where the pursuer already has a private law remedy against the defender if the statute was broken, for example for breach of contract, it is presumed that Parliament did not intend that the pursuer should have the additional remedy of suing in delict for breach of statutory duty. Although the position is not clear, it is submitted that the existence of a right to seek judicial review should not be presumed to exclude the possibility of a civil remedy for breach of statutory duty: judicial review is simply a procedure and damages are available only if the pursuer has a private law remedy. Accordingly, the right to seek judicial review, while a factor to be taken into consideration by the courts, should not be conclusive in deciding whether or not Parliament intended that the pursuer should also have the private law remedy of suing in delict for breach of statutory duty.[3]

1 [2010] UKSC 37.
2 [1911] 2 KB 149, 80 LJKB 842, 104 LT 659, 75 JP 289, CA.
3 *Hague v Deputy Governor of Parkhurst Prison* [1992] 1 AC 58, [1991] 3 All ER 733, HL, at 752 per Lord Jauncey.

11.3 Where a statute provides a penalty for breach of statutory duty, the general presumption is that Parliament did not intend that there should be the additional sanction of delictual liability for breach of statutory duty.[1] There are two exceptions to this rule.[2]

First, if it is apparent that the statutory obligations were passed for the protection of a particular class of individuals, then a delictual action for breach of statutory duty may lie if the pursuer belongs to that class and has suffered injury or loss. This explains how employees were able to sue for breach, for example, of the Factories Acts, even though this legislation imposed criminal penalties on employers who were in breach.[3] Similarly, performers whose work was recorded by record companies without their permission, in breach of the Dramatic and Musical Performers' Protection Act 1958, were held to have been intended by Parliament to be able to pursue private law remedies for breach of statutory duty in spite of the fact that the statute also provided criminal sanctions.[4] But it must be clear that the pursuer falls within the class. So, for example, in *RCA Corpn v Pollard*[5] it was held that companies who had exclusive recording contracts with performers could not sue for breach of statutory duty under the 1958 Act.

If the statute is not designed to protect a particular class and provides penalties for breach, no action for breach of statutory duty will lie.[6] But it may be difficult to determine whether or not the legislation was designed to protect a particular class. In *Cutler v Wandsworth Stadium Ltd (in liquidation)*,[7] for example, the appellant brought proceedings against a licensed dog track to compel it to allow him space at the track to carry on his profession as a bookmaker. Statute provided that the occupier of a licensed track 'shall take such steps as are necessary to secure that ... there is available for the bookmakers space on the track where they can conveniently carry on bookmaking in connection with dog races run on the track'. The House of Lords held that the purpose of the legislation was to protect those members of the public who wished to place bets by ensuring that there was a choice of bookmakers at the track: it was not to give bookmakers the right of a place at the track. Accordingly, the appellant was not entitled to a remedy for breach of statutory duty. But it could equally be argued that it was Parliament's intention to protect the rights of bookmakers to earn their living. The decision in *Cutler* was ultimately a matter of policy. It is interesting to note that the courts are more prepared to construe statutes as giving a delictual remedy for breach of statutory duty where the pursuer has been physically injured[8] than, as in *Cutler*, where the pursuer has suffered only pure economic loss as a result of the breach of the statutory obligations.

Nevertheless, in the leading Scottish case of *Pullar v Window Clean Ltd*,[9] the Inner House of the Court of Session refused to accept that planning legislation which *inter alia* provided that window sashes should be so constructed to enable the window to be cleaned from the inside, was intended to protect window cleaners. There was therefore no breach of statutory duty when a window cleaner fell from the outside sill because the sashes had not been constructed in accordance with the legislation: 'The solution in each case must depend upon what the intention of Parliament was in enacting the obligation in question, and what persons consequently have a right to enforce it or to found upon it as a basis for a claim in damages.'[10]

1 See, for example, *Morrison Sports Ltd v Scottish Power* [2010] UKSC 37.
2 *Lonrho Ltd v Shell Petroleum Co Ltd (No 2)* [1981] 2 All ER 456 at 461 per Lord Diplock.
3 See also *Littlejohn v Wood & Davidson Ltd* 1997 SLT 1353, OH (Merchant Shipping Act 1988, s 31(1) intended to protect a particular class of persons ie persons on board ships: civil claims for damages allowed in spite of existence of criminal sanctions).

4 *Ex parte Island Records Ltd* [1978] Ch 122, [1978] 3 All ER 824, CA.
5 [1983] Ch 135, [1982] 3 All ER 771, CA.
6 *Morrison Sports Ltd v Scottish Power* [2010] UKSC 37.
7 [1949] AC 398, [1949] 1 All ER 544, HL.
8 As in the case of the Factories Acts.
9 1956 SC 13, 1956 SLT 17.
10 1956 SC 13 at 20 per the Lord President (Clyde).

11.4 Even when the legislation is designed to protect a particular class, there may be other factors which deny an action for breach of statutory duty, albeit that the statute does *not* provide criminal sanctions for its breach. In *X (minors) v Bedfordshire County Council*,[1] children sued a local authority (i) for personal injuries sustained by being removed from their parents in care proceedings; and (ii) for personal injuries sustained by not being removed from their parents in care proceedings. Although the children were clearly within the class of persons the care legislation was designed to protect, the House of Lords held that Parliament did not intend that the children should have a private law right to sue for breach of the statute. This was because the legislation involved an administrative system designed to promote the social welfare of the community and the local authority's duties were expressed in broad language. Moreover, Parliament could not possibly have intended that a local authority should be liable *without proof of fault* merely because a court subsequently decided that children should not have been taken into care and vice versa.[2] In short, given the discretion inevitably involved in child care legislation, bona fide mistakes would arise and such mistakes were not to be compensated in the absence of fault.[3]

In *Lonrho Ltd v Shell Petroleum Co Ltd (No 2)*[4] Lord Diplock maintained that there was a second exception where a private law remedy could arise for breach of statutory duty even though the statute provided criminal penalties for its breach:

'The second exception is where the statute creates a public right (ie a right to be enjoyed by all those of Her Majesty's subjects who wish to avail themselves of it) and a particular member of the public suffers ... "particular, direct and substantial" damage other and different from that which was common to all the rest of the public.'[5]

The extent of this exception has not been developed and need not be discussed further.

Once it has been decided as a matter of construction that Parliament intended that a delictual action should lie for breach of statutory duty, a person who has suffered harm must show that the statute was intended to protect a person in his position, ie that the pursuer falls within the class to be protected and that the damage sustained is of the kind that the statute was designed to prevent. In *Gorris v Scott*,[6] for example, statutory regulations required that sheep or cattle being shipped from a foreign country to the UK had to be put in pens. The defendant failed to provide the pens and as a result the plaintiff's sheep were washed overboard in a storm. The plaintiff's action for breach of statutory duty failed because the court held that the purpose of the pens was to prevent animals from being infected by contagious diseases, not to prevent them from being swept overboard. If the sheep had died as a result of a contagious disease, a delictual claim for breach of statutory duty would have been successful.

The defender must, of course, have broken the statutory duty which was incumbent upon him. Whether or not the defender's conduct constitutes a breach will depend on the interpretation of the particular provision. Statutes may impose absolute liability, strict liability, or reasonable practicability. If a breach of the statutory duty is established, ie the defender has broken the duty,[7] there is no need for the pursuer to prove fault. But the pursuer must establish that the breach of statutory duty caused the harm.[8] Unless, as in the case of the Occupiers' Liability (Scotland) Act 1960,[9] the defence is expressly stated to be available, *volenti non fit injuria* cannot be pleaded.[10] This is because a person cannot agree to take a risk of harm which Parliament has legislated to prevent arising. However, the pursuer's damages may be substantially reduced as a result of contributory negligence.

1 [1995] 2 AC 633, [1995] 3 All ER 353, HL.
2 On potential liability at common law for negligence see beyond paras 11.5 ff. In *Thames Trains Ltd v Health and Safety Executive* [2003] EWCA Civ 720, the Court of Appeal held that the HSE did not owe a statutory duty giving rise to a private action by passengers who had sustained personal injuries in a train crash caused by faulty signals: but its failure to exercise its powers carefully could give rise to a claim in negligence (cf strict liability for breach of statutory duty).
3 See also, for example, *O'Rourke v Camden London Borough Council* [1998] AC 188, [1997] 3 All ER 23, HL.
4 [1982] AC 173, [1981] 2 All ER 456, HL.
5 [1981] 2 All ER 456 at 461.
6 (1874) LR 9 Exch 125.
7 For examples see discussion of Part I of the Consumer Protection Act 1987, the Animals (Scotland) Act 1987 and the Occupiers' Liability (Scotland) Act 1960, above.
8 On causation generally, see Chapter 6 above.
9 Occupiers' Liability (Scotland) Act 1960, s 2(3).
10 See, for example, *Wheeler v New Merton Board Mills Ltd* [1933] 2 KB 669, CA.

B. PUBLIC LAW ISSUES

11.5 Ministers of the Crown, local authorities and other governmental agencies are often given statutory powers to implement policy. This will often involve the exercise of discretion. Consider the following examples:

(1) A minister is given the power to send some criminals to an open prison: if such a criminal should escape, steal and damage a person's motor car, is the minister liable in delict?[1]

(2) A local authority is given the power to inspect and approve the plans of buildings: if the local authority approves the plans for the foundations of a house, is the local authority liable to the owner of the house if the foundations were unsuitable and have to be repaired?

(3) A minister is empowered to give information to the public on the risks of HIV infection: is the minister liable to a person who contracts HIV through injecting heroin if the information only disclosed the risk of infection from sexual contact and omitted the danger of infection from drug abuse?

In *X (minors) v Bedfordshire County Council*,[2] the House of Lords recognised that if a state agency exercised its statutory powers carelessly, there could be liability at common law in negligence. But before there can be liability in negligence, the careless exercise of the statutory powers must amount to a breach of a pre-existing duty of care owed by the agency to the pursuer. Traditionally, the courts have been reluctant to impose on a state agency a duty of care to exercise its powers carefully unless three hurdles were overcome.

(1) If the agency's statutory discretion involves broad issues of policy, the issue is non-justiciable. The paradigm is when an authority has to allocate scarce resources. If, for example, a local authority chose to spend resources on library provision rather than on increasing the number of fire engines, a person who suffered burns in a fire which could not be contained because of the absence of the fire brigade would be unable to sue because the issue of whether more resources should have been spent on fire engines as opposed to books is non-justiciable. In *Kent v Griffiths*[3] Lord Woolf MR recognised that the allocation of resources in respect of the provision of sufficient ambulances and enough staff to man them were matters which were probably not justiciable. In *Ryder v Highland Council*,[4] the Lord Ordinary (Tyre) thought that

the authority's decision not to operate a 24-hour treatment service to remove snow and ice from the A9 was not a justiciable issue.

(2) Where the statutory discretion operates at an operational as opposed to a broad policy level, for a long time it was argued that a duty of care could not be imposed unless the purported exercise of the power was beyond the ambit of the statutory discretion. In determining this issue, the courts adopted quasi-administrative law principles. In particular, it was considered that this hurdle could only be overcome if the exercise of the discretion was such that no reasonable state agency would have acted in this way. In other words, where the mistake, albeit careless, was one which a reasonable state agency or local authority could have made in the bona fide exercise of its powers, a duty of care could not be imposed and accordingly liability at common law for negligence could not arise. So for example, if a fire authority prioritised calls, provided the prioritisation was not unreasonable, the decision would fall within the ambit of the statutory discretion and no liability would arise even if, with hindsight, the prioritisation was mistaken. However, because of developments discussed in (3) below, it is submitted that this 'public law' hurdle is no longer a precondition for the imposition of a duty of care although it remains crucial if the pursuer is seeking judicial review rather than damages for negligence.

(3) The reason why the 'public law' hurdle is now of little, if any, significance is because before the court will impose a duty of care the three-fold *Caparo* criteria have to be satisfied, namely reasonable foreseeability of harm to the pursuer, proximity between the pursuer and defender, and that it is fair, just and reasonable to impose the duty.[5] This enables the courts to decline to impose a duty of care either because of the absence of proximity or on the broader 'fair, just and reasonable' criteria. In *Hill v Chief Constable of West Yorkshire*,[6] for example, the House of Lords held that the chief constable did not owe a duty of care to the mother of the last victim of the Yorkshire Ripper. Not only was there no proximity but Lord Templeman also considered that it would not be fair, just and reasonable to impose a duty of care on the chief constable in relation to his function of investigating crime. Similarly, in *X (minors) v Bedfordshire County Council*[7] it was not thought fair, just and reasonable to impose a duty of care on a local authority or its social workers when exercising their discretion whether or not to take potentially abused children into care. In so doing,

the courts were in effect granting to state agencies blanket immunity from liability in negligence when exercising their discretionary powers.[8]

1 Of course, the criminal will be liable in delict.
2 [1995] 2 AC 633, [1995] 3 All ER 353, HL.
3 [2001] QB 36 at 53.
4 [2013] CSOH 95.
5 See *Caparo Industries plc v Dickman* [1990] 2 AC 605, [1990] 1 All ER 568, HL.
6 [1989] AC 53, [1988], 2 All ER 238, HL.
7 [1995] 2 AC 633, [1995] 3 All ER 353, HL.
8 See also *Forbes v City of Dundee District Council* 1997 SLT 1330, 1997 SCLR 682, OH (not fair, just and reasonable to impose a duty of care on a local authority to ensure that steps were built in accordance with building regulations: the pursuer could, of course, sue the owner/occupier of the building); *Onifade v Secretary of State for Social Security* 1999 GWD 17-819 (no duty of care to prevent pursuer from suffering economic loss as a consequence of an erroneous decision by an adjudication officer refusing the pursuer income support); *Santander v Keeper of the Registers of Scotland* [2013] CSOH 24 (not fair, just and reasonable to impose a duty of care on the Keeper to prevent the bank suffering economic loss when the Keeper registered a forged discharge of a standard security in favour of the bank. The bank and the Keeper were both victims of the forger's crime, but the bank had given the forger the original loan and had sufficient assets to take the risk that she might default and forge a discharge).

11.6 However, the courts can no longer grant blanket immunity as a matter of course. First, in *Osman v United Kingdom*[1] the European Court of Human Rights held that to strike out a claim on the ground that the police enjoyed blanket immunity was a breach of the claimant's right under Article 6 of the European Convention on Human Rights which provides that 'In the determination of his civil rights and obligations … everyone is entitled to a fair and public hearing'. After a period of consternation on the scope of *Osman*,[2] the European Court of Human Rights then took the view that there was no breach of Article 6 merely because an action was dismissed due to the absence of a duty of care, provided that the claimant had had the opportunity to argue that in the circumstances of her case it was fair, just and reasonable to impose a duty and that it would be disproportionate to the harm sustained not to do so.[3] Second, the European Court of Human Rights considered[4] that where a local authority failed to take steps to protect a child who was the subject of abuse, there could be a breach of the *child's* right under Article 3 of the Convention which provides that 'No one shall be subjected to torture or to inhuman or degrading treatment or punishment'. Similarly, failure to have and follow fair procedures when taking a child into care was held by the Court to constitute a breach of the *parent's* right under Article 8 of the Convention 'to respect for his private and family life'.[5] In these cases the claimants obtained substantial damages for breach of their Convention rights in circumstances where damages were not available in delict because of the judges' refusal to impose a duty of care.

As a result of these developments, the courts are now more ready to impose a duty of care on a local authority. In *Barrett v Enfield London Borough Council*,[6] the House of Lords distinguished *X (minors) v Bedfordshire Council* and held that once a child had been taken into care, a local authority could owe the child a common law duty to prevent him suffering mental harm caused by the authority's failure to provide suitable support: it was irrelevant that the local authority's decisions involved the exercise of discretion on the part of professional social workers. In *D v East Berkshire Community NHS Trust*[7] it was accepted that a local authority owed a duty of care to *a child* in relation to the investigation of suspected abuse and the initiation and pursuit of care proceedings.[8] But the House of Lords held that a local authority did not owe the child's *parents* a duty of care to prevent them suffering mental harm if they were wrongly suspected by doctors or social workers of abusing their child: where there was a potential conflict of interests between the parent and child in care proceedings, the child's welfare was the paramount consideration. It was therefore not fair, just or reasonable to impose such a duty. In *Trent Strategic Health Authority v Jain*[9] the plaintiffs were the proprietors of a nursing home. The authority took proceedings under the Registered Homes Act 1984 to cancel the plaintiffs' registration. They did so under an emergency procedure where the plaintiffs had no right to be heard. On appeal the owners of the home were fully exonerated. However, by then the home had been shut for four months and their business was ruined. Nevertheless, the House of Lords held that the authority did not owe them a duty of care when the authority applied to have their registration revoked. The purpose of the authority's statutory powers was to protect the residents of care and nursing homes: in an emergency it could be necessary to have the proprietor's registration cancelled immediately. There was therefore a potential conflict of interest between the owners and the residents in the homes. Therefore, the authority did not owe the proprietors a duty of care when exercising their statutory powers[10]

There are other areas where the pursuer has failed to satisfy the *Caparo* tripartite criteria. In cases where a pursuer alleges that the police or local authority were under a duty to prevent him suffering harm as a result of a third party's criminal activities, it is often impossible to establish a sufficient degree of proximity. This is because the pursuer must show that the defender knew that she was at a greater risk than an ordinary member of the public if the third party regained or retained his liberty. In *Thomson v the Scottish Ministers*,[11] for example, the pursuer was the mother of a woman who was murdered by a prisoner who had been given short leave from jail. The Inner House held that the prison authorities did not owe the victim a duty of care to prevent her being harmed by the prisoner when he was released. There was no evidence that she was the subject of a special or distinct risk if the prisoner was released and therefore there was no proximity between her and the prison authorities.

But even where there is sufficient proximity because the pursuer knows that he is in danger from a particular person and has made his fears known to the relevant authority,[12] the House of Lords held in *Van Colle v Chief Constable of Hertfordshire*[13] that the core principle of public policy laid down in *Hill v Chief Constable*[14] *viz* that the police do not owe a common law duty of care to protect individuals against harm caused by criminals, should normally prevail. The imposition of such a duty of care would distort, by encouraging defensive action, the manner in which the police would otherwise deploy their limited resources and would cause resources to be diverted from the performance of the public duties of the police. Accordingly it is only when the police have voluntarily assumed responsibility for the pursuer's safety, for example to provide protection, that such a duty will be imposed.

1 [1999] 1 FLR 193.
2 See, for example, *Barrett v Enfield Borough Council* [2001] 2 AC 550 per Lord Browne-Wilkinson at 559–560; *Kent v Griffiths* [2001] QB 36 per Lord Woolf MR at 50.
3 *Z v United Kingdom* [2001] 2 FLR 612.
4 *Z v United Kingdom* [2001] 2 FLR 612 ('appeal' from *X (minors) v Bedfordshire County Council* [1995] 2 AC 633); *E v United Kingdom* (2003) 36 EHRR 31 (action against Scottish local authority for failure to protect children from sex abuse by their stepfather).
5 *TP and KM v United Kingdom* [2001] 2 FLR 549.
6 [2001] 2 AC 550. See also *S v Gloucester County Council* [2000] 3 All ER 346 (local authority owed a duty of care to a child not to be sexually abused by a foster parent).
7 [2005] AC 373.
8 To that extent, *X (minors) v Bedfordshire County Council* was not followed as being inconsistent with the child's rights under the European Convention on Human Rights.
9 [2009] UK HL 4.
10 This case arose before the Human Rights Act 1998. The court thought that had it been in force the plaintiff would have obtained compensation for breaches of Article 6 and Article 1 of the First Protocol: 'Every natural or legal person is entitled to the peaceful enjoyment of his possessions. No one shall be deprived

of his possessions except in the public interest and subject to the conditions provided for by law.'
11 [2013] CSIH 63.
12 As happened in *Osman v UK* [1999] 1 FLR 193.
13 [2008] 3 WLR 593: see also *Brooks v Comr of Police of the Metropolis* [2005] 1WLR 1495.
14 [1989] AC 53, discussed above para 11.5.

11.7   On the other hand, the courts have become more ready to accept that an employee of a state agency may owe a direct duty of care to the claimant for which the local authority is vicariously liable if the employee is negligent. In *Phelps v Hillingdon London Borough Council*,[1] the House of Lords held that while, in the performance of their duties under the Education Acts, education authorities owed no relevant duty of care to school children, nevertheless individual employees of the authorities might owe a common law duty of care if they had assumed responsibility for the child: if this duty was breached then the local authority would be vicariously liable. Consequently, the local authority in this case could be vicariously liable for an educational psychologist's failure to assess and provide appropriate assistance for a pupil with special needs.[2]

Once a duty of care is established, the pursuer must prove that there was a breach of duty. As we have seen,[3] it can be very difficult to establish professional negligence. In *Bradford-Smart v West Sussex County Council*,[4] for example, a girl was bullied on a bus going to and from school. The Court of Appeal held that the school would not be in breach of its duty towards the girl if it had only failed to take steps which were unlikely to do much good. A reasonable body of opinion would have taken the view that the school had done enough to protect her from bullying and accordingly her claim failed as she could not prove that the school had been negligent.

The pursuer must also prove that the defender's negligence was the cause of the harm sustained. He must show that he was worse off as a result of the carelessly delivered service than if the service had not been provided at all. In *Gibson v Orr*,[5] a bridge carrying a public road collapsed. The police assumed control of the hazard. They coned off the north side and positioned a police vehicle on the bridge as a warning to drivers on the south side. After an hour, they left without having received confirmation that any barrier or warning was in place on the south side. The pursuer was injured when the car in which he was a passenger was driven onto the bridge from the south side and fell into the river. In a fully reasoned speech, the Lord Ordinary (Hamilton) held that the police authority owed the pursuer a duty of care. By purporting to take control of the hazard, the police constables entered into proximate relationships with those road users likely to be immediately and directly affected by that hazard. Moreover, unlike the case of the investigation of crime where the *Hills* core principle would apply, there were no policy reasons why it would not be fair, just and reasonable to impose the duty. The difficulty is that the accident would have happened in exactly the same way even if the service had not been provided at all. However, the whole point of the defender's duty was to prevent an accident occurring after the officers had taken control and assumed responsibility for potential road users. If the duty of care had been performed, the accident in which the pursuer was injured would not have happened.

This is quite different from the situation where, owing to its operational carelessness, a fire brigade increases the risk of damage to the pursuer's life or property ie when the pursuer's position is worse off as a consequence of the careless delivery of the service. In *Duff v Highland and Islands Fire Board*,[6] it was held that a fire brigade owed a duty of care not to be careless when engaged in fire fighting. The defender had attended to a fire in the pursuer's chimney which restarted after the brigade had left, causing the destruction of the pursuer's house![7] This decision was followed in *Burnett v Grampian Fire and Rescue Service*[8] where the Lord Ordinary (Macphail) held that while it might be arguable that there was insufficient proximity when a fire brigade fails to turn up at all, a duty of care arises when the fire brigade has assumed responsibility to protect the pursuer's property from fire.

1 [2001] 2 AC 619.
2 See also *A v Essex County Council* [2003] 1 FLR 615 (local authority vicariously liable for social workers' failure to inform potential adoptive parents that the child to be adopted was seriously disturbed).
3 On professional liability, see Chapter 7 above.
4 [2002] EWCA Civ 7.
5 1999 SC 420. Cf *Alexandrou v Oxford* [1993] 4 All ER 328 (no duty of care to owner of property which police had inspected in response to a burglar alarm).
6 1995 SLT 1362.
7 In *Capital and Counties plc v Hampshire County Council* [1997] QB 1004, [1997] 2 All ER 865, CA, the Court of Appeal held that a fire brigade did not owe a duty of care to a member of the public to answer calls for help because there was no proximity at that stage. Once the brigade had turned up and begun fighting the fire, a duty of care arose not to increase the risk of injury or damage caused by the original fire as a result of carelessness in carrying out the operations. In *OLL v Secretary of State for the Home Dept* [1997] 3 All ER 897, following *Capital and Counties plc*, Moy J held that the coastguard service was under no enforceable

private law duty to respond to an emergency call: if it did, it was only liable in negligence for positive acts which directly caused greater injury than would have occurred if it had not intervened at all.

8 2007 SCLR 192.

11.8 We have been considering potential liability in negligence for the careless exercise of statutory powers. A similar approach has been taken when a local authority or state agency has failed to use a statutory power which it was not obliged to exercise under the legislation. In *Stovin v Wise and Norfolk County Council*,[1] a local authority had a statutory power to direct a landowner to remove a wall which was a danger to users of the highway. Before the plaintiff was injured in a road accident, the local authority had known the wall was a hazard but had not exercised the power to have the danger removed. The House of Lords held that while the local authority had a public law duty to consider whether or not to exercise the power, this did not automatically confer a common law right on an individual to obtain damages if injured as a consequence of the authority's decision not to exercise its powers. A common law duty of care would only arise from such an omission if (i) the local authority's failure to exercise the power was irrational (the 'public law' hurdle), and (ii) the legislation did not exclude the right of a person to seek damages if harm was sustained because the power was not exercised. However, in *Gorringe v Calderdale MBC*[2] Lord Hoffman held that it was 'difficult to imagine a case in which a common law duty can be founded simply upon the failure (however irrational) to provide some benefit which a public authority has power (or a public duty) to provide'.[3] Here the local authority had not provided a warning on a stretch of road of the danger of driving too fast. This omission could not in itself generate a common law duty of care when the authority's failure to exercise its powers under s 39 of the Road Traffic Act 1988 to promote road safety did not give rise to a private law remedy for breach of statutory duty. Accordingly, the possibility raised in *Stovin v Wise* of deriving a common law duty of care merely from a failure to exercise a statutory power would appear to be closed.

In *MacDonald v Aberdeenshire*[4] the Inner House accepted that Scots Law differed from English law in that 'road authorities are liable in negligence, but only in respect of hazards, in the sense of defects that are unlikely to be noticed by road users who exercise reasonable care and skill'.[5] Since the duty is restricted to the removal of hazards that would *not* be noticed by a reasonably skilful driver, the scope of the duty is narrow. Applying the Scottish test would give the same result as in *Stovin* as the hazard there was obvious. Similarly, there would be no liability if the authority failed to clear snow as the reasonable driver would easily recognise the hazard.

1 [1996] AC 923, [1996] 3 All ER 801, HL.
2 [2004] UKHL15, [2004] 2 All ER 326, [2004] 1 WLR 1057, [2004] RTR 443, HL.
3 [2004] UKHL 15 at para 32.
4 [2013] CSIH 83.
5 Per Lord Drummond Young at para 71.

11.9   There is little doubt that this is one of the most difficult areas of the law of delict. If the statute provides for a private right to sue for breach of statutory duty, there is no difficulty. If this is not the case, there is a presumption that a common law duty of care does not arise. Put another way, the failure to exercise a statutory power or fulfil a statutory duty should not give rise to liability since the law of delict provides reparation for harm wrongfully caused not recompense for the failure to receive a benefit, for example having the roads gritted for ice or snow. Where harm is caused by a state agency in exercising its statutory powers, a duty of care can be imposed but for policy reasons it may not be fair, just or reasonable to do so. However, a duty may arise, even in these circumstances, if the state agency has nevertheless assumed responsibility for the personal safety of the pursuer or his property.

Article 2 of the European Convention provides that 'Everyone's right to life shall be protected by law. No one shall be deprived of his life intentionally.' A State Agency can therefore be liable for a breach of Article 2 if it has failed to take sufficient measures to protect a person's life: this could include the person being killed by a third party. But before there is a breach of Article 2 it has to be shown that the public authority had or ought to have known at the time of a real and immediate risk to the life of an identified individual from the criminal acts of a third party[1] and that it failed to take reasonable measures to avoid that risk. This is a very high test. In *Van Colle v Chief Constable of Herefordshire*[2] the state had called Van Colle as a witness in a trial. Since there was no evidence to suggest that the accused was violent, it could not have been reasonably anticipated that the accused would kill him: consequently there was no breach of Article 2. For the same reason there was no breach of Article 2 in *Mitchell v Glasgow City Council*,[3] or *Thomson v Scottish Ministers*.[4]

It is important to appreciate that in this section we have been concerned with the possibility of delictual liability arising from the exercise of a discretionary power by a minister of the Crown, a local authority or another governmental agency. Where there is no degree of discretion involved, unless the statute provides the state agency with immunity, liability will arise if the ordinary criteria for delictual liability are satisfied. In *Kent v Griffiths*,[5] for example, the plaintiff suffered brain damage because an ambulance which she had summoned failed to arrive within a reasonable time of her call. No explanation was given for the delay: indeed, the crew had falsified the time records. The Court of Appeal held that since there was an ambulance available and there had been no alternative demands on the crew, they owed the plaintiff a duty of care to arrive within a reasonable time of her call; by accepting the call they had assumed responsibility for the patient. This was not a case which involved policy or resource issues but consisted of a routine task which had been carried out carelessly, to the plaintiff's cost. Similarly, the driver of a ministerial motor car or a local authority bus owes the same *Donoghue v Stevenson* duty of care[6] to a fellow road user as an ordinary driver and will be liable in delict if the duty of care is breached. In other words, the defender owes the pursuer a duty of care independent of her status as an employee of a state agency. In these circumstances, the state agency will be vicariously liable for the delict of its employee provided, of course, the employee was acting within the scope of her employment at the time the accident occurred.[7]

1 There could also be a breach of Article 2 if a state agency fails to prevent a person killing herself when there was a real and immediate risk that she might do so, for example if she was in a mental hospital suffering from depression: *Savage v South Essex Partnership Trust* [2008] UKHL 74; *Rabone v Pennine Care NHS Trust* [2012] UKSC 2 In *Smith v Ministry of Defence* [2013] UKSC 41 the Supreme Court held that the court's jurisdiction to protect persons from a breach of Article 2 extended to members of the armed forces serving abroad.
2 [2008] 3 WLR 593.
3 [2009] UKHL 11, 2009 SLT 265, discussed above para 10.3.
4 [2013] CSIH 63.
5 [2001] QB 36. See also *Aitken v Scottish Ambulance Service* [2011] CSOH 49 (a child died in hospital after arriving by ambulance. There had been a delay of 21 minutes between the emergency call being answered and the ambulance dispatched. Proof before answer allowed to establish whether there had been breach of a duty of care which arose when the ambulance service assumed responsibility for the welfare of the child).
6 See *Donoghue v Stevenson* 1932 SC (HL) 31, 1932 SLT 317.
7 On vicarious liability, see Chapter 12 below.

CHAPTER 12

Employers' liability and vicarious liability

A. EMPLOYERS' LIABILITY

12.1　It is an implied term of the contract of employment that an employer will take reasonable care for the safety of his employees. If an employer does not take reasonable care, he will be in material breach of contract. In these circumstances, an employee may withdraw his labour and sue for damages. An employer may be in breach of his contractual obligations even if the employee has not suffered any harm. In addition to his contractual obligations, an employer owes a *Donoghue v Stevenson* duty of care[1] to his employees to prevent them from suffering physical or psychiatric harm as a result of the employer's negligent conduct. Accordingly, an employee who is injured may sue his employer in delict as well as for breach of contract; but the employee cannot be compensated twice for the same loss. If the employee does not suffer any harm, there can be no liability in delict though there might still be a remedy for breach of contract.[2]

The obligation to take reasonable care for the safety of his employees is personal to the employer, ie it cannot be delegated by the employer to senior employees or a third party.[3] However, in a modern industrial context, in order to *fulfil* the obligation of reasonable care, an employer may have to appoint a safety officer and/or safety committee. The scope of the duty incumbent on an employer includes taking reasonable care to supply the employee with proper plant and equipment, to select competent fellow workers and to provide a safe system of working; but it is a *general* duty to take reasonable care. For example, an employer can be liable for failure to *devise* a safe system of working.[4] Where an employer fails to instruct an employee to use protective devices or clothes, or fails to provide adequate training, a breach of the duty to take reasonable care can arise: *Pickford v ICI plc*.[5] An employer may also have to train employees to protect themselves from violent third parties they may meet in the course of their employment, for example school children![6]

Moreover, it cannot be overemphasised that at common law the employer is only expected to maintain the standards of the reasonable person in his position, ie it is only to take reasonable care. An employer is not expected to ensure that an employee is never harmed. In assessing whether or not a particular employer has taken reasonable care, the calculus of risk will be relevant.[7] The court will therefore consider such factors as the nature of the danger, the employer's knowledge of the danger, the extent of the harm, the probability of the harm arising and the cost of eliminating the risk.[8]

1 See *Donoghue v Stevenson* 1932 SC (HL) 31, 1932 SLT 317, and Chapter 3 above. The existence of a contract between the employer and employee is an important factor in establishing the 'foreseeability of harm' criterion.
2 *Rothwell v Chemical and Insulating Co* [2008] 1 AC 281 (pleural plaques do not constitute harm and therefore no delictual liability) discussed above at para 5.2.
3 *Hislop v Durham* (1842) 4 D 1168. In *MacIver v J & A Gardner Ltd* 2001 SLT 585, it was held that an employer owed a duty of care to a ship's master who was the safety officer in charge of the ship. On non-delegable duties, see *Woodland v Swimming Teachers' Association* [2013] UKSC 66.
4 *McGregor v AAH Pharmaceuticals Ltd* 1996 SLT 1161, OH.
5 *Pickford v ICI plc* [1996] ICR 566, [1996] IRLR 622, CA.
6 *McLeod v Aberdeen City Council* 1999 GWD 23-1115.
7 *Brisco v Secretary of State for Scotland* 1997 SC 14; *McErlean v J & B Scotland Ltd* 1997 SLT 1326; *Mcginnes v Endeva Service Ltd.* 2006 SLT 638. On the calculus of risk generally, see paras 5.10 ff above.
8 *Latimer v AEC Ltd* [1953] AC 643, [1953] 2 All ER 449, HL; *Hatton v Sutherland* [2002] 2 All ER 1; *Barber v Somerset County Council* [2004] UKHL 13.

12.2   In *Davie v New Merton Board Mills Ltd,*[1] for example, an employee was injured when a piece of a chisel he was using broke and a splinter entered into his eye. The defect in the chisel was latent and arose as a result of the metal used for the chisel not having been tempered properly by the manufacturer. The employer had bought the chisel from a reputable retailer who had in turn bought it from a reputable wholesaler who had purchased it from the manufacturer. In these circumstances, the House of Lords held that the employer had taken reasonable care and the employee's action against the *employer* failed. The employee could, of course, have sued the manufacturer in delict for breach of the manufacturer's *Donoghue v Stevenson* duty of care which he owed to the ultimate consumer of the product.[2] However, the view was taken that this was placing too heavy an onus on an employee. Accordingly, under the Employers' Liability (Defective

Equipment) Act 1969,[3] if an employee suffers physical harm as a result of a defect in equipment[4] provided by the employer and the defect is attributable wholly or partly to the fault of a third party,[5] for example the manufacturer, then the defect is deemed to be also attributable to negligence on the part of the employer. In other words, the employee can sue the employer without the need to prove that the employer was negligent. The *employer* will then seek redress against the third party either in contract or, theoretically at least, in delict.

The employer has to take reasonable care in selecting competent workers who will not cause harm to the other employees. If the employer fails to do so and an employee is injured as a result, the employee can sue the employee for breach of the duty of care.[6] Again it must be emphasised that the employer is only expected to take reasonable care. Before the employer can be negligent, he must know that the employee he has appointed could be a danger to fellow workers.[7] The contract of employment is not a contract *uberrimae fidei*; the employer must therefore make reasonable enquiries to determine whether or not an aspirant employee would be a source of danger to fellow employees if he were to be engaged. For example, the employer should ask whether or not an applicant for a job as a van driver has a clean driving licence and whether or not he has been convicted of careless or reckless driving.[8]

The duty to provide a safe system of working is owed to the particular employee. And so if an employer knows that an employee is an epileptic or has only one eye, the standards required to constitute reasonable care may be greater in respect of that employee than the other workers. Accordingly, the employer may be negligent vis-à-vis that employee even if his conduct would not amount to negligence if the employee were not epileptic or had two eyes.[9]

1 [1959] AC 604.
2 See *Donoghue v Stevenson* 1932 SC (HL) 31, 1932 SLT 317. On product liability generally, see Chapter 8 above.
3 Employers' Liability (Defective Equipment) Act 1969, s 1(1).
4 The courts have taken a wide view of the meaning of 'equipment' in order to protect employees: see, for example, *Knowles v Liverpool City Council* [1993] 4 All ER 321, [1993] 1 WLR 1428, HL (council employee injured by a defective flagstone: flagstone held to constitute equipment).
5 The pursuer is not obliged to identify the third party who was at fault: *Edwards v Butlins Ltd* 1998 SLT 500, 1997 GWD 21-1052.
6 The duty extends to providing adequate supervision of employees whose behaviour at work might injure a fellow worker: *Gibson v British Rail Maintenance* 1995 SC 7, 1995 SLT 953 (pursuer injured by a ball which was being used in a game played by two other employees: employer liable because foreman was

absent when the game was being played); *Ward v Scotrail Railways Ltd* 1999 SC 255 (pursuer suffered a psychiatric disorder as a result of a fellow employee's sexual molestation: employer would be in breach of the duty if he failed to stop the harassment); *Waters v Commissioner of Police of the Metropolis* [2000] 4 All ER 934 (plaintiff claimed to have been raped and buggered by a fellow officer in her police residential accommodation: defendant did not investigate her complaint and she suffered victimisation and harassment from the other officers for bringing a complaint. The House of Lords held that the defendant was in breach of duty in their failure to prevent her fellow officers from taking retaliatory steps against the plaintiff).

7 See, for example, *Hudson v Ridge Manufacturing Co Ltd* [1957] 2 QB 348, [1957] 2 All ER 348.
8 Subject to the offences being spent under the Rehabilitation of Offenders Act 1974.
9 *Paris v Stepney Borough Council* [1951] AC 367, [1951] 1 All ER 42, HL.

12.3 The employer's general duty includes taking reasonable steps to prevent the employee suffering *psychiatric*[1] as well as physical harm.[2] In *Hatton v Sutherland*[3] the Court of Appeal held that where an employee has sustained psychiatric harm there are no special control mechanisms and the ordinary principles of employers' liability apply. Accordingly, the employee must show that the employer was in breach of the duty of care. As we have seen,[4] there will be no breach unless it can be shown that the harm sustained by the pursuer was a reasonably foreseeable consequence of the employer's conduct. But by its nature psychiatric harm is less foreseeable than physical harm. Moreover, in *Hatton* the court took the view that an employer is usually entitled to assume that an employee can withstand the normal pressures of work unless the employer knows that the employee is particularly vulnerable. This could arise, for example, where the employer was aware that the employee had had a nervous breakdown before[5] or the employee's doctor had informed him that the working conditions were causing the employee to suffer depression[6] or there have been unexplained and uncharacteristic absences from work. There can be liability if the psychiatric injury was caused by an excessive workload, ie where the employee was required to perform duties far beyond those agreed in her contract.[7]

An employer does not have a general duty to monitor employees to see whether they are at risk of suffering psychiatric harm and taking steps to prevent them doing so.[8] But even if psychiatric harm was reasonably foreseeable, there is no liability unless the employee can show that there were reasonable steps which the employer should have taken to prevent him suffering mental harm.[9] The economic costs to the business of reducing the risk and fairness to other employees will be important factors in determining whether or not the employer had taken reasonable care. If the only way to prevent the employee suffering mental harm was to dismiss him from the job, an employer is not in breach if the employee chooses to continue working.[10] In short, while an employer's general duty of care to protect his employees includes psychiatric as well as physical harm, it will be very difficult to establish a breach of duty in respect of psychiatric harm caused by stressful work unless the employer knew that the employee was particularly vulnerable and there were reasonable – as opposed to difficult or expensive – steps to reduce the pressure on the employee.

Where an employee suffers psychiatric harm from witnessing the physical – or mental – injuries of a third person, for example a fellow employee,[11] the employer does not owe a duty of care unless the employee was within the area of risk of potential physical harm[12] or the *Alcock* criteria for liability in respect to psychiatric injury to secondary victims are satisfied.[13] In *Keen v Tayside Contracts*,[14] for example, a worker was instructed by his employer to assist the emergency services at the scene of a road accident. There he saw the crushed and burned bodies of the victims. The pursuer's supervisor refused him permission to leave the scene of the accident even though he asked to do so. The pursuer claimed that the employer was negligent in (a) failing to instruct supervisors to let employees leave the scene of an accident where there were dead and mutilated bodies and (b) failing to provide post-incident support for employees who had been disturbed by seeing the victims. The Lord Ordinary (Paton) dismissed the action. Although acting in the course of his employment, the pursuer was a secondary victim since the psychiatric harm was caused by witnessing the victims of the road accident: the *Alcock* criteria could not be satisfied as there was no relationship of love and affection between the victims and the pursuer.[15]

---

1 Stress in itself does not per se constitute psychiatric harm though it may lead to a psychiatric disorder if allowed to continue unabated.

2 *Fraser v State Hospitals Board for Scotland* 2001 SLT 1051; *Cross v Highland and Islands Enterprise* 2001 SLT 1060; *Green v Argyll & Bute Council* 2002 GWD 9-295. In *McCarthy v Highland Council* [2011] CSIH 51 the defender was found liable for the psychiatric injury suffered by a teacher as a result of their failure to provide her with a dedicated male support worker after she had been assaulted on several occasions by a pupil who required special educational needs.

3 [2002] 2 All ER 1 approved by the House of Lords in *Barber v Somerset County Council* [2004] UKHL 13.

4 Paras 5.4 ff above.

5 *Walker v Northumberland CC* [1995] 1 All ER 737.

6 *Stevenson v East Dunbartonshire Council* 2003 SLT 97; *Barber v Somerset County Council* [2004] UKHL 13.

7 *Flood v University of Glasgow* 2010 SLT 167. The excessive workload enabled the Inner House to distinguish the case from *Hatton*.

8 *Chapman v The Lord Advocate* 2006 SCLR 186; *Donaldson v The Scottish Ministers* 2009 SLT 240 (prison officer had been suffering from stress but employer was told that he was fit to return to work: therefore employer could not reasonably foresee that he would suffer a psychiatric disorder).

9 If the employer has taken reasonable steps there will be no breach of duty: see for example *Pratt v Scottish Ministers* 2013 SLT 590.

10 *Walker v Northumberland CC* [1995] 1 All ER 737.

11 See, for instance, *Robertson v Forth Road Bridge Joint Board* 1995 SC 364; *Hunter v British Coal Corporation* [1999] QB 140.

12 In which case the employee is a primary victim and is protected by the employer's general duty to take reasonable care of his employees. It can be difficult to determine whether or not an employee has sufficient proximity to the accident which caused the harm to the third party to be regarded as a participant and therefore a primary victim. See *Robertson v Forth Road Bridge Joint Board* 1995 SC 364; *Campbell v North Lanarkshire Council* 2000 SCLR 245; *Young v Charles Church (Southern) Ltd* 2000 SCLR 373; *Salter v UB Frozen & Chilled Foods Ltd* 2003 SLT 1011.

13 Namely that there was a relationship of love and affection between the employee and the person who was injured, proximity to the accident or its immediate aftermath and direct visual observation of the accident or its aftermath.

14 2003 SLT 500.

15 This is consistent with the decision of the House of Lords in *Frost v Chief Constable of South Yorkshire Police* [1999] AC 455 where the injuries to the third parties witnessed by the plaintiffs were also caused by their employer. For discussion, see para 4.5 above. In *Donaldson v the Scottish Ministers* 2009 SLT 240 the pursuer suffered a psychiatric illness from watching one prisoner assaulting another prisoner. The Lord Ordinary (Woolman) held that the pursuer had not demonstrated what the employee should have done to avoid the incident.

12.4   The employer must provide a safe environment in which his employee works.[1] Where an employee works at a place which is not under the control of his employer, the employer can still be liable for failing to inspect the premises to ensure that the employee is not exposed to unnecessary risks.[2] It has been held that there can be a breach of the duty if the employer has not taken reasonable steps to protect an employee from the risk of illness arising from passive smoking.[3]

At common law the onus lay on the employee to prove that the harm sustained was a breach of the employer's duty of care, ie that the employer was negligent. Since the nineteenth century, safety at work has been the subject of statutory regulations. These provide detailed safety requirements for machinery, particular processes and operations. Although earlier statutes provided criminal sanctions in cases of breach, the courts allowed an employee who was injured as a result to sue the employer in delict for breach of statutory duty. Moreover, as the statutes often imposed strict liability, an employee who sued for breach of statutory duty did not have to establish negligence. But, of course, the employee had to show that the employer was in breach of the statutory obligations.[4]

The Health and Safety at Work etc Act 1974 lays down the minimum standards required of employers for safety at the workplace. It is, however, a criminal statute and it is expressly enacted that its breach does not give rise to a private law remedy for breach of statutory duty. Confusingly, the morass of safety legislation, in particular the Factories Act 1961, continued in force for a while and breach of these provisions did give rise to an action for breach of statutory duty. But now much of this legislation has been repealed and replaced by statutory regulations implementing EU directives.[5] Breach of these detailed regulations will, in general, continue to give rise to delictual liability. Discussion of these regulations is outside the compass of the current work. Nevertheless, where an employee is injured as a result of a breach of these regulations, it is important to remember that he will still be able to sue for breach of statutory duty and plead the employer's negligence at common law in the alternative. As in all cases of breach of statutory duty, *volens* is not a defence unless expressly allowed in the statutory regulations, but the employee's damages may be reduced on the grounds of contributory negligence.

An employer may owe the employee a duty of care under the Occupiers' Liability (Scotland) Act 1960, as well as the general duty of care owed to employees at common law.[6]

1 For example, that the level of noise in the workplace will not cause deafness. The pursuer must establish the level of the noise: *Robinson v Midlothian Council* [2009] CSOH 109.

2 *Crombie v McDermott Scotland Ltd* 1996 SLT 1238, 1996 Rep LR 122, OH; *Muir v North Ayrshire Council* 2005 SLT 963 (pursuer was a home help who was injured in the house of a client: employer could be liable as they knew the environment in which she was working).

3 *Rae v Strathclyde Joint Police Board* 1999 GWD 12-571.

4 See, for example, *Thomson v Kvaerner Govan Ltd* 2004 SLT 24, HL.

5 See, for example, the Provision and Use of Work Equipment Regulations 1998, and the Manual Handling Operations Regulations 1992. On the Provision and Use of Work Equipment Regulations 1998, see *Smith v Northamptonshire CC* [2009] UKHL 27, where the Supreme Court stated that courts should be careful not to impose upon employers responsibilities that went far beyond those at which the Directive and Regulations were aimed; on the Manual Handling Operations Regulations 1992, see for example, *MacDonald v Wood Group Engineering (North Sea) Ltd* [2010] CSOH 165. On the Workplace (Health, Safety and Welfare) Regulations 1992, see for example, *Munro v Aberdeen City Council* [2009] CSOH 129; *Gillie v Scottish Borders Council* [2013] CSOH 76. On the Noise at Work Regulations 1989, see *Robinson v Midlothian Council* [2009] CSOH 109.

6 *Hill v Lovett* 1992 SLT 994, OH.

B. VICARIOUS LIABILITY

(1) Introduction

12.5   In certain circumstances a person may be liable for the delicts committed by another. This is known as vicarious liability. Although the doctrine arises out of several relationships, the most common by far is that of employer and employee.[1] An employer is vicariously liable for the wrongs committed by the employee in the course of his employment. This arises when the employee concerned harms a third party or another employee provided the delict was committed in the course of employment. Although the employer and employee are jointly and severally liable, in practice the pursuer will sue the employer who is more likely to have funds or be insured. Where it is an employee who has been injured, the employer is obliged by statute to have insurance so that funds are available if he is found to be vicariously liable.[2] Where an employee has been negligent, if the employer is found vicariously liable, the employer can, in theory at least, recover the damages he has paid from the employee, since the employee's wrongful conduct constitutes a breach by the employee of the contract of employment.[3] In practice, an employer – or his insurers – do not exercise this right to sue the employee for breach of contract.

1 In child abuse cases vicarious liability has attached when the relationship is 'akin to employment': *Various Claimants v Catholic Child Welfare Society* [2012] UKSC 56.
2 Employers' Liability (Compulsory Insurance) Act 1969. In Scotland, it has been held that failure to insure can result in the directors of a company being personally liable in a claim for damages for breach of statutory duty: *Quinn v McGinty* 1999 SLT (Sh Ct) 27. In England, it has been held by the Court of Appeal that no civil liability lies for breach of the Employers' Liability (Compulsory Insurance) Act 1969: see *Richardson v Pitt-Stanley* [1995] QB 123, [1995] 1 All ER 460, CA.
3 *Lister v Romford Ice and Cold Storage Co Ltd* [1957] AC 555, [1957] 1 All ER 125, HL.

(2) Wrongs of an employee

12.6   The first issue is to determine whether the relationship of employer and employee exists between the person who committed the delict and the person alleged to be vicariously liable: whether the person who committed the wrong is working under a contract of employment (*locatio operarum*) or is an independent contractor working under a contract for services (*locatio operis faciendi*). The traditional test for distinguishing between a contract of employment and a contract for services is that of 'control':[1] an employer has the power to control not only what the employee should do but also *how* he should do it. If A has a cleaner who regularly cleans A's house, there is a contract of employment since A can tell the cleaner not only what to do but the manner in which the work is to be done. On the other hand, if A wishes to have a suit dry cleaned, while he may tell the cleaners what to do, A does not have the power to tell them how to carry out the dry-cleaning process: here A is simply entering into a contract for the services of the dry cleaner and not a contract of employment.

The 'control' test remains a useful criterion where the work involved is relatively unskilled. But it is of less value where the alleged employer is a company or large organisation and the work involved is specialist and sophisticated. The courts have therefore had to develop other criteria. Where a person works as an integral part of an organisation, he is likely to be working under a contract of employment, particularly if there is some element of control.[2] Although the parties' expressed intention in their contract is an important factor, the 'label' they have used to describe their relationship is not decisive. As Lord Denning MR observed in *Massey v Crown Life Insurance Co:*[3]

'If the true relationship of the parties is that of master and servant under a contract of service [a contract of employment], the parties cannot alter the truth of that relationship by putting a different label upon it.'

On the other hand, if the relationship between the parties is ambiguous, the 'label' in the contract may be a crucial factor in determining the true relationship between them.[4] An important consideration is the economic reality of the situation. If, for example, the worker supplies his own equipment and materials and takes the 'economic risk' inherent in the enterprise, it is more likely that he is an independent contractor than an employee.[5] On the other hand, where the worker purchases equipment using money lent to him by the other party to the contract who has an option to purchase the equipment for a nominal sum at the end of the contract, then the court would be likely to hold that this is a contract of employment although technically the worker owns the equipment. Other important factors include the payment of National Insurance contributions, the pension position, the payment of Schedule D or Schedule E taxation, whether or not the worker is paid a fee or a sum on a regular basis and the arrangements for termination of the contract.

1 *Yewans v Nokes* (1880) 6 QBD 530. On vicarious liability, see Aidan O'Donnell, SULI *Delict* Chapter 4.
2 *Stevenson, Jordan and Harrison Ltd v MacDonald and Evans* (1952) 69 RPC 10, [1952] 1 TLR 101, CA.

3 [1978] ICR 590 at 594, [1978] 2 All ER 576 at 579, CA.
4 *Massey v Crown Life Insurance Co* [1978] ICR 590 at 594, [1978] 2 All ER 576 at 579, CA.
5 See, for example, *Ready Mixed Concrete (South East) Ltd v Minister of Pensions and National Insurance* [1968] 2 QB 497, [1968] 1 All ER 433.

12.7 The courts can therefore consider a wide range of factors. This has long been recognised as the proper approach in Scots law.[1] It should be emphasised that in the vast majority of cases it will be clear whether the contract between the parties is one of employment or for services. However, in hard cases, ie where the nature of the contract is ambiguous, the multiple tests approach gives the courts considerable discretion in determining whether or not a contract of employment exists. Where the issue is whether a worker is an employee for the purpose of the doctrine of vicarious liability, it is thought that the courts would be reluctant to find that a worker was not an employee if this would mean that the pursuer would not obtain reparation because the defender was without requisite funds or insurance. Nevertheless, there are occasions when this happens. In *Toms v Royal Mail Group plc*[2] a driver was assigned to the defender by an employment agency with whom the driver had entered into a temporary worker agreement. When he was driving for the PO at night, the driver fell asleep at the wheel. There was an accident in which the driver's son and stepson were killed. Although the PO had control over the driver, the Lord Ordinary (Glennie) held that there was no mutuality of obligations between them so as to create a contract of employment. Therefore, the PO could not be vicariously liable for the driver's negligence. This case exposes a serious gap in the protection of third parties who are injured by temporary agency workers.

Having established that a contract of employment exists between the parties, the employer will be vicariously liable for the wrongs committed by the employee 'in the course of the employment'.[3] In other words, before an employer is vicariously liable, the employee's acts or omissions which constitute the delict must fall within the scope of his employment. This will arise when the delict is a mode or method – albeit wrongful – of the kind of work the employee is engaged to do. The classic exposition of the doctrine in Scots law is to be found in the judgment of the Lord President (Clyde) in *Kirby v National Coal Board:*[4]

'But, in the decisions, four different types of situation have been envisaged as guides to the solution of this problem. In the first place, if the master actually authorised the particular act, he is clearly [vicariously] liable for it. Secondly, where the workman does some work which he is appointed to do, but does it in a way which his master has not authorised and would not have authorised had he known of it, the master is nevertheless still responsible, for the servant's act is still within the scope of his employment. On the other hand, in the third place, if the servant is employed only to do a particular work or a particular class of work, and he does something outside the scope of that work, the master is not responsible for any mischief the servant may do to a third party. Lastly, if the servant uses his master's time or his master's tools for his own purposes, the master is not responsible.'

1 See, for example, *Short v J & W Henderson Ltd* 1946 SC (HL) 24, 1946 SLT 230; *United Wholesale Grocers Ltd v Sher* 1993 SLT 284, OH.
2 2006 SLT 431.
3 An employer is not vicariously liable unless all the aspects of the employee's conduct which constitute the delict have occurred in the course of employment. Thus, if A and B commit a delict, the employer of A is only vicariously liable if the combined conduct of both A and B amounts to a delict in the course of A's employment: *Credit Lyonnais Bank Nederland NV* (now known as *Generale Bank Nederland NV*) *v Export Credits Guarantee Department* [2000] 1 AC 486. Thus, if A's conduct per se does not constitute a delict, A's employer is not vicariously liable if B's conduct would be outwith the scope of A's employment if A had carried out B's acts or omissions. See also *Royal Bank of Scotland v Bannerman Johnstone Maclay* 2003 SC 125.
4 1958 SC 514 at 532–533, 1959 SLT 7.

12.8 Taking these four situations in turn: (1) If an employer has expressly or impliedly authorised the wrongful conduct, the employee is acting within the scope of the employment and the employer is vicariously liable for the delict. In *Neville v C & A Modes Ltd*[1] for example, the pursuer was suspected of shoplifting by employees of the defender. She was forcibly taken from the street back into the shop and there accused of theft. The pursuer argued that the defender was vicariously liable for defamation of character. The Inner House held that the defender's employees had a duty under their contracts of employment to protect the defender's property and take action to prevent theft. The employees' action had therefore been authorised by the defender, ie was within the scope of their employment, albeit that it may have been defamatory in the circumstances of this case.[2]

1 1945 SC 175, 1945 SLT 189.
2 On defamation, see Chapter 15 below.

12.9 (2) If the employee does work which he was authorised to do, but does it in a way which the employer has not authorised and would not have authorised, nevertheless the employer is vicariously liable because the employee's act is still within the scope of his employment. In other words, the wrongful conduct is a mode – albeit a wrongful mode – of carrying out the work the employee was authorised to do. An example will illustrate the point. A is employed by B as a van driver. A drives the van carelessly or over the speed limit. As a result of his negligent driving, A injures C. In an action for reparation, B is vicariously liable for A's negligent driving. The careless driving is a mode – albeit a wrongful mode – of carrying out the work A was authorised to do. B would still be vicariously liable even if he instructed A not to drive carelessly or over the speed limit.

An employee's act or omission does not cease to be within the scope of his employment merely because the conduct is fraudulent. In *Taylor v Glasgow District Council*,[1] for example, a building control officer had been given actual authority to issue building warrants and completion certificates. He issued false documents as part of a fraudulent scheme with a development company. The company sold the property to Taylor who sustained economic loss. It was held that the defender could be vicariously liable for the fraudulent conduct of its employee because he had been given actual authority to issue the documents. The fact that the defender did not benefit from the fraud was irrelevant: the only question was whether the employee's conduct was an improper mode of doing what he was authorised to do.

Although the courts were prepared to treat fraudulent misconduct as an improper mode of doing what the employee was authorised to do, for many years they were reluctant to include other intentional wrongs. In *Trotman v North Yorkshire County Council*,[2] for example, the Court of Appeal held that sexual misconduct on the part of a teacher was not an unauthorised mode of carrying out his teaching duties; consequently, the local authority was not vicariously liable for the assault. However, in *Lister v Hesley Hall*[3] the House of Lords held that an employee's unauthorised actions could still be within the scope of his employment if the wrongful behaviour was so closely connected with his employment that it would be fair and just to hold the employer vicariously liable. In *Lister* the warden of a school boarding house sexually abused boys who were in his care. He had been employed to look after the children and this would involve physical proximity between them if the warden was to fulfil his responsibilities. There was therefore a very close connection between the nature of the warden's employment and the sexual assault, the risks of which were inherent in that position. In these circumstances it was fair and just to hold the employer vicariously liable for the assaults.[4] It has been suggested[5] that *Lister* was a case where the employer had assumed responsibility for the welfare of the children and should therefore be liable for the conduct of the persons to whom the children's care had been delegated. Put another way, the local authority had undertaken a direct responsibility to the children (and their parents) which had been breached when they entrusted their care to an employee who was a potential danger to them. Analysed in this way, the local authority would have been in breach of a direct or personal duty of care owed to the children, analogous to the personal duty owed by an employer to his emplyoyees[6] and non-delegable in the same way.[7] However, this was not the approach adopted by their Lordships in *Lister*, where the case proceeded as one of vicarious – rather than direct or personal – liability.

In *Various Claimants v Catholic Child Welfare Society*[8] the Supreme Court accepted that a relevant factor in determining whether an employer should be vicariously liable is the risk to others which an employer creates when he entrusts duties, tasks and functions to an employee. This is known as enterprise risk. It is certainly a satisfactory rationale of the sexual abuse cases. However, it has been used in other contexts. In *Brink's Global Services v Igrox*,[9] for example, an employee was instructed to fumigate a container. Because he was employed by the firm he gained access to the container. He delayed the fumigating process, opened the container and stole silver bars from it. The Court of Appeal held that theft by an employee from the very container he had been instructed to fumigate was a risk reasonably incidental to the purpose for which he was employed. There was therefore a sufficiently close connection between the theft and his employment that it was fair and just that the employer should be vicariously liable. The difficulty with this approach is, of course, how to determine what risks are inherent in a particular job.

1 1997 SC 183, 1997 SLT 537.
2 [1999] LGR 584, CA.
3 [2001] UKHL 22, [2002] 1 AC 215, [2001] 2 All ER 769, [2001] 1 WLR 1311, HL.
4 Accordingly, *Trotman* was overruled.
5 M Loubser and E Reid 'Vicarious Liability of Intentional Wrongdoing' 2003 JR 143.
6 Discussed at paras 12.1 ff above.
7 In *Gorrie v Marist Brothers* 2002 SCLR 436, the pursuer was the victim of sexual abuse by one of his teachers. He claimed that the defender was in breach of a primary duty owed to the pursuer to take reasonable care to appoint fit and proper persons as teachers.
8 [2012] UKSC 56.
9 [2010] EWCA Civ 1207.

12.10 *Lister v Hesley Hall*[1] is a case where the House of Lords was prepared to abandon well-settled rules for the imposition of vicarious liability in order to avoid a result that their Lordships considered unjust in the circumstances, namely that the local authority would not be vicariously liable for the sexual assaults perpetrated by their employee on children in their care. Purporting to proceed on the basis of principled but practical justice, the House found the local authority to be vicariously liable for their employee's delicts because his wrongful conduct was closely connected to the risks inherent in the acts he was authorised to do. In these circumstances, it might be thought that the close connection criterion should be restricted to cases of an employee's intentional wrongdoing and that the traditional rules should remain to determine whether an employer is vicariously liable for his employee's negligence.[2] However in *Majrowski v Guy's and St Thomas's NHS Trust*,[3] Lord Nicholls does not appear to limit the test in this way. He said:[4]

'A precondition of vicarious liability is that the wrong must be committed by an employee in the course of his employment. A wrong is committed in the course of employment only if the conduct is so closely connected with the acts the employee is authorised to do that, for the purposes of the liability of the employer to third parties, the wrongful conduct may fairly and properly be regarded as done by the employee while acting in the course of his employment.'

And in *Sharp v Highland and Islands Fire Board*[5] the Lord Ordinary (Macphail) simply accepted that *Lister* was the leading authority on vicarious liability in both English and Scots law.

On the other hand, *Majrowski* was concerned with the question whether an employer could be vicariously liable for his employee's harassment of a fellow employee:[6] in applying the closely connected test to hold that an employer could be, the House of Lords was doing so in the context of an intentional wrong. *Sharp* was concerned with the vicarious liability of an employer for his employee's assault on an opponent during a football match which was part of a training course *viz* an intentional wrong. When the scope of the *Lister* criteria was discussed in the Inner House in *Wilson v EXEL UK Ltd*[7] and *Vaickuviene v Sainsbury*,[8] again the context was that of intentional wrongs: assault in *Wilson* and murder in *Vaickuviene*. It is therefore still not certain whether the *Lister* closely connected with employment test has absorbed the traditional tests for determining whether the employee's wrong was within the course of his employment or whether it is restricted to cases where the employee has committed an intentional wrong.

1 [2001] UKHL 22, [2002] 1 AC 215, [2001] 2 All ER 769, [2001] 1 WLR 1311, HL.

2 The test has been applied in the context of fraud: *Dubai Aluminium Co Ltd v Salaam* [2003] 1 All ER 97; *Royal Bank of Scotland v Bannerman Johnstone Maclay* 2005 SC 437.
3 [2007] 1 AC 224.
4 Ibid at 229.
5 2005 SLT 855.
6 On harassment, see above para 1.12.
7 [2010] CSIH 35.
8 [2013] CSIH 67. *Wilson* and *Vaickuviene* are discussed at para 12.14.

12.11 (3) If the employee is employed to do a particular task or a particular class of work, and does something outside the scope of his work, then the employer is not vicariously liable since the employee was not acting within the scope of his employment. For example, A is employed by B to pack goods at B's warehouse. A decides to deliver goods to a customer and drives B's van. If A injures C as a result of A's careless driving, prima facie B is not vicariously liable because A was not employed as a driver and was therefore not authorised to drive B's van. A's driving of the van is outside the scope of his employment and B is therefore not vicariously liable.

It may be difficult to determine what is the scope of a worker's employment. Obviously the terms of the contract are important, but the courts are not prepared to accept that for the purpose of vicarious liability the scope of employment is limited to the employee's express contractual duties. In the example above, if, to B's knowledge, A had delivered goods to a customer in the van on previous occasions, driving the van could well fall within A's employment, even though A's job description in his contract is that of a packer. Moreover, given that the pursuer has *ex hypothesi* been injured or suffered harm, courts will be reluctant to allow an employer to escape vicarious liability by arguing that the employee's failure to follow the employer's detailed instructions resulted in the employee acting outside the scope of employment (no vicarious liability) as opposed to engaging in a wrongful mode of carrying out the work the employee was authorised to do (vicarious liability).

12.12 Thus in *Rose v Plenty*,[1] a milkman was expressly instructed by his employer not to use boys to help him deliver milk or to give boys lifts in his milk float. In breach of this order, he continued to use a 13-year-old boy to help him. The lad was injured as a result of the milkman's negligent driving of the float. The employers argued that they were not vicariously liable because the employee was acting outside the scope of his employment. In other words, his particular work was delivering milk without the help of young boys and therefore he was acting outside the scope of his employment when he delivered milk with the help of a 13-year-old lad. However, the Court of Appeal held[2] that the express prohibition did not change the scope of the milkman's employment. As Lord Denning MR explained:[3]

'In considering whether a prohibited act was within the course of the employment it depends very much on the purpose for which it is done. If it is done for his employer's business, it is usually done in the course of his employment, even though it is a prohibited act ... But if it is done for some purpose other than his master's business, as, for instance, giving a lift to a hitchhiker, such an act, if prohibited, may not be in the course of his employment ... In the present case it seems to me that the course of Mr Plenty's [the milkman's] employment was to distribute the milk, collect the money and to bring back the bottles to the van. He got, or allowed this young boy, Leslie Rose, to do part of that business which was the employer's business. It seems to me that although prohibited, it was conduct which was within the course of employment ... I agree it is a nice point in these cases on which side of the line the case falls.'

1 [1975] ICR 430, [1976] 1 All ER 97, CA.
2 Lord Denning MR and Scarman LJ; Lawton LJ dissented.
3 *Rose v Plenty* [1976] 1 All ER 97 at 100–101.

12.13 In certain situations it will be a question of degree whether the employee's conduct is or is not within the scope of his employment. In *Williams v Hemphill (A & W) Ltd*,[1] members of the Boys' Brigade were at a camp at Benderloch. A company of Girl Guildry was also at the camp. The girls were to return to Dollar by train. A lorry driver was instructed by his employer to take the boys back to Glasgow. He was persuaded by some of the boys to return to Glasgow via Connell, Stirling and Dollar railway stations, so that the boys could catch a glimpse of the girls. The shortest route back to Glasgow was via Loch Lomond. There was an accident and one of the boys, who had not instigated the change of route, was injured. The employers would not have authorised the route the driver had taken. The question was whether, by deviating from the authorised route, the driver was no longer acting within the scope of his employment with the result that the employer would not have been vicariously liable. The House of Lords held that it was ultimately a question of degree whether, as a result of the deviation, the employee was no longer engaged on the employer's business. In this case, the dominant purpose of the journey was to transport the boys to Glasgow and the driver was still engaged on that task when the accident occurred in spite of not having taken the most direct route. As Lord Pearce explained:[2]

'In weighing up, therefore, the question of degree whether the admittedly substantial deviation of the vehicle with its passengers and baggage was such as to make the lorry's progress a frolic of the servant unconnected with or in substitution for the master's business, the presence of the passengers is a decisive factor against regarding it as a mere frolic of the servant. In the present case the defenders remained liable, in spite of the deviation, for their driver's negligence.'[3]

In this context, 'frolic' does not connote triviality. Instead the court must consider whether the employee's conduct amounts to 'an unrelated and independent venture of his own: a personal matter, rather than a matter connected to his authorised duties'.[4]

(4) If an employee uses his employer's time or his employer's equipment for the employee's own purpose, the employer is not vicariously liable because the employee is no longer acting within the scope of his employment. As Lord Pearce indicated, in these circumstances the employee is acting on a 'frolic' of his own. So, for example, if, during the time he is supposed to be working, an employee goes shopping, the employer will not be vicariously liable for any delict the employee may commit since shopping is clearly outside the scope of the employment. Similarly, if a van driver, without authorisation, uses his employer's van to help a friend move house, the employer is not vicariously liable if an accident occurs during the move because that is outside the scope of the employment.

1 1966 SC (HL) 31, 1966 SLT 33.
2 1966 SC (HL) 31 at 46.
3 Lord Pearce did indicate, however, that there must be limits set by common sense: for example, if the deviation involved going to Glasgow via Inverness!
4 *Ward v Scotrail Railways* 1999 SC 255 per Lord Reed at 264.

12.14 Difficulties may arise if the employee's delictual act or omission occurs at the workplace. In *Kirby v National Coal Board*,[1] a miner during a temporary break went to a prohibited place in order to smoke. When he struck a match, there was an explosion and the pursuer was injured. The court held that by going to the prohibited area in order to smoke, he was no longer acting within the scope of his employment – mining – and consequently the defender was not vicariously liable. On the other hand, in *Century Insurance Co Ltd v Northern Ireland Road Transport Board*,[2] an explosion took place when an employee lit a cigarette while transferring petrol. The House of Lords held that this was an unauthorised mode of doing his job which was to transfer petrol and that the employer therefore remained vicariously liable.

Where a person is injured at work as a result of horseplay by other employees, the employer may escape vicarious liability if the horseplay constitutes 'a frolic of their own'. In *Smith v Crossley Bros Ltd*,[3] an apprentice was injured by fellow employees during initiation rites.[4] It was held that the employer was not in breach of the general duty of care to provide competent fellow workers.[5] Nor was the defendant vicariously liable because the actings constituted a frolic and were outside the scope of the workers' employment. On the other hand, in *Harrison v Michelin Tyre Co Ltd*[6] the employer was held to be vicariously liable when an employee who was standing on a duckboard was injured as a result of a fellow employee jumping on the other end of the duckboard for a lark. The court took the view that a reasonable person would consider that, even though the act was unauthorised, it was nevertheless 'part and parcel' of the job and accordingly not outside the scope of employment.[7] If the *Lister* closely connected test is applied, it is thought that the employer in *Smith* would have been held to have been vicariously liable. In *Wilson v EXEL UK Ltd*[8] an employer was not vicariously liable when one employee assaulted another by pulling her pig tail. The assault had no connection with the employee's tasks. In *Vaickuviene v Sainsbury*,[9] an employee whose job was to stack shelves murdered a fellow employee on the employer's premises during working hours. The employer was held not to be vicariously liable. The employment simply provided the murderer with the opportunity to carry out his own personal campaign of harassment of his victim with tragic consequences. (The employer might have been in breach of their common law duty of care to provide the victim with competent and non-dangerous fellow employees.)

It is generally accepted that travel to and from work is outside the scope of employment and that the employer is not vicariously liable for an employee's wrongs at that time. However, where the employer retains an element of control, vicarious liability may continue before or after work. Thus in *Bell v Blackwood, Morton & Sons Ltd*,[10] an employer was held to be vicariously liable when the pursuer was injured by a fellow employee when leaving work. The employers had attempted to prevent employees from rushing downstairs to catch their buses and had supervised the descent of the stairway from time to time. In these circumstances, the employees were still within the scope of their employment when on the stairway where the accident occurred. Where an employee works at two places, it has been held that he is within the scope of his employment when travelling between them.[11]

1 1958 SC 514, 1959 SLT 7.
2 [1942] AC 509, [1942] 1 All ER 491, HL.
3 (1971) 95 So Jo 655, CA.
4 The unfortunate lad had a compressed-air pipe placed in close proximity to his rectum.
5 See para 12.2 above.
6 [1985] 1 All ER 918, [1985] ICR 696.
7 An owner of a night club has been held to be vicariously liable for assaults carried out by 'bouncers' on a customer who had kicked in the door of the premises: the bouncers were not on a frolic of their own but had been attempting to preserve the integrity of the club, albeit in a *very* unauthorised way! See *Vasey v Surrey Free Inns plc* [1996] PIQR P373 CA. Post-*Lister*, it has been accepted that such assaults are sufficiently closely connected with the risk of physical harm inherent in the nature of a bouncer's job for vicarious liability to be imposed: *Mattis v Pollock (t/a Flamingo's Nightclub)* [2003] 1 WLR 2158, CA. See also *Ashmore v Rock Steady Security Ltd* 2006 SLT 207; *Honeybourne v Burgess* 2006 SLT 585.
8 [2010] CSIH 35. See also *Shields v Crossroads (Orkney)* [2013] CSOH 144.
9 [2013] CSIH 67.
10 1960 SC 11, 1959 SLT (Notes) 54, OH.
11 *Thomson v British Steel Corpn* 1977 SLT 26, OH.

12.15 The law on vicarious liability is in a state of flux. Uncertainty prevails. The courts have had difficulties in keeping the *Lister* criteria within acceptable limits. In *Wilson v EXEL UK Ltd*,[1] the Inner House reaffirmed that the ultimate question was whether or not the employee's actings could be said to be within the course of his employment. The traditional tests were still relevant. A broad approach should be adopted in the sense that the context of the act complained of should be looked at and not just the act itself. Time and place were always relevant but would not be conclusive. The fact that the employment provides the opportunity for the act to occur at a particular time and place is not necessarily enough. The 'frolic of his own' criterion could still be useful. In *Vaickuviene v Sainsbury*,[2] Lord Carloway observed[3] that if the traditional tests establish that the employee's actings were within the scope of his employment there is no need to consider whether it is fair and just to impose vicarious liability. Where the traditional tests do not point to the employee's actings being within the scope of his employment, then resort can be made to the *Lister* close connection test where the enterprise risk or creation of risk will be a relevant factor.

1 [2010] CSIH 35.
2 [2010] CSIH 67.
3 Ibid at para 25.

12.16   In certain situations, an employee may be hired out to work under the instructions of another employer. For example A, a general contractor, may hire equipment from B to be operated by an employee of B but under A's instruction. If the 'borrowed' employee is negligent and injures one of A's employees or a third party, who is vicariously liable, A or B? The general rule is that the employer with whom the borrowed employee has a contract of employment remains vicariously liable even though the employee works under the general instructions of another. And so in our example, B remains vicariously liable. B will only escape vicarious liability if he has delegated to A not only the power to control what B's employee does but also *how* the employee should do the job. The onus rests on B to establish that the full plethora of control has passed from B to A. This will be almost impossible to establish where B's employee operates sophisticated equipment.

This principle was settled by the House of Lords in the leading case of *Mersey Docks and Harbour Board v Coggins and Griffith (Liverpool) Ltd*.[1] The plaintiff hired a mobile crane to the defendant which was to be operated by an employee of the plaintiff. It was agreed in the contract of hire that the operator of the crane was to be treated as an employee of Coggins. The craneman injured a worker while operating the crane negligently. The question arose whether the plaintiff or the defendant should be vicariously liable. The House of Lords held that *in a question with the injured third party*, vicarious liability could not be determined by the contractual arrangements made between the plaintiff and defendant to which the injured person had not been a party. Prima facie the plaintiff was the employer and was vicariously liable unless it could be established that full control of the craneman had passed to Coggins. While Coggins could tell the craneman what to do, since he was a highly skilled worker they could *not* tell him *how* to do his job. Accordingly, Mersey Docks had failed to discharge the onus which lay upon them to prove that their employee had been transferred *pro hac vice* to Coggins. Therefore, as far as the injured person was concerned, he could sue Mersey Docks as vicariously liable for the negligence of their employee, the craneman. But because of the terms of their contract of hire with Coggins, Mersey Docks could recover the damages from Coggins since they had agreed to treat the crane man as their employee.[2]

1 [1947] AC 1, [1946] 2 All ER 345, HL.
2 This principle has been accepted as part of Scots law: see *Park v Tractor Shovels Ltd* 1980 SLT 94, OH; *Royal Bank of Scotland v Bannerman Johnstone Maclay* 2005 SC 437 (proof allowed on whether or not an employee had been transferred *pro hac vice* to act as financial controller for customer of the defenders).

(3) Vicarious liability for independent contractors

12.17 As a general rule, a person is not vicariously liable for the wrongs of an independent contractor whom he hires to undertake a particular job, for example a taxi driver, a plumber, a builder etc. If, for example, A, a general contractor, hires the services of B, an independent contractor, and through his negligence B causes harm to C, an employee of A, A is not vicariously liable for B's delicts. If C is injured by the negligence of an employee of B, B will, of course, be vicariously liable to C. However, A may be liable in delict to his employee, C, if A's act in hiring B is a breach of A's general duty to take reasonable care for the safety of his employees.[1] But this is a breach of A's personal duty of care towards his employees – it is not *vicarious* liability for B's delictual act. To succeed against A, C must show that A did not take reasonable care in hiring B's services, for example if A knows that B is incompetent or unqualified. The duty is analogous with that of taking reasonable care to provide an employee with competent fellow workers. However, in *Marshall v William Sharp & Sons Ltd*,[2] the defender hired the services of a worker who was paid an hourly rate for work done. The defender had full control over the actings of the worker concerned. The pursuer, an employee of the defender, was injured as a result of the worker's negligence. The Inner House held that the defender was *not* in breach of his personal duty to the pursuer to provide a competent independent contractor to work with him. Nevertheless, the court found that the defender was vicariously liable in spite of the fact that the person who had injured the pursuer was an independent contractor. It is submitted that this decision can be supported on the ground that the defender had the power to control not only what the independent contractor could do but how he should do it. This is not usually the case when a person hires an independent contractor, for example a taxi driver or a plumber. Accordingly, unless the hirer has the full plethora of control over an independent contractor, he will not be vicariously liable for the wrongs of an independent contractor in carrying out a job.

In building contracts, an employer is liable to third parties for loss sustained as a result of an independent contractor carrying out hazardous operations on the site.[3] But the main contractor is *not* liable for the delicts of the sub- or sub-sub-contractors; nor is the sub-contractor liable for the wrongs of the sub-sub-contractor. Thus a main contractor cannot sue a sub-contractor for damage to property owned by the main contractor as a consequence of a sub-sub-contractor's negligence.[4]

1 On an employer's duty to take reasonable care, see paras 12.1 ff above.
2 1992 SCLR 104, 1991 SLT 114.
3 This may be a general principle if the operation being carried out by the independent contractor is inherently hazardous: *Stewart v Malik* 2009 SLT 205. See also *Morris Amusements Ltd v Glasgow City Council* [2009] CSOH 84.
4 *MTM Construction Ltd v William Reid Engineering Ltd* 1998 SLT 211, 1997 SCLR 778, OH.

(4) Principal and agent

12.18 A principal can be vicariously liable for the wrongs of his agent. This will arise if: (i) the acts of the agent were expressly authorised by the principal; or (ii) the principal ratified the agent's acts after they were done; or (iii) the delict is within the actual or ostensible authority of the agent. For vicarious liability to arise it is not enough that X permits Y to do a particular act, for example drive X's car: instead, X must have delegated a task or duty to Y.[1] The principle is important in the context of employment where an employer prima facie escapes vicarious liability because the employee is working outside the scope of his employment: the employer may still be vicariously liable as principal if in the circumstances the employee is acting within his actual or ostensible authority as the employer's agent at the time of the wrongful act.[2] A partnership can be vicariously liable for the delicts of its agents, the partners, provided the wrongful conduct can fairly and properly be regarded as done by the partner while acting in the ordinary course of the firm's business: such conduct can include fraud.[3]

The committee of a club or other unincorporated association are not vicariously liable for the wrongs of the other members of association.[4]

1 *Morgans v Launchbury* [1973] AC 127, [1972] 2 All ER 606, HL.
2 *Taylor v Glasgow District Council* 1997 SC 183, 1997 SLT 537.
3 See, generally, *Dubai Aluminium Co Ltd v Salaam* [2003] 2 AC 366, [2003] 1 All ER 97.
4 *Harrison v West of Scotland Kart Club* 2004 SC 615.

C. CONCLUSION

12.19 The discussion of vicarious liability is important because it illustrates how the common law developed an exception to the principle that a person is not obliged to make reparation unless he has caused harm as a result of his own *culpa* or fault. As a result of industrialisation, it became apparent that those who were injured by the wrongs of workers would, in practice, have little likelihood of obtaining compensation from the worker himself. Accordingly, the doctrine of vicarious liability arose to enable the pursuer to sue the employer, in addition to the employee, since the employer was more likely to have funds or be insured.

CHAPTER 13

Delict and the family

It is now proposed to consider delictual liability in the context of family relationships. We will be concerned with delictual liability *between* members of the family and the rights of members of the family to seek reparation if a relative is injured or killed.

A. TITLE TO SUE

13.1 At common law, spouses could not sue each other in delict. If a woman was injured as a result of her husband's negligent driving, she could not obtain reparation. This rule was clearly anachronistic, especially as the loss would ultimately fall on her husband's insurance company. The position was changed by s 2 of the Law Reform (Husband and Wife) Act 1962, which provided that each of the spouses had 'the like rights' to bring proceedings against the other in respect of a delict 'as if they were not married'. The 1962 Act has been repealed,[1] but of course the common law does not revive.

A spouse is not liable for the wrongs of the other spouse unless liability is established on a basis other than marriage itself. So for example, a wife could be vicariously liable for a delict committed by her husband if she were his employer and the delict arose in the course of his employment.

As a general rule, a child or young person under the age of 16 has no active legal capacity.[2] However, a child under 16 can instruct a solicitor in connection with any civil matter provided she has a general understanding of what it means to do so. A child of 12 or more is presumed to be of sufficient age and maturity to have such understanding, although a child under 12 may instruct a solicitor if she in fact has such an understanding.[3] If the child has the capacity to instruct a solicitor, she has capacity to pursue or defend a civil action.[4] Accordingly a child with sufficient capacity can pursue an action in delict. If the child does not have such capacity, the action must be brought by the child's legal representative who will usually be the child's parents.[5]

The Age of Legal Capacity (Scotland) Act 1991 does not affect the delictual responsibility of children and young persons under the age of 16.[6] Thus a child under the age of 16 can, theoretically at least, be sued if the child has committed a delict. Parents are not vicariously liable for the wrongs committed by their children. But where a child causes harm as a result of a parent's negligence, the parent may be liable for a breach of a duty of care which the parent owed to the pursuer. For example, if a child runs in front of a car and the driver is injured trying to avoid the child, the mother may be liable in delict if she has not taken reasonable care to ensure that the child was not on the road.[7] Because the 1991 Act does not affect the age of delictual responsibility, a child who has been injured may have any damages awarded reduced on the ground of contributory negligence.[8] In *McKinnell v White*,[9] for example, a child of five was held to be 50 per cent contributorily negligent because he ran in front of a speeding motorist. The Lord Ordinary (Fraser) took the view that by the age of five a child brought up in an urban environment should have been aware of the danger of road traffic. It has always been competent for a child to sue his or her parent in delict.[10]

Where a foetus sustains injury *in utero*, the unborn baby has no right to sue in delict unless and until it has been born alive. Only on birth does a child obtain legal personality. However, provided the defender owed a duty of care towards the foetus, if the baby is born alive, an action in delict can be brought on the child's behalf in respect of the harm sustained *in utero*. This is sometimes said to be a consequence of the civil law principle *nasciturus pro iam nato habetur quotiens de eius agitur*, namely that in a matter affecting its interests, an unborn child *in utero* should be deemed to be born (the *nasciturus* doctrine).[11] It is submitted that there is no need to rely on the *nasciturus* doctrine to achieve this result. Given that the defender owes a *Donoghue v Stevenson* duty of care[12] to the foetus, based on reasonable foreseeability of injury *in utero*, then if there is a breach of the duty which causes harm to the foetus, a wrong will be committed when the baby is born. It is at that stage, ie when the baby is born alive, that the wrong is completed because, while the breach of duty took place during the pregnancy, harm for the purpose of delictual liability is not sustained by the child until the child is born.[13] It is only then that *constituent harm* arises as a result of the breach of the duty of care: *damnum injuria datum*.

Because it is competent for a child to sue a parent, a mother who injures her foetus during the pregnancy could be sued by her child in delict, provided the child is born alive. A mother clearly owes a duty of care to the foetus. If during her pregnancy she fails to take reasonable care, for example if she abuses drugs or falls down the stair when drunk, then she can be liable if her breach of duty of care results in harm to the child when born alive. It would therefore appear that a mother carries a potential litigant in her womb for nine months! Similarly, a father who injures his wife's foetus through, for example, negligent driving may be liable in delict if the child is born alive suffering from harm as a result of the injuries sustained *in utero.*

In practice, it is likely that where a foetus is injured *in utero* the mother will also have sustained physical or psychiatric harm. If the defender owed her a duty of care which has been broken, the mother may sue for the harm she has suffered. Where the mother miscarries as a result of the defender's breach of duty, she may obtain damages for the loss of her baby. Of course, in these circumstances, the unborn child has no title to sue because the child has not been born alive.

1 By Schedule 3 to the Family Law (Scotland) Act 2006.
2 Age of Legal Capacity (Scotland) Act 1991, s 1(1)(a).
3 ALC(S)A 1991, s 2(4A).
4 ALC(S)A 1991, s 2(5A).
5 Children (Scotland) Act 1995, s 1(1)(d). If the parent is the defender, for example if the child was injured as a result of her mother's careless driving, a curator ad litem will be appointed to represent the child.
6 ALC(S)A 1991, s 1(3)(c).
7 *Hardie v Sneddon* 1917 SC 1, 1916 2 SLT 197.
8 On contributory negligence, see paras 6.12–6.13 above.
9 1971 SLT (Notes) 61, OH. See also *McCluskey v Wallace* 1998 SC 711 (four-year-old child, 20 per cent contributory negligence). There is no general rule to determine the degree of a child's contributory negligence. The danger to which the child is exposed and the child's capacity to appreciate that risk are important: *Galbraith's Curator ad Litem v Stewart (No 2)* 1998 SLT 1305, OH (eight-year-old child, no contributory negligence).
10 *Young v Rankin* 1934 SC 499, 1934 SLT 445.
11 *Cohen v Shaw* 1992 SCLR 182n, 1992 SLT 1022, OH.
12 See Chapter 3 above.
13 *Hamilton v Fife Health Board* 1993 SC 369, 1993 SLT 624.

B. PERSONAL INJURIES TO A RELATIVE

13.2 In *Robertson v Turnbull*,[1] it was held that where a person was injured, the defender did not owe a threshold duty of care to the victim's spouse or relatives who had suffered economic loss as a result of the injuries sustained. So, for example, members of the injured person's family could not sue in delict for loss of support.[2] The victim can, of course, sue for loss of future earnings as derivative economic loss.[3] Moreover, at common law, a pursuer who was injured could not recover damages for the economic loss suffered by a relative as a result of the pursuer's injuries, for example where a spouse had given up work in order to nurse her injured husband.[4]

The common law on this point has now been superseded by s 8 of the Administration of Justice Act 1982. This provides that where a person has sustained personal injuries, the injured person can recover damages which amount to reasonable remuneration for necessary services rendered to the pursuer by a relative.[5] The services rendered by the relative must be physical services, such as nursing.[6] Thus it has been held that s 8 of the 1982 Act did not apply when a relative had donated bone marrow to the pursuer who would otherwise have died.[7] The quantification of damages by reference to the number of hours of providing services and a modest notional hourly rate is well established.[8] But the courts often take a broad view when reaching an appropriate figure.[9] The damages can be reduced to take into account the injured person's contributory negligence.[10]

The pursuer, ie the injured person, then accounts to the relative for any damages recovered under this provision.[11] Originally, damages could only be awarded in respect of services rendered up to the date of the action;[12] but now damages can be awarded for services likely to be rendered by a relative to the injured person in the future.[13] Damages are not available under s 8 of the 1982 Act if the relative expressly agreed that no payment should be made in respect of the services rendered or to be rendered.[14] Where the injured person has died before the action is concluded, the deceased's executor may recover damages for necessary services rendered by a relative before the victim died.[15]

Where a person who was not in employment was injured, at common law he had no right to sue for loss of earnings since *ex hypothesi* he was not earning. This was particularly unfair to wives who had given up their jobs to look after the home or children. Section 9(1) of the Administration of Justice Act 1982 gives an injured person who has been providing unpaid personal services to a relative[16] the right to sue for damages if the pursuer is unable to continue to do so as a result of the injuries sustained. The personal services must be services which (a) were or might have been expected to have been rendered by the pursuer before the injuries;

(b) were of a kind which when rendered by a person other than a relative would ordinarily have been obtainable on payment; and (c) the injured person but for the injuries in question might have been expected to render gratuitously to a relative.[17]

In *Ingham v John G Russell (Transport) Ltd*[18] the Inner House refused to restrict the concept of personal services to services which were rendered to the person of the relative, such as nursing, as opposed to the relative's property, such as cleaning the relative's house. It was enough that the services had been rendered *in person* by the injured person and therefore included maintenance or DIY services rendered by the injured person to his spouse. It is therefore clear that an injured woman, for example, can recover damages if she is unable to provide unpaid housekeeping and child-rearing services for her spouse, cohabitant or children. Because the personal services must have been rendered gratuitously before s 9 applies, the Administration of Justice Act 1982 recognises the fact that work in the home is still prima facie unpaid but that its economic value is such that justice demands that the injured person should receive compensation for the inability to continue to provide it, even though technically the pursuer has not suffered any patrimonial loss, ie loss of earnings.

Where the injured person's expectation of life has been diminished as a result of her injuries, in assessing the amount of damages under s 9(1), the court is to assume that the pursuer would have lived until the notional date of death.[19] In other words the pursuer can obtain damages for the inability to provide gratuitous personal services to a relative during the lost years.

Where the injured person has died, a relative may claim as a head of loss a reasonable sum in respect of the loss of gratuitous personal services rendered to the relative by the deceased.[20] Before he can do so, the pursuer must be a relative who has the right to claim damages for loss of support by the deceased under the Damages (Scotland) Act 2011. Accordingly, it is to the provisions of the 2011 Act that we shall now turn.

1 1982 SC (HL) 1, 1982 SLT 96. This case removed the doubts raised by *dicta* in *Dick v Burgh of Falkirk* 1976 SC (HL) 1 that a defender could owe a duty of care to the victim's relatives. *Turnbull* is consistent with the settled policy of the law not to grant remedies to third parties in respect of injuries to other people: for discussion see *D v East Berkshire Community Health NHS Trust* [2005] AC 373 per Lord Rodger at paras 100ff.

2 This is an example of non-recoverability of secondary economic loss. Similarly, a child cannot sue for economic loss incurred as a result of serious injuries suffered by his mother (she was in a persistent vegetative state): *Buckley v Farrow* [1997] PIQR Q78, CA.

3 On loss of future earnings, see paras 16.15 ff below.

4 *Edgar v Lord Advocate* 1965 SC 67, 1965 SLT 158.

5 'Personal injuries' means (a) any disease and (b) any impairment of a person's physical or mental condition: s 13(1) of the 1982 Act. 'Relative' includes the injured person's spouse or divorced spouse, civil partner or former civil partner, opposite sex and same sex cohabitants, any ascendant or descendant, any brother, sister, uncle or aunt or their issue and any person accepted by the injured party as a child of the family: any relationship by affinity is treated as a relationship by consanguinity and the half blood is treated as a relationship of the whole blood; a stepchild is treated as a child and illegitimacy is irrelevant: s 13(1) of the 1982 Act.

6 BNA nursing and home help rates can be useful but are by no means conclusive of what reasonable remuneration should be in a particular case. See, for example, *Kennedy v Lees of Scotland* 1997 SLT 510 (use of agency rates rejected as unsuitable where victim had not received substantial nursing, but only short visits from relatives).

7 *Duffy v Lanarkshire Health Board* 1998 SCLR 1142, 1998 Rep LR 119, OH. In *Sturgeon v Gallacher* 2003 SLT 67, the pursuer ran a farm in partnership with his wife. After he had been injured in an accident, his son laboured on the farm for £50 a week. The Lord Ordinary (Emslie) held that the son's work did not constitute necessary services for the purpose of Administration of Justice Act 1982, s 8 as they were rendered to the partnership, not the pursuer. The pursuer could, however, include the extra outlay (the son's wages) in his claim for loss of earnings.

8 *Wallace v Glasgow* City Council [2010] CSOH 88, per Lord Tyre at para 30. Reversed on another point in *Wallace v Glasgow City Council* [2011] CSIH 57.

9 *Kerr v Stiell Facilities* [2009] CSOH 67 following *Clark v Chief Constable of Lothian and Borders* 1993 SC 320.

10 *Yale v Forbes* 2004 SLT (Sh Ct) 13.

11 Administration of Justice Act 1982, s 8(2). But where the relative is the defender, it has been held that a claim under s 8 is incompetent: *Kozikowska v Kozikowski* 1996 SLT 386. It was thought contrary to public policy that the pursuer should remunerate the person she blamed for her injuries – *sed quaere*?

12 *Forsyth's Curator Bonis v Govan Shipbuilders* 1989 SCLR 78, 1989 SLT 91.

13 Administration of Justice Act 1982, s 8(3).

14 Administration of Justice Act 1982, s 8(1) and (3). See *Denheen v British Railways Board* 1988 SLT 320n, 1986 SLT 249, OH.

15 See, for example, *McManus' Executrix v Babcock Energy Ltd* 1999 SC 569; *Murray's Executrix v Greenock Dockyard Co Ltd* 2004 SLT 346.

16 For the definition of 'relative', see the Administration of Justice Act 1982, s 13, discussed at note 5 above.

17 Administration of Justice Act 1982, s 9(3).

18 1991 SC 201, 1991 SLT 739.

19 Administration of Justice Act 1982, s 9(1A). Damages for loss of expectation of life are discussed at paras 13.4 and 16.12 beyond.

20 Administration of Justice Act 1982, s 9(2); *Ingham v John G Russell (Transport) Ltd* 1991 SC 201, 1991 SLT 379. It can be difficult to quantify the value of such services, particularly when the deceased was simply 'a normal, average married man living in family who did the correspondingly normal, average things which a father and husband does around the house, the garden and the family car': *Beggs v Motherwell Bridge Fabricators Ltd* 1997 SCLR 1019, 1998 SLT 1215 at 1223 per the Lord Ordinary (Eassie). See also *Farrelly v Yarrow Shipbuilders Ltd* 1994 SCLR 407, 1994 SLT 1349n, OH; *McManus' Executrix v Babcock Energy Ltd*

1999 SC 569. *Murray's Executrix v Greenock Dockyard Co Ltd* 2004 SLT 346 (£2,100 awarded as deceased only occasionally helped out).

C. DEATH OF A RELATIVE

13.3 If a person dies as a result of another's wrong, two potential claims arise. First, the deceased's own claim which can transmit to the deceased's executor who can pursue the action for the benefit of the deceased's estate. Second, a dependent claim by the deceased's relatives.

(1) The deceased's claim

13.4 Where a person is killed outright as a result of the defender's wrong, the deceased's executor cannot raise an action in delict in respect of the death.[1] In these circumstances, the only claims are those of the deceased's relatives. However, if a person is injured and subsequently dies as a result of the injuries, the deceased's right to sue in delict in respect of personal injuries transmits to the executor who can sue on behalf of the deceased's estate. This complex area of the law is now regulated by the Damages (Scotland) Act 2011.[2]

Where a person dies the rights which vested in the deceased immediately before his death to sue for damages in respect of personal injuries transmit to the executor.[3] As a result, the executor can raise an action or, if an action has been raised by the deceased before he died, continue the action on behalf of the deceased's estate.[4] The executor may sue in respect of patrimonial loss, for example loss of earnings sustained by the deceased, but only up to the date of death.[5] In other words, patrimonial loss attributable to any period after the deceased's death, for example loss of future earnings, is non-transmissible to the executor. This is necessary to prevent double compensation given that the defender may have to meet claims for loss of support brought by the deceased's relatives.

The deceased's right to damages for non-patrimonial loss by way of solatium is also transmissible to the executor,[6] but again in assessing damages for solatium the court is to have regard only to the period ending immediately before the deceased's death.[7] Solatium is damages for pain and suffering arising from the personal injuries. In assessing damages for solatium, the court is entitled to have regard to the extent to which the deceased suffered because he was aware that his expectation of life had been reduced as a result of the injuries.[8]

The effect of these provisions can be illustrated by the following example. A is seriously injured as a result of the negligent driving of B. A dies two years after the accident.[9] If A had begun an action against B, A's executor can continue the action provided it has not been concluded.[10] If A had not begun proceedings, A's executor can bring an action against B.[11] However, the executor's claims for patrimonial loss and solatium are restricted to losses incurred by the deceased at the date of death: any patrimonial loss referable to a period after the date of death cannot be recovered by the executor. If the action is successful,[12] the damages awarded become part of the deceased's estate. This means that they will be distributed to the deceased's legatees if there is a will or to a surviving spouse or civil partner and the deceased's heirs according to the rules of intestate succession where the deceased died without a will. If A has relatives, they may have a claim against B if A's death *was* as a result of the personal injuries A has sustained. It is to the relative's dependent claim that we now turn.

1 Where death is caused by a fatal accident, the deceased's executor can obtain damages for the deceased's fear of impending death. However, it has been questioned whether Parliament intended the court to carry out 'the difficult – and often distasteful – task of trying to assess the feelings of pain and apprehensions of mortality of someone so abruptly and severely injured as so be in the imminent and real danger of death within a period of minutes': *Beggs v Motherwell Bridge Fabricators Ltd* 1998 SLT 1215 at 1223–1224 per the Lord Ordinary (Eassie). The sum awarded was £250! The deceased's immediate family may also have such a claim: see para 13.6 below. In England no damages are awarded under this head; *Hicks v Chief Constable of South Yorkshire Police* [1992] 2 All ER 65, HL.

2 References in this chapter are to the Damages (Scotland) Act 2011 unless otherwise stated.

3 Damages (Scotland) Act 2011, s 2(1)(a).

4 D(S)A 2011, s 10. Where the action was brought by the deceased it is not concluded while an appeal is competent or before any appeal taken has been disposed of, s 10(2).

5 D(S)A 2011, s 2(2).

6 Damages (Scotland) Act 2011, s 2(1). See, for example, *McManus' Executrix v Babcock Energy Ltd* 1999 SC 569. This case was distinguished in *Murray's Executrix v Greenock Dockyard Co Ltd* 2004 SLT 346 on the ground that the deceased while dying of an insidious disease had suffered less than McManus.

7 D(S)A 2011, s 2(2).

8 D(S)A 2011, s 1(1) and (2). Otherwise no damages by way of solatium are recoverable in respect of loss of expectation of life: s 1(3). In an action in respect of personal injuries, damages can also be awarded in respect of patrimonial loss arising from the fact that the injured person's expectation of

life has been reduced: s 1(1) and (2): discussed at para 16.16 beyond. Where
the action is brought by the executor, however, only patrimonial loss arising
before the date of death can be recovered: s 2(2). Where the injured person has
no dependent relatives who could sue for loss of support should the victim
die, the rule that patrimonial loss can only be claimed by an executor up until
the date of death may tempt the defender to delay settling the claim until the
victim dies.

9 It is irrelevant whether or not the death was a result of A's injuries.

10 Damages (Scotland) Act 2011, s 10(1)(b). An action is not concluded while any
appeal is competent or before any appeal taken has been disposed of: s 10(2).

11 D(S)A 2011, s 10(1)(a).

12 Any defences, for example *volens*, which B could use in an action by A are good
against an action brought by A's executor. Similarly, damages can be reduced
as a result of A's contributory negligence.

(2) The dependent claims

13.5   Where a person dies in consequence of personal injuries
sustained by him as a result of the defender's conduct, then if the
defender would have been liable to pay damages to the deceased
if he had lived, she is also liable to pay damages to a certain class
of the deceased's relatives.[1] It will be seen that a relative's right
to sue is *dependent* on the defender being liable to pay damages
if an action had been brought by the deceased in respect of the
personal injuries sustained. Accordingly, the relative's claim can
be defeated if the deceased would not have succeeded against the
defender, for example if the defender did not owe a duty of care
to the deceased or had not broken the duty or the deceased was
volens. The relative's damages can also be reduced on the grounds
of the deceased's contributory negligence.[2]

By s 4(2) of the 2011 Act it is expressly enacted that the relative's
claim cannot be brought if the defender had discharged his liability
to the deceased before he died. In other words, if the deceased had
settled his claim before he died, this automatically excludes the
deceased's relative's dependent claim. But because of the amount
of damages which can be awarded to the deceased's relatives
for non-patrimonial loss, the dependent claims are often more
valuable than the deceased's claim. This led to a cruel dilemma
where the victim was diagnosed with mesothelioma and knew
that he would die within a very short time: should he accept a
settlement which would exclude his family's right to sue after
he had died or refuse and lose the financial support which could
make his last months more bearable? To ease this dilemma, the
2011 Act provides that where the personal injury is mesothelioma,

a settlement does not exclude the deceased's relatives' rights to claim damages for non-patrimonial loss.[3]

The nature of the dependent claim turns on whether the pursuer is a member of the deceased's immediate family or a wider class of relatives specified in the Damages (Scotland) Act 2011.

1 D(S)A 2011, ss 3 and 4. Personal Injuries means any disease and any impairment of a person's physical or mental condition: s 14(1). Where a child who has been born alive dies from injuries sustained *in utero* the parents have title to sue as the child could have sued the defender when the child was born alive: *Hamilton v Fife Health Board* 1993 SC 369. There would be no claim under the 2011 Act if the child was not born alive.
2 See, for example, *Beggs v Motherwell Bridge Fabricators Ltd* 1998 SLT 1215, 1997 SCLR 1019, OH (deceased 20 per cent contributorily negligent).
3 D(S)A 2011, s 5.

(a) The immediate family

13.6   The deceased's immediate family consists of the following relatives:[1]

(1)   the deceased's spouse or civil partner;
(2)   the deceased's cohabitant, ie any person not being the spouse or civil partner of the deceased who immediately before the death was living with the deceased as husband and wife or in a relationship which has the characteristics of the relationship between civil partners;
(3)   the deceased's children: this includes children who have been accepted by the deceased as children of the family. A posthumous child is included;[2]
(4)   the deceased's parents: this includes any person who accepted the deceased as a child of his or her family;
(5)   the deceased's brothers and sisters: this includes any person brought up in the same household as the deceased and who was accepted as a child of the family in which the deceased was a child;
(6)   the deceased's grandparent or the deceased's grandchild.

It will be clear that relatives now include members of the deceased's de facto family, thus reflecting contemporary family structures.

Any relationship by affinity is treated as a relationship by consanguinity;[3] any relationship of the half blood is treated as a relationship of the whole blood; and the stepchild of any person is treated as his child.[4] But in a claim for damages for non-patrimonial loss persons who would qualify only by affinity, for example the deceased's mother-in-law or father-in-law or son-in-law or daughter-in-law are excluded and step-parents and step-children are excluded unless they qualify because they had accepted the deceased as a child of their family or the deceased had accepted them as a child of the deceased's family.[5]

Members of the deceased's immediate family may claim damages for the following:

(1) Damages for patrimonial loss

    (a) Loss of support

A relative can claim damages to compensate the relative for any loss of support which the relative has sustained or is likely to sustain as a result of the deceased, A's, death. This covers both loss of support up until the date of proof and loss of support in the future. The loss of support constitutes the multiplicand and an appropriate multiplier is found by reference to the Ogden tables.[6] These claims can be substantial.

The 2011 Act introduces a set of rules by which a relative's loss of support – and consequently the multiplicand – is to be calculated. The total amount available to support the deceased, A's, relatives is an amount equivalent to 75% of A's net income.[7] Where the relatives are A's surviving spouse, civil partner or cohabitant and/or a dependent child, the total 75% constitutes the family's loss of support.[8] A dependent child is a child who, at the date of A's death, had not attained the age of 18 and to whom A owed an obligation of aliment, ie A's child or a child whom A had accepted as a child of A's family.[9] In the case of other members of A's immediate family, including A's child or accepted child who is 18 or over, the loss of support is the actual amount of that loss, ie what support the relative in fact received from A.[10] Where the pursuers are A's surviving spouse, civil partner or cohabitant and/or a dependent child and another immediate relative, the sum awarded to the last is deducted from the 75% of A's income and the balance is the loss of support for the former. For example:

A's net income is £40K. The total available for loss of support is £30K. If A's only relative is A's wife, she will have the full £30K as loss of support. If A is survived by

A's wife and a dependent child, the loss of support for A's wife and child is £30K. If A is survived by his wife, a dependent child and A's mother whom he has supported by giving her £5K a year, then A's mother's loss of support is £5K and the wife and child's loss is £25K.

While the 2011 Act does not expressly do so, it is submitted that in applying this formula as a general rule the income of the surviving immediate relative should be ignored. However, by s 7(2) of the 2011 Act, the court may apply a different percentage 'if satisfied that it is necessary to do so for the purpose of avoiding a manifestly and materially unfair result'. This discretion should be used only in exceptional circumstances: otherwise the courts could run a coach and four through the utility of the 75% rule. But it might be used if A's surviving spouse or civil partner was very wealthy and A had not contributed much to the family expenses. Conversely, it could be used when A had many dependent children and could not have spent anything like 25% of his net income on himself.

No account is taken of any patrimonial gains which accrue to the relative by way of succession or settlement as a result of A's death. Similarly no account is taken of insurance monies, pensions etc which the relative may receive.[11] If the deceased had obtained a provisional award of damages before his death, in assessing the relative's loss of support the court takes into account such part of the provisional award as was intended to compensate the deceased for any period beyond the date when he died.[12]

Unless a claim falls under the provisions of the 2011 Act, no person can obtain damages by reason of relationship to the deceased.[13] For the purpose of the legislation, loss of support has been narrowly construed. In *Mackintosh v Morrice's Executors*,[14] H and W were killed in a car crash. Before they died, they had transferred large sums to their daughters who were the pursuers in the action. This had been done to avoid the incidence of inheritance tax when the couple died. H and W were in good health and it was probable that they would have survived for seven years from the date of transfer so that no inheritance tax would have been payable. The accident took place within the seven years. The daughters claimed sums representing the inheritance tax which they had paid but which would not have been due if their parents had not died prematurely in the car crash. Their claims failed because such claims are restricted to any loss of support sustained by them as a result of their parents' deaths. A sum representing a diminution in the value of their parents' estates which the pursuers inherited as residuary legatees could not be regarded as support given to them by their parents while they were alive. Their claim as their parents' executrices also failed because executors can only recover patrimonial losses sustained by deceased persons during their lifetimes:[15] and since there was no liability to pay inheritance tax until they died, the loss to the parents' estates was sustained after they had died and therefore did not transmit to their executrices.

(b) Funeral expenses

The relative can recover any reasonable expenses incurred by the relative in relation to A's funeral.[16]

(c) Loss of A's personal services

The relative is entitled to include as a head of damages a reasonable sum in respect of the loss of gratuitous personal services rendered to the relative by A.[17] 'Personal services' has the same meaning as in s 9(1) of the Administration of Justice Act 1982.[18]

(2) Damages for non-patrimonial loss

By s 4(3)(b) of the 2011 Act a member of the deceased's immediate family can claim such sum of damages as the court thinks just by way of compensation for all or any of the following:

(a) distress and anxiety endured by the relative in contemplation of the suffering of A before A's death;

(b) the grief and sorrow of the relative caused by A's death;[19]

(c) the loss of such non-patrimonial benefit as the relative might be expected to derive from A's society and guidance if A had not died.

In making such an award, the court is not obliged to ascribe any of the award to any of these heads of loss.

The amount of damages to be awarded for non-patrimonial loss is entirely a matter for the discretion of the court. There is no official tariff. Juries have tended to make more generous awards than judges sitting without a jury. In order to reduce the disparity between judicial and jury awards in *Hamilton v Ferguson Transport (Spean Bridge) Ltd*[20] the Inner House directed judges to consider the awards made by juries as well as judges in similar cases. In addition, the Inner House took the view that in jury trials the judge should suggest a spectrum of the level of damages for non-patrimonial loss which would be appropriate; this spectrum is for the assistance of the jury and is not binding on them.[21] It will be interesting to see whether as a consequence the level of damages for non-patrimonial loss awarded by judges and juries will converge.

What is clear is that in contemporary Scotland life is considered to be more precious than it may have been thought to be by earlier generations. Consequently the loss of a life of a close relative seems a greater loss than before. This change has resulted in higher awards of damages for loss than used to be the case. In *Ryder v First Aberdeen Ltd*,[22] for example, an award of £40K was thought to be appropriate for a son's loss of his mother.[23]

1 Damages (Scotland) Act 2011, ss 4(5)(a) and 14(1).
2 *Cohen v Shaw* 1992 SLT 1022.
3 See *Monteith v Cape Insulation Ltd* 1998 SC 903.
4 D(S)A 2011, s 14(2).
5 D(S)A 2011, s 4(5)(a) and (b).
6 *McManus' Executrix v Babcock Energy Ltd* 1999 SC 569. The multiplicand only applies to the calculation of future loss of support: D(S)A 2011, s 7(1)(d). On multiplicands and multipliers see paras 16.5 ff beyond.
7 D(S)A 2011, s 7(1)(a).
8 D(S)A 2011, s 7(c)(i).
9 D(S)A 2011, s 7(3).
10 D(S)A 2011, s 7(1)(b).
11 D(S)A 2011, s 8(1).
12 D(S)A 2011, s 8(3).
13 D(S)A 2011, s 8(5).
14 2007 SC 6.
15 See also *Milligan's Executors v Hewats* [2013] CSOH 60 (executors could not sue the deceased's solicitors since the deceased had not sustained any loss before he died).
16 D(S)A 2011, s 4(3)(a).
17 D(S)A 2011, s 6(1).
18 D(S)A 2001, s 6(2). For discussion of s 9(1) of the 1982 Act see para 13(1) above. See for example, *McGee v RJK Building Services Ltd* [2013] CSOH 10.
19 The pursuer is entitled to establish the gravity of her grief and sorrow by bringing evidence that she sustained a psychiatric disorder as a consequence of the death: *Gillies v Lynch* 2003 SCLR 467. However, damages for psychiatric

disorder will only arise if the defender owed an independent duty of care to the pursuer to prevent her sustaining psychiatric harm: for discussion, see above paras 4.2 ff. In *Cruickshank v Fairfield Rowan Ltd* 2005 SLT 462, the Lord Ordinary (Brodie) confessed at 466 'to some difficulty with the notion that it is possible to discern in the circumstances of one family, bonds of affection that are stronger or a degree of emotional investment in the future of a child that is more profound, than in the circumstances of another family, and so in the circumstances in the one case to be very special and in the other case not'.

20 [2012] CSIH 52.
21 See for example *Kelly v Upper Clyde Shipbuilders* 2 July 2012, OH.
22 [2013] CSOH 95.
23 See also *McGee v RJK Building Services Ltd* [2013] CSOH 10. In *Currie v Esure Services* [2014] CSOH 34 parents were awarded £42K each in respect of the loss of their son: the deceased's brother was awarded £22.5K.

(b) Specified relatives

13.7 The specified relatives include the deceased's ascendants and descendants (other than a parent or grandparent or a child or a grandchild), former spouse or civil partner, but not a former cohabitant, uncles and aunts, nephews and nieces and cousins. Such relatives include the appropriate 'in-laws', and half blood is to be treated as full blood. A step-child who has not been accepted as a child of the deceased's family is to be treated as a child.[1]

Specified relatives can claim damages for patrimonial loss arising from A's death. In relation to loss of support, the relative must establish the actual value of the support he received from A. The relative cannot take advantage of the 75% rule. Relatives can also claim for reasonable funeral expenses and loss of A's gratuitous personal services. A specified relative is not entitled to damages for non-patrimonial loss. The fact that the deceased had no legal obligation to support the specified relative is irrelevant: reparation is made for the loss of *de facto* financial support both before the date of death and in the future.

1 D(S)A 2011, ss 14(1)(e)–(g) and (2).

Transmission

13.8 The right of a relative of A to a dependent claim under the Damages (Scotland) Act 2011 can transmit to the executor of the relative if the relative dies before an award of damages is made.[1] For example, if A dies leaving his wife, B, B's right to sue as a member of A's immediate family transmits to her executor if she dies before an award of damages has been made to her. In determining the amount of damages payable to the relative's executor, the court can only have regard to the period ending immediately before the relative's death.[2] This proviso, while obviously important in respect of the relative's claim for loss of support, could also affect a claim for non-patrimonial loss under s 4(3) of the 2011 Act if the relative died shortly after the deceased person.

1 D(S)A 2011 s 9(2).
2 D(S)A 2011, s 9(2).

CHAPTER 14

Delict and road traffic

A. INTRODUCTION

14.1 In modern society, motor vehicles which are driven carelessly are a major cause of accidents. Accidents involving vehicles are probably the area of the law of delict with which ordinary people are most likely to be involved. Where a person suffers personal injuries or damage to property as a result of a road accident, the general principles of delictual liability apply. Indeed, the paradigm of a duty of care based on reasonable foreseeability of harm[1] is the duty of care which a driver owes to other road users. The pursuer must establish a breach of duty on the part of the defender, causation and harm, as in any other action for reparation.[2] However, because of the frequency of such accidents, the common law has been supplemented by statutory provisions designed to ensure that victims of road accidents receive compensation. Moreover, the practices of insurance companies are of particular importance in this area. The 'peculiarities' of delictual liability for careless driving are discussed in this section.

1 On duty of care generally, see Chapter 3 above.
2 See Chapters 5 and 6 above.

B. THE STANDARD OF CARE

14.2 As stated above, before a driver is liable in delict the pursuer must establish that he was in breach of duty; in other words, that the defender did not reach the standard of care of the reasonable driver in his situation and was therefore negligent. In road traffic cases, considerable assistance in establishing that the defender did not exercise reasonable care is provided by the Highway Code, an HMSO publication. The Road Traffic Act 1988 provides:[1]

'A failure on the part of a person to observe the provisions of the Highway Code shall not in itself render that person liable to criminal proceedings of any kind but any such failure may in any proceedings (whether civil or criminal ...) be relied upon by any party to the proceedings as tending to establish or negative any liability which is in question in those proceedings.'

Although a breach of the terms of the Highway Code will not per se establish negligence,[2] if the conduct averred is in fact in breach of the Code then this will be highly persuasive in establishing that the defender did not take reasonable care.[3]

Under the Road Traffic Act 1988, it is a criminal offence to cause death by dangerous driving;[4] to cause serious injury by dangerous driving;[5] to drive dangerously;[6] to drive without due care and attention;[7] to cause death while driving without due care and attention when unfit to drive through drink or drugs;[8] and to cause death by driving without due attention or reasonable consideration.[9] Moreover, statutory regulations designed to protect road users provide offences where vehicles are (1) constructed in such a manner as to create a hazard[10] and (2) used in such a way as causes danger to other road users.[11] Although breach of these statutory provisions and regulations does not give rise to delictual liability for breach of statutory duty,[12] a conviction will be important evidence in establishing negligence on the part of the defender.

1 Road Traffic Act 1988, s 38(7).
2 For example, merely because the defender was driving above the speed limit does not in itself establish that he was not taking reasonable care: speed is not per se the cause of an accident. See *Colborne v Wallace* 1993 GWD 17-1121 per the Sheriff Principal (Nicholson).
3 See, for example, *Robertson v J Sidney Smith* 1999 GWD 4-214. Although the Highway Code is within judicial knowledge, its provisions cannot be used in place of evidence: *Cavin v Kinnaird* 1993 SCLR 618, 1994 SLT 111.
4 Road Traffic Act 1988, s 1. For these purposes, dangerous driving means driving which falls below what would be expected of a competent and careful driver when it would be obvious to a competent and careful driver that driving in that way would be dangerous. The 1988 Act was amended by the Road Traffic Act 1991.
5 RTA 1988, s 1A.
6 RTA 1988, s 2.
7 RTA 1988, s 3.
8 RTA 1988, s 3A. It is enough to be above the prescribed limits for alcohol.
9 RTA 1988, s 2B.
10 For example, it is an offence to drive a vehicle which exceeds the maximum length stipulated in the Road Vehicles (Construction and Use) Regulations 1986 (SI 1986 No 1078).
11 For example, it is an offence to carry an object on a vehicle which overhangs that vehicle in excess of a distance prescribed in the regulations, without the leading edge being suitably marked.
12 On breach of statutory duty, see Chapter 11 above.

C. THE NATURE OF THE LOSSES

14.3 Where there has been a road accident, any damages for death or personal injury will be assessed according to the ordinary principles of delict.[1]

Where a motor car is damaged in an accident, the owner is entitled to the value of the car if it is 'a write off' or the cost of repair. In addition, the owner is entitled to loss of use of the damaged car while it is being repaired or replaced. This is calculated as being the reasonable cost of hiring a car while the damaged vehicle is off the road. Car hire companies usually require the motorist to produce an acceptable debit or credit card 'up front' so that they will be paid for the rental which the motorist will eventually recover from the defender's insurer. However, there are accident hire companies or credit hire companies which do not require a debit or credit card 'up front'. Instead, when the motorist seeks a replacement car while his own is off the road, the company assesses the merits of his case. If satisfied that the claim is unanswerable, the company provides a car and then pursues the motorist's claim against the defender's insurer. For these services, the accident or credit hire company charges an additional fee beyond the 'spot rate' for simple car hire.

In *Dimond v Lovell*[2] the House of Lords held that compensation for loss of use of a damaged car was restricted to the spot rate for hiring a car from a company other than an accident or credit hire company, ie the additional fee element charged by an accident or credit hire company was not recoverable. Given the number of claims involved, this was a very important decision for insurance companies who would have to meet only the reasonable cost of hire of the car and not the additional fees charged by an accident or credit hire company. In *Lagden v O'Connor*,[3] however, the motorist was unable to afford the cost of hiring a replacement car from a car hire company: unless he was able to use the services of an accident or credit hire company, he would have been unable to have a replacement car at all. In these circumstances the House held that the motorist's loss could be calculated on the basis of the accident or credit hire company's charges including the additional fee. In reaching this conclusion, the majority of their Lordships held that the impecuniosity of the plaintiff should be taken into account: Lord Wright's opinion in *The Liesboch*[4] that a claimant's lack of means should *not* be taken into account when assessing his loss was no longer to be followed. The court realised that there could be difficulties in determining when a motorist was so

278 Delict and road traffic

impecunious that he was entitled to use the services of an accident or credit hire company but thought that the fear this would lead to an increase in litigation and delay in reaching settlements was exaggerated.[5] This remains to be seen.

1 On death, see Chapter 13 above; on personal injury, see beyond Chapter 16.
2 [2002] 1 AC 384.
3 [2004] 1 All ER 277.
4 [1933] AC 449.
5 For example, there are persons who are quite well off but do not have credit or debit cards and persons who are unable to hire a car without using an agreed overdraft facility. Why should the latter not recover the cost of borrowing to hire the replacement car?

D. OBTAINING COMPENSATION

14.4 It is obvious that cars and other motor vehicles create considerable hazards to road users, whether they be pedestrians, cyclists or other drivers. To ensure that there is a fund available to provide compensation in the event of delictual liability as a result of a road accident, the owner of a vehicle is obliged to take out insurance. A motor vehicle must be insured in respect of 'third-party liability', ie it must be insured in respect of delictual liability for a person other than the owner himself. This compulsory third-party insurance covers liability for causing death or personal injuries or property damage to the victim. It is a criminal offence to drive a vehicle which does not have a valid third-party liability policy of insurance[1] or to allow a vehicle to be driven without such insurance.[2]

Although it is only third-party liability insurance which is compulsory, many drivers purchase additional insurance to cover their own losses which are incurred in an accident for which they are wholly or partly responsible. These losses include, for example, the cost of repair of the insured's own vehicle and the cost of hiring an alternative vehicle for a limited period while the insured's vehicle is being repaired. These are known as insured losses. Where a driver purchases additional insurance as well as third-party liability insurance, this is known as a comprehensive policy of insurance. Comprehensive insurance does not usually cover death or personal injuries sustained by the driver as a result of his own negligence. It is common practice for the insurer to require the holder of a comprehensive policy to meet the first part of a claim made under that policy. This is typically between the first £50 and £300 of the claim. This sum of money is known as uninsured loss. Any loss not covered by the comprehensive policy, such as a claim in respect of death or personal injury of the driver, is an uninsured loss.

To summarise the position. If, as a result of negligent driving, A causes physical harm or property damage to B, B can sue A in delict and his compensation will be covered by A's compulsory third-party insurance. If B has a comprehensive insurance policy, he may elect to claim for his insured losses under the policy but he is not obliged to do so; he must, of course, sue A for any uninsured losses. If the accident was not the result of A's negligence, B cannot sue A; but if B has a comprehensive policy of insurance, he can claim under the policy for insured losses even if the accident was the result of B's negligence.

Where a person suffers property damage as a result of another driver's negligence, if he elects to claim for insured losses under his comprehensive policy of insurance then the principles of subrogation apply. This means that the insurer 'steps into the shoes' of the insured and is entitled to sue the negligent driver to recover the monies paid out under the comprehensive policy of insurance. In these circumstances, the action is raised in the name of the insured rather than in the name of the insurance company. The defender is cited personally but, again under principles of subrogation, the defender's compulsory third-party insurance company will in effect take over the defence if the action has been intimated to them.

In practice, insurers may have inter-office agreements whereby actions do not have to be raised even if delictual liability is disputed. In order to reduce their overall expenses, the insurers accept that they will meet their own outlays under the appropriate insurance policies without attempting to recover these from each other in defended civil proceedings. However, such agreements, often known as 'knock for knock' agreements, are becoming less common because insurers are battling to minimise losses. Insurers who previously would have 'confirmed' a 'knock for knock' agreement with the third-party insurers are resorting to litigation to recover their outlays under their comprehensive insurance policy in full.

It should be emphasised that whether or not a comprehensive insurer confirms a 'knock for knock' agreement with a negligent driver's third-party insurer, this does not affect the insured driver's right to sue the negligent driver personally in delict to recover his uninsured losses. If he is successful, he is entitled to look to the defender's compulsory third-party insurer for any sums not recovered from the defender which are due under the decree provided appropriate intimation of the action has been made to the insurance company.

An insurance company may be entitled under general principles of contract to refuse to indemnify the insured losses. This could arise, for example, if the insured was in material breach of the terms of the policy of insurance by not paying the premiums or if the policy could be rescinded by the insurance company on the ground of misrepresentation. However, where a pursuer successfully obtains decree against a negligent driver and seeks to recover his compensation from the defender's compulsory third-party insurer, under the Road Traffic Act 1988 the insurance company cannot refuse payment on the ground that under general principles of contract it is not bound to indemnify the insured defender unless the insurance company takes steps to obtain a declarator from the court that it is entitled to avoid the policy.

Similarly, should a driver cancel a compulsory third-party liability policy of insurance, the insurer remains liable for any losses suffered by a third party in a subsequent accident caused by the negligence of the driver provided the contract has not been rescinded. The insurance company can then recover its outlays from the 'former' insured driver. In these circumstances, the insurer is known as a 'Road Traffic Act insurer'. The Road Traffic Act insurer will escape liability if the company does not retain an insurable interest in the vehicle. This would occur, for example, if the 'former' insured driver sold the car with the actual policy document in the glove compartment!

1 Road Traffic Act 1988, s 143(a).
2 RTA 1988, s 143(b).

Motor Insurers' Bureau

14.5   The legislation requiring owners of vehicles to have third-party liability insurance was clearly designed to protect third parties. Such protection is not afforded where an individual flouts the law and drives a vehicle without appropriate insurance cover, although, of course, it is possible in these circumstances that the defender will have sufficient assets to meet a successful action for reparation.

In order to protect third parties in this situation, a body called the Motor Insurers' Bureau (MIB) entered into an agreement with the Ministry of Transport on 17 June 1946 to provide from 1 July 1946 compensation for victims of road accidents where the injured parties were unable to obtain compensation due to the defender's lack of appropriate third-party insurance. There have been various revised agreements since then, but the present text covering accidents on or after 31 December 1988 provides compensation for victims of those accidents in respect of death, personal injury and property damage. The December 1988 Agreement followed an EEC Directive[1] on motor insurance requiring member states to extend third-party insurance to include property damage.

Clause 2 of the agreement provides that the MIB will 'pay or satisfy or cause to be satisfied to or to the satisfaction of the person or persons in whose favour the judgment was given' any sum due under the decree or judgment which remains unsatisfied for a period of seven days from the time at which the decree or judgment should have been in force. The MIB's liability includes any element of interest or expenses included in the decree.

This obligation is subject to certain conditions, the most important being that notification of the commencement of the proceedings must be given to the MIB before, or within seven days after, the commencement of the proceedings. The claimant must take all reasonable steps to obtain judgment or decree against all those liable for the death, personal injury or property damage, and against any principal where such a person is a servant or agent. Additionally, the MIB will have no liability where the claim is in respect of damage to a motor vehicle where the claimant knew or ought reasonably to have known that at the time of the use of the vehicle it was not properly insured in terms of the Road Traffic Act 1988.

Similarly, where the claim is in respect of personal injury, the MIB has no liability where the claimant was a passenger in or on a vehicle which he knew or should reasonably have known was not insured in terms of the Road Traffic Act 1988, although this exception applies only where the decree the MIB is being asked to satisfy is obtained against the owner or person using the vehicle in which the claimant was a passenger. The MIB has no liability if the accident does not take place on a road or highway to which the public has access.[2]

The MIB is not liable where the vehicle in which a person was injured was being used in the course or furtherance of a crime. Thus, a car passenger could not claim when he was injured in a car accident when in possession of cannabis with intent to supply.[3]

The MIB's liability in respect of property claims is limited by the fact that there is currently a £175 excess payable, ie the first £175 is not paid. The Bureau's maximum liability is £250,000. The MIB is only required to compensate for damage which is required to be insured against by law, ie under compulsory third-party insurance.

Where an offending driver cannot be traced, this agreement is of no effect. However, a sister agreement, referred to as 'the MIB untraced drivers' agreement' then comes into play. There have been a number of revised agreements. For accidents on or after 14 February 2003, the relevant agreement is that of 7 February 2003. It covers property damage as well as personal injury. Application must be made within three years of the injury being sustained or within nine months if there is a claim for property damage.

Owing to the expenses involved in pursuing a claim against an uninsured driver, the MIB has now arranged free legal expenses cover for which the pursuer can apply when a claim is being brought against such a driver. The scheme, MIBLES, is available in respect of claims made on or after 13 November 2003.

1 Second Council Directive 84/5, OJ L8 11.1.84 p 17. This Directive has been held not to be directly effective: *Evans v Motor Insurers' Bureau* [1999] Lloyd's Rep JR 30.
2 *Clarke v Kato* [1998] 4 All ER 417, [1998] 1 WLR 1647, HL (MIB not liable where accident took place in car park).
3 *Delaney v Pickett* [2011] EWCA Civ 1532.

CHAPTER 15

Defamation and verbal injury

A. INTRODUCTION

15.1 The law has long recognised a person's interest in her honour and reputation. Accordingly, where A makes a false statement about B with the intention of harming B's honour or reputation then B has a delictual action against A. In Roman law, there was a specific remedy, the *actio injuriarum*, which provided compensation (solatium) for insult *(contumelia)*. In order to succeed, it had to be established that a false statement was made with the intention of insulting the victim. It followed, therefore, that the action lay even if the statement had only been made to the victim herself, ie where the statement had not been made to a third party. If the statement had been published to a third party and, as a result, the victim suffered economic (patrimonial) loss, in the later Roman Empire such loss could, in theory at least, be recovered under general principles of *culpa*: *damnum injuria datum*. Accordingly, where intention to insult could not be established, but the statement was made carelessly to a third party, the only damages that could be obtained were for patrimonial loss: but, if intention to insult could be established, solatium would also be available under the *actio injuriarum*. Given the influence of Roman law, Scots law could have developed a simple set of principles:

(1) if A makes an untrue statement about B to B, with the intention of insulting B, then B can sue A for solatium even if the statement is not published to a third party, provided intention to insult can be proved;

(2) if A makes an untrue statement about B to C, then B could recover damages for patrimonial loss on the basis of *culpa* but only obtain solatium if intention to insult could also be established.

But since *culpa* covers both intentional and unintentional, but careless, conduct, the fact that the remedies were originally based on two separate, if related, principles, ie *culpa* and the *actio injuriarum*, was overlooked.[1] Moreover, the law in this area was influenced by the English law of libel and slander with its emphasis on the defendant's malice. As a result, the Scots law of defamation and verbal injury is complex and contentious, and it is difficult to reconcile all the authorities.

The modern law appears to proceed on two major wrongs: defamation and verbal injury. These will be considered in turn.

1 For discussion of the confusion, see T B Smith *A Short Commentary on the Law of Scotland* (W Green, 1962) pp 724–732.

B. DEFAMATION

15.2 Defamation is the delict which is committed when a person makes an injurious and false imputation against the character or reputation of another person. The victim is usually a natural person but could be a trading company,[1] partnership or voluntary association. However, since legal persons such as companies have no feelings, they can only recover for patrimonial loss. Because, by statute, it does not have corporate status, a trade union cannot sue.[2] A local authority also cannot sue,[3] but if individuals, for example councillors, are defamed by attacks on a council, they can sue in their own right. Under the Damages (Scotland) Act 2011,[4] where a person has died, the executor can continue any action raised by the deceased before his death and recover damages – solatium – for non-patrimonial loss such as hurt feelings and damages for patrimonial loss: if no action has been raised by the deceased, the executor can raise an action but can only recover in respect of patrimonial loss to the estate.

For an action to be successful, it must be shown that the defender made a false statement which was defamatory of the pursuer with the intention to harm the pursuer's character or reputation. However, and this is very important, if the pursuer proves that the statement concerned the pursuer (a question of fact) and is defamatory (a question of law), then the court presumes that the statement is false and was made with the intention to harm him. The onus thereafter lies on the *defender* to prove either that the statement was true (*veritas*) or that it was made without the intention to harm the pursuer. The onus on the defender to justify the 'essence or sting' of any attack on an individual's reputation has been held not to be a disproportionate interference with the right to freedom of expression under Article 10 of the European

Convention on Human Rights.[5] Moreover, the law will also presume that a person will be upset if defamed and it is therefore not necessary for the pursuer to prove non-patrimonial loss in respect of insult; but if patrimonial loss is also claimed, such loss has to be established by the pursuer.

1 *Incorporation of Fleshers of Dumfries v Rankine* Dec 10 1816 FC. If the individual board members are also defamed, they can sue in their own right. If the defamation is actually of the individuals, the company cannot sue.

2 Trade Union and Labour Relations (Consolidation) Act 1992, s 10(1); *Electrical, Electronic, Telecommunication and Plumbing Union v Times Newspapers Ltd* [1980] QB 585, [1980] 1 All ER 1097.

3 *Derbyshire County Council v Times Newspapers Ltd* [1993] AC 534, [1993] 1 All ER 1011, HL. Similarly, the government cannot sue *qua* government; cf individual ministers. This principle has been extended to political parties: *Goldsmith v Bhoyrul* [1998] QB 459, [1997] 4 All ER 268, QBD.

4 Section 2(1)(b) (i) and (3).

5 *Berezovsky v Forbes Inc (No 2)* [2001] EWCA Civ 1251.

(1) The false statement

15.3 The pursuer must establish that the defender made a statement about the pursuer: this is a question of fact. The statement will usually take the form of words, written or spoken. Scots law does not make a distinction between oral and written communication for the purpose of the law of defamation.[1] However, any form of communication can amount to a statement so that it could consist of a television or radio broadcast, a picture, cartoon or effigy.[2] In Scots law the statement does not have to be communicated to a third party: it is enough if it is communicated only to the victim himself.[3] In these circumstances, however, only solatium for insult can be awarded. Before damages for patrimonial loss can be awarded, the statement must have been published to third parties.[4] If a defamatory statement is repeated, every person who repeats the statement commits a separate delict. So, for example, if A makes a defamatory statement about B to a newspaper reporter who repeats it to his editor who publishes it in his newspaper, then the editor and the reporter, as well as A, are liable to B in delict.[5]

It should be emphasised that once the pursuer has established that a defamatory statement was made by the defender, the law *presumes* that the statement is false. The onus then lies on the defender to show that the facts in the statement were true (*veritas*). But before the pursuer has the benefit of this presumption, the statement must be defamatory. It is to that concept that we now turn.

1 In English law such a distinction is made: oral communication constitutes slander; written communication constitutes libel.
2 In *Monson v Tussauds Ltd* [1894] 1 QB 671, CA, placing a waxworks effigy of the plaintiff who had been acquitted of murder in the Chamber of Horrors along with convicted murderers constituted a slanderous statement.
3 *Ramsay v Mackay* (1890) 18 R 130.
4 If the pursuer published the statement to a third party, he is personally barred from claiming patrimonial loss: *Will v Sneddon, Campbell and Munro* 1931 SC 164, 1931 SLT 125.
5 See, for example, *Carroll v British Broadcasting Corpn* 1997 SLT (Sh Ct) 23; *Lord Robertson of Port Ellen v Newsquest (Sunday Herald) Ltd* 2006 SCLR 792; *Buchanan v Jennings* [2005] 1AC 115.

(2) Defamatory nature of the statement

15.4   A defamatory statement is one which 'tends to lower [the pursuer] in the estimation of right thinking members of society generally'.[1] Although it is settled that some types of statement are clearly defamatory, the categories of defamation – like the categories of negligence[2] – are never closed. The question whether or not a statement is defamatory is one of law, to be decided by the court.[3] The test is objective, ie whether the reasonable person would decide that this type of statement was defamatory. The statement must be read in the context of the publication as a whole.[4]

The meaning of the material is that which an ordinary, reasonable, fair-minded reader would infer from the language, not what the author intended the statement to mean.[5] It is the general view of society as a whole which is important, not the views of the section of society in which the pursuer moves. As the mores of society change, what might once have been regarded as derogatory by right-thinking members of society in the past, may not be so regarded by them today. Thus, for example, in 1934 it was thought to be defamatory falsely to state that a woman had been the victim of rape.[6] That might not be regarded as defamatory today when victims of rape are treated with sympathy rather than shunned.

The following are examples of defamatory statements but it must always be remembered that these are only examples and that other types of defamatory statements may arise.

1 *Sim v Stretch* [1936] 2 All ER 1237, HL, at 1240 per Lord Atkin.
2 *Donoghue v Stevenson* 1932 SC (HL) 31 at 70 per Lord MacMillan.
3 Accordingly, the defence can make a plea to the relevancy of the issue.
4 *Charleston v News Group Newspapers Ltd* [1995] 2 AC 65, [1995] 2 All ER 313, HL (defendant published pornographic photograph superimposing the plaintiffs' heads on the bodies: accompanying article explained that the plaintiffs had

been victims of an illicit computer game. The meaning of the material had to be determined on the basis that the reasonable person would have read the article and not simply looked at the photograph and headlines). See also *Norman v Future Publishing Ltd* [1999] EMLR 325; *McCann v Scottish Media Newspapers Ltd* 1999 GWD 10-473; *Lord Robertson of Port Ellen v Newsquest (Sunday Herald) Ltd* 2006 SCLR 792.

5 *Charleston v News Group Newspapers Ltd* [1995] 2 AC 65, [1995] 2 All ER 313, HL; *McCann v Scottish Media Newspapers Ltd* 1999 GWD 10-473.
6 *Youssoupoff v Metro-Goldwyn-Mayer Pictures Ltd* (1934) 50 TLR 581, CA.

(a) Imputations on moral character

15.5 It is defamatory to undermine a person's moral character. Thus it is defamatory to call a woman a prostitute or an adulteress or even to suggest that she lacks 'proper womanly delicacy'.[1] At one time it was clearly defamatory to state that a person was homosexual.[2] But with the increasing tolerance of homosexuality, it has been observed judicially that an allegation of homosexuality should no longer be regarded as defamatory per se.[3] In *Cowan v Bennett*,[4] the sheriff stated that an imputation of homosexuality is not defamatory. A man is not lowered in the esteem of 'right thinking' persons on the basis of his sexual orientation alone. Nevertheless, allegations that a nun was dishonest, unchaste and a lesbian have been held to be capable of amounting to defamation.[5]

Defamatory statements are not restricted to imputations on sexual morality. Thus it is defamatory to call a person a hypocrite.[6] It appears no longer to be defamatory merely to call a person a liar or a 'stranger to the truth':[7] but to call a person a thief and a liar has been held to be defamatory.[8] To state that a woman whose child had died was a heartless and uncaring mother is defamatory.[9]

1 *Cuthbert v Linklater* 1935 SLT 94. But would this be regarded as defamatory today?
2 *AB v XY* 1917 SC 15, 1916 2 SLT 210; *Kerr v Kennedy* [1942] 1 KB 409, [1942] 1 All ER 412.
3 *Quilty v Windsor* 1999 SLT 346.
4 2012 GWD 37-738.
5 *Prophit v British Broadcasting Corpn* 1997 SLT 745, OH.
6 *Stein v Beaverbrook Newspapers Ltd* 1968 SC 272, 1968 SLT 401; *Lord Robertson of Port Ellen v Newsquest (Sunday Herald) Ltd* 2006 SCLR 792.
7 *Carroll v British Broadcasting Corpn* 1997 SLT (Sh Ct) 23. Cf *Watson v Duncan* (1890) 17 R 404.
8 *Gilbert v Yorston* 1996 SCLR 1122, 1997 SLT 879, OH.
9 *McCabe v News Group Newspapers Ltd* 1992 SLT 707, OH.

(b) Imputations of criminality

15.6   It is defamatory to accuse a person of a serious crime which ordinary people do not commit or condone, such as murder,[1] theft,[2] or being a paedophile. It would not perhaps be defamatory to accuse a person of careless driving (or tax evasion?). If the defender pleads *veritas*, he can rely on the fact that the pursuer committed such a crime even if the offence is 'spent' under the Rehabilitation of Offenders Act 1974.[3] Similarly, it is defamatory to say that a person should be in jail since this implies that he is guilty of a crime. It is also defamatory to say that a person was responsible for enabling a person to commit a horrendous crime.[4]

1 *Waddell v British Broadcasting Corpn* 1973 SLT 246; *Berezovsky v Forbes Inc (No 2)* [2001] EMLR 45, CA.
2 *Sutherland v British Telecommunications plc* 1989 SLT 531.
3 Rehabilitation of Offenders Act 1974, s 4.
4 *Lord Robertson of Port Ellen* v *Newsquest (Sunday Herald) Ltd* 2006 SCLR 792.

(c) Imputations against competence or conduct

15.7   Statements which disparage a person's professional competence or conduct are defamatory, for example, to accuse a doctor of gross professional negligence[1] or a professor of his inability to teach[2] – or write textbooks on delict? Allegations of conduct which is unprofessional in the circumstances are also defamatory: for example, to allege that an athlete refused to play a curling match for Scotland at an international competition,[3] to accuse a solicitor of conducting a case for his own – as opposed to his client's – interests,[4] or to say that a prison warden had sexual relations with a prisoner.[5]

1 *Simmers v Morton* (1900) 8 SLT 285, OH.
2 *Auld v Shairp* (1875) 2 R 940.
3 *Munro v Brown* [2013] CSOH 117.
4 *McRostie v Ironside* (1849) 12 D 74.
5 *Winter v News Scotland Ltd* 1991 SLT 828.

(d) Imputations of financial unsoundness

15.8   It is defamatory falsely to allege that a person is insolvent[1] or is unwilling[2] or unable to pay his debts.[3]

1 *AB v CD* (1904) 7 F 72.
2 *Outram v Reid* (1852) 14 D 577.
3 *Mazure v Stubbs Ltd* 1919 SC (HL) 112, 1919 2 SLT 160.

(e) Disparaging public character

15.9 Persons who enter public life are expected to be able to withstand a degree of criticism[1] – or even ridicule[2] – in respect of the way in which they carry out their public duties. However, although the test may be stricter, allegations of, for example, dishonesty in carrying out a public office would, it is thought, constitute defamation. Statements undermining a public figure's sexual morality, ie concerned with his private as opposed to public life, are, of course, defamatory. In England, it has been held to be potentially defamatory to call a famous actor 'hideously ugly': this could lead an ordinary person to infer that he was repulsive and consequently lower him in the public's estimation and make him an object of ridicule.[3]

1 *Mutch v Robertson* 1981 SLT 217.
2 *McLaughlan v Orr Pollock & Co* (1894) 22 R 38 at 42 per Lord McLaren; *Brooks v Lind* 1997 Rep LR 83, 1997 GWD 13-570 (pursuer was said to be part of the council 'mafia' and a joint venture he was involved in was described as 'sheer lunacy and gross administration': held not to be defamatory); *MacLeod v Newsquest (Sunday Herald) Ltd* 2007 SCLR 555 (political journalist awarded the prestigious Tartan Bollocks award for making the biggest gaffe of the year!); *Curran v Scottish Daily Record and Sunday Mail* [2011] CSIH 86 (Tommy Sheridan called Ms Curran a 'scab' for failing to support him politically: not defamatory as well within the latitude permitted by the law where comments are made about persons acting in their public capacity).
3 *Berkoff v Burchill* [1996] 4 All ER 1008, [1997] EMLR 139, CA.

(f) Imputations on health

15.10 It is defamatory falsely to allege that a person is insane or has obnoxious physical defects or is suffering from certain illnesses, such as venereal disease or AIDS.

(g) Innuendo

15.11 A statement or action may appear to be harmless, yet when taken in the context of the facts and circumstances in which it was made, a defamatory meaning may be inferred. For example, it is not prima facie defamatory to display a wax effigy of a person in a waxworks: but to put it in the Chamber of Horrors along with those of convicted murderers implies that the person concerned is also a murderer.[1] Similarly, to announce the birth of twins to a married couple in a newspaper appears innocuous until it is appreciated that they married only a month before, thus implying pre-marital sexual intercourse.[2] In this situation, Scots law allows a pursuer to plead the facts and circumstances from which the defamatory meaning of the statement or act can be drawn. This is known as 'the doctrine of innuendo'.

The onus rests on the pursuer to state the meaning of the acts or statement in the light of the relevant facts and circumstances. In *Cuthbert v Linklater,*[3] for example, the pursuer argued that the defender, an author, had defamed her when a female character in his novel took a Union Jack from Edinburgh Castle and placed it in a men's public urinal. An ardent Scottish nationalist, the pursuer had in fact taken a Union Jack from Stirling Castle and had tossed it at a guard. Consequently, by innuendo, a reasonable reader would assume that the character in the novel was meant to be her and that she was capable of acting indelicately. The court accepted the argument.[4]

The test on whether an innuendo can be inferred is that of the ordinary reasonable person,[5] ie whether a reasonable person would regard the words as offensive if placed in the same position as the pursuer. The question whether the statement or act plus the innuendo placed upon them by the reasonable person amounts to defamation is a matter of law to be decided by the court. It is a question of fact whether the statement or act was taken as having a defamatory meaning by those to whom it was actually communicated.

1 *Monson v Tussauds Ltd* [1894] 1 QB 671, CA.
2 *Morrison v Ritchie & Co* (1902) 4 F 645.
3 1935 SLT 94.
4 See also *Wragg v D C Thomson & Co Ltd* 1909 2 SLT 315, where a newspaper published an article that a certain George Reeves had shot his wife twice and then killed himself. The paper omitted to mention that the incident took place in the USA. At the time it was published, George Reeves, a famous music hall artiste, was appearing in Glasgow. The court held that there was an innuendo that the incident referred to him.
5 *Duncan v Associated Scottish Newspapers Ltd* 1929 SC 14 at 21 per Lord Anderson; *Lord Robertson of Port Ellen v Newsquest (Sunday Herald) Ltd* 2006 SCLR 792.

(3) Intention to harm the pursuer

15.12 Once it has been established that a statement is defamatory, not only is it presumed to be false but it is also presumed that the statement was made with the intention of harming the particular pursuer (malice). A defender can rebut the presumption of falsehood by pleading *veritas*, ie that the statement was in fact true.[1] The question then arises whether or not the defender can rebut the presumption of malice by proving that he did not intend to harm the particular pursuer.

Authority suggests that the presumption of intention to harm cannot be rebutted. In *Hutton (E) & Co v Jones*,[2] a newspaper published an article about an apparently fictitious character, Artemus Jones. This article contained material which would have been defamatory if Artemus Jones was an actual person. However, there was a 'real' Artemus Jones who sued the newspaper. The defence was that since the newspaper did not know of the existence of the plaintiff, it could not have intended to defame him. The House of Lords rejected this defence.

Although *Hutton v Jones* was an English case, Scots law appears to be similar. In *Outram v Reid*,[3] a newspaper published a list of bankruptcies including 'John Reid, wine and spirit merchant, Glasgow'. There were two John Reids who were wine and spirit merchants in Glasgow, one of whom was indeed bankrupt, while the other was solvent. The latter successfully sued in defamation even though the defender was not aware of his existence. Similarly, the unfortunate couple, the birth of whose twins was prematurely announced, sued successfully in spite of the fact that the defender did not know of their existence nor had intended any harm.[4] And Mr Reeves was also able to sue even though the story concerned another Mr Reeves who lived in America.[5]

Although the issue appears to be settled, it is the present writer's view that the solution adopted by the courts is unprincipled. Instead, the courts should have accepted that the defender did not have the intention to insult the pursuers in these cases and accordingly no solatium should have been awarded for the pursuers' hurt feelings. However, as is clear from the Scottish decisions, there was an element of fault on the part of the defenders in publishing the statements. In *Outram v Reid*,[6] for example, the defender omitted the address of the bankrupt Mr Reid which had been published in the Official Gazette: if it had been published in the newspaper, the confusion would have been avoided. Again, in *Morrison v Ritchie & Co*,[7] the defender was criticised by the court for failing to check that the facts in the announcement were accurate. Given that it is (at least) arguable that the defenders were at fault in these cases, the pursuers were entitled to damages for patrimonial loss on general principles of *culpa* but not solatium. They would also have had to establish patrimonial loss which would have been difficult in *Morrison*. But until the issue is reconsidered by the Inner House, it must be accepted that the presumption of intention to insult is now irrebuttable and solatium as well as damages for patrimonial loss can be recovered in these circumstances.[8]

It is unlikely that the matter will be litigated. The Defamation Act 1996[9] provides a statutory defence. The publisher can make an offer of amends. An offer of amends can be made even if the statement was not made innocently.[10] The offer must contain a correction and an apology which can then be published: it should also provide for compensation.[11] Once the offer is accepted, the aggrieved party can no longer sue for defamation but can enforce the offer by proceedings in court.[12] The court can award compensation if this has not been agreed by the parties.[13] If an offer of amends is made but not accepted by the aggrieved party, this is a defence in any subsequent action for defamation.[14] But this defence is not available if the defender knew or had reason to believe that the statement referred to the aggrieved party *and* was false and defamatory of the pursuer: but it is presumed until the contrary is shown that the defender did not know and had no reason to believe that was so.[15]

1 On *veritas*, see para 15.13.
2 [1910] AC 20.
3 (1852) 14 D 577.
4 *Morrison v Ritchie & Co* (1902) 4 F 645.
5 *Wragg v D C Thomson & Co Ltd* 1909 2 SLT 315.
6 (1852) 14 D 577.
7 (1902) 4 F 645.
8 In *Munro v Brown* [2011] CSOH 117 it was irrelevant that the defender believed that the pursuer had refused to play in the curling match when he made the statement to that effect which was subsequently established to be untrue.
9 Defamation Act 1996, ss 2–4.
10 Ie even if the publisher intended to refer to the pursuer or did not take reasonable care in relation to the publication.
11 DA 1996,s 2(4).
12 DA 1996, s 3(2) and (3).
13 DA 1996, s 3(5).
14 Defamation Act 1996, s 4(2). There is no time limit in which the pursuer has to accept or reject the offer. Though it might be reflected in an award of expenses, the pursuer's failure to accept could last for an indefinite period so that the pursuer could still accept the offer after a long delay: see *Moore v The Scottish Daily Record and Sunday Mail* 2007 SLT 217.
15 DA 1996, s 4(3). In *Milne v Express Newspapers* [2003] 1 All ER 482, it was held that the defence will not be lost unless the publisher was in bad faith, ie 'reason to believe' that a statement was false meant choosing to ignore or shutting the mind to information which should have led to a belief, not merely a suspicion, that the allegation was false.

(4) Defences

(a) *Veritas*

15.13 As we have seen, if a statement is defamatory, the law presumes that it is false. This presumption can be rebutted. The onus lies on the defender to prove that the statement was true. In *H v H*[1] the defender distributed leaflets alleging that a solicitor had acted dishonestly, unprofessionally and maliciously when preparing a child welfare report in relation to family proceedings involving the defender's grandchild. The most that the defender could establish was an element of carelessness by the solicitor and the defence of *veritas* failed. If truth (*veritas*) is established, this is a complete defence. What is necessary to establish *veritas* will depend on the nature of the defamatory statement. To allege that someone is a murderer can be justified by proof of one act of murder; but to say someone is a thief implies that he is currently dishonest and *veritas* is not established simply by showing he was twice convicted of petty theft 23 years before.[2]

If more than one fact is alleged, *veritas* will operate only if all the facts which are defamatory are proved true.[3] Conversely, if some non-defamatory facts are admitted to be false, then the defence will still succeed if the defamatory facts can, nevertheless, be shown to be true.[4] By s 5 of the Defamation Act 1952 it is provided that:

'in an action for defamation in respect of words containing two or more distinct charges against a pursuer, a defence of *veritas* shall not fail by reason only that the truth of every charge is not proved if the words not proved to be true do not materially injure the pursuer's reputation having regard to the truth of the remaining charges.'[5]

If, however, the allegations are not separable but are part and parcel of a single defamatory allegation, the section does not apply.

1 [2012] CSOH 126, [2013] CSIH 82. See also *Munro v Brown* [2011] CSOH 117.
2 *Fletcher v Wilsons* (1885) 12 R 683.
3 *Fairbairn v Scottish National Party* 1979 SC 393, 1980 SLT 149.
4 *Sutherland v Stopes* [1925] AC 47, HL.
5 Section 5 does not have to be construed so as to bring lesser meanings of the words complained of within the adjective 'distinct': *Berezovsky v Forbes Inc (No 2)* [2001] EMLR 45, CA.

(b) *In rixa*

15.14 Statements made *in rixa*, ie during a quarrel, an argument or a brawl, do not give rise to an action in defamation unless the pursuer can prove that they were made with intent to injure.[1] The defence is more likely to succeed if the defender has apologised. It is *not* a defence that the statement was made as a joke.[2]

1 *Christie v Robertson* (1899) 1 F 1155; *Carroll v British Broadcasting Corpn* 1997 SLT (Sh Ct) 23.
2 *Prophit v British Broadcasting Corpn* 1997 SLT 745. Cf *Cowan v Bennett* 2012 GWD 37-738. There the sheriff thought that business cards suggesting the pursuer was a paedophile were not defamatory as right-minded persons would regard them as a joke albeit in extremely poor taste! It is thought that this part of the judgment is wrong.

(c) Vulgar abuse

15.15 If the words used amount to mere vulgar abuse, then no action in defamation lies. To call someone a 'bitch' or a 'dickhead' is not actionable, since it is not meant to be taken seriously.[1]

1 For example, *MacLeod v Newsquest (Sunday Herald) Ltd* 2007 SCLR 555. Was this what the sheriff was thinking in *Cowan*?

(d) Fair retort

15.16 If A makes a statement about B, B is entitled to the opportunity to reply. If B's retort is defamatory, it is not actionable unless A can prove that it was said with intent to injure.[1] Where B's retort is published by a newspaper, the newspaper also has the defence: and the newspaper's defence is not lost if A subsequently establishes B's intention to injure.[2]

1 *Gray v Scottish Society for the Prevention of Cruelty to Animals* (1890) 17 R 1185; *Carroll v British Broadcasting Corpn* 1997 SLT (Sh Ct) 23
2 *Curran v Scottish Daily Record* [2011] CSIH 86.

(e) Honest comment

15.17 Where a defamatory remark takes the form of an opinion, for example that a novel is badly written or an actor gave a bad performance, the defender can plead the defence of fair comment. In order to succeed, the defender must prove: (1) that the statement is a comment on a fact or facts; (2) that the facts upon which the comment is made are true;[1] and (3) that the facts concern some matter of public interest. The comment must explicitly or implicitly indicate at least in general terms, what are the facts on which the comment is being made: however it is no longer necessary that the reader should be in a position to judge for himself how far the comment was well founded.[2] If these criteria are established, the onus shifts to the pursuer to show that the comment was made with the intention of harming the pursuer. The comment must be honestly made and relevant to the facts upon which it was based. For example, a theatre critic who criticises a play must honestly hold the opinion that the play is bad[3] and must restrict his comments to the play rather than the playwright.[4]

In *Spiller v Joseph*,[5] the Supreme Court held that the defence should be known as honest comment rather than fair comment.

1 Where the statement contains facts and opinion, the defence of fair comment is not lost if the facts upon which the opinion is based are true even if other facts are false: Defamation Act 1952, s 6.
2 *Spiller v Joseph* [2010] UKSC 53.
3 *Turner v Metro-Goldwyn-Mayer Pictures Ltd* [1950] 1 All ER 449, [1950] WN 83, HL; *Telnikoff v Matusevitch* [1992] 2 AC 343, [1991] 4 All ER 817, HL.
4 *Merivale v Carson* (1887) 20 QBD 275, CA.
5 [2010] UKSC 53.

(f) Privilege

15.18 A person who makes a defamatory statement may have the defence of privilege. In certain situations, public policy demands that a person should be free to speak without fear of litigation on the grounds of defamation. There are two forms of privilege: absolute privilege and qualified privilege.

15.19

(i) Absolute privilege

Where a statement is protected by absolute privilege, it cannot form the basis of an action for defamation or verbal injury.[1] It does not matter that the statement is defamatory or was made with the intention to harm the victim (malice). The following situations are covered by absolute privilege:

(a) Statements made in the Westminster Parliament. Any statement made in the Westminster Parliament has the protection of absolute privilege. This includes statements made in parliamentary committees. The statement does not have to be relevant to the proceedings. It is not restricted to statements made by members of either House: it would include, for example, a statement made by a witness giving evidence to a Select Committee. It does not extend to statements made by members of Parliament outside the Houses.[2] Where the conduct of a person in or in relation to proceedings in the Westminster Parliament is in issue in defamation proceedings, that person can waive, for the purpose of the defamation action, the privilege that prevents proceedings in Parliament from being impeached or questioned in court.[3] This is to enable an MP, for example, to rely on his own conduct in Parliament in order to pursue an action of defamation while, of course, retaining the defence of absolute privilege for statements he has made in Parliament!

(b) Statements made in judicial proceedings. A statement made by a judge in the course of judicial proceedings is protected by absolute privilege even if it was made maliciously.[4] However, the statement must be made while the judge is acting judicially, ie it must be relevant to the case which is subject to the proceedings.[5] Advocates or solicitors pleading the case also enjoy absolute privilege,[6] provided the statement is relevant to the case. Witnesses giving evidence have absolute privilege as long as the evidence is pertinent to the case.[7] Any findings of fact by a jury are subject to absolute privilege. But parties to a civil action do not enjoy absolute privilege – only qualified privilege.[8] Absolute privilege extends in like way to the participants in quasi-judicial proceedings or tribunals, for example, courts martial, public inquiries, arbitrations, children's hearings, employment tribunals and disciplinary tribunals.[9]

(c) Reports authorised by the Westminster Parliament. Reports of proceedings and papers etc published by or under the authority of either House of Parliament attract absolute privilege.[10] Fair and accurate reports of proceedings before a court are absolutely privileged provided they are published contemporaneously with the proceedings.[11]

(d) Any statement made in proceedings of the Scottish Parliament and any publication of any such statement authorised by the Scottish Parliament are absolutely privileged.[12]

(e) Miscellaneous. The Lord Advocate is absolutely privileged in respect of what she does in relation to prosecutions on indictment. This protection extends to procurators fiscal and Advocates Depute acting on the Lord Advocate's instructions. Ministers of the Crown are also protected provided the statement is made in the proper exercise of their functions. Reports of the various ombudsmen are also absolutely privileged.

1 On verbal injury, see para 15.25 below.
2 *Buchanan v Jennings* [2005] 1 AC 115.
3 Defamation Act 1996, s 13; *Hamilton v Al Fayed* [2001] 1 AC 395.
4 *Haggart's Trustees v Lord President Hope* (1824) 2 Sh App 125, HL; *Primrose v Waterston* (1902) 4 F 783, 10 SLT 37.
5 *Watt v Thomson* (1870) 8 M (HL) 77.
6 *Rome v Watson* (1898) 25 R 733, 5 SLT 377. The privilege extends to written pleadings.
7 *Watson v McEwan* (1905) 7 F (HL) 109. This privilege extends to statements made in precognitions: *B v Burns* 1994 SLT 250.
8 See para 15.20 below.
9 *Thomson v Ross* 2001 SLT 807 (Scottish Solicitors Discipline Tribunal).
10 Parliamentary Papers Act 1840.
11 Defamation Act 1996, s 14. Courts include any court in the UK, the European Court of Justice, the European Court of Human Rights and United Nations' international criminal tribunals.
12 Scotland Act 1998, s 41.

15.20

(ii) Qualified privilege

When a statement is protected by qualified privilege, the defender is assumed to have acted in good faith and an action of defamation or verbal injury[1] will not succeed unless the pursuer can show that the statement was made with the intention of harming the pursuer (ie with malice). Qualified privilege arises in the following circumstances:

(a) Duty or interest to speak. Where a person has a legal duty to speak, the statement is protected by qualified privilege. The protection extends to situations where there is a moral or social duty to speak, for example, to report a crime or inform a reporter to a children's hearing of child abuse. Complaints to the chief constable about the conduct of police officers attracts protection if an action of defamation is brought against the complainer by the officer who was the subject of the complaint.[2] Similarly, a letter to the deputy chief executive of the prison service about the unfitness of an employee to serve as an officer has been held to attract qualified privilege.[3] A person who gives a reference enjoys qualified privilege.[4] Whether a situation involves a duty to speak which attracts qualified privilege is a question of law to be determined by a court.

Qualified privilege also arises where a person has an interest to speak, for example, replying to criticism.[5] In these situations, the person who receives the statement must have a reciprocal interest in the information. So, for example, a complaint about the conduct of a police officer is protected by qualified privilege if made to the relevant chief constable but not if made to a newspaper editor.

(b)   Reports of proceedings in Parliament in the press or other media attract only qualified privilege. The position is the same in respect of reports of judicial and other quasi-judicial proceedings.[6]

(c)   Parties to a civil action enjoy only qualified privilege in respect of statements made in civil proceedings. If, however, the pursuer can prove that the statement was made with the intention of harming the pursuer (ie maliciously), then an action for defamation or verbal injury may lie.[7] This delict is often called 'judicial slander'.

(d)   Under the Defamation Act 2013,[8] the publication of statements in peer-reviewed scientific or academic journals is subject to qualified privilege.

(e)   Under the Defamation Act 1996,[9] the publication of certain types of reports is subject to qualified privilege.

1   On verbal injury, see para 15.25 below.
2   *Fraser v Mirza* 1993 SC (HL) 27, 1993 SLT 527.
3   *Quilty v Windsor* 1999 SLT 346. In *Pearson v Educational Institute of Scotland* 1997 SC 245, 1998 SLT 189, a report on the competency of the pursuer to be head of a college, which the union had sent on to a government department, was held to attract qualified privilege.
4   *Farquhar v Neish* (1890) 17 R 716. However, even if not made maliciously, the writer of the reference may be liable in negligence: *Spring v Guardian Assurance plc* [1995] 2 AC 296, [1994] 3 All ER 129, HL, discussed at para 4.17 above.
5   *Campbell v Cochrane* (1905) 8 F 205; *Carroll v British Broadcasting Corpn* 1997 SLT (Sh Ct) 23.
6   *Richardson v Wilson* (1879) 7 R 237, 17 SLR 122; *Cunningham v Scotsman Publications Ltd* 1987 SC 107, 1987 SCLR 314, OH.
7   *Williamson v Umphray and Robertson* (1890) 17 R 905, 27 SLR 742.
8   Section 6.
9   Defamation Act 1996, s 15 and Sch 1. Detailed treatment is outwith the scope of the present text. It should be noted that by para 12 of Sch 1, qualified privilege extends to fair and accurate reporting of a public meeting: this includes a press conference and a press release distributed at such a conference. See *McCortan Turkington Breen (a firm) v Times Newspapers Ltd* [2000] 4 All ER 913; *Thomson v Ross* 2002 SLT 807.

15.21   As we have seen, where a statement is subject to qualified privilege, it can be the subject of an action of defamation or verbal injury[1] if the pursuer acted maliciously. In the present writer's view, this simply means that the defender intended to harm or insult the pursuer, although it has been contended that it is sufficient to show that the defender was not motivated by duty or interest. But if that were so, at least in the case of duty or interest to speak, qualified privilege would not attach in the first place. However, as the authorities stand,[2] malice can be established if it can be shown that the defender abused the privileged occasion – as well as proving that he intended to injure the pursuer. Nevertheless, proof of malice is difficult.[3] It may be inferred from extreme language, a previous personal vendetta between the parties or the fact that the defender did not believe that the statement was true.[4] It is not enough simply to establish that the statement was defamatory.[5]

1 See para 15.25 below.
2 See especially *Fraser v Mirza* 1993 SC (HL) 27, 1993 SLT 527 at 531 per Lord Keith of Kinkel.
3 For an example of the difficulties, see *Fraser v Mirza* 1993 SC (HL) 27, 1993 SLT 527.
4 *Horrocks v Lowe* [1975] AC 135, [1974] 1 All ER 662, HL.
5 *Adam v Jackson* [1917] AC 309.

(g) The *Reynolds* defence

15.22 In *Reynolds v Times Newspapers*[1] the House of Lords held that qualified privilege would protect the publication of material which the writer was under a moral or social duty to publish and the intended recipients had an interest in receiving. In determining whether the defence was appropriate the court should consider all the circumstances of the case including the nature, status and source of the material. This is known as the 'duty–interest' test or 'right to know' test. The public has an interest in the maintenance of free expression through the promotion of a free press: on the other hand, publishers, editors and journalists have a duty to act responsibly. Responsible journalism for this purpose is not determined by whether the published material was in fact true or false: the question is whether the public has an interest in its publication irrespective of its truth and whether there was some evidence to support the allegations.[2] In *GKR Karate v Yorkshire Post Newspapers Ltd (No 2)*[3] qualified privilege applied to an article in a local newspaper alleging malpractice by a karate instructor who gave classes in the area. The journalist had a social and moral duty to write the article and the local inhabitants had a proper interest in knowing about the alleged malpractices as they might attend the classes. In writing the piece, the journalist had acted responsibly on information supplied to her from reliable sources. On the other hand, in *Grobbelaar v News Group Newspapers Ltd*[4] qualified privilege did not attach to a massive and relentless campaign of vilification in which Grobbelaar's guilt was unequivocally asserted, with some of the allegations going far beyond what could be supported by the evidence the newspaper had obtained.

In *Jameel v Wall Street Journal*,[5] the House of Lords recognised that the *Reynolds* public interest defence was 'a 'different jurisprudential creature' from the law of privilege, although it is a natural development of that law'.[6] In particular when it applies, 'There is no question of the privilege being defeated by proof of malice because the propriety of the conduct of the defendant is built into the conditions under which the material is privileged'.[7] These conditions are:

(a) the subject matter of the published material must be in the public interest. This is to be decided by the judge. But everything which engages the public's interest is not necessarily in the public interest. Investigative journalism which is intended to uncover political or economic subterfuge will usually be in the public interest but not celebrity 'tittle tattle';

(b) the inclusion of the defamatory material must be justified. The defamatory material must be part of the story and the more serious the allegation, the more important that it makes a real contribution to the public element in the subject matter of the publication. Allowance has to be made for editorial judgment at the time of publication; and

(c) the steps taken to gather and publish the information must have been responsible and fair: the responsible journalism test. This is an objective test *viz* the publisher must have taken the care that a responsible publisher would take to verify the material published.[8] A publisher cannot claim that he acted responsibly by relying on information that came to his knowledge after the date of publication of the defamatory material.[9]

In *Seaga v Harper*,[10] the Privy Council held that the *Reynolds* defence was not restricted to the press and media but extended to publications made by any person who published material of public interest in any medium, so long as the conditions applicable to responsible journalism were satisfied.

There is no general rule that it is not in the public interest to publish details to support an accusation of criminal conduct that is being investigated by the police. However allegations against ordinary individuals are less likely to be in the public interest than allegations against persons who perform public functions especially when they are about the alleged performance of those functions. In *Flood v Times Newspapers*,[11] the defendant published an article in which it was stated that the police were investigating a detective for corruption. The article named the detective as Flood. It also contained details of the accusations which involved the sale of sensitive information to Russian exiles who wished to avoid extradition back to Russia. While the article did not state that Flood was guilty, it suggested that there were reasonable grounds to suspect he was or, at least, grounds for investigating whether he was guilty. After the investigation, Flood was completely exonerated. The Supreme Court held that the defendant was entitled to the *Reynolds* defence. The publication of an article on alleged police corruption was in the public interest. In this case details of the allegations were also in the public interest, including the name of the suspected officer. This was also a matter of editorial judgment with which the courts should be slow to interfere. The protection for the individual lay in the need for verification of the alleged facts. Here the journalist had taken reasonable steps to have the material verified and the *Reynolds* defence applied.

This development shows the importance to be given to a responsible free press in a democratic society which is enshrined in Article 10 of the European Convention on Human Rights.

1 [2001] 1 AC 127.
2 *Loutchansky v Times Newspapers Ltd (No 2)* [2002] QB 783.
3 [2002] EMLR 410.
4 [2001] 2 All ER 437.
5 [2007] 1 AC 359.
6 Ibid per Baroness Hale at 408.
7 Ibid per Lord Hoffmann at 381.
8 *Bonnick v Morris* [2003] 1 AC 300.
9 *Loutchansky v Times Newspapers Ltd (No 1)* [2002] QB 321.
10 [2009] 1 AC 1.
11 [2012] UKSC 11.

(h) Responsibility of publication

15.23 By s 1 of the Defamation Act 1996, a person has a defence to an action of defamation if he can show that: (i) he was not the author, editor or publisher of the defamatory statement; (ii) he took reasonable care in relation to its publication; and (iii) he did not know and had no reason to believe that what he did caused or contributed to the publication of a defamatory statement. The defence is designed to protect persons concerned with printing, processing, producing, distributing or selling newspapers, books, films, CDs, software etc which contain the defamatory material.[1]

1 See, for example, *Godfrey v Demon Internet Ltd* [2001] QB 201, [1999] 4 All ER 342, [2000] 3 WLR 1020, QBD.

(5) Damages

15.24   In an action for defamation and verbal injury,[1] the pursuer is entitled to an award of solatium in respect of insult and hurt feelings and compensation for any patrimonial loss. Where the case is one of defamation, insult is presumed but any patrimonial loss must be averred and proved. Although patrimonial loss, if it has been sustained, is relatively easy to assess, solatium is more difficult because it involves no little degree of speculation. In practice, solatium is usually a modest sum in Scots law.[2] Everyone is assumed to be of good character, so solatium is unlikely to be increased if the pursuer is particularly good. But the more eminent the pursuer, the greater the loss of reputation, and more will consequently be awarded as solatium. In general, the worse the allegation, the greater the sum that will be awarded; in particular, the sum may be increased if the defender has persisted in the defamatory allegations against the pursuer.[3] However, at the end of the day, solatium is intended to compensate non-patrimonial loss:[4] a person who brings an action primarily to clear his name will receive only a nominal sum.[5]

An award of solatium can be mitigated as a result of a number of factors. First, if the pursuer's character or reputation is already tainted before the defamatory statement, evidence can be led by the defender to show that the pursuer did not therefore suffer as much as an ordinary person.[6] An immediate retraction of the statement and an apology will mitigate the loss.[7] This will also be the case if the pursuer provoked the defender into making the defamatory statement.[8] If the statement has been published by more than one person, the defender can mitigate the damages the pursuer should receive if the pursuer has already received damages in respect of the same words, or words to the same effect, from a third party.[9] So, for example, if A and B defame C using the same words, if C sues A, A can plead mitigation if C has already received damages from B.

1 On verbal injury, see para 15.25 below.
2 See, for example, *Gilbert v Yorston* 1996 SCLR 1122, 1997 SLT 879, OH (no evidence that any third party believed the defamatory material: no effect on pursuer's career. Pursuer was awarded £1,500 as solatium).

3 *Baigent v British Broadcasting Corpn* 1999 GWD 10-474 (awards of £60,000 and £50,000 were made against the BBC: the attack on the pursuers' personal integrity and professional ability was very vindictive); *Munro v Brown* [2011] CSOH 117; *Kinley v Devine* [2014] CSOH 67.
4 *Stein v Beaverbrook Newspapers Ltd* 1968 SC 272, 1968 SLT 401.
5 *Gilbert v Yorston* 1996 SCLR 1122, 1997 SLT 879, OH.
6 *Corrigan v Monaghan* 1923 SC 1, 1922 SLT 634.
7 *Morrison v Ritchie & Co* (1902) 4 F 645.
8 *Paul v Jackson* (1884) 11 R460.
9 Defamation Act 1952, s 12.

C. VERBAL INJURY

15.25 Where a statement is made which is not defamatory,[1] the law will not presume that it is false, made with intent to injure and caused insult to the victim. It does not follow that where the non-defamatory statement has undermined a person's character or reputation that he is without a remedy. Scots law recognises that non-defamatory statements can amount to civil wrongs which are actionable in delict. These are known as verbal injuries.

The most common situation where an action will lie for verbal injury occurs in cases where a non-defamatory statement is made which holds up the pursuer to public hatred, ridicule and contempt. In *Paterson v Welch*,[2] the defender stated that the pursuer had made the comment that if children from the poorer classes were allowed to attend Madras College, this would 'contaminate the genteel children' currently attending that school. To state that a person holds a controversial opinion is not defamatory, ie it does not lower him in the estimation of right-thinking persons. However, the court was prepared to allow the case to proceed as an action for verbal injury provided the pursuer could aver and prove that: (1) the statement was false; (2) the statement was intended to injure the pursuer; and (3) that injury had in fact been sustained by the pursuer.[3] Thus, unlike a case of defamation, where falsity, intention to injure and injury are presumed, in cases of verbal injury the onus lies on the pursuer to prove these facts.

In *Steele v Scottish Daily Record and Sunday Mail Ltd*[4] the defender made a statement in its newspaper's legal advice and consumer rights page that the pursuer, a car dealer, had acted harshly in refusing to cancel a hire purchase agreement with a customer who had got into financial difficulties. 'Have a heart, that's my message to Motor Dealer, Mr Steele' ran the headline. The statement was not defamatory since it merely suggested that the pursuer was a hard businessman. Nevertheless, the Inner House held that Steele would have an action if he could prove that the statement was false, that it was intended to harm him and had, in fact, caused him harm. The case failed on the basis that the article was not intended to hold Steele up to public hatred, ridicule and contempt, but had been written to persuade him to give his unfortunate customer a better deal. Therefore, before an action can lie for verbal injury on this ground, the effect of the statement, apart from being false, must have been intended to cause the pursuer to be despised or condemned by ordinary members of the public.[5]

While it is not defamatory falsely to state that a person is homosexual,[6] an action could lie in verbal injury if the victim could demonstrate malice on the part of the defender and patrimonial or non-patrimonial loss.

An action for verbal injury will also lie if A makes a false statement about the state of B's property, for example that B's house is falling down[7] (slander of property). Similarly, an action will lie if A falsely alleges that B does not own property which he wishes to sell[8] (slander of title), or if A falsely states that B's business is not run well[9] (slander of business). To succeed in these situations, B must prove that the statement was false, intended to harm B economically and actually caused B patrimonial loss.[10] But because there is no intention to injure the pursuer's character or reputation, solatium cannot be awarded.[11]

Finally, an action for verbal injury may lie if A defames B with the intention of harming C. Because C has not been defamed, ie C's reputation has not been directly attacked, C cannot sue A in defamation. But if C can prove that A's defamatory statement in respect of B was false, was intended to harm C and did harm C, then in principle C should have an action for verbal injury against A.[12] So, for example, if a person defames a woman by calling her a prostitute, not only can she sue in defamation but her husband could have an action based on verbal injury if he could prove that the statement was false, that it was made to injure him and in fact did so. Unlike his wife's case of defamation where these three requisites are presumed in her favour, in his action for verbal injury the onus lies on the husband to establish these facts.

A defender in an action of verbal injury can rely on the same defences that are available in an action of defamation.[13]

1 On the categories of defamatory statements, see paras 15.44 ff above.
2 (1893) 20 R 744.
3 *Paterson v Welch* (1893) 20 R 744 at 749 per the Lord President (Robertson).
4 1970 SLT 53.

5 *Steele v Scottish Daily Record and Sunday Mail Ltd* 1970 SLT 53. See also *Burns v Diamond* (1896) 23 R 507, (1896) 3 SLT 274.
6 Discussed at para 15.5 above.
7 *Argyllshire Weavers Ltd v A Macaulay (Tweeds) Ltd* 1965 SLT 21, OH.
8 *Philp v Morton* (1816) Hume 865.
9 *Craig v Inveresk Paper Merchant Ltd* 1970 SLT (Notes) 50, OH.
10 *Argyllshire Weavers Ltd v A Macaulay (Tweeds) Ltd* 1965 SLT 21, OH.
11 Unlike the 'public hatred, ridicule and contempt' cases where, as in defamation, both solatium and damages for patrimonial loss are recoverable. Unlike defamation, insult must be proved before solatium can be obtained.
12 *North of Scotland Banking Co v Duncan* (1857) 19 D 881 at 887 per Lord Deas. Cf *Broom v Ritchie & Co* (1905) 6 F 942, where the distinction between defamation and verbal injury was not clearly drawn.
13 Discussed at paras 15.13 ff above.

D. *CONVICIUM*

15.26 It is an essential requirement of defamation and verbal injury that the statement is false. Some writers have argued that Scots law recognises another form of verbal injury, *convicium*, where *veritas* is no defence.[1] *Convicium* involves holding the pursuer up to public hatred, ridicule and contempt, and in so far as it ever had an independent existence in Scots law, it is thought that it has been overtaken by the genus wrong of verbal injury where the statement has to be false before it is actionable.[2]

In the present writer's view, it is too late for the courts to revive this delict, particularly since it could undermine freedom of speech, given that *veritas* is no defence. Instead, the legislature must give consideration to whether it is desirable to introduce a statutory remedy for unwarranted intrusions into an individual person's privacy.[3] The scope of the remedy – where *veritas* would be no defence – would be determined after balancing an individual's interest in privacy against the public interest in freedom of speech. This is clearly a task for the Scottish Parliament rather than the judiciary, who would have to develop principles which were, arguably, never part of Scots common law.[4]

1 See, in particular, Walker *Delict* (2nd edn, 1981) p 736.
2 See para 15.25 above.
3 There is also potential liability if the defender's conduct amounts to a breach of the pursuer's rights under Article 8 of the European Convention on Human Rights (right to respect for his private and family life, his home and his correspondence): see, for example, *Martin v McGuiness* 2003 SCLR 548. See also discussion of confidential information at paras 1.19 ff above.
4 This chapter is strongly influenced by Dr Kenneth Norrie's seminal article 'Hurts to Character, Honour and Reputation: a Reappraisal' 1984 JR 163.

Part IV

DAMAGES

INTRODUCTION

The purpose of this last chapter is to give a short account of the law of damages. At the outset it is important to remember that no obligation to make reparation arises unless the victim has sustained constituent harm. As we have seen[1] harm is a constituent part of an actionable wrong: *damnum injuria datum*. Moreover, even if the victim has sustained constituent harm there is no liability unless that harm was a reasonable and probable consequence of the defender's wrongful conduct.[2] If the harm was a reasonable and probable consequence of the defender's wrongful conduct, then there has been a *breach* of the defender's duty of care and the defender's liability to make reparation is triggered. Accordingly, once a wrong has been established, the defender is obliged to compensate the pursuer for the *losses* he or she has incurred as a result of the harm sustained by the pursuer which was constitutive of the delict.

Scots law recognises two kinds of reparable losses *viz* non-patrimonial loss and patrimonial loss.

(a) Non-patrimonial loss
    Solatium is the traditional name given to damages for non-patrimonial loss. Non-patrimonial losses can be regarded as invasions of the victim's personality rights in the broadest sense. Thus, solatium can be awarded in relation to the following: victims of defamation and verbal injury for the affront to their dignity caused by the wrong; wrongful conception; wrongful interference with the corpse of a relative, particularly a child; grief arising from the death of a relative; wrongful imprisonment; assault, in particular non-consensual medical procedures; and for pain and suffering arising from personal injuries. Obviously the assessment of an award of solatium is not scientific involving a degree of artificiality and a considerable element of discretion on the part of the judge or jury.
(b) Patrimonial loss
    Patrimonial losses are the economic losses arising from the harm sustained by the victim. These losses derive from or are parasitic upon the harm that the victim has sustained and

which was constitutive of the delict. For example, if A suffers personal injuries, he may receive compensation for past loss of earnings, future loss of earnings, loss of pension rights, past and future medical expenses, ie economic losses which *derive* from the personal injuries. Where A's property is damaged, the derivative patrimonial loss is the cost of repair or replacement and if after repair the property is worth less than before it was damaged, the pursuer can recover the diminution in value. (The owner of damaged property may, of course suffer non-patrimonial loss, for example anger and distress if his papers constituting a lifetime's scholarship are destroyed in a fire.) One of the difficulties with reparation for 'pure' economic loss is that unlike personal injury or damage to property cases, the harm which is constitutive of the delict is itself economic loss and as we have seen[3] it is only in exceptional circumstances that liability arises.

1 Para 5.2 above: *Rothwell v Chemical and Insulating Co Ltd* [2008] 1 AC 281.
2 Paras 5.4 ff above: *Muir v Glasgow Corpn* 1943 SC (HL) 102.
3 Paras 4.10 ff above.

CHAPTER 16

Damages

A. REMOTENESS OF LOSSES

16.1 It will be remembered that Scottish courts once took the view that delictual liability would not be imposed upon a defender if the harm sustained by the pursuer was too remote.[1] However, in the present writer's view, these cases should now be analysed as situations where the court was unwilling to impose a duty of care on the defender, ie the duty of care was being used as a threshold device to deny delictual liability. But even where there has been a breach of a duty of care and the defender is liable to make reparation to the pursuer in respect of the losses arising from the constituent harm he or she has sustained, it does not follow that the defender must compensate the pursuer for every loss arising from that harm. Some losses are 'too remote'. Consider the following example:

As a result of his careless driving, A knocks down a pedestrian, B. B will recover solatium[2] for his or her pain and suffering and damages for derivative economic loss. The latter will include loss of wages between the date of the accident and the date of the action; future loss of earnings from the date of the action, if B is unable to work or can work only at a lower-paid job;[3] the cost of medical treatment and nursing up to the date of the action and the cost of such care in the future. However, if as a result of the accident, B was unable to give instructions to his stockbroker to purchase shares which he had intended to buy, or if B was unable to post his football coupon, the profits B would have made on the shares or the dividend he would have won if the coupon had been posted are not recoverable even though they arise from the fact that B was incapacitated as a result of the accident. These losses are too remote and cannot therefore be recovered.

What criteria do the courts use to determine whether or not losses are too remote? The classic statement of the rule on remoteness of losses in Scots law was articulated by the Lord Ordinary (Kinloch) in *Allan v Barclay*:[4]

'The grand rule on the subject of damages is, that none can be claimed except such as naturally and directly arise out of the wrong done; and such, therefore, as may reasonably be supposed to have been in the contemplation of the wrongdoer.'

However, there is a potential contradiction inherent in this statement. While many losses which are reasonably foreseeable also directly arise from the wrong done, it is possible to envisage situations where a loss directly arises from the wrong but is not reasonably foreseeable and vice versa, ie a loss which is reasonably foreseeable but does not arise directly from the wrong.

This problem has been a matter of particular concern in England. In *Re Polemis and Furness, Withy & Co Ltd*,[5] the Court of Appeal held that the question whether particular losses can be recovered depends only on whether they were the direct consequence of the wrongful act. Provided some harm was reasonably foreseeable so that there was a breach of a duty of care, the defendant is liable to compensate for all the harm directly resulting from the breach of duty even if those losses were unforeseeable.

In this case, stevedores carelessly allowed a plank to fall into the hold of a ship. The falling plank caused a spark which in its turn ignited petrol vapour in the hold. The vapour caused a fire which destroyed the vessel. The court held that while the fire was not a reasonably foreseeable consequence of allowing the plank to fall, some damage to the vessel was. In the light of these findings, the court was prepared to hold that since it was reasonably foreseeable that some form of harm would result from the negligent act, damages in respect of losses caused by the fire, albeit not reasonably foreseeable, were nevertheless recoverable as a direct consequence of the foreseeable harm. Although this case is often cited as authority for the proposition that reasonable foreseeability plays no part in determining the extent of recoverable losses, such a conclusion may not be entirely justified. If it had been held that it was not foreseeable that the plank would cause any damage at all, the court might well have held that the consequences of the fire were too remote.

However, it may appear illogical to insist that some harm to the pursuer must be foreseen as a reasonable and probable consequence of the defender's act or omission before there is a breach of a duty of care, ie delictual liability, yet allow the pursuer to recover losses directly arising from that breach which were not reasonably foreseeable. In *Overseas Tankship (UK) Ltd v Morts Dock and Engineering Co, The Wagon Mound,*[6] the Privy Council declined to follow *Re Polemis*. In this case, a ship was being bunkered when some oil being loaded on board spilt into the harbour as a result of the carelessness of the appellant's employees. Morts' employees were welding nearby when the spillage happened. Molten metal from their operations fell onto some debris which caught fire; this in turn set the oil alight, causing substantial fire damage to the wharf owned by Morts. It was found as a fact that it was not reasonably foreseeable that the oil could have been ignited in such a way. Although it was reasonably foreseeable that the oil spillage would cause some harm to the respondent's dock, ie by fouling the dock, nevertheless the court held that the appellants were not liable for the losses caused by the unforeseeable fire. If *Re Polemis* had been applied, it is arguable that the appellants would have been liable for the losses caused by the fire, because some harm, ie the fouling of the dock, was foreseeable and the fire could be regarded as a *direct* result of the breach of duty[7] – albeit that the fire was unforeseeable. However, since harm by fire was not reasonably foreseeable as a probable consequence of the spillage, it is submitted that in this case there was no breach of duty of care, ie there was no delictual liability, and therefore it is not a remoteness of losses case at all.[8]

1 See para 5.17 above.
2 For the calculation of solatium, see para 16.12 below.
3 For the calculation of loss of future earnings, see paras 16.13 ff below.
4 (1864) 2 M 873. The case was concerned with whether an employer could recover damages for the loss of his injured employee's services. In other words, it was concerned with the defender's liability rather than remoteness of losses. Today it would be analysed as an example of non-recoverability of secondary economic loss. However, the passage has always been regarded as an authoritative statement of remoteness of losses.
5 [1921] 3 KB 560, CA.
6 [1961] AC 388, [1961] 1 All ER 404, PC.
7 Although in this case it is equally arguable that the fire was *indirectly* caused as a result of the molten metal falling on the oil.
8 Cf *Hughes v Lord Advocate* 1963 SC (HL) 31, 1963 SLT 150, where personal injuries caused by fire were reasonably foreseeable: only the extent of the injuries was not.

16.2 The Scottish courts have not given authoritative guidance on the matter; instead, reliance is simply placed on Lord Kinloch's 'grand rule'. In *Kelvin Shipping Co, The Baron Vernon v Canadian Pacific Railway Co, The Metagama,*[1] Viscount Haldane LC opined[2] that when 'a collision takes place by the fault of the defendant's ship, the damage is recoverable, in an action for damages if it is the natural and reasonable result of the negligent act, and it will assume that character if it can be shown to be such a consequence as in the ordinary course of things would flow from the situation which the offending ship created.'[3]

Although there are *obiter dicta* that *Re Polemis* does not reflect the law of Scotland,[4] in *Campbell v F and F Moffat (Transport) Ltd*[5] the Lord Ordinary (Lord Cameron of Lochbroom) held that the test was not whether the loss was reasonably foreseeable but whether it arose naturally and directly out of the wrong. In that case, the pursuer was injured in a road accident and, as a result, his employment was terminated in 1989. Two years later, his former employer closed the mill where the pursuer had worked and gave the employees working at that date *ex gratia* redundancy payments. In his action for damages, the pursuer sought compensation for the loss of the redundancy payment he would have received if his employment had not been terminated two years earlier as a result of the accident. Lord Cameron took the view that this loss was not so utterly speculative that it could not amount to a natural and direct consequence of the accident.

It is submitted that in Scots law it is too simplistic to see the question of remoteness of damages in terms of reasonable foreseeability on the one hand and direct consequences on the other. The courts use a combination of both tests in assessing whether the loss is a natural consequence of the delictual act. It is only if the loss is utterly speculative[6] that the loss will be too remote and not recoverable in an award of damages. On the other hand, what is clear is that in a case of personal injuries, the defender takes her victim as she finds him. If, for example, A, as a result of her carelessness, burns B, if B has a predisposition to cancer which is triggered by the burn, with the result that B dies, A is liable for B's death even if that was not reasonably foreseeable as a consequence of the burn. In this situation, reasonable foreseeability of death is treated as irrelevant or, alternatively, the defender is deemed to have reasonably foreseen that the pursuer could have been an ill, as opposed to healthy, person.[7] Moreover, as we have seen, where the pursuer is a primary victim, the defender is liable for causing mental or psychiatric illness, even though such illness was not reasonably foreseeable: a case of an eggshell personality rather than an eggshell skull![8]

1 1928 SC (HL) 21, 1928 SLT 117.
2 Ibid.
3 However, this case was clearly concerned with the existence of liability rather than remoteness of losses.

4 See, for example, *Cowan v National Coal Board* 1958 SLT (Notes) 19, OH, per the Lord Ordinary (Cameron).
5 1992 SCLR 551, 1992 SLT 962, OH.
6 As it is submitted is the case in the examples of the loss of profits on the shares and the loss of a football pools' dividend: see para 16.1 above.
7 *McKillen v Barclay Curle & Co Ltd* 1967 SLT 41. This is known as 'the thin skull' or 'the eggshell-skull rule'.
8 *Page v Smith* [1996] AC 155, [1995] 2 All ER 736, HL: discussed at para 4.2 above.

16.3   In *Simmons v British Steel*,[1] Lord Rodger summarised[2] the relevant principles thus:

'These authorities suggest that, once liability is established, any question of the remoteness of damage is to be approached along the following lines which may, of course, be open to refinement and development. (1) The starting point is that a defender is not liable for a consequence which is not reasonably foreseeable. (2) While a defender is not liable for damage that was not reasonably foreseeable, it does not follow that he is liable for all damage that was reasonably foreseeable: depending on the circumstances, the defender may not be liable for damage caused by a *novus actus interveniens* or unreasonable conduct on the part of the pursuer, even if it was reasonably foreseeable. (3) Subject to the qualification in (2) if the pursuer's injury is of a kind that was foreseeable, the defender is liable, even if the damage is greater in extent than was foreseeable or it was caused in a way that could not have been foreseen. (4) The defender must take his victim as he finds him (5) subject again to the qualification in (2), where personal injury to the pursuer was reasonably foreseeable, the defender is liable for any personal injury, whether physical or psychiatric, which the pursuer suffers as a result of the wrong-doing.'

With the greatest respect it is thought that this summary is not without difficulties. In particular it appears to confuse issues of initial liability (factors (3) and (5)) with those of remoteness of losses.[3]

In the present writer's view the law on remoteness of losses can be summarised as follows:

(i)   the victim must have sustained harm which is constitutive of delictual liability: normally this means that the harm sustained was a reasonable and probable consequence of the defender's wrongful conduct.[4]
(ii) The defender is liable for the non-patrimonial and patrimonial losses for which the constitutive harm is the legal cause provided such losses are reasonably foreseeable. There is therefore no liability to make reparation for unforeseeable losses or losses where the constitutive harm is not the legal cause, ie there has been causative fade.[5]

(iii) In the case of personal injuries only, the defender takes his victim as he finds him and is liable for unforeseeable non-patrimonial and patrimonial losses provided that the defender's wrongful conduct is the legal cause of these losses. This is known as the 'egg shell skull' or 'thin skull' rule. Thus, for example, where the constitutive harm is a foreseeable physical injury, the defender can be liable for the patrimonial and non-patrimonial losses arising from an unforeseeable mental illness always provided the physical injury materially contributed to the mental illness or its recurrence.[6]

1 2004 SC (HL) 94. The case is an unexceptional example of the application of the thin skull rule in respect of liability for the victim's unforeseeable mental illness following foreseeable physical injuries caused by the negligence of the defender. However the House of Lords held that both the Lord Ordinary (Hardie) and the Second Division failed to apply the relevant principles!

2 Ibid at 115; the authorities cited by Lord Rodger have been removed.

3 Lord Rodger's *dictum* was followed with approval in *Spencer v Wincanton Holdings Ltd (Wincanton Logistics Ltd)* [2009] EWCA Civ 1404. In the present writer's view that was a case on legal causation and not remoteness of losses. For discussion of the case see para 6.7 above.

4 But where the pursuer is a primary victim, ie is within the area of risk of physical harm, mental illness can be constitutive even if it is not reasonably foreseeable and the victim did not suffer any foreseeable physical harm: *Page v Smith* [1996] AC 155. It is thought that the decision is unprincipled on this point.

5 Where a claimant's suicide was the result of depression caused by a personal injury which was a consequence of the defendant's negligence, the suicide was held not to break the chain of causation; see *Corr v IBC Vehicles* [2008] 1 AC 884. This was an extreme case: normally damages would at least be reduced as a result of the victim's contributory fault. There was no causative fade in *Spencer v Wincanton Holdings Ltd (Wincanton Logistics Ltd)* [2009] EWCA Civ 1404 (plaintiff's fall while filling his car at a garage was still a consequence of losing his leg as a result of an accident at work).

6 *Simmons v British Steel* 2004 SC (HL) 94.

16.4   It cannot be stressed enough that the thin skull rule only applies where the victim has suffered personal injuries. In all other cases the losses must be reasonably foreseeable. Thus where the constituent harm is damage to property, any losses sustained by the owner must be reasonably foreseeable before the defender is liable to pay solatium or compensation in respect of them. In *Yearworth v North Bristol NHS Trust*,[1] for example, on the advice of the defendants the claimants had provided samples of semen which would be put into cold storage by the hospital fertility unit. This was done because the men were undergoing chemotherapy which might render them infertile. Owing to the negligence of the hospital the semen thawed and the sperms died. The men suffered mental distress when they were told that the sperms were lost and they would therefore not be able to have children as a result of IVH if they became infertile. (Fortunately, they regained their fertility after the chemotherapy ended.) The Court of Appeal held that the sperm constituted property which was owned by the men. The damage to the sperm was the constituent harm. Therefore, the defendants would only be liable for the claimants' non-patrimonial loss if the men's distress arising from the wrongful destruction of their sperms was reasonably foreseeable which in the circumstances the court held it was.

Where the intentional wrongs are concerned, different principles apply and the defender is liable to make reparation for all losses suffered by the pursuer which directly arise from the wrong – whether or not these losses are reasonably foreseeable. The intention to injure the pursuer, which is normally an essential requisite of these delicts, disposes of any question of remoteness of losses.[2]

1 [2009] EWCA Civ 37. In *Attica v British Gas* [1988] QB 304 the plaintiff obtained damages for mental illness caused by seeing her house destroyed by fire due to the negligence of the defendants since mental harm to the owner of the property was reasonably foreseeable as she actually witnessed the fire.
2 *Smith New Court Securities Ltd v Scrimgeour Vickers (Asset Management) Ltd* [1997] AC 254, [1996] 4 All ER 769, HL; *Barry v Sutherland* 2002 SLT 413.

B. CALCULATION OF DAMAGES

(1) Introduction

16.5 The purpose of an award of damages is to compensate the pursuer for those losses which arose as a result of the delict. It is intended, so far as money can, to place the pursuer in the financial position he would have been if the wrong had not occurred.[1] Where the claim is in respect of damage to property, damages are relatively simple to assess, ie the cost of repair or replacement of the property.[2] If after repair the property is worth less than before it was damaged the pursuer can recover the diminution in value.[3] It is now settled that if the cost of repair is greater than would reasonably be expected because of the owner's impecuniosity at the time the property was damaged, the pursuer can recover for the increased costs of repair.[4] In *Network Rail Infrastructure Ltd v Conarken Group Ltd,*[5] the defendants damaged the plaintiff's rail infrastructure. This led to the temporary closure of the line. Under track access agreements, the plaintiffs had to pay compensation to train operating companies who had suffered financial loss as a result of the consequent disruption of their schedules. The Court of Appeal held that the cost of repair and the loss of revenue flowed naturally from the damage to the rails. The economic loss sustained by the plaintiff in compensating the operating companies under the agreements was therefore not too remote. As it was in the public interest to have punctual and reliable train services and because the track agreements had been carefully drafted, the defendants were liable to pay damages in respect of the compensation the plaintiffs had paid to the train operators.

Greater difficulties arise in calculating damages in wrongful conception and wrongful birth, pure economic loss and personal injury cases and these deserve fuller treatment.

1 See, for example, *O'Brien's Curator Bonis v British Steel plc* 1991 SC 315, 1991 SCLR 831, 1991 SLT 477 at 480 per the Lord President (Hope); *Cantwell v Criminal Injuries Compensation Board* 2002 SC (HL) 1.
2 The pursuer still incurs a reparable loss even though he could have pursued a contractual claim against a third party to repair the property: *Ford Motor Co Ltd v HLM Design Ltd* 1997 SLT 837, OH.
3 *Hunter v National Specialist Steeplejacks* 2004 GWD 3–49.
4 *Alcoa Minerals of Jamaica v Herbert Broderick* [2002] 1 AC 371; *Lagden v O'Connor* [2004] 1 All ER 277. In these circumstances, the pursuer is not in breach of his duty to mitigate the loss by waiting until he could afford the repairs.
5 [2011] EWCA Civ 644.

(2) Wrongful conception and wrongful birth

16.6   As we have seen,[1] the infringement of a parent's right not to have a child is reparable in Scots law. Applying the remoteness of losses rule, the parents should be entitled to receive compensation for the losses which are reasonably foreseeable as a direct consequence of the wrongful conception. These would include the mother's pain and suffering during the pregnancy and birth of the child; any loss of the mother's earnings during the pregnancy; and the cost of rearing the child. However, in *McFarlane v Tayside Health Board*[2] the House of Lords held that parents could not recover as damages the cost of bringing up a healthy and normal child conceived as a result of medical negligence. Their Lordships did so on grounds of legal policy. Departing from the principle that the function of the law of delict is corrective justice, ie to compensate the pursuer for the losses arising from a wrong, the House held that as a matter of distributive justice compensation for the cost of alimenting a healthy and normal child could not be condoned. To do so would be: (i) disproportionate to the defender's fault; (ii) a further inroad to the principle that pure economic loss is prima facie not recoverable in delict (albeit that the economic loss in such cases is derivative, ie *derives* from the wrongful conception); (iii) to regard the child as a financial liability and nothing else; (iv) to necessitate an attempt to balance the cost of a child's upbringing against the unquantifiable rewards of parenthood; and (v) a potential drain on the limited resources of the NHS which would affect the community's sense of how such resources should be allocated.

The 'principle' in *McFarlane* that the cost of rearing a healthy and normal child could not be recovered in wrongful conception cases was reaffirmed by the House of Lords in *Rees v Darlington Memorial Hospital NHS Trust*.[3] In this case, the child was normal and healthy but the mother was blind. A majority of their Lordships[4] held that the mother's disability was not a ground for distinguishing *McFarlane*. However, they took the view that an award of solatium did not adequately recognise the wrongful infringement of the mother's freedom to limit the size of her family.[5] Accordingly, she should receive a conventional – non-compensatory – award of £15,000 to afford some measure of recognition of the wrong she had suffered.[6]

McFarlane involved the wrongful[7] conception of a healthy and normal child. What of the situation where a handicapped child is born but the mother lost the opportunity to terminate the pregnancy as a result of the defender's failure to carry out the appropriate pre-natal tests? In *McLelland v Glasgow Health Board*[8] an Extra Division held that in wrongful birth cases the principle in *McFarlane* also applied to exclude the cost of the child's basic maintenance: however, any increased costs attributable to the child's special needs could be recovered. In England, the Court of Appeal reached a similar conclusion in *Parkinson v St James and Seacroft University Hospital Trust*.[9] Accordingly, it would appear that while the basic costs of alimenting a handicapped child cannot be recovered, any extra expenditure involved in attempting to make the child's upbringing as normal as possible can.

These decisions illustrate once again the readiness of the House of Lords to depart from the application of recognised rules of delictual liability to avoid a result which is not consonant with their Lordships' view of what is desirable in terms of social and economic policy.

1 Paras 4.7–4.9 above.
2 2000 SC (HL) 1.
3 [2004] 1 AC 309, [2003] 4 All ER 987.
4 Lords Bingham, Nicholls, Millet and Scott; Lords Steyn, Hope and Hutton dissenting.

5 *Quaere* whether this also applies to a father's freedom to do so?
6 There can be few more blatant examples of judicial 'legislation'.
7 Ie a conception arising from a failed sterilisation as a result of medical negligence.
8 2002 SLT 446. It should be noted that the father as well as the mother received solatium in respect of the birth of the handicapped child.
9 [2002] QB 266. This decision was approved by Lords Steyn, Hope and Hutton in *Rees*.

(3) Pure economic loss claims

16.7   In some situations when delictual liability for pure economic loss has been recognised, it is relatively simple to calculate the loss. For example, in the case of a disappointed legatee, the loss is the value of the lost legacy.[1] Where a surveyor has been negligent and failed to discover defects, the loss to the purchaser is either the cost of repair or the diminution in the value of the property.[2] But difficulties have arisen in quantifying loss when the pursuer has been induced to enter into a transaction as a result of the defender's misrepresentation.

1 *White v Jones* [1995] 2 AC 207, [1995] 1 All ER 691, HL; *Holmes v Bank of Scotland* 2002 SLT 544.
2 *Patel v Hooper & Jackson* [1999] 1 All ER 992, CA.

(a) Fraudulent misrepresentation

16.8   It is well settled that when A has entered into a transaction as a result of B's fraudulent misrepresentation, B is liable for all A's losses arising directly from the transaction, even though some of them might not be reasonably foreseeable.[1] This would include losses which A incurs as a result of a general fall in the market value of the assets involved in the transaction.

1 *Smith New Court Securities Ltd v Scrimgeour Vickers (Asset Management) Ltd* [1997] AC 254, [1996] 4 All ER 769, HL; *Barry v Sutherland* 2002 SLT 413.

(b) Negligent misrepresentation

16.9   What is the position if A has entered into a transaction as a result of B's negligent misrepresentation? When the misrepresentation takes the form of *advice*, ie B advises A to enter into a particular transaction, then B is liable for all the losses incurred by A as a consequence of entering into the transaction, provided such losses are reasonably foreseeable.[1] Again, this could include losses which A incurs as a result of a general fall in the market value of the assets involved in the transaction.

However, when the misrepresentation takes the form of B providing *information* which A uses to decide whether or not to enter a particular transaction, the House of Lords[2] has imposed a cap on B's potential liability. In other words, B is only liable for that part of A's loss which was a reasonably foreseeable consequence of the information being wrong. Consider the following examples:

(i) B *advises* A to lend £10 million to C, using C's property as security. C defaults. Owing to a general fall in the market value of property, C's property is now worth only £5 million. A can recover from B all foreseeable losses arising from his entering into the transaction with C, ie £10 million – £5 million = £5 million.

(ii) B tells A that C's property is worth £15 million. In fact, it is worth only £12 million. A decides to lend C £10 million, using C's property as security. C defaults. Owing to a general fall in the market value of property, C's property is now worth only £5 million. A's loss is £10 million – £5 million = £5 million. However, B is only liable to the extent that his information was wrong, ie the difference between the negligent valuation and the actual value at the time the information was given: £15 million – £12 million = £3 million.

There are difficulties in defending the judicial reasoning for applying a cap in negligent information cases.[3] Nevertheless, it appears to be settled law. Moreover, where the pursuer has been contributorily negligent in entering into the transaction (which is often the case), the House of Lords has held that the deduction should be made from the pursuer's total loss, not the loss recoverable after the cap has been fixed.[4] So if, in example (ii), A was 20 per cent contributorily negligent, A's damages would be £5 million – £1 million = £4 million: and A would still recover £3 million from B.

It should also be remembered that in cases of fraudulent as well as negligent misrepresentation, the pursuer must take reasonable steps to mitigate his loss.[5]

1 *Bristol and West Building Society v Rollo Steven and Bond* 1998 SLT 9, OH; *Hamilton v Allied Domecq plc* 2005 SC 437. The pursuer's transaction must be within the nature and scope of the defender's duty of care: *Newcastle Building Society v Paterson Robertson and Graham* 2001 SC 734. Where, as a consequence of negligent advice, the pursuer loses a right in land, the potential development value of the land can be recovered: *Paul v Ogilvy* 2001 SLT 171. The time spent by the

pursuer in dealing with the problems resulting from the defender's negligence is a recoverable head of loss but not the time spent in preparation for the litigation: *Lomond Assured Properties v McGrigor Donald* 2000 SLT 797.

2 *South Australia Asset Management Corpn v York Montague Ltd* [1997] AC 191, [1996] 3 All ER 365, HL.

3 See eg Joe Thomson 'Damages for Misrepresentation' 1997 SLT (News) 301.

4 *Platform Home Loans Ltd v Oyston Shipways Ltd* [2002] 2 AC 190, [1999] 1 All ER 833, HL.

5 *Standard Chartered Bank* v *Pakistan National Shipping Corpn* [1995] 2 Lloyd's Rep 365.

16.10 Difficulties can arise in determining when the pursuer has sustained the loss. In some cases a loss is sustained as soon as the pursuer enters into a transaction after being given negligent advice. For example after consulting his solicitor, A agrees to guarantee her son's business debts. She grants a standard security over her house in favour of her son's creditor. The business fails and the creditor enforces the standard security. She sues the solicitor alleging that she had not been advised sufficiently on the nature of the transaction and the standard security. Following the English case of *Foster v Outred & Co*,[1] A's loss would be held to have arisen when she granted the standard security and not when the creditor enforced it: the loss would be the difference in value between an encumbered and unencumbered property. On the other hand, there is no reason to believe that the business will fail. Nevertheless in *Osborne & Hunter Ltd v Hardie Caldwell*[2] the Second Division held that while as a general rule there may be no loss until there is default, each case turns on its own facts: in this case it was negligent to advise anyone to lend money to the borrower and accordingly the client sustained a loss as soon as he parted with his money. In *Law Society v Sephton & Co*[3] the House of Lords, approving *Foster v Outred*, held that loss occurred when a contingent liability depressed the value of property or led to a party to a bilateral transaction receiving less than he should have done or to be worse off than if he had not entered into the transaction but that the mere possibility of an obligation to pay money in the future does not of itself constitute loss until the contingency in fact occurs.

1 [1982] 1 WLR 86.
2 1999 SLT 153.
3 [2006] 2AC 543.

(4) Personal injury claims

16.11 Where a party suffers personal injuries as a result of the delictual conduct of the defender, he is entitled to obtain solatium in respect of non-patrimonial losses such as pain and suffering and compensation for any derivative economic loss which he has sustained. Again, 'the objective' is, so far as money can, to compensate the injured party for the consequences of the wrongful act.[1] The pursuer can claim in respect of loss, injury and damage suffered. It is now the practice to divide the claim into various heads of losses. Although it is sensible and convenient to do so, it is always important to remember that these are not several discrete claims but a *single* claim which can be regarded as falling into several parts for the purposes of quantification.[2] Compensation for the pain and suffering as a result of physical injury is known as solatium; compensation in respect of derivative economic loss is known as damages.

1 *Admiralty Comrs v SS Susquehanna (Owners)* [1926] AC 655, HL.
2 *Irving v Hiddleston* 1998 SCLR 350, 1998 SLT 912, OH.

(a) Solatium

16.12 It is, of course, clear that no money sum can in effect compensate for non-patrimonial losses such as pain and suffering. In *Wright v British Railways Board*[1] Lord Diplock said that

'such loss is not susceptible of *measurement* in money. Any figure at which the assessor of damages arrives cannot be other than artificial and, if the aim is that justice meted out to all litigants should be even handed instead of depending on idiosyncrasies of the assessor, whether jury or judge, the figure must be "basically a conventional figure derived from an experience of awards in comparable cases".'[2]

In *McMillan v McDowall* the judge opined that 'While the assessment of solatium is not a precise science and has frequently been called a jury question, the view of [a Lord Ordinary] in a similar case must be treated with respect.'[3]

The court therefore approaches the question of solatium on the basis of comparing one case with another and making a determination taking into account the severity and nature of the injuries sustained by the pursuer. The court assesses solatium as at the date of the proof and does not attempt to assess solatium as it would have been at the date of the injury itself.

In making an award of solatium the court takes into account not only the extent of the injury but also the pursuer's awareness of pain.[4] No award can be made if, as a result of his injuries, the pursuer has been rendered permanently unconscious. Such awards are made not only in respect of physical injury. A person who, for example, suffers from an identifiable psychological condition can be awarded damages where the condition arises as a consequence of a delict.[5] Where the pursuer had suffered abuse as a child, he was awarded £75,000 as solatium.[6] In *Maclean v Lothian and Borders Fire Brigade*,[7] an award of solatium took into account the pursuer's loss of congenial employment.

In making its assessment of solatium, the court takes into account not only the pain and suffering which has been experienced by the pursuer but also the pain and suffering which he is likely to have in the future. A global award is made. The award also takes into account the pursuer's loss of amenity. Everything which reduces the pursuer's enjoyment of life, which has been sustained as a result of the accident, will be reflected in the award of solatium. It has been held in England that the important element in such a claim is the fact of deprivation of amenity and not whether the injured person is aware of such deprivation.[8] Also included in an award of solatium is the pain and suffering occasioned when the pursuer is, was, or at any time will be, likely to become aware that his expectancy of life has been shortened by his injuries.[9]

1 [1983] 2 AC 733, [1983] 2 All ER 698, HL.
2 [1983] 2 All ER 698 at 699 (Lord Diplock's emphasis). It is submitted that the position is the same in Scots law.
3 *McMillan v McDowall* 1993 SLT 311, OH, at 312 per T G Coutts QC.
4 *Lim Poh Choo v Camden and Islington Area Health Authority* [1980] AC 174, [1979] 2 All ER 910, HL.
5 *Clark v Scottish Power plc* 1994 SCLR 202, 1994 SLT 924; *Lawson v Scotdem Ltd* 1999 GWD 8-393. Distress has, on occasion, been the subject of an award of solatium even in the absence of physical injury or mental illness: *Fraser v D M Hall & Son* 1997 SLT 808; *McLelland v Greater Glasgow Health Board* 2002 SLT 446 (distress to a parent caused by the wrongful birth of a handicapped child).
6 *J v Fife Council* 2009 SLT 160.
7 1998 SCLR 1004, OH.
8 *Lim Poh Choo v Camden and Islington Area Health Authority* [1980] AC 174, [1979] 2 All ER 910, HL. Of course, if the person has been rendered unconscious, he will not obtain compensation for pain and suffering.
9 Damages (Scotland) Act 2011, s 1 (2).

(b) Patrimonial loss

16.13 Having assessed damages in respect of solatium the court must then turn to the question of patrimonial loss. The court first assesses the pursuer's past loss, ie loss incurred between the date of the accident and the date of the proof. It then attempts to assess the pursuer's future loss.

16.14 **(i) Damages for patrimonial loss to the date of proof** If the pursuer has been out of work since the date of his accident, he will be entitled to be compensated for his loss of income. This loss can take various forms such as loss of wages or salary, a reduction in a share of partnership profits or loss of a dividend in a single-employee company.[1] In addition, the pursuer will frequently have a claim for expenses. The general rule is that reasonable expenses are recoverable. Consequently, reasonable medical expenses can be recovered even if it is shown at a later stage that they are unnecessary.[2] Expenses need not be confined to medical or nursing services. By s 8 of the Administration of Justice Act 1982, when a person has sustained personal injuries or has died in consequence of the personal injuries he has sustained, the defender is liable to pay damages in respect of necessary services which have been, or will be, rendered to the injured person by a relative in consequence of the injuries in question. Section 9 of the Administration of Justice Act 1982 also imposes an obligation upon the wrongdoer to pay to the injured person a reasonable sum by way of damages when he is unable, as a result of the accident, to render gratuitous personal services to his family.

In calculating loss of earnings, the pursuer's income tax must be taken into account and his liability to pay National Insurance contributions.[3] Accordingly, in so far as past patrimonial loss is concerned, the wages which form the basis of the calculation are the pursuer's net earnings.

16.15 **(ii) Damages for future patrimonial loss** This head of claim is by far the most important in assessing damages in respect of personal injury. The first stage is to assess damages in respect of future loss of earnings. This is done by taking the loss of the pursuer's net earnings at the date of proof and calculating that on an annual basis. The courts do not attempt to speculate on future rates of taxes and National Insurance contributions, but base their calculation on the rates current at the date of proof.[4] No allowance is made for possible increases in the pursuer's earnings if he had not been injured. The figure produced is known as the 'multiplicand'.

16.16 The second stage is to find a 'multiplier'. The Ogden tables provide actuarial calculations of lump sums which are required to provide incomes for different persons at different ages. In *Wells v Wells*,[5] the House of Lords laid down that the rate of return on the investment of the damages should be 3 per cent, and that the Ogden tables should be used as the *starting point* for finding the appropriate multiplier. The traditional Scottish approach was to use the Ogden tables as a check on the multiplier which was found by less scientific methods. Nevertheless, the guidelines laid down by the House of Lords in *Wells* have been followed by the Scottish courts.[6] After taking the appropriate multiplier for the tables, there will usually be a deduction to take into account contingencies relating to the pursuer other than death, for example early retirement or redundancy.[7]

In cases where the victim's expectation of life has been diminished, in assessing the amount of future patrimonial loss, the court is to assume that the pursuer will live until the date when his death would have been expected had he not been injured. This is known as the notional date of death. In other words, the multiplier is to be determined on the basis of the notional date of death rather than the date when it is expected that the pursuer will actually die. The period between the expected date of death and the notional date of death is known as the lost period. In calculating the multiplicand in respect of the lost years the court will consider what the pursuer would have earned had he not been injured and what benefits he would have received and then deduct from that amount 25% of the total: the 25% reduction represents what would have been the pursuer's living expenses during the lost period had the injuries not been sustained.[8]

1 *Anthony v Brabbs* 1998 SLT 1137.
2 *Clippens Oil Co Ltd v Edinburgh and District Water Trustees* 1907 SC (HL) 9, 15 SLT 92; *Rubins v Walker* 1946 SC 215.
3 *British Transport Commission v Gourlay* [1956] AC 185, [1955] 3 All ER 796, HL; *Cooper v Firth Brown* [1963] 2 All ER 31, [1963] 1 WLR 148.
4 *British Transport Commission v Gourlay* [1956] AC 185.
5 [1999] 1 AC 345. The House of Lords felt empowered to lay down a 3 per cent return because the pursuer would be assumed to invest the damages in index-linked government stock rather than in equities which might give a higher return but which, of course, are a less safe investment. Under s 1 of the Damages Act 1996, the Lord Chancellor and the Secretary of State for Scotland have the power to prescribe the rate of return. This has now been reduced to 2.5 per cent: Damages (Personal Injury) (Scotland) Order 2002 (SI 2002 No 46), art 3.
6 *McNulty v Marshalls Food Group Ltd* 1999 SC 195; *McManus' Executrix v Babcock Energy Ltd* 1999 SC 569.
7 Sometimes the multiplier produced by the Ogden tables is not suitable in a particular case where, for example, the injured person may be able to return to relatively well paid work after retraining: see for example *McGhee v Diageo plc* [2008] CSOH 74; *Brand v Transocean North Sea Ltd* [2011] CSOH 57.
8 Damages (Scotland) Act 2011, s 1.

16.17   The third stage is for the court to multiply the multiplicand by the multiplier to give a lump sum. So, for example, if the multiplicand is £20,000 and the multiplier is 10, then the total sum awarded is £200,000. The pursuer is expected to live off the income and capital, the theory being that the lump sum will have been consumed by the date the pursuer dies!

Where a pursuer is severely injured, damages can be awarded for the cost of her maintenance, nursing and medical care in the future. Again, the multiplicand/multiplier method is adopted. The court assesses the cost of maintenance and care on an annual basis and then applies a multiplier based on the Ogden tables.[1]

Loss of pension rights can also be taken into account in assessing future patrimonial loss,[2] as can the pursuer's general loss of value in the labour market. In *Hill v Wilson*,[3] damages were awarded for impairment to earning capacity as opposed to loss of future wages. It is particularly difficult to assess damages when the injured person is a child. In such a case, 'it has never been suggested that damages should be assessed on such a basis, namely on a basis which provides not only reasonable compensation but in effect a guarantee of future financial security'.[4] In some cases, the court will abandon the multiplicand/multiplier method of calculating future patrimonial loss. This would happen where, for example, the pursuer has been able to continue working albeit on light work at a reduced wage, or there is evidence that the pursuer will be able to resume employment in the very near future, even though the job may be lower paid than previously.[5]

Personal injury cases can be tried by jury. Juries tend to award higher damages than judges, particularly in relation to solatium. Although a court can order a new trial if the sum awarded is excessive, it will not do so unless the damages awarded are beyond what a reasonable jury would award and there is serious injustice: the fact that a judge would have awarded considerably less is not sufficient.[6] In complex cases, particularly those involving future loss of earnings special cause may be shown for withholding jury trial.[7]

1 For the courts' approach before *Wells v Wells* [1998] 3 All ER 481, [1998] 3 WLR 329, HL, see *O'Brien's Curator Bonis v British Steel plc* 1991 SC 315, 1991 SCLR 831, 1991 SLT 477.
2 *Mitchell v Glenrothes Development Corpn* 1991 SLT 284, OH (conventional multiplicand/multiplier method used); *Cantwell v Criminal Injuries Compensation Board* 2002 SC (HL) 1.
3 1998 SC 81, 1998 SLT 69, OH.
4 *O'Connor v Matthews* 1996 SLT 408 at 412, per the Lord Ordinary (Marnoch).
5 *Stevenson v British Coal Corpn* 1989 SLT 136; *McGhee v Diageo plc* [2008] CSOH 74.
6 *Girvan v Inverness Farmers Dairy (No 2)* 1998 SC (HL) 1.
7 See for example *Lewendon v International Paper (UK) Ltd* [2011] CSOH 116.

(5) Interest

16.18 Having assessed the quantity of damages, the court is obliged to consider the question of interest. Interest is payable under the Interest on Damages (Scotland) Act 1958, as amended by the Interest on Damages (Scotland) Act 1971.

Although solatium is awarded as a lump sum, it is important for the purpose of awards of interest to distinguish past and future solatium. Interest is only awarded on past solatium.[1] Past solatium is a sum awarded for the pursuer's pain and suffering until the date of proof. But if the pursuer is experiencing pain and suffering and loss of amenities at the date of the proof, the court will estimate damages to compensate the pursuer for the fact that these may continue in the future. So, for example, a court might award a total sum of £10,000 by way of solatium, made up of £6,000 for past solatium and £4,000 for future solatium. Interest on past solatium is paid at the average court rate for the period between the date of the accident and when the 'pain' diminished: this could, of course, have occurred before the date of the proof. If the pursuer is still suffering pain at the date of proof, interest will be awarded on past solatium at half the average court rate.[2]

Subject to the court's discretion, interest on damages for patrimonial loss runs from the date of the accident.[3] Again, although a global sum is awarded, damages are divided between past and future loss. In the case of past losses, interest is awarded at one half of the average court rate from the date of the accident to the date of proof. There is no interest payable on awards in respect of future patrimonial loss.[4] The rules applicable to interest in respect of personal injuries operate without prejudice to the general rule which awards interest at the court rate from the date of decree until the date of payment by the defender.

1 *Smith v Middleton* 1972 SC 30; *J v Fife Council* 2009 SLT 160.
2 *Keicher v National Coal Board* 1988 SLT 318; *Preston v Grampian Health Board* 1988 SLT 435.
3 *Macrae v Reed & Mallik Ltd* 1961 SC 68, 1961 SLT 96.
4 *Hill v Wilson* 1998 SLT 69.

(6) Deductions from awards

16.19 Deductions may have to be made from an award of damages for patrimonial loss. Section 10 of the Administration of Justice Act 1982 prohibits the taking into account for the purposes of reduction of damages any benefit the pursuer received in respect of: (a) any contractual pension or benefit[1] (b) any pension or retirement benefit to which s 2(1) of the Law Reform (Personal Injuries) Act 1948 applied; (c) any benefit payable from public funds in respect of any period after the date of the award of damages which is designed to secure to the injured person or any relative of his a minimum level of subsistence; (d) any statutory redundancy payment;[2] (e) any payment made to the injured person or to any relative of his by the injured person's employer following upon the injuries in question where the recipient is under an obligation to reimburse the employer in the event of damages being recovered in respect of his injuries; and (f) any payment of a benevolent character made to the injured person or to any relative by any person following upon the injuries in question. The section directs, however, that any remuneration or earnings from employment, any unemployment benefit payable from public funds payable prior to the date of the award of damages, or any payment of a benevolent character made by the person responsible for the accident to the injured person, shall be taken into account. Any savings to the pursuer as a result of being maintained in hospital or accommodation provided by a care home service is deducted.[3]

Prior to the introduction of the Social Security Act 1989, in assessing damages for patrimonial loss a deduction was made of only one-half of the value of certain specified benefits, ie sickness, invalidity or disablement benefit, which the pursuer had received during a period of five years from the date of the accident; but in *Hodgson v Trapp*[4] the House of Lords held that the full value of other benefits, such as attendance and mobility allowances, was to be deducted. However, the Social Security Act 1989 made major changes and the law was consolidated in the Social Security Administration Act 1992, Part IV (ss 81–104): Part IV has now been restated, with amendments, in the Social Security (Recovery of Benefits) Act 1997.

When damages are awarded, heads of loss are relevant for the purpose of the Social Security (Recovery of Benefits) Act 1997:

(1) compensation[5] for earnings lost during 'the relevant period';
(2) compensation for the cost of care incurred over the relevant period; and
(3) compensation for loss of mobility during the relevant period.

The following benefits paid over the relevant period are deducted as follows:

From head (1):   disability working allowance, disablement pension, incapacity benefit, income support, invalidity pension and allowance, jobseeker's allowance, reduced earnings allowance, severe disablement allowance, sickness benefit, statutory sick pay, unemployability supplement and unemployment benefit;

From head (2):   attendance allowance, the care component of disability living allowance and any disablement pension increase;

From head (3):   mobility allowance and the mobility component of disability living allowance.[6]

The 'relevant period' is five years from the date of the accident or five years from first claiming benefit as a consequence of a disease. Thus, benefits paid over that five-year period are recoverable from the relevant head of loss. Payments which are paid thereafter are not recoverable. When damages are paid *before* the end of five years, the relevant period ends at the date of payment; therefore, benefits paid after that date but before the five-year period ends are not recoverable.[7] The person paying damages, the compensator, deducts the amount of recoverable benefits from the pursuer's compensation[8] which he then pays to the Secretary of State.[9]

1 *Lewicki v Brown & Root Wimpey Highland Fabricators Ltd* 1996 SC 200, 1996 SCLR 680, 1996 SLT 1283 (payment under employer's long-term disability scheme held to be a contractual benefit and not deducted: cf if it had been treated as earnings or remuneration from employment). Where the pursuer's claim is in respect of loss of earnings and loss of a contractual retirement pension, then s 10(a) applies to the claim for loss of earnings so that his ill-health pension is not deducted but s 10(a) does *not* apply to the claim for loss of a contractual retirement pension so that his ill-health pension has to be brought into account: *Cantwell v Criminal Injuries Compensation Board* 2002 SC (HL) 1.
2 Reversing *Wilson v National Coal Board* 1981 SC (HL) 9, 1981 SLT 67. An *ex gratia* non-statutory payment falls to be deducted: *Duncan v Glacier Metal Co Ltd* 1988 SCLR 320, 1988 SLT 479, OH.
3 Administration of Justice Act 1982, s 11 (a) and (b).
4 [1989] AC 807, [1988] 3 All ER 870, HL.
5 Compensation includes interest on an award of damages for loss of earnings: *Griffiths v British Coal Corpn* [2001] 1 WLR 1493.
6 Social Security (Recovery of Benefits) Act 1997, Sch 2.
7 SS(RB)A 1997, s 3. See *Mitchell v Laing* 1998 SC 342. This case provides an excellent example of literal construction of a statute by the Lord President (Rodger).
8 SS(RB)A 1997, s 6. The compensator obtains a certificate specifying the amount of recoverable benefits paid to the pursuer.
9 SS(RB)A 1997, s 7.

16.20 A major effect of the legislation is to abolish the provision that only one-half of the specified benefits should be taken into account in assessing damages. Under the Social Security (Recovery of Benefits) Act 1997, all the specified benefits received by the pursuer during the relevant period are fully to be taken into account. Benefits received after the relevant period are not affected and are not to be taken into account. The position is therefore that both pursuers and defenders are worse off under the new legislation.

As far as the pursuer is concerned, he is worse off by not keeping half the value of any sickness, invalidity or disablement benefit received during the relevant period. He is, however, better off in that after the relevant period, those benefits which would have previously been deducted in full when assessing damages under the rule in *Hodgson v Trapp*,[1] for example attendance and mobility allowances, are no longer taken into account. Most importantly, awards of solatium are no longer subject to deduction of recoverable benefits. The defender is worse off in that (i) he now pays the specified benefits in full during the relevant period, whereas before he paid only half their value to the pursuer as damages, and (ii) he can no longer take advantage of the rule in *Hodgson v Trapp*, ie that the full value of other benefits paid to the pursuer would be deducted when assessing the damages.

When the compensation is less than a prescribed sum, it will be treated as a small payment, and no deduction in respect of benefits paid during the relevant period will be made.[2]

1 [1989] AC 807, [1988] 3 All ER 870, HL.
2 Social Security (Recovery of Benefits) Act 1997, Sch 1.

C. PROVISIONAL AND INTERIM DAMAGES

16.21 The normal rule in actions of damages for personal injuries is that the damages are assessed once and for all at the date of proof. As a consequence, pursuers used to delay bringing proceedings for a considerable period until they could ascertain the full extent of their loss. Pursuers often suffered hardship during the period between the accident and the date of proof. The situation was particularly unfair if the pursuer's physical condition was likely to deteriorate as a result of the injuries at some time in the future after the date of the proof. In *Stevenson v Pontifex and Wood*[1] the Lord President (Inglis) observed:[2]

'I hold the true rule of practice based on sound principle to be, that though the delict ..., be of such a nature that it will necessarily be followed by injurious consequences in the future, or though it may for this reason be impossible to ascertain with precise accuracy at the date of the action ... the amount of loss which will result, yet the whole damage must be recovered in one action.'[3]

A pursuer's position in these circumstances has, to some extent, been alleviated by s 12 of the Administration of Justice Act 1982, which provides that the court is entitled to make an award of provisional damages in respect of personal injuries. Such an award can be made when it is proved, or admitted, that there is a risk that at some definite or indefinite time in the future, the pursuer will, as a result of the act or omission of the defender, which gave rise to the cause of the action, develop some serious disease or some serious deterioration in his physical or mental condition.[4] Provisional damages can only be awarded where the defender was, at the time of the accident giving rise to the cause of action, either a public authority or an insured person.[5] The purpose of this provision is therefore to give the pursuer an opportunity to claim damages in circumstances where his position is likely to worsen but where he cannot assess the full extent of his loss because the condition will take some time to deteriorate.

Before an award of provisional damages can be made, the pursuer must establish that there is a risk[6] that at some time in the future he will develop some serious disease or some serious deterioration in his physical or mental condition. Although assessment of the risk may be difficult,[7] it is clear that the risk must be more than *de minimis*.[8] There must be evidence that there is the possibility of a *serious* deterioration in the pursuer's condition.[9] If, for example, the pursuer's health or disability will become worse incrementally, there are no grounds for an award of provisional damages because there is no 'clear cut and severable threshold' when the pursuer could apply for damages in the future on the basis that a serious deterioration had in fact taken place.[10] Although the deterioration must be as a consequence of the wrongful conduct of the defender that led to the pursuer's personal injuries in the first place, nevertheless in deciding whether or not the deterioration is serious, account must be taken of the effect of such deterioration upon the pursuer's physical abilities in the context of his ordinary life: '[s]eriousness cannot be assessed in a vacuum'.[11] Damages can only be deferred in respect of the serious deterioration in the pursuer's condition.[12]

1 (1887) 15 R 125.

2 (1887) 15 R 125 at 129.
3 See also *Dunlop v McGowans* 1979 SC 22, 1979 SLT 34 at 39 per the Lord Justice-Clerk (Wheatley).
4 Administration of Justice Act 1982, s 12(1)(a).
5 AJA 1982, s 12(1)(b).
6 Cf the approach of the Lord Ordinary (Dervaird) who suggested (*obiter*) that if there was no risk but a certainty that there would be a deterioration, this would not be a suitable ease for provisional damages: *Prentice v William Thyne Ltd* 1989 SLT 336n, OH, at 337.
7 *Potter v McCulloch* 1987 SLT 308, OH, at 310 per the Lord Ordinary (Weir).
8 *White v Inveresk Paper Co Ltd* 1987 SC 143, 1988 SLT 2, OH, at 6 per the Lord Ordinary (Murray).
9 *White v Inveresk Paper Co Ltd* 1987 SC 143, 1988 SLT 2, OH, at 5 per the Lord Ordinary (Murray). See also *Potter v McCulloch* 1987 SLT 308, OH, at 310 per the Lord Ordinary (Weir); *Meek v Burton's Gold Medal Biscuits Ltd* 1989 SLT 338n, OH, at 339 per the Lord Ordinary (Prosser). In *Bonar v Trafalgar House Offshore Fabrication Ltd* 1996 SLT 548, OH, the Lord Ordinary (Gill) held that the court must determine what the apprehended deterioration is: contingent liability cannot be imposed on a defender unless the nature and extent of that liability is clear.
10 See also *Prentice v William Thyne Ltd* 1989 SLT 336n, OH ('clear and sensible threshold'); *Robertson v British Bakeries Ltd* 1991 SLT 434 ('recognisable threshold').
11 *Robertson v British Bakeries Ltd* 1991 SCLR 450n, 1991 SLT 434, OH, at 439 per the Lord Ordinary (Osborne).
12 *Meek v Burton's Gold Medal Biscuits Ltd* 1989 SLT 338n, OH.

16.22 Even if the pursuer satisfies the statutory criteria, the court is not obliged to defer the award of damages. The interests of the defender in not being called upon to pay further damages at some indefinite time in the future must also be considered.[1] Accordingly, an application for provisional damages is unlikely to be successful unless the medical evidence establishes that the deterioration is likely to take place in, say, a period of not more than ten years. Moreover, the court has the discretion to stipulate a time limit after which the pursuer is unable to claim further damages for a deterioration in his condition.[2] In *McColl v Barns*,[3] for example, where it was established that there was a risk that post-traumatic epilepsy might occur within seven years of the date of the accident, the pursuer was allowed to apply within that period for a further award of damages if the risk should in fact materialise. In the course of his judgment, the Lord Ordinary (Morison) said:[4]

'In my opinion this is a most appropriate case for such an order to be made. An assessment made to reflect the possibility of the condition occurring would be unrealistic and impracticable. If no assessment were made and the risk were to materialise, the pursuer would be unjustly deprived of compensation for a serious injury which would be a result of the accident. Since the additional risk becomes negligible after a period of seven years from the date of the accident I shall restrict the order ... to that period ...'.

The court is also entitled to award interim damages. Interim damages are to be distinguished from provisional damages in so far as they do not depend upon a pursuer suffering from a continuing disability, the eventual seriousness of which cannot be ascertained. Interim payments can be made in the Court of Session in terms of Rule of Court 89A(1) and will be awarded if the court is satisfied that the defender or defenders have admitted liability or that if the action proceeded to proof the pursuer would succeed in a question of liability without any substantial finding of contributory negligence on his part.[5] The court must be satisfied that it is 'practically certain' that the pursuer will succeed on the question of liability and that any finding of contributory negligence will not be so large as to have a material effect on the assessment of the amount the pursuer is likely to recover as damages.[6] An interim award is taken into account in making the final award and will not be made against the defender unless that defender is either a person who is insured in respect of the pursuer's claim or is a public authority or 'is a person whose means and resources are such as to enable him to make interim payment'.[7]

Lump sum payments are particularly unsuitable in some cases of catastrophic injury, particularly when a child is seriously injured and requires constant care. The sums involved in these cases can run into millions. Yet the victim might live for a long time and the lump sum might prove inadequate to pay for his care. Conversely, the victim may die earlier than expected giving rise to a windfall to his family which in the case of medical negligence will have been at the taxpayer's expense. To avoid these outcomes, in cases of severe catastrophic injuries, the parties have been prepared to settle in agreements which include periodical payments.[8]

1 *Paterson v Costain Mining Ltd* 1988 SCLR 70, 1988 SLT 413, OH.
2 Administration of Justice Act 1982, s 12(2).
3 1992 SCLR 907, 1992 SLT 1188, OH; see also *Lappin v Britannia Airways Ltd* 1989 SLT 181n, OH (five years).
4 *McColl v Barns* 1992 SLT 1188 at 1190.
5 See, for example, *Hutcheson v Ascosmit Co* 1992 SLT 1115.
6 *Cowie v Atlantic Drilling Co Ltd* 1995 SC 288, 1995 SCLR 335, 1995 SLT 1151; *Cleland v Campbell* 1998 SLT 642, OH.
7 Rule of Court of Session 89A(1).
8 *D's Parent and Guardian v Greater Glasgow Health Board* [2011] CSOH 99.

D. PRESCRIPTION AND LIMITATION

16.23   A pursuer may lose her right to obtain reparation if she does not begin proceedings against the defender within certain prescribed periods. By s 6 of the Prescription and Limitation (Scotland) Act 1973[1] the obligation to make reparation for a delictual act[2] is extinguished after five years. The five-year prescriptive period runs from the date on which the delict is complete, ie when the pursuer suffers *damnum* (harm).

'The right to raise such an action accrues when *injuria* concurs with *damnum*. Some interval of time may elapse between the two … and … in such circumstances time is to run from the date when *damnum* results, not from the earlier date of *injuria*.'[3]

This could cause injustice in cases where the damage suffered is latent and the pursuer does not discover that, for example, his house is unstable as a result of defective foundations until five or more years after the damage was in fact sustained. In such situations, time begins to run only when the pursuer first became or could with reasonable diligence have become aware of the damage.[4] Where the pursuer was the victim of sexual abuse, it has been held that he had sustained injuries, ie the *damnum* had occurred, at the time of the abuse even though he was seeking reparation for a psychiatric disorder which did not present itself until 40 years later: the defender's obligation to make reparation was therefore extinguished by the long negative prescription (20 years).[5]

There are, however, important exceptions to the general rule. First, liability for defective products under Part I of the Consumer Protection Act 1987 is extinguished after ten years.[6] Liability for defamation prescribes after 20 years.[7] Importantly, delictual liability in respect of personal injuries or death no longer prescribes.[8] However, a claim for damages for personal injuries, death, defamation and harassment[9] must be brought within a period of three years. This is known as a limitation period. If the action is not commenced within the three-year period, the pursuer cannot enforce his rights unless the defender waives his right to defend the action on the ground that the limitation period has expired.

In the case of personal injuries or property damage as a result of a defective product, the action is not competent if it is brought after a period of three years from the date when the pursuer knew that it was reasonably practicable for him to be aware that there was a defect in the product, that the injury or damage was caused by the product, that the injury or damage was sufficiently serious to bring an action for reparation and that the defender was liable under s 2 of the Consumer Protection Act 1987.[10] A similar limitation period applies to actions brought in relation to death caused by a defective product.[11] In respect of defamation actions, it is simply stated that the three-year limitation period runs from the date when the right of action accrued.[12]

1 In this section references are to the Prescription and Limitation (Scotland) Act 1973, as amended, unless otherwise stated.

2 PL(S)A 1973, Sch 1, para 1(d). Periods during which the pursuer was induced to refrain from bringing the action by reason of the debtor's fraud or error induced by the words or conduct of the debtor are not reckoned as part of the prescriptive period: s 6(4)(a). See *BP Exploration Operating Co Ltd v Chevron Transport (Scotland)* 2002 SC (HL) 19. Any period under which the original creditor was under a legal disability does not count: s 6(4)(b).

3 *Dunlop v McGowans* 1980 SC (HL) 73, 1980 SLT 129 at 132–133 per Lord Keith of Kinkel; see also *Renfrew Golf Club v Ravenstone Securities Ltd* 1984 SLT 170, OH; *Strathclyde Regional Council v Border Engineering Contractors Ltd* 1997 SCLR 100, 1998 SLT 175, OH; *Osborne & Hunter Ltd v Hardie Caldwell* 1999 SLT 153; *K v Gilmartin's Exrix* 2002 SC 602.

4 PL(S) Act 1973, s 11(3). See for example *David T Morrison & Co v ICL Plastics Ltd* 2013 SLT 413. However, the long-stop 20 years' prescription begins to run from the date the damage occurred: s 7. In theory, therefore, a claim for reparation for latent damage could prescribe after 20 years without the five-year prescriptive period being triggered.

5 *K v Gilmartin's Exrx* 2002 SC 602. The abolition of the long negative prescription in respect of death and personal injuries by the Prescription and Limitation (Scotland) Act 1984, s 6(1) and Sch 1, para 2 is not retrospective.

6 PL(S)A 1973, s 22A, Sch 1, para 2(ggg). In this case the ten years run from the date the product is first put on the market, not the date when the damnum occurs.

7 PL(S)A 1973, s 7(2) and Sch 1, para 2(gg).

8 PL(S)A 1973, ss 6(2)and 7(2) and Sch 1, para 2(g).

9 PL(S) A 1973,s 18B.

10 Prescription and Limitation (Scotland) Act 1973, s 22B.

11 PL(S)A 1973, s 22C.

12 PL(S)A 1973, s 18A(1).

16.24 An action for damages for personal injuries must commence within three years from the date on which the injuries were sustained.[1] However, the three-year period does not begin to run from the date when the injuries were sustained unless it was reasonably practicable for the pursuer to be aware of all the following facts: that the injuries were sufficiently serious to bring an action of damages;[2] that the injuries were caused by an act or omission; and that the defender was responsible for the act or omission.[3] So, for example, where a pursuer sustained personal injury as a result of the defender's delictual conduct but the pursuer did not know that he was injured, as in the case of an insidious disease, the three-year period only begins to run when it was reasonably practicable for him to realise that the illness was attributable to the defender's acts or omissions, ie when he knows he is ill. Similarly, the three-year period will only begin when the pursuer knows that the defender is responsible for the delictual conduct; if this knowledge arises after the date when the injuries were sustained, the three-year period only begins to run from the later date. A similar limitation period applies to actions for damages brought in relation to death which has resulted from personal injuries and actions for damages for harassment.[4] In all these limitation periods, time does not run against a pursuer who is or was under legal disability by reason of non-age or unsoundness of mind.[5]

However, in the case of the limitation periods in respect of actions for damages in respect of personal injuries or death from personal injuries, actions for defamation or verbal injury and harassment, the court has a discretion to allow the action to proceed outwith the three-year period if 'it seems equitable to do so'.[6] All the circumstances of the case are taken into consideration, including the length of time in bringing the action, whether the pursuer was responsible for the delay, whether there is an action available against the pursuer's solicitor if the solicitor was responsible for the delay, the inconvenience to the defender etc.[7] The issue is entirely a matter for the discretion of the presiding judge. In practice, the power is used sparingly in claims for personal injuries or death from personal injuries as a result of the knowledge provisions which have to be satisfied before the three-year limitation period begins to run.

1 PL(S)A 1973, s 17(1) and (2). If the act or omission which caused the injuries was continuing, the three-year period runs from the date when the injuries were sustained or the date when the act or omission ceased, whichever is later: see *Mather v British Telecommunications plc* 2001 SLT 325.
2 *Blake v Lothian Health Board* 1993 SLT 1248, OH.
3 *Kirk Care Housing Association Ltd v Crerar and Partners* 1996 SLT 150, OH. The onus rests on the pursuer to prove when he was actually aware of these facts or did not have constructive knowledge of them: *Agnew v Scott Lithgow Ltd (No 1)* 2001 SC 516; *W v Glasgow City Council* [2010] CSIH 70; *A v Glasgow City Council* 2010 SC 411.
4 Prescription and Limitation (Scotland) Act 1973, ss18 and 18B.
5 PL(S)A 1973, ss 17(3), 18(3), 18A(2), 22B(4) and 22C(3). No causal connection is required between the period of non-age and the delay: *Paton v Loffland Bros North Sea* 1994 SLT 784.
6 PL(S)A 1973, s 19A.
7 For examples, see *McCullough v Norwest Socea Ltd* 1981 SLT 201, OH; *Carson v Howard Doris Ltd* 1981 SC 278, 1981 SLT 273; *Donald v Rutherford* 1983 SLT 253, 1984 SLT 70; *Whyte v Walker* 1983 SLT 441, OH; *Clark v McLean* 1994 SCLR 564, 1995 SLT 235; *Gorrie v Marist Brothers* 2002 SCLR 436; *Harrison v West of Scotland Kart Club* [2008] CSOH 33; *Bowden v Poor Sisters of Nazareth* [2008] UKHL 32, 2008 SC (HL) 146; *Sinclair v Morrison* [2009] CSOH 81; *Chinn v Cyclacel Ltd* [2013] CSOH 17; *A v N* [2013] CSOH 161.

Index